THE
BIG
ONE

THE
BIG
ONE

BILL CROMARTIE

GRIDIRON PUBLISHERS
Atlanta, Georgia

The Big One by Bill Cromartie
Copyright © by William Kelly Cromartie

Printed in the United States of America

Library of Congress Cataloging-in-Publication data:
1. History. University of Michigan — Football
2. History. The Ohio State University — Football
3. History. College sports — United States
4. History. Football — United States
Library of Congress Catalog Number: 94-78051

ISBN 0-932520-56-1

1st Edition — 1979
2nd Edition — 1982
3rd Edition — 1989
4th Edition — 1994

Published in Atlanta, Georgia

GRIDIRON PUBLISHERS
P.O. Box 724201
ATLANTA, GEORGIA 31139
(404) 431-0962

DEDICATED TO
WOLVERINES AND BUCKEYES
EVERYWHERE

TABLE OF CONTENTS

ACKNOWLEDGMENTS

A special acknowledgment is extended to both the University of Michigan and The Ohio State University for their generous cooperation in helping the author gather material for this book.

We would like to thank the Sports Information Directors of both institutions—Michigan's Will Perry and Bruce Madej, and Ohio State's Marv Holman and Steve Snapp, along with UM's Jim Schneider and OSU's Bryan Ramsey.

A special thanks is also extended to Don Canham, former Athletic Director at Michigan, and to Ms. R. Ruth Jones of the Ohio State Photo Archives.

A book of this type would be impossible to write without the newspaper files (1897-present) of the *Detroit Free Press,* the *Detroit News,* the *Columbus Dispatch,* the *Columbus Citizen Journal,* the *Ann Arbor News,* and the *Chicago Tribune,* among others.

These newspapers were the source of the vast majority of the factual material included here. And to their sportswriters, both past and present, we sincerely extend a grateful and admiring salute.

They were eyewitnesses to the color, the drama, and moments of comedy, as it unfolded year after year. With their old typewriters (and new computers) they recorded the facts and quotations which we can draw upon—now and in the future.

Thanks, men. You've done a great job. And I have enjoyed reading your every word spread over almost 100 years of this grand old Michigan-Ohio State football rivalry.

PREFACE

It was early afternoon on a late November Saturday in 1946. My father and I were at his favorite fishing spot on the Kinchafoonee Creek leading to his farm in southwest Georgia.

We had been there only a short time when he told me to pull in my line. We were going to the car to listen to a football game. Leave all this good fishing," I thought, "to listen to a football game?" As a young boy who had never listened to a football broadcast, I simply couldn't understand the priorities.

The game daddy wanted to hear was between Georgia and Georgia Tech. It was truly a big game that year, as the unbeaten Bulldogs were ranked No. 3 behind Army and Notre Dame, while the Yellow Jackets had lost only once and rated seventh. The winner would go to the Sugar Bowl.

The broadcast, coming in loud and clear, somehow made a tremendous impression on me. Heretofore, football and baseball had been games to become excited about only through playing them on the school grounds or in the back yard. Yet, here I was, supposedly on a leisure fishing trip, completely wrapped up in a contest being played 200 miles away.

That was my induction into the world of football fandom.

With Charley Trippi leading a 34-0 rout of Tech, then a few weeks later starring in a 20-10 win over North Carolina and Charlie "Choo-Choo" Justice in the Sugar Bowl, I developed an instant loyalty to Georgia, a university which I graduated from a dozen years later.

After absorbing all the other New Year's Day bowl games, including Illinois' 45-14 trouncing of UCLA in the Rose Bowl, which began the pact between the Big Nine and Pacific Coast Conference, I couldn't wait for the '47 football season to begin.

Except for my allegiance to the Bulldogs, college football, as I observed it back then, was the Big Nine first and everybody else scrambling for runner-up. I devoured all available newspaper stories for Big Nine news and accounts of games with such big-sounding names as Minnesota, Wisconsin Northwestern and Purdue; Illinois, Iowa, Indiana and, of course, Michigan and Ohio State. They all seemed such far-away places.

These were names I associated with real football, played in huge stadiums, before huge crowds, and games which seemingly were always played in the snow or sleet or mud which, somehow, magnified the image of ruggedness and toughness.

These were names that were entrancing as spoken by the radio announcers on the old "CBS Football Roundup," an all-Saturday afternoon network program that brought the audience "live," in-progress spot coverage of the nation's big games, many of which were always from the campuses of the Big Nine.

And how great it was to see conference teams on the newsreel at the theater each week in nearby Albany — timed so you could see that particular part of the program twice and the movie only once.

In 1975, I tested a technique for a book on a subject which I was quite familiar. The result was *Clean Old-Fashioned Hate,* a game-by-game history of the Georgia-Georgia Tech rivalry, now in its sixth edition.

I then tackled Alabama-Auburn in *Braggin' Rights,* before taking on Big Ten football from a perspective of the Michigan-Ohio State series in *The Big One.*

These books represent an attempt to depict the traditional and intense college football rivalries as institutions in their own right.

The concept of the football rivalry as its own institution is not an invention of mine nor anyone else. People do not create institutions. The process, instead, is that individuals, organizations, schools, museums — even football rivalries — exhibit qualities and characteristics such as endurance, class, appeal interest and tradition to the point that institutional status is bestowed.

So it is in the case of Michigan-Ohio State on the football field.

The Big One is presented with the hope that it will be regarded as a factual and non-partisan account of the games and background of the historic old rivalry.

By the way, no fish were caught that sunny Saturday afternoon back in 1946, but I was "hooked" — and hooked good.

— Bill Cromartie

1897

THE START OF
SOMETHING BIG

"The most important games of the gridiron today in this section are those between the University of Michigan and Ohio State University at Ann Arbor, and the University of Chicago and Beloit at Chicago," declared the *Detroit Free Press*.

The date of the dispatch was Saturday, October 16, 1897. The time in history had arrived that Michigan and Ohio State would be together on the football field for the very first time.

When the whole swinging thing began, Michigan had been playing football for 18 years and Ohio State for seven. Why it took that long for the two Midwest giants to come eye-to-eye in football is nowhere fully explained. It may be sufficient to observe that in those years, it just wasn't that important, no matter how momentous an event it has become today. It's now more than a game. Much more.

Michigan's football history had begun on May 30, 1879, and resulted in a 1-0 win over Racine (Wisconsin) at White Stockings Grounds (also known as the 23rd Street Grounds) in Chicago. The park was the former home of Chicago's National Baseball League team, the White Stockings, later to become the Cubs.

Ohio State's first official kick of the ole pigskin came 11 years later in Delaware – Delaware, Ohio, that is – a small town about 20 miles north of Columbus and the home of Ohio Wesleyan. The Buckeyes journeyed to Delaware for a game that was played on the morning of May 3, 1890. OSU won 20-14.

1

MICHIGAN – 1897

Michigan had been playing football for 18 years before the first game against Ohio State. This was the first U-M team to meet, and defeat, the Buckeyes. The score was 34-0 and the game was played on Regents Field in Ann Arbor on Saturday, October 16, 1897.

1st row – C. A. Barabee, W. C. Steckle and Howard Felver.

2nd row – W. P. Baker, J. W. Bennett, J. R. Hogg, J. E. Eagen and S. Keena.

3rd row – Ward Hughes (manager), R. S. Lockwood, H. S. Pingree and C. C. Teetzel.

4th row – F. C. Hannon (scored first touchdown in the series), and N. B. Ayers.

Players not pictured, but who played in that first game – M. B. Snow, W. H. Caley, H. E. Lehr, G. D. Stewart, William Talcott, John McLean and W. Savage. (Photo courtesy of Michigan Athletic Department.)

OHIO STATE – 1897

The Buckeyes began playing intercollegiate football in 1890, but this was the first OSU team to face Michigan.

1st row – James Brophy, J.E. Mackey, W.T. Leonard, Albert Engensperger, Charles Richards, Charles Steinle and Waite.

2nd row – Ross Purdy, Harry Urban, Harry Hawkins, Harry Saxbe and Scott.

3rd row – Fred Butcher, Charles Benedict, and John Segrist.

4th row – Claude Culbertson, Robert King, W.E. Sykes, Enos, manager, R.E. Dwyer, Miller and Charles Segrist. (Photo courtesy of OSU Photo Archives.)

Detroit News
Saturday, October 16, 1897

"MICHIGAN MAKES A TOUCHDOWN!"

It was a "hot time in the old town" back in 1897 as shown by this illustration from the University of Michigan yearbook of the time. (Photo courtesy of The Michiganensian.)

Thus, Michigan and Ohio State were both victorious in their first football games and a tradition was established. It seems that the two teams have been winning ever since, and for the great majority of the time, they have.

As the 1897 Buckeye-Wolverine date approached, Michigan had played 97 games and emerged with a 68-26-3 (.717) record. However, Ohio State's program got off to a more modest beginning. When it came time for the Bucks' initial confrontation with U-M, the Ohioans' 58-game record was 28-27-3. The next 10-year period would produce a successful .735 winning percentage and the Buckeyes were off and running.

Again, to the modern observer, it's hard to imagine that Michigan and Ohio State played a total of 155 football games before ever meeting each other. What a waste of thrills!

But back to 1897. This was a period in which men's overcoats were advertised in Columbus and Detroit for $7.50, and a solid oak chest of drawers for $3.50, and a piano for $185.00. It was a time that the Yarnell Institute, with establishments located in both Michigan (Northville) and Ohio (Willoughly) could cure, well, just about anything. Their advertisements claimed success over the ills of the "Opium User," the "Cocaine Victim," the "Tobacco Slave," and the "Whiskey Inebriate." Yarnell's treatment, it said, "Always restores the nervous system of the patient to its normal state of vigor."

As for the '97 football season, OSU Coach David Edwards and his Buckeyes blanked Ohio Medical 6-0 and lost to Case 14-0, both in Columbus. It was now time to pack the game gear and head for Ann Arbor.

The Wolverines in their 1897 season had defeated Normal 24-0 and were then held to a scoreless tie by Ohio Wesleyan. A few days later, the Michigan board of control of athletics announced that it would sever athletic relations with Ohio Wesleyan. It was reported that Wesleyan had allowed its coach to play in the game. The young man's name? Fielding Harris Yost, who four years later would launch a career at Michigan that would eventually make him the Wolverines' all-time winningest coach and a legend of the college game.

"The Ohio team has a reputation of putting up a fast game," a *Free Press* reporter wrote on game day. "It will be the first hard game that Michigan has had and the followers of the team are hoping to get some idea of the strength of the line on today's play." It would have been enlightening if the reporter had explained how

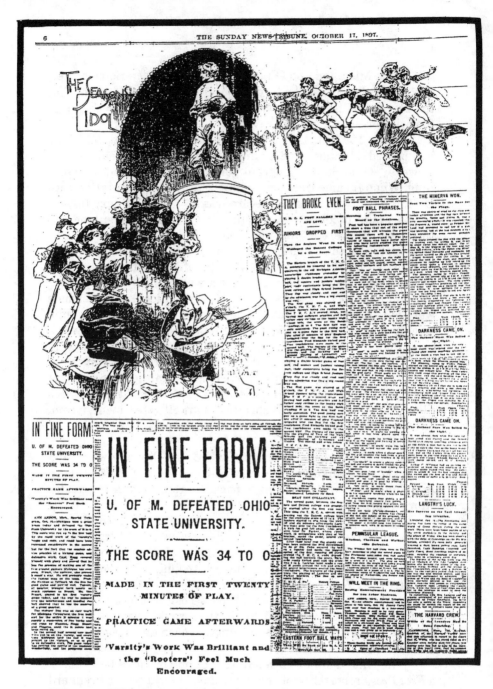

Who was "The Season's Idol" when Michigan and Ohio State first met back in 1897? According to the Sunday News-Tribune *of Detroit it was the collegiate football player. Although the Victorian Era had not ended, the illustration suggests that the game of football was capable of inspiring decidedly non-Victorian emotions. Also note in the sub-head that "Varsity's (UM) Work Was Brilliant and the 'Rooters' Feel Much Encouraged."*

the 0-0 draw with Wesleyan could not be regarded as a "hard game."

As things turned out, Ohio State's "fast game" reputation was just that – a reputation. Michigan won the series' first game with ease, 34-0, at Regents Field on the U-M campus.

The Wolverines scored all the game's points in the first half and could have just about named their point total had they chosen to do so. Luckily for the Columbus visitors, Michigan Coach Gustave Ferbert called off his Wolves completely during the second half of the mismatch and the game itself was called to a halt five minutes early.

Michigan kicked off and "The Big One" had begun – the series that in later years would transcend the boundaries of the two states involved and evolve into a "national series" in the truest sense.

It was now Ohio State vs. Michigan, and nothing would ever be the same again for either team, for either of the institutions, nor for their respective alumni and followers.

Unable to move the ball on the first possession, OSU punted to midfield and U-M rushed right in for a touchdown. Hannan blasted over for the score, Hogg kicked the goal and the Wolverines led, 6-0. (In 1897 a touchdown had a point value of four; conversions two and field goals four.)

Before intermission, Stuart had registered three touchdowns, Hogg and Pingree one each, and Hogg kicked five successful conversions. Michigan had the big game won.

"In the second half," reported the *Detroit News*, "several new men were put in on the 'varsity' and every time Michigan took the ball it was punted to the visitors, so as to get in on defensive work."

The Wolverines went on to post four more wins in 1897 before losing a season-ending game to Chicago, 21-12, played indoors at the Chicago Coliseum before 10,000 fans, a huge crowd in those days. The defeat cost Michigan a share (with Wisconsin) of the Intercollegiate Conference of Faculty Representatives championship. The ICFR, only in its second year, would later become known as the Western Conference, the Big Seven, the Big Eight, the Big Nine, and finally the Big Ten. However, the original title is still the official name of the Conference.

OSU's loss to Michigan was obviously a shattering experience. The Buckeyes failed to win any of their remaining six games and finished the 1897 season with a disastrous 1-7-1 record. Not

OCTOBER 17, 1897

GETTING TO WORK

MICHIGAN DEFEATED OHIO STATE BY A HANDY SCORE.

ALL SIX TOUCHDOWNS MADE IN THE FIRST TWENTY MINUTES.

TEAM TURNED TO A KICKING GAME IN THE SECOND HALF

STUART, NEW HALFBACK, PROVED HIS REPUTATION FOR SPEED.

Latest News of What Capt. Hogg's Men Have Been Doing.

Detroit Free Press

before, nor since, has an Ohio State football team lost seven games in one season. And the mere 18 points the team managed to score still stands as an all-time low for a campaign.

Just as 1897 was the beginning of the series, it also turned out to be the beginning of a long period of frustration for OSU. It would take 16 games spread over a 22-year period before the Buckeyes could claim a victory over Michigan, and each loss until then did its share in intensifying the rivalry. The pattern of mutual institutional "hate" was forming. It would get worse, or better, depending on one's outlook.

1900

0-0 IN '00

Michigan and Ohio State had not met since their series inaugural in 1897 and both teams chalked up impressive records during the three-year hiatus. The Wolverines were 23-5-0, including a perfect 10-0-0 season in 1898 which presented the Maize and Blue with their first Western Conference championship.

During the same period, OSU, not yet a member of the Conference, won 19, lost six and tied one, and its 9-0-1 record the previous year was the team's first unbeaten season.

The pre-game buildup for the 1900 Ohio State-Michigan game began early in the week and by Saturday had ballooned into wild excitement. And there's little wonder. Both teams were 7-1-0 and more than anxious to christen the 20th century with a victory over a rival that, after only one game, and that three years ago, had already achieved "most hated" status.

OSU's lone loss had been to Ohio Medical, 11-6. Were the Buckeyes "looking ahead?" Michigan's only blemish was a 28-5 licking at the hands of a powerful Iowa team that finished unbeaten that year.

"A big group of rooters from OSU will leave tomorrow morning on a special train for Ann Arbor, and the team will not lack for encouragement," a reporter for the *Detroit Free Press* wrote.

On the day of the game, November 24, the *Free Press* reported, "A thousand shouting students from Columbus came up to Ann Arbor to cheer their team on to an expected victory over Michigan.

9

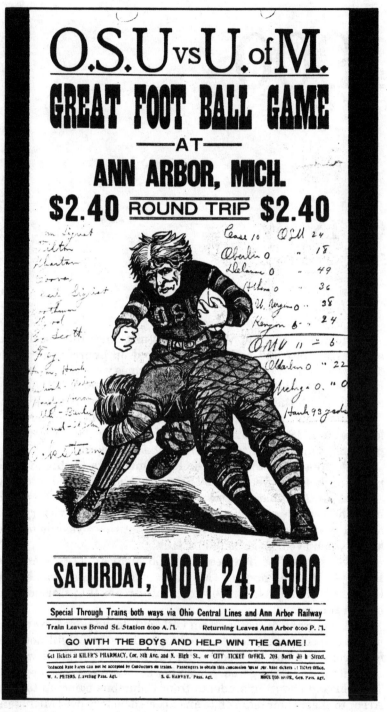

A railroad advertisement for the 1900 game. Today the fare would be quoted as "$1.20 each way on a roundtrip." (Courtesy of OSU Photo Archives)

The whole university, co-eds and all, apparently followed the team into the enemy's country, and made a demonstration which was the feature of the game. They had songs and yells and, led on by official yell-masters, fairly took the breath of the home crowd away, for there has never before been such a large number of outsiders at a game played at Ann Arbor. The cheering is usually all one way, but the scenes enacted today make the contest the most typical college game which has ever been played on Regents Field."

As for the game, neither side had a score or a victory to cheer about. It ended all even – Michigan 0, Ohio State 0. "It was a remarkably close struggle with plenty of good football, and the work of the two teams on a slippery field was unusually free from loose playing," said the *Free Press.*

OSU had the better of the first half; U-M the second half. The Buckeyes won the toss of the coin and chose a strong wind to their backs. Michigan elected to kickoff, forced a punt, and missed on a long field goal try. On the Bucks' next series of downs, James Westwater fumbled the snap from center on punt formation and put the Wolverines in good shape at the OSU 21-yard line. Unable to pick up a first down, the ball went back to visitors at the 15.

Ohio State then went to work. James McLaren ripped off a 20-yard gain and Westwater rambled for 23 more. Suddenly, the ball was on Michigan's 52-yard line. (A football field measured 110 yards in length until 1912). However, two runs netted only eight yards and OSU punted. (A fourth down wasn't added until 1912).

The remainder of the half continued one of punt-swapping and neither team made a serious threat.

Also in 1900, games were divided into two halves, so it was now time for the Buckeyes to buck the breeze. On their first two possessions they had punts blocked and the latter such mistake gave Michigan the ball at the OSU 22-yard line. Once again the Bucks held, this time at the 15. U-M later reached the enemy's 13-yard line but couldn't cash in. Late in the game, Everett Sweeley punted to State's three-yard line and OSU was able to control the ball until time ran out. The series' first tie had been recorded.

Each team had one game remaining on the schedule. Ohio State cracked Kenyon 23-5 for an 8-1-1 season. Michigan lost to Chicago 15-6 to finish 7-2-1.

The year 1900 would be Langdon "Biff" Lea's only season as head coach at Michigan. He was replaced by a man who was

11

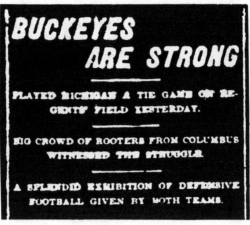

BUCKEYES ARE STRONG

PLAYED MICHIGAN A TIE GAME ON RE-
GENTS' FIELD YESTERDAY.

BIG CROWD OF ROOTERS FROM COLUMBUS
WITNESSED THE STRUGGLE.

A SPLENDID EXHIBITION OF DEFENSIVE
FOOTBALL GIVEN BY BOTH TEAMS.

Detroit Free Press

REJUVENATED CHAMPIONS

Played Better Football Than Michigan,

Ohio State Proved Her Right to Recognition in
Western Football.

Michigan Presented Her Very Strongest Eleven and Tried
Everything in Her Football Repertoire Without Shak-
ing the Perfect Defense of O. S. U.

Columbus Dispatch

destined to become one of collegiate football's all-time, all-time legends. And on the horizon were new heights for not only Michigan, but the Western Conference.

Until the turn of the century there had been little opposition, outside the East, in the annual scrap for the mythical national championship. During the era, the press in other sections of the country gave extensive coverage to the Eastern powers, especially those of Yale, Harvard, Princeton and Pennsylvania.

Word had begun to spread, however, about the strength of the relatively new Western Conference. In 1900 the league added two more members, Iowa and Indiana, to bring its total to nine. And when the "Big Nine" posted a phenomenal 42-3-3 record against non-conference foes and outscored them 1326-102, the Eastern football establishment began to ask, "Who is this new kid on the block?"

In reality, though, during the Western Conference's five-year existence, its members had anchored themselves as a group that warranted closer attention. Their 182-29-12 (.843) "outside" record spoke very well for itself. Furthermore, the conference had outscored its opposition by a staggering total score of 5173-696, for an average game score of 23-3.

The Eastern powers had good cause to take note of Midwestern football.

1901

RUN FOR THE ROSES

Should anybody ever devise a "Top Ten" for the most "well-known" or "popular" or "famous" teams in the history of college football, the 1901 University of Michigan club not only needs to be included, but it would rank very near, or at, the top of the list.

As a starter, the '01 Wolverines had the distinction of winning the first Rose Bowl game. Next, the team had a perfect (really *perfect*) 11-0-0 record, scoring 550 points and allowing its opponents nothing. Not a single score of any kind all year.

And its colorful new coach, Fielding H. Yost, better known as "Hurry Up" Yost, added even more personality and appeal to this more than memorable football team.

Michigan was the fifth stop in five years on Yost's coaching circuit and his brief career had already established the man as a winner. In 1897 he led Ohio Wesleyan to a 7-1-1 record, including a 6-0 win over Ohio State and a scoreless tie with Michigan, a game in which he participated as a player and triggered the severing of athletic relations between the two schools.

Yost then went to Nebraska where he was also 7-1-1. In 1899 he moved next door to Kansas and turned the Jayhawks into a 10-0-0 winner. From the plains, Yost went West, all the way to Palo Alto, California, and a stint at Stanford. His 1900 Stanford team won seven, lost two and tied one. That gave Yost a 31-6-2 coaching record and when he got wind that Michigan was looking for a new coach, he applied, was hired, and in typical "hurry up" style, hopped a train headed for Ann Arbor.

FIELDING HARRIS "HURRY UP" YOST

His first Michigan team (1901) won all 11 games on the schedule, scoring 550 points to none for opponents. The season was capped by a 49-0 rout of Stanford in the first Rose Bowl game. (Photo courtesy of Michigan Athletic Department.)

The front cover and first inside page of the Official Program for the first Michigan-Ohio State game played in Columbus (1901). The author, almost by accident, discovered this rare piece of memorabilia in the Main Library on the Ohio State campus. Interesting features include the football-shaped pages, color printing (the OSU jersey in scarlet, the "M" in blue), the tattered stockings of the "M" player, the gold cord tying the 14-pages together to resemble the laces of an actual football, and the tremendous amount of hand labor required in the assembly of the book. Numerous advertisements filled the inside pages and no price was quoted anywhere. It was certainly a unique piece of work.

Yost was born in the tiny town of Fairview, West Virginia in 1871. He attended college at Ohio Normal for two years before returning to his hometown of Fairview. In 1895, at the age of 24, he enrolled at the West Virginia School of Law where he also played tackle for the Mountaineers for two years. Even though he had received a law degree, Yost went to Ohio Wesleyan as head coach and his colorful career had begun. As evidenced by the spat with Michigan, he had not yet ended his playing career.

A vagabond as a young adult, Yost found a home in Ann Arbor.

The 1901 Maize and Blue had smashed Albion, Case, Indiana, Northwestern, Buffalo (128-0) and Carlisle by a combined score of 319-0 as the team was readying for its first trip ever to the hostile territory of Columbus, Ohio, and the date with the Buckeyes.

The *Detroit Free Press* reported, "There were 375 Michigan students who made a flying trip over the Ann Arbor and Hocking Valley railroads in a special train to see their representatives give battle to the Ohio men, and they did some incessant rooting at the game."

Under normal circumstances, Ohio State's figures leading up to the big game would be impressive – a 4-0-1 record by a combined 77-5 score – but when compared to Michigan's staggering statistics of that year, the Buckeyes didn't seem to stand much of a chance.

But the Bucks played a rough and tough game that November 9 and held their high-powered opponents to a respectable score of 21-0 at Ohio Field before 4,000 lovers of the game. The contest was OSU's 100th all-time football game.

The final margin could have been much greater but the gutty Buckeye team held Michigan four times within the five-yard line to deny scores. Obviously, Ohio State was more than ready for this particular game.

OSU returned the opening kickoff to their own 43 and immediately gained 15 yards but were held and had to punt. A little later in the game, Michigan recovered a fumble at the Ohio 35-yard line and marched to the two before being stopped.

James Westwater punted and here came Michigan again, but a fumble at the OSU four-yard line halted the drive. Another Westwater kick gave U-M good field position and they crunched back to the Ohio three, again to be held out. Westwater was called upon once more and punted his team out of immediate danger, but moments later OSU found the relentless opposition near its goal again. Could the Buckeyes do it again? Could they

At the first Michigan-Ohio State game to be played in Columbus, in 1901, carriages and wagons served as a grandstand for many of the fans in attendance. (Photo courtesy of OSU Photo Archives.)

hold for the fourth straight time? Yes they could! Michigan was halted at the four as the Ohio faithfuls screamed to the heavens.

Another OSU punt was in order, followed by another Michigan march, this time to the 10-yard line where it became third (and last) down and one yard to go for a first down. Their power game having come up short all afternoon, the Wolverines resorted to trickery – and it worked. On a fake field goal attempt, Everett Sweeley surprised the defense with a run and a pickup of five yards. Neil Snow then struggled to the two, and Hugh White powered over for the touchdown. The Wolverines had finally cracked the stubborn Buckeye defense for a score. Bruce Shorts kicked his only successful conversion of the day and U-M led 6-0. (By 1900 touchdowns had come to count for five points; conversions one point.)

Later in the first half, Michigan took a punt at the OSU 40-yard line and scored in just one play. Bill Heston ripped through the Ohio defense on a play described by a reporter for the *Free Press* thusly: "Only (James) Kittle stood as an obstacle and Referee Wrenn, in trying to get out of the way of Heston, got in the road of Kittle. The California halfback (Heston) made a touchdown under those circumstances." Michigan now led, 11-0.

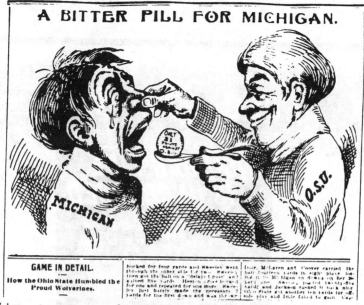

A BITTER PILL FOR MICHIGAN.

GAME IN DETAIL.

How the Ohio State Humbled the Proud Wolverines.

This cartoon appeared in the Columbus Sunday Dispatch *the day after the 1901 Michigan-Ohio State game, and clearly indicates that the Buckeyes considered the 21-0 defeat as, well, at least a moral victory. It could have been because U-M's "Point-A-Minute" team that year averaged 53 points in the other 10 games. Also note the headline reading, "How the Ohio State Humbled the Proud Wolverines."*

A few moments later Snow scored on a short run and the half ended with the score 16-0. The weary OSU players welcomed the break.

Early in the second half, Snow scored from the five-yard line to conclude the day's point-making. "Only at one stage of the game did the ton of human beef represented by Ohio's team make any material progress toward a touchdown," said the *Free Press*. That came late in the game when the Bucks reached Michigan's 20-yard line. The Buckeyes were winless in their three games against Michigan, and it was reported that the happy Wolverine fans celebrated long and loud in Columbus that night.

"The game showed up the superior condition of the Michigan men," said the *Free Press*. "On almost every scrimmage some Ohio man would stretch out on the ground and take the full time. This playing for wind was so apparent that the Michigan players finally burlesqued it. The Ohio men could not stand the gag and their

oit Free Press

SUNDAY NOVEMBER 10, 1901—FORTY-EIGHT PAGES,—FIVE PARTS. PRICE: FIVE CENTS.

PART ONE.

MICHIGAN LINE IS UNCROSSED

Only Once Did Ohio Threaten Goal.	Harvard Scored On Penn. at Will.
ANN ARBOR BOYS GOT SCORE OF 21.	NEW WOODRUFF TRICK PLAY FAILED
Chicago Held Northwest Team to 6-5	West Point Tied Princeton in Fierce Game.

FOOTBALL RESULTS AT A GLANCE.

Fullback Neil Snow scored two touchdowns in UM's 21-0 win over OSU in 1901. Later that season he registered five TDs in the first Rose Bowl game.

doctors and trainers ran more yards than both teams put together."

There was also a "considerable wrangle" between the coaches before the game. Yost insisted that the regulation 35-minute halves be played, while OSU's coach, John Eckstorm, wanted 25-minute halves. The game's umpire (Hoagland) told Eckstorm that if he wouldn't agree to the rules, the game would be forfeited to Michigan.

The Wolverines went on to defeat Chicago, Beloit and Iowa. Ohio State won only one of its three remaining games to conclude a 5-3-1 autumn.

Meanwhile, out in sunny Pasadena, California, the Tournament of Roses Committee had decided that football should replace polo as the main athletic event to cap the New Year's Day festivities. The original plan called for an "East-West" game, so in 1901 they invited Michigan to play Stanford (3-1-2), coached by Charles Frickert, who had replaced Yost. The Wolverines routed the host team 49-0 and prompted a reporter for the *New York Times* to write, "The score is quite in proportion to the general superiority of the Eastern men at the game of football."

Snow scored five touchdowns that January 1, 1902 afternoon, which is still a Rose Bowl record. Heston gained 170 yards in 18 carries and Michigan rushed for 503 yards while Stanford struggled to get 67.

There would not be another Rose Bowl football game for 14 years.

The first Rose Bowl game as reported by The New York Times *shared the spotlight with Pommery Champagne and the big White Sale at Siegel Cooper Company.*

1902

MERCY

Fielding Yost had his incredible "Point-A-Minute" gridiron machine clicking on all eight cylinders (or was it all 16?) in 1902. The "Point-A-Minute" label tagged on that particular squad was almost a reality. The team averaged nearly a point for every minute of playing time in the 11 games. Prevailing rules of the era called for two 35-minute halves, but most of Michigan's games in 1902 were not played in their entirety.

Albion, Case, Michigan Agricultural College and Indiana fell before the onslaught of the mighty Maize and Blue by an average score of 79-2. Then came a "close" 23-0 victory over Notre Dame.

Ohio State also had a perfect record (4-0-0) and had not allowed a point when it came time to "face the music" at Ann Arbor on October 25.

Meanwhile, back in Columbus, the *Dispatch* reported, "No football game in years has created such an interest in this city. For days and days the contest has been food for speculation and comment. . . .How much Columbus cared who won the game is best illustrated by the fact that more than 500 telephone calls were answered by the Dispatch."

Once the callers discovered the final score, they were a very disappointed group.

Michigan 86, Ohio State 0. It could have been worse. Officials mercifully decided enough was enough with 10 minutes left on the clock. No Buckeye protest is recorded. (Had today's point standards been in effect, the 1902 game would have ended with a final score of 101-0.)

ALBERT HERRNSTEIN

Scored an all-time series record six touchdowns in the 86-0 win over Ohio State in 1902. He later was head coach at OSU. (Photo courtesy of Michigan Athletic Department.)

BUCKEYES NOT IN IT

Michigan Gave Ohio a Terrific Drubbing.

Piled Up a Heartbreaking Score of 86 to 0.

2,200 Rooters From Columbus Saw Balloon Go Up.

The Finest Game of Foot Ball in Wolverine's Gridiron History—Every Man a Star, and Yost is Happy.

The Detroit News

The Wolverines led at intermission 45-0 and in the second half added 41 more points to make the slaughter complete. A. E. Herrstein tallied six touchdowns, James Lawrence, Phil Palmer and Dan McGugin added two each, while Bill Heston, Joe Maddock and Paul Jones recorded one apiece. Heston's score was on a 70-yard run. Lawrence kicked eight conversions and Everett Sweeley three.

Fifteen touchdowns equals 75 points; 11 goals equals 11 points. It all added up to 86 points, and never before nor since has Ohio State suffered as bad a defeat on the football field.

The following are some observations by newsmen representing the *Detroit Free Press*, the *Detroit News-Tribune* and the *Columbus Dispatch*, all of whom were at Ferry Field that day: "Ohio State never got near enough to Michigan's goal to see what the crossbars looked like. . . .Ohio came up from Columbus anticipating victory and 2,300 jubilant rooters followed the team. . . .

Fully 5,000 cheered and sang, and between the Michigan rooters and Ohio's, each led by a brass band, there was pandemonium until it became apparent that Ohio was doomed. . . .Today's avalanche is likely to dishearten Ohio and result in a breaking off of football relations. . . .Lincoln, Ohio's big left guard, was ruled out for smearing his fist over Carter's nose. . . .Capt. 'Buck' Coover weeping at the bitter defeat of his team and Ohio rooters equally disconsolate at the humiliating score. . . .it was spirit and inferior might pitted against giant veterans. . . .The Scarlet and Gray reserves were drawn on heavily."

Michigan followed with a 6-0 squeaker over Wisconsin. The next week Yost went to Minneapolis to scout the Minnesota-Illinois game while his Wolverines stayed home and annihilated Iowa, 107-0. Then came wins over Chicago (11-1-0 that year) and Oberlin. That set the stage for a Western Conference title match between Michigan and Minnesota in the season's finale. The Wolverines prevailed, 23-6.

Final record: 11-0-0, 644 points scored to the opponents' 12.

OSU returned to Columbus to lick its wounds before rebounding with wins over Kenyon and Ohio Wesleyan, ties against Illinois and Indiana, and a loss to Case for a 6-2-2 season.

But in the Buckeyes' battles with Michigan, they were still winless (0-3-1) and had yet to score, while the Wolverines had 141 points.

1903

GAME 5

WHAT'S A COACH TO DO?

It was the first week in November and Coach Perry Hale and his Ohio State Buckeyes were mentally preparing themselves for a second trip in two years to Ann Arbor and another dreaded date with awesome Michigan, a team that had smothered Hale and his boys 86-0 just one year before.

The Wolverines, unbeaten in their eight games in 1903, were averaging 55 points per outing and had surrendered just one touchdown. If there was one single ray of hope for OSU, it stood in the fact that just one week before, Minnesota proved that Fielding Yost and his Michigan players were human and not supernatural beings. The Golden Gophers scored in the last minute to tie the Wolverines 6-6 in a classic duel at Minneapolis.

The Bucks had lost to Case, 12-0, but won the other six games on the schedule by an overwhelming point margin of 193-11. But, once again, they proved to be no match for their rivals from up North. The Wolverines won by a final of 36-0 as Herbert Graver scored five touchdowns before a Regents Field crowd of 5,000 on November 7, and the game was not nearly as close as the final score indicated. Michigan led at halftime, 36-0.

Ohio State kicked off at 2:45 in the afternoon and "The Big M" moved right in for a touchdown. On the game's first scrimmage play, Graver set the tone for things to come with a 50-yard gain around the left side, all the way to Ohio's 28. Two more runs gained eight yards before Graver traveled the final 20 for the score. Thomas Hammond was perfect with his first of six conversions and U-M was ahead, 6-0.

25

The Detroit News-Tribune
SPORTING SECTION
DETROIT, MICHIGAN, SUNDAY MORNING, NOVEMBER 8, 1903.

OPENING OF THE DEER SEASON.

BATTLE
ROYAL

BETWEEN PENNSY AND HAR-
VARD AT PHILADELPHIA.

HARVARD WON OUT FINALLY
BY A SCORE OF 17 TO 10.

PENNSY TOOK ADVANTAGE OF
HARVARD'S FUMBLES.

OFFER BY
GRIFFITH

MAY RESULT IN SALE TO HIM
OF DETROIT BALL CLUB.

SCORING
MACHINE

WELL LUBRICATED AT D. A. C.
YESTERDAY.

VARSITY'S
BAD DAY

MICHIGAN OUTPLAYED BY O.
S. U. IN SECOND HALF.

FIRST HALF RESULTED IN 36
POINTS, HOWEVER.

FUMBLES AND A WEAK DE-
FENSE CAUSE OF SLUMP.

YESTERDAY'S FOOT
BALL RESULTS.

The Doctor: "Well, I guess we are in good shape now to take care of all the hunters that'll come along."

The big sports news in Michigan in early November of 1903 was the opening of deer season and "Varsity's Bad Day" of football against Ohio State. Bad day? One sub-head says, "Fumbles and a weak defense cause of slump." Slump? The Wolverines won 36-0.

Michigan scored again on its next possession with a snappy, 55-yard drive requiring only four plays. Graver got three yards, Person another three, Joseph Maddox 30, and Graver the final 19. Later in the first half, Michigan made it 18-0 after recovering a fumble at the OSU 35. Heckin bulled for five and here was Herbert Graver again, racing 30 more for the touchdown.

Two minutes and 50 seconds later came another score. Michigan began at Ohio's 54-yard line after receiving a punt and hammered out a nine-play drive. Graver went to the 44; Harrison Weeks to the 39; Weeks to the 29; Maddock to the 27; F. C. Longman to the 22; Graver to the 12; Weeks to the seven, and Maddock to the five. John Curtis took his turn and scored to make Michigan's bulge 24-0.

Graver added two more first-half touchdowns, the latter on a 30-yard excursion, and the scorekeeper was through for the day.

OSU captured two of its last three games, all in Columbus, and posted a final record of 8-3-0.

Michigan blanked three remaining opponents (Wisconsin, Oberlin, Chicago) for a third straight undefeated season, during which time the overall record was 30-0-1 by an unbelievable total score of 1759-18.

As for the Wolverine-Buckeye series, it now stood 4-0-1.

1904

GAME 6

"WE SCORED! WE SCORED!"

The second half had just begun at Columbus and the score was: Michigan 5, Ohio State 0.

Michigan had the ball at its 44-yard line and Frank Longman rammed into the line on second down. The pigskin popped away and was rolling freely. In shot OSU's Bill Marquardt, who picked up the bouncing ball and sped away from the heap of tangled humanity. A race was on.

"Vainly Harry Hammond ran after the fleet Ohio fullback, plunged at him on Michigan's five-yard line and missed," reported the *Detroit News*.

William B. Marquardt won the race and Ohio State had finally scored on Michigan! With the partisan crowd of 8,000 roaring uncontrollably, Ralph Hoyer cooly added the conversion and the score was suddenly 6-5 in favor of OSU. "The fame of the Wolverines made this feature especially gratifying to Ohio," said the *News*. The place went absolutely crazy. The Buckeyes actually led mighty Michigan, "Champions of the West," as they were now being called.

"Once Ohio had scored, Michigan plunged in with desperation," the *News* reported. OSU's lead, however, lasted just eight minutes and the Wolverines proceeded to place a 31-6 victory in the football record books. Nevertheless, the Buckeye rooters were happy. Just to score on Michigan in those days was a feat within itself, and no OSU team had ever done it before.

OHIO SCORED ON MICHIGAN

Longman's Fumble Allowed Marquardt to Get the Ball.

HARRY HAMMOND'S PURSUIT FAILED AT FIVE-YARD LINE.

Michigan Got Going After That and Scored Rapidly.

Even the Detroit News *thought OSU's first score in the series, in 1904, was more significant than the final score of the game.*

BILL HESTON

Michigan's great All-America scored five touchdowns against OSU in the 1901-02-04 games. One was a 70-yarder — still the longest scoring run from scrimmage in series history. (Photo courtesy of Michigan Athletic Department.)

BILL MARQUARDT

Scored Ohio State's first touchdown ever against Michigan. His run tied the game 5-5 and Ralph Hoyer's conversion made it 6-5, but the Wolverines came back for a 31-6 victory. (Photo courtesy of OSU Photo Archives.)

Both teams entered the October 15 battle undefeated, untied and unscored upon. U-M had registered 248 points against four opponents and OSU had tallied 184, also against four foes.

Following Ohio's go-ahead touchdown, Michigan's great running back Bill Heston scored on a short plunge to cap a methodical eight-minute march. Tom Hammond kicked the PAT and U-M was back on top to stay, 11-6.

Hammond later added field goals of 32 (the first field goal in series history) and 25 yards for a 19-6 advantage. Heston blasted over for two more touchdowns, Hammond converted both times, and Michigan won the sixth game of the series going away.

"The victory was dearly won by Michigan in the gruelling, smashing style that left a trail of men knocked out after every play," typed a *News* reporter.

Also making the news in the 1904 contest was a heated scramble for possession of the "game ball" after the game ended. There was an unwritten rule that the ball belonged to the winning team but on this particular day Ohio State wanted it. As the game ended a Buckeye player grabbed the pigskin and ran to OSU's side of the field and hurled the football high into the crowd.

"Yost, followed by both teams, ran after him and the rooters gazed on breathlessly while a Michigan man and a Buckeye man scrambled up over the high bleachers' front," said the *News*. "The Wolverine struggled through the crowd of Ohio spectators. The Buckeye, no other than Capt. (James) Marker, who had played brilliantly, clambered on the rail and shouted: 'Ohio, Ohio, be gentlemen; give me that ball!' The ball popped out of the crowd, Marker jumped down and handed it to the referee, who delivered it to Capt. Heston of Michigan."

OSU went on to defeat Case and Kenyon but lost to Indiana, Illinois, Oberlin and Pop Warner's Carlisle Indians for a final record of 6-5-0.

Even back in the early 1900s, what effect did losing to Michigan have on the Ohio State football team? Once the Buckeyes played their big rival, was their season "over"? Did OSU just "play out" its remaining schedule? According to cold calculations, there was a definite pattern. For example, in the last five seasons (1900-04), in games leading up to the meeting with Michigan, OSU has an impressive 25-2-1 record. In games *after* the Ohio-Michigan encounter, the Bucks' record fell to only 7-10-2.

As for the Wolverines, after the Ohio State game in 1904, Coach Yost and his crew won six more games for another undefeated season. One of those games, the following week in fact, deserves special mention.

The opponent was West Virginia, Yost's alma mater. The Mountaineers went to Ann Arbor ostensibly as innocent lambs. Whether it was unavoidable in the dimensions of the mismatch, or whether "Hurry Up" had another motivation, was never explained. The remarkable fact is that the Michigan troops followed the policy of "take no prisoners" and humiliated Yost's "old school" by a final score of 130-0.

Since Yost had been at Ann Arbor he was yet to taste defeat. His phenomenal record now swelled to 43-0-1 and in the process his mighty teams walloped their opposition by a per game average score of 52-1.

Teams that represented the Big Nine had definitely become the monsters of the Midwest. In 1904 Conference members won 56 and lost only four against non-Conference competition, to increase the all-time record (1896-1904) to 378-46-17 and a winning percentage of .881.

Meanwhile, back in Columbus and the rest of Ohioland, Bill Marquardt was a touchdown hero.

1905

TWINKLIN' HEELS, TREMBLIN' HUMANITY, A 113-YARD RUN, ANOTHER MICHIGAN WIN

It was November 11, 1905, and time for the seventh meeting between Michigan and Ohio State. The Buckeyes had not lost a game all fall, which was dandy on its own merit. However, the Wolverines hadn't suffered defeat in the past *five* falls!

Michigan was embarked upon college football's all-time string of games without a loss, now extended to 53 – all but six by shut-outs.

Once again, OSU was no match for the men from Michigan. Sparked by a 113-yard run by Alfred Barlow, the Wolverines clobbered the Bucks 40-0 on the home turf of Regents Field.

Playing all its games in Columbus, OSU was 6-0-2, suffering ties with Otterbein and Case. Michigan had beaten nine opponents by an average score of 41 to a flat zero, including triumphs over powerhouses Vanderbilt (18-0) and Nebraska (31-0).

It was late in the game and U-M had Ohio State salted away for another year, with a 28-0 cushion, when the most electrifying run in series history brought the crowd of 8,000 to its feet.

Under the rules of the day, a missed field goal attempt became a "live ball" and could be run back by the defensive team at its option.

"Barlow, the little sub-quarterback, stood beneath his own goal posts, shading his eyes from the sun," wrote a reporter from the *Detroit News*. "He saw Stolp swing his foot on the ball. Then he saw the oval mount high and go wide of the posts. As it came to

REGENTS FIELD – ANN ARBOR

Scene of five Michigan-Ohio State games – 1897, 1900, 1902, 1903
and 1905. This wide photograph was printed on separate, facing

---

him three yards back of the line and to the right of the posts, he
swung to the right and broke through the maze of crimson and grey
players, bearing down on him. One got him by the heel, but he
shook the tackler off. Another tackler was brushed out of the way.
A third was beaten out. A fourth was knocked galley-west by
Stuart. A fifth loomed for an instant in the runner's path, then
flew, tumbling head over heels to one side, as Curtis bumped into
him. Another stood waiting, and was knocked over by Garrels.
Still a seventh, the last, came on, and was diving for the sub-
quarter's twinkling heels when Hammond knocked him to one
side. The little runner sped away down a clear field to the limit,
and over – 113 yards in all, with a touchdown at the end. The cheering was deafening. The south bleacher was a mass of trembling
humanity, over which thousands of little maize and blue pennants
waved furiously triumphant." Barlow had made his record run
and every step of the way had been recorded by the reporter from
Detroit.

As for the rest of the game, Michigan received the opening
kickoff and in 13 pounding plays reached Ohio's 35-yard line.
"Everything was pointing to a straightforward walk for the first
score, when Tom Hammond's grip on the leather relaxed, and a
Buckeye fell on the ball on the Ohio 35-yard line," typed the *News*
reporter.

OSU couldn't move and lined up in punt formation. In stormed
the Wolverines. "Up shot the leather, straight into the air. The
wind carried it backwards. From the Michigan stands rose shrill
yells of delight and loud guffaws," reported the *News*. John Curtis
had blocked the kick and the ball bounded all the way into Ohio's

pages in the 1906 Michiganensian, perhaps from different plates made with different exposures. Also note the lines running up and down, as well as across the field. The resulting grid pattern is the origin of the term "gridiron" for a football field.

endzone, where Harry Patrick fell on it for a touchdown. Hammond's goal-after was good and U-M was on its way, 6-0.

The Wolverines then made it 12-0 on a fumble recovery at the OSU 30. "Stolp was stopped so suddenly that he dropped the ball in astonishment," said the *News*. John Garrels recovered and W. J. Embs' short plunge capped the quick drive. Hammond's kick was once again on target. Garrels scored just before intermission. Curtis converted and Michigan was in command, 18-0.

Early in the second half, Curtis' touchdown run and Hammond's PAT made it 24-0. A little later, Hammond kicked a 20-yard field goal for four more Wolverine points.

Then came Barlow's run to glory.

Garrels scored his second touchdown of the day on a streaking 40-yard run late in the game and Hammond's ninth kicking point of the game concluded the scoring. In three games against Ohio State, Hammond kicked 14 conversions and three field goals for a total of 26 points.

After seven games between the two rivals, the W-L-T figures were 6-0-1 in Michigan's favor, along with a decided 248-6 advantage in scoring.

The Buckeyes won twice more that year before dropping the season's finale to Indiana. With the exception of the Michigan disaster, all the games were played in Columbus and the final record was 8-2-2.

Michigan rolled on. There were two more shutouts (Wisconsin and Oberlin) for a 55-0-1 record since Fielding Yost had become coach at Ann Arbor in 1901.

MICHIGAN'S ALFRED BARLOW

Returned a missed field goal 113 yards in the 1905 game – the longest run in the history of the Michigan-Ohio State rivalry. (Photo courtesy of Michigan Athletic Department.)

Then it happened. And it happened on Thanksgiving Day (November 20) at Chicago before a throng of 27,000 souls. Coach Amos Alonzo Stagg had led his University of Chicago Maroons to an 8-0-0 season record and had allowed only one touchdown. Chicago ended the remarkable Michigan unbeaten streak by blanking the Wolverines by a scant margin of 2-0.

The score came on a safety midway through the second half, when Chicago punted from the Michigan 43-yard line. The ball went into the endzone, but instead of downing it, U-M's Danny Clark attempted to run it out and was tackled behind the goal.

It was the Wolverines' first defeat in five years to the day. On Thanksgiving Day in 1900, Chicago had beaten Michigan 15-6. The streak started the following season and lasted for 56 games (55-0-1 record). During that ultrasuccessful stretch, the Yostmen accumulated 2821 points (50.4 per game) to the opponents' 40 total points. An incredible feat, and even today it stands as the longest unbeaten streak among the major teams in collegiate football. Not Yale, nor Harvard, nor Pennsylvania, the grid powers of that era matched it. Nor has Notre Dame, Southern California, Alabama, Oklahoma, Nebraska, Texas or any other team.

Just as incredible as the streak was the coaching record of Yost. The loss to Chicago in 1905 marked the first time in his nine-year career as coach that he failed to win (or share) a Conference championship while at the helm. He had coached at Ohio Wesleyan, Nebraska, Kansas, Stanford and Michigan. "Hurry Up's" overall record read 86-7-3 at the conclusion of the 1905 season.

Tom Hammond kicking and William Clark holding. Hammond kicked 14 conversions and 3 field goals in the 1903-04-05 games against Ohio State. (Photo courtesy of Michigan Athletic Department.)

For the record, the awesome power of the Big Nine was again reflected in the members' performance against "outside" teams in 1905. It was 55-3-1.

However, the big sports news of 1905 wasn't Michigan's win over Ohio State, nor Alfred Barlow's 113-yard run, nor the coaching record of Yost, nor the power of the Big Nine. Rather, the big news was football fatalities. In 1905, 14 youths died as results of injuries suffered on the gridiron. In the past five years, an astonishing total of 71 young men lost their lives from injuries received while playing high school and college football.

The public, the press, college officials, Congress and especially President Teddy Roosevelt were up in arms and demanding that either sweeping rule changes be made to modify the brutal features of the game, or that the game be abolished. On December 28, 1905, representatives of 62 colleges met and made major rules changes. Many of the reforms were proposed by John Wilhelm Heisman, who was coaching at Georgia Tech at the time and for whom the Heisman Trophy is named.

College football, for all its popularity and appeal both to players and spectators, had come to the brink of extinction. Such was the feeling of the critics. It was a close call, but football came out with a future.

1906

GAME 8

U-M GOT REAL
KICK OUT OF IT

Michigan's John Garrels had already missed on three field goal attempts as the scoreless game ticked down to its final four minutes. The line of scrimmage was Ohio State's 36, and John Garrels was poised and ready for his fifth try.

"It was not a person in the color-bedecked stands that thought he would make the score when they saw him drop back for the kick," reported the *Detroit News*. "Yet it was Michigan's only chance to win. It had to be taken. Yost's face was ashen gray, his lips drawn with anxiety as he watched the preparations for the kick.

"Not a sound was heard as the ball whirled from Lowell, the doughty center, to Bishop, the heady quarterback (and holder). Even Ohio State's derisive howls were stilled. The ball rose beautifully from the toe of Garrels' boot, and sped straight between the posts and over the bar.

"The pandemonium that broke loose in the Michigan bleacher outdid in volume and sincerity in noise-making anything that has been seen on University Field in the history of Ohio State athletics."

Garrels' field goal gave Michigan a four-point lead and the Wolverines forced a safety just before the final whistle and once again the Buckeyes were victims to the Maize and Blue, this time by a 6-0 score.

The Wolverines opened the 1906 season with a 28-0 win over Case and anxiously awaited their next game, which would be in

The Detroit Free Press *celebrated Michigan's 1906 victory over Ohio State with a graphic cartoon in its Sunday sports section.*

two weeks against Ohio State in Columbus. The Buckeyes had walloped Otterbein, Wittenberg and Muskingum by a combined score of 109-0 and were oozing over with confidence for Michigan's October 20 invasion.

The first half of the game was void of any serious touchdown threats by either team, and except for Garrels' two missed field goal tries, the game was one of stout defensive action and numerous punts.

The kick-back game continued into the second half with nine punts (five by OSU) before the Wolverines set their game-winning drive in motion. Taking a punt at their own 44-yard line, the move forward began. Garrels burst for seven yards, E. D. Kanaga rammed for three (first down) before two straight five-yard cracks by Paul Magoffin resulted in another first down at the OSU 47. (Remember, the playing field was 110 yards long in 1906.) John Curtis worked three yards, then five. Kanaga's three-yard smash got another first down at the Buckeye 36. Ohio stood up and stopped the next two running plays cold. Coach Fielding Yost then called upon Garrels again for a FG attempt. The kick was good: Michigan 4, Ohio State 0.

With just moments remaining in the game and OSU backed up to its own five-yard line, a bad snap from center that Ohio's Walter Barrington could only fall on, gave the winners their final two points.

Michigan later defeated Illinois (28-9) and Vanderbilt (10-4) before dropping a 17-0 game to Pennsylvania and a final 4-1-0 season. Ohio State, still not a member of the Western Conference, won the five games left on its schedule for a successful 8-1-0 autumn.

Or was it "successful"? Probably not; not when it involved having to endure still another defeat at the hands of Michigan – for still another year.

Had the game of football suddenly become too big at the University of Michigan? Obviously, A. A. Andell, president of the institution, thought so. Andell called a meeting of Western Conference faculty representatives in March of 1906, and among the regulations agreed upon was limiting the football season to only five games. It was, apparently, the Association's first attempt to de-emphasize the fast-growing and immensely popular sport.

As evidence of that popularity, the public howled in Michigan and throughout the Midwest. And it's most ironic that the adoption of the rule to reduce the number of games would lead directly to Michigan's withdrawal from the Conference in just one year.

1907

GAME 9

PASS IT ON, BOYS

The forward pass, now in its second season as a legal offensive maneuver in football, was being used sparingly by teams across the Nation.

A year earlier the *Detroit News*, in a sports editorial, had this to say: "Notwithstanding the assurance of the rules committee that the game would be more open and sportsmanship this season (referring to 1906) it is now evident that for this season at least football for the local schools is spoiled. . . .The forward pass was introduced to make 10 yards possible. The object was to make the game more open and put an end to the grueling mass play. . . . Several coaches say that it is useless to try the pass more than once. . . .The tendency of all fans is that the game is spoiled for this year."

Fielding H. Yost, however, was not reluctant to use this new toy. "The working of the forward pass contributed more to Ohio State's defeat than any other feature of the Wolverine play," reported the *News*. Yost ordered 10 passes in his afternoon offensive game plan, seven were completed, and Michigan won again from the Buckeyes, 22-0, in the first Wolverine-OSU game played at the new Ferry Field in Ann Arbor, before 7,000 excited fans.

In response to a new rule by the Western Conference, requiring members to reduce football schedules to only five games, Michigan decided it would not be in its best interest to comply and was now playing as an independent. And remember, it was Michi-

In the 1907 game, Paul Magoffin (top) caught a scoring pass from William Wasmund (bottom) – the first TD pass in series history. (Photo courtesy of The Michiganensian.*)*

gan's president who initiated the five-game policy. The Conference was back to seven teams as Northwestern also left the family, but for one year only.

The Wolverines opened 1907 with three straight whitewash jobs: against Case (9-0); Michigan Agricultural College (46-0); and Wabash (22-0) before Ohio State came calling. The Buckeyes had topped Otterbein (28-0), Muskingum (16-0) and Denison (28-0), before being held to a 6-6 tie by Wooster.

The lineup of opposition for both Michigan and Ohio State in '07 is notable by its absence of the "big name" powers of today, but it should be remembered that neither school was a Conference member and thus had limited options in scheduling.

"When Capt. Schory led his Buckeyes on the field at 2:20 the south bleachers held 2,000 singing, cheering rooters for OSU, all waving their scarlet and gray pennants defiantly at the 5,000 Michiganders seated on the north bleachers," was how the *News* described the scene just before the kickoff that cold, wet and windy October 26 afternoon.

Ohio won the toss and elected to take the wind. Michigan kicked off and the game quickly settled into a punting duel. It continued that way until six minutes before intermission when the Wolverines drove for a touchdown. From the nine-yard line, John Loell scored. "The lad took the leather, banged through Claggett, surged along with half the Ohio State line-up on him, half the Michigan bunch pulling and hauling and shouting, until he had covered nine yards and fallen across the line," reported the *News-Tribune*. Walter Graham tacked on the conversion and once again Ohio State trailed Michigan, 6-0.

OSU answered with drives to Michigan's 30-yard line and later to the 20, but both times field goal tries were no good and U-M carried its touchdown lead into halftime.

Early in the second half, Michigan used what newspapers referred to as "the stunt", which was simply a forward pass, to take an 11-0 lead. From the Buckeye 45-yard line, W. S. Wasmund threw to Walter Rheinschild, who slapped the ball to an approaching Mason Rumney, and this fancy new play resulted in a 20-yard gain. On the next snap came the first touchdown pass of the Michigan-Ohio State series and the *News* described the historic play this way: "Wasmund threw unerringly to Magoffin, who ducked past Carr and fled down field, straightarming Barrington enroute for 25 yards and the second touchdown."

Graham's kick for the goal was wide. Wolverines 11, OSU 0.

Bill Wasmund-to-Paul Magoffin. Touchdown pass. Football strategy would never be the same again.

Rheinschild added touchdown runs of 10 and 35 yards later in the game, Allerdice was successful with a conversion on the last score for the final 22-point victory.

Michigan's next engagement would represent the school's 200th football game and in it the Wolverines defeated Vanderbilt 8-0. The all-time grid record stood at 162-33-5 for a winning percentage of .822. Pennsylvania, however, ruined the Wolverines' chances for a perfect season with a 6-0 win in the last game.

Ohio went on to topple Kenyon, Oberlin, Heidelberg and Ohio Wesleyan, but couldn't defeat Case and recorded a final 7-2-1 season.

But why couldn't Ohio State beat Michigan? Or even score on Michigan? The bitter frustration had now soured into a "psyche." The Wolverines led OSU in series touchdowns, 45-1, in points scored, 274-6 and in victories, 8-0. The Buckeyes' lone salvation up to this point had been a scoreless tie seven years ago.

41

1908

GAME 10

ALLERDICE TO
THE RESCUE

The 1908 game marked the ninth time in the 10-game history of the series that Ohio State had to face an unbeaten Michigan outfit.

The Wolverines opened the season with a 16-0 shutout of Case. However, the next week U-M journeyed to East Lansing and got a huge shock from a team the newspapers referred to as "Farmers" – Michigan Agricultural College, now Michigan State. The score was 0-0. The last two times these intrastate teams met had resulted in 46-0 (1907) and 119-0 (1902) routs by Michigan.

The Wolverines then defeated Notre Dame 12-6 and extended their hex over the Irish to a perfect eight-for-eight in clashes between these Midwest gridiron giants. That brought the schedule to October 24 and time for the annual "whupping" of Ohio State. The Buckeyes were waiting with a 2-2-0 record; and it became a 2-3-0 record after Michigan beat the Bucks 10-6 in a rugged match played in the rain at Ohio Field as David Way Allerdice scored all of the Wolverines' points.

Early in the game, U-M's Allerdice and OSU's Walter Barrington missed long field goal attempts. However, 11 minutes into the contest, Allerdice hit one for a Michigan lead. Prentiss Douglass returned a punt 25 yards to Michigan's 52-yard line. Douglass then broke free for 20 yards, A. W. Benbrook plowed for seven more, Douglass was stopped at the line, and Allerdice, standing at the 38-yard line, slammed the ball forward. It was

OHIO STATE HOLDS YOST'S HUSKIES TO SMALL SCORE

Buckeye Team Leads at End of First Half, but Michigan Scores Touchdown in Second, Making Final Score 10 to 6—Frequent Penalties Rob Wolverines of Opportunities to Increase Total.

In the early days of the series, when Ohio State was yet to win a game, the size of Michigan's victory margin was often the main feature of the game story, as indicated by this Detroit Free Press *headline in 1908.*

good, but barely. The ball struck the crossbar and bounced over. Michigan 4, OSU 0.

Fifteen minutes later, Ohio scored. It came suddenly and without warning – just as the Bucks' only other touchdown in the series came back in 1904. With the ball on OSU's 25-yard line, Millard Gibson dropped back in punt formation – but he didn't punt. Gibson darted left, ran over two Wolverines, zig-zagged by four more, and was off to the races with Douglass in hot pursuit. A merry chase was on. Douglass caught him, but a split second too late. Gibson fell just over the goal – touchdown. An 85-yard touchdown run! Barrington padded the score with a conversion and Ohio State led Michigan, 6-4.

"Ohio rooters went wild for fifteen minutes and whooped it up until the whistle blew at the end of the half, showing Michigan two points behind on the scoreboard," reported the *Detroit Free Press*. "Then bedlam did break loose and Ohio sports offered even money that they would win."

It'll never be known how many "takers" the OSU boosters got, but whatever the number, they were destined to be losers, as was the Buckeye team.

Play in the first half had been fast and furious. "Both sides were weary, and at no time did it seem possible that either side would score again," said the *Free Press*.

43

MILLARD GIBSON

His 85-yard touchdown run with a fake punt during the 1908 game was the Buckeyes' only TD in a 10-6 loss to Michigan. Gibson's run is still the third longest in series history. (Photo courtesy of OSU Photo Archives.)

Except for one quick scoring strike, both teams were stymied in the second half. Michigan stayed bogged down by fumbles and penalties; Ohio stayed bogged down by Michigan.

With 15 minutes left to play, the Yostmen won the game. From the OSU 49-yard line, Allerdice passed to Leroy Ranney, who caught the ball at the 40 and went all the way to the 10 before being dragged down by a gang of defenders. Douglass pounded to the three, and Allerdice scored. Allerdice also kicked the point-after and Michigan had the ball game in the bag, 10-6. Neither club threatened after that.

"The students' special left immediately after the game, leaving the squad to follow leisurely tomorrow," the *Free Press* reported. There was, it is suspected, a hot time on the old choo-choo back to Ann Arbor that Saturday night in '08.

The Wolverines then feasted on some Southern meat, ripping Vanderbilt 24-6 and Kentucky 62-0. In the final two games, they found Eastern opposition somewhat tougher. Pennsylvania topped U-M for the third straight year, 29-0, and Syracuse won 28-4. The 29-point margin by the Quakers was Michigan's most lopsided defeat since a 44-0 loss to Cornell in 1892, 155 games ago. In addition, the Wolverines had not lost back-to-back games in 15 years.

Ohio State went on to win four of its remaining five games and one was of special significance. On November 14, the Bucks went to Nashville, Tennessee, and beat Vanderbilt 17-6. It was the school's 100th all-time football win.

The Wolverines' series lead went to 9-0-1; the scoreboard lead to 286-12.

45

Scene at the main entrance to Ohio Field in the early 1900s, as spectators begin arriving in their horseless carriages, and passing the time of day on what appears to be a perfect autumn afternoon for football. Ohio State and Michigan played eight games here. (Photo courtesy of OSU Photo Archives.)

1909

GAME 11

AGAIN, IT'S ALL ALLERDICE

The natives were growing restless.

"Football at Ohio State, as in most of the larger colleges, towers over all other sports in importance . . . .One must admit that the two most important Ohio games were lost (to Michigan and Case). . . .Every team of importance in the state was successfully defeated until the Case game, when on a slippery field the Scientists won undisputed claim to the Trophy Cup (Ohio Conference championship). . . .Among many, at least two things were demonstrated conclusively. . . .In the first place, it became evident that a change was needed in our playing schedule, for we had arrived at the point where we should drop most of the Ohio teams and fill these dates with out-of-state elevens. . . .Our schedule for the coming year includes but one out of state game. . . .The time is at hand. . . .We shall step into a broader field and make Ohio State the great Middle Western football power that everyone feels she should be – that everyone knows she can be," read an account in the Ohio State yearbook, *Makio*, in capsuling the 1909 season. The sentiments were basically the same as those in press reports coming out of Columbus, Cleveland, Cincinnati, Dayton and other Ohio cities.

Another loss to Michigan, plus six other defeats to teams within the State (Oberlin, Wooster, Western Reserve and three to Case) in the past three years had the alumni, fans and friends of the Scarlet and Gray squirming.

48

In the five years, 1906 through 1910, OSU's 49-game schedule included only seven out-of-state opponents – Michigan five times and Vanderbilt twice. Everybody was demanding a more intersectional and prestigious schedule. The unrest that began to surface in 1909 became the cornerstone to the Buckeyes' entry into the Western Conference three years later.

Another fact that stuck in the craw of OSU supporters was that their Buckeyes had *never* defeated any of the nine teams that made up the Western Conference.

As for the 1909 Ohio State-Michigan game, Dave Allerdice scored 19 points to lead the Wolverines to an easy 33-6 win at Ferry Field in Ann Arbor on October 16. Michigan had played only one game, a 3-0 win over Case. Ohio had tuned up by scoring 127 points in games against Otterbein, Whittenberg and Wooster and had allowed no points by those foes.

It took only seven minutes for U-M to take the lead for keeps. A bad snap from center sailed way over the head of an OSU punter and the ball bounced all the way to the 15-yard line. George Lawton blasted to the nine, then to the one, and Charles Freeney went over for the score. Allerdice kicked the conversion and Michigan was on top, 6-0.

On Ohio's next series of downs, a fumble at U-M's 40 provided an opening for another Wolverine score. Two plays gained 20 yards to the Bucks' 45. From there, that lad David Way Allerdice tallied on a beautiful, twisting run. He also converted, and the score was 12 to zip.

Later in the first half, it was Allerdice again. His 40-yard run to the OSU one-yard line set up Lawton's TD plunge. Again, Allerdice was on target with his trusty toe and Michigan's advantage went to 18-0.

U-M kicked off, Allerdice recovered another OSU bobble and, when the drive stalled at the 25, Allerdice kicked a field goal. The scoreboard showed Michigan a 21-0 leader. (In 1909 the field goal dropped in value from four to three points.)

Just after intermission, Michigan drove down to OSU's 10-yard line and the *Detroit News* reported, "The bleachers were a tumult. 'We want fifty; we want fifty!' roared the Michigan rooters. And booming across from the Ohio section came the appeal: 'Hold'em varsity; hold'em varsity!' And Ohio held."

But later in the game, Allerdice added another field goal, Stanfield Wells scored a touchdown, and Allerdice kicked his third field goal of the day. In three games against Ohio State, Allerdice

MICHIGAN SWAMPS OHIO STATE ON FERRY FIELD BY SCORE OF 33 TO 6

The Detroit News

DAVID WAY ALLERDICE

In three games against Ohio State (1907-08-09), Allerdice scored two touchdowns and kicked six conversions and four field goals. (Photo courtesy of Michigan Athletic Department.)

scored two touchdowns, kicked six conversions and four field goals for a total of 30 points.

"The Ohioans made but one touchdown, and this smacked strongly of flukeishness," said the *News*.

Under the prevailing rules, a punt was a "live" and could be recovered by the kicking team. OSU punted and as the ball rolled towards the goal line, Michigan's Charles Freeney let it go, thinking it would bounce beyond the goal for a touchback. But while Freeney was "thinking", in roared Ohio's Chelsea Boone, a center, who snatched up the ball directly in front of the goal and scored. Leslie Wells converted.

It was OSU's third touchdown against Michigan and all three had been colored with a freakish tint.

Michigan rooters did not get their "fifty" that day, but they did get another victory over Ohio State.

After clobbering OSU, the Wolverines edged Marquette 6-5; blasted Syracuse 44-0; lost to Notre Dame for the first time, 11-3; beat Pennsylvania for the first time, 12-6, and closed out the season with a big 15-6 win over previously unbeaten Minnesota, which brought back the chants of "Champions of the West".

Ohio followed up with victories over Denison, Ohio Wesleyan, Vanderbilt and Kenyon; losses to Case and Oberlin, and a 7-3-0 season.

The OSU won-lost numbers weren't all that bad, but there was dissatisfaction nevertheless. And as it seems always to happen in college football, dissatisfaction leads to coaching changes. For the 1910 season, Howard Jones of Yale was named to replace A. E. Herrnstein who had compiled a 28-10-1 in four seasons at OSU. Herrnstein was a former Michigan player. In fact, in the 1902 slaughter of the Bucks in Ann Arbor, he had scored six touchdowns.

Jones would be the first of four Ohio State coaches whose job were to last only one season.

1910

GAME 12

A 3-3 "WIN"

" 'What's the score?' Yelled a hack driver Saturday evening while driving north on High Street as crowds were coming down from the Michigan-Ohio State football game. One urchin, who had saved his nickels to get inside the big gates, was on the job with the ready reply: 'Three to three, Ohio State,' " reported the *Columbus Dispatch* in its Sunday edition.

And that just about sums up the story of the 1910 duel between the two rivals as they swapped first-half field goals for the 3-3 standoff. The Scarlet and Gray was happy over the knotted situation, simply because they didn't lose to their visitors from Ann Arbor.

Based on the season's results leading up to the game, if OSU ever had a chance to topple Michigan, this would be the year. After a 3-3 tie with Case in the opener, U-M had to score in the last minute to down the Farmers of Michigan State, 6-3. Thus, Michigan took a shaky 1-0-1 record to Columbus. Ohio was 4-0-0 and had outscored the opposition 105-5.

Could this, then, be the year?

The followers of the Maize and Blue didn't think so. It was reported that a special train with 10 coaches, crammed with rooters, went to Columbus; and it's for certain the people didn't go to witness a defeat.

"The Ohioans were more optimistic over the outcome of the game today than they have ever been before when Michigan was

52

the contender. . . .None of the wiser heads would make arbitrary statements. All said it would be a tight game. . . .The majority of undergraduates made no bones about stating without qualification that the Crimson and Gray would top the Maize and Blue," wrote a *Detroit News* reporter.

The story continued, "Yost was not optimistic. He took his men into a room at their hotel this morning, locked the door and succeeded in making them realize the importance of getting down to real business later in the day."

There had been a major rule change in 1910. The length of games was reduced from 70 minutes (two 35-minute halves) to an hour (four 15-minute quarters). And all of the scoring came within a seven-minute span in the second quarter of that year's Michigan-Ohio State game.

Early in the period, Michigan received a punt at its own 42-yard line and 11 plays later had three points. Joe Magidsohn gained four, Don Green got three, and Magidsohn came back with five and a first down. Green's gain of six carried to OSU's 51-yard line. Neil McMillan went to the 46 for a first down; George Thomson to the 37 and Magidsohn to the 33 for another first down. Green lost four and then was stopped for no gain. Thomson kept it going as he threw a perfect pass to Stanfield Wells for a 15-yard pickup and a first down at Ohio's 23-yard line.

Even though it was first down, Yost was anxious for points – even three. And he got them as Fred Conklin booted good with 11 minutes left before halftime. A writer for the *Columbus Dispatch* obviously didn't think too much of the first-down decision when he wrote, "He (Yost) evidently held State too cheaply and considered his team would win no matter how loosely he picked his plays. If such were his intentions he was badly fooled."

A Michigan fumble indirectly led to OSU's tying of the game. Robert Clare fell on Green's bobble at the U-M 53-yard line. A few plays later, Wells punt backed the Wolverines deep. Thomson tried to kick his team out of trouble but got off a short one that Ohio took at the Wolverines' 35.

Quarterback Archie Egbert burst through for 10 yards and a first down at Michigan's 25. What's this? Coach Howard Jones, in his first and only year at OSU, emulated Yost and opted to try for a tie game right then and there. He got one, too, as Wells dropkicked the ball through the uprights. The score was 3-3 with four minutes remaining in the quarter.

That was it. Neither team, at least offensively, could mount a threat for the remainder of the afternoon.

SPORTING SECTION — The Columbus Sunday Dispatch. — All the News and Gossip of the Sporting World

The Columbus paper declares that "Michigan Not Ohio State's Master" after a 3-3 gridlock in 1910.

Other observations from the writers at the game from Detroit and Columbus, included: "The State men were in better condition than the Wolverines and played the game without a whimper. . . . Yost will say nothing. He is disgusted. . . . Wells drop-kicked and the Ohio student body went nutty. . . . From there on the Michiganders seemed to go to pieces – if they had ever been together."

Michigan concluded its strange 1910 season with an 11-0 win over Syracuse, a 0-0 tie with Penn and, for the second year in a row, handed Minnesota its only loss, 6-0. There was also supposed to be a game with Notre Dame but the Irish cancelled out because of two alleged ineligible players on the U-M squad. The two teams would not get back together for 33 years.

The Wolverines averaged only 3.3 points per game in 1910, yet they finished unbeaten with a 3-0-3 record. Michigan's scoring ratio was a far cry from the "point-a-minute" Yost teams of just a few years earlier, but they were still winning.

OSU's remaining five games resulted in wins over Ohio Wesleyan and Kenyon, ties with Denison and Oberlin, and a fourth straight defeat by Case – the Buckeyes' only loss in a 6-1-3 season.

"Coach Jones didn't disclose any of the fancy stuff in holding Michigan to a tie," observed a *Tribune* reporter. "Joe Fogg of the Case team was there with peering eyes, but he took nothing back with him other than a genuine respect for the State men, who held Michigan to the same score as Case did."

An Ohio State coach "holding back" against Michigan? If the Columbus writer's opinion was correct, there's little wonder Mr. Jones' stay at OSU lasted for only one year.

1911

GAME 13

AGAIN? YEP, AGAIN

Michigan 19, Ohio State 0. The victory was just that clean. Just that methodical.

The Buckeyes had three good chances early in the game for at least a field goal, but the attempts were either too weak or too wide, and OSU's hopes of beating Michigan faded away before 5,000 onlookers at Ferry Field on October 21.

The series now read: 11-0-2; the scoreboard 341-21.

Michigan opened up with wins over Case (24-0), Michigan State (15-3), and were anxiously awaiting Ohio State's arrival the following week. No opponent had scored on OSU in its first three games – but the Buckeyes themselves had produced a mere nine points. There was a 6-0 win over Otterbein, a 3-0 victory over Miami (Ohio) and a scoreless tie against Western Reserve.

"Headed by their band, the Wolverines trotted on the field 15 minutes before time for the game. The Ohio State squad was a bit late, failing to appear on the lot until after the time set for the game to start. They finally appeared at 2:35 and looked rangy and fast," reported the *Detroit News*.

Michigan kicked off and the 13th series game was on. Midway through the first quarter, Ohio's Earl Foss missed field goal attempts from the 20 twice, and then from 18 yards out, thus spoiling a good chance for his team to break on top.

"The Wolverines were below par during the opening minutes. No pop, no fire, no tearing, ripping, smashing by the Michigan team could be seen. . . .It was evident that if the Wolverines were to do anything they must get into the spirit of a real battle," said the *News*.

Following OSU's last field goal miss, Michigan worked down to Ohio's 10-yard line but was stopped. State punted out to mid-field and here came U-M again. George Thomson ripped off seven yards to the OSU 48. Otto Carpell got three, Stanfield Wells 10, Neil McMillan one, Thomson seven, Wells six, and Carpell five as the scrimmage line reached the OSU 16. A penalty cost Michigan five yards and Thomson got three back. Then a Thomson-to-Fred Conklin pass netted 16 yards and a first down at the State two. Wells crashed over. Conklin's conversion was wide but the Yostmen led 5-0 and held on for the rest of the first half.

Michigan kicked off to open the third quarter, immediately forced a punt and drove down close enough for a field goal. Starting from the Ohio 45, Carpell carried to the 39, Wells ripped to the 27, James Craig was stopped for nothing and Thomson managed only one. Thomas Bogle came on for a successful three-pointer and the Wolverines' lead was upped to 8-0.

Later in the period, Michigan drove 32 yards in six plays to Ohio's 23 but flubbed a field goal attempt. OSU punted and the Wolverines drove back again, to the eight-yard line. The Scarlet defense held and took possession of the ball. Unable to move, the Buckeyes sent William Wright into his own endzone to punt. In crashed Conklin who blocked the kick and also recovered it for a touchdown. Conklin then kicked the conversion and the score stood at 14-0, Michigan.

Late in the game, Thomson scored from the one-yard line to cap an 11-play, 51-yard drive. Wells carried four times for 22 yards to spark the march. Conklin's missed PAT kept the final score to 19. Michigan was on the enemy two-yard line when the game ended.

A week later, Ohio State played its 200th all-time football game and a 3-0 win over Ohio Wesleyan made the milestone contest a success. Case (along with Michigan) continued to be a real thorn in Ohio's side as the Roughriders made it five straight, 9-0, and increased their dominance over the Buckeyes to 10-4-2. It would be, however, the last time Case would ever defeat Ohio State in football. Winding up 1911, the Bucks beat Kenyon, tied Oberlin, lost to Syracuse, topped Cincinnati and recorded a 5-3-2 autumn.

After the game against the Buckeyes, Michigan's schedule turned intersectional and included teams from Tennessee, New

YOST'S MEN BEAT OHIO STATE

Take Hard Fought Contest from Buckeyes by 19 to 0.

VISITORS FAIL AT KICKING.

Gains by Wells and Thomson Are Features of Ann Arbor Game.

York, Pennsylvania and Nebraska. All the games were exciting and low-scoring affairs. The Wolverines edged Vanderbilt 9-8, were tied by Syracuse 6-6, lost to Cornell 6-0, squeaked by Penn 11-9 and tied Nebraska 6-6. In the past two seasons, Michigan had averaged only 7.9 points per game but lost only one time. The key, of course, was that the Wolverines surrendered only 3.4 points per game. The two-season record was a weird 8-1-5, bringing Fielding Yost's 11-year coaching record at Ann Arbor to a glowing 83-7-7. The average score of Yost's games was Michigan 34 and opponents 2½.

TIMEOUT

OHIO STATE JOINS THE BIG BOYS

On April 6, 1912, it became official: Ohio State University was admitted to the Western Conference.

OSU joined Chicago, Illinois, Indiana, Iowa, Minnesota, Northwestern, Purdue and Wisconsin and the association moved from eight teams to the "Big Nine." There was rejoicing by Buckeye fans everywhere.

It is a well recognized fact that the athletic life of the University is one great interest around which to develop a real college spirit. . . .While the athletic rivalry Ohio State has had in Ohio has been keen and the competition for the most part worthy, still there has been something lacking. The bounds have seemed too prescribed; the victories gained, to lack something of a true ring. . . .It is surely fitting that we should have sought for recognition by, and competition with, other universities like our own, where there is similarity of aims and ideals, a real community of interest. . . .Our State has been well received in the Conference. We have been styled "a new rival well worthy of the steel" by our opponents.

L. W. St. John
The *Makio*
Ohio State Yearbook

1912

GAME 14

THE "LAST" GAME

The 1912 meeting was billed as the last game between Michigan and Ohio State. Little did they know!

" 'Good-bye Michigan,' Makes Ohio State Sad" headlined a story in the *Detroit News* the Monday after the game. "Ohio State is sad," the article began. "It is not because Michigan beat the Buckeyes, but because the Maize and Blue and the Red and Gray have clashed for the last time. The Ohioans have entered the cloistral ranks of the Conference, and are barred from engagements with such wicked schools as Michigan. . . .It is a matter of real regret to the student body. Michigan has always been the big game. . . .Even the students at the U. of M. have hardly been more ardent followers of the fortunes of the men of Yost than have the Ohio bunch. . . .But the old friends are parted and the string of 12 Michigan victories and two tie games is broken off short."

As for the game, played at Ohio Field on October 19, Michigan scored first and fourth quarter touchdowns, shutdown OSU completely, and walked away from the rivalry unbeaten in 14 games with a 14-0 victory.

The game was Fielding Yost's 100th since he arrived as Michigan's coach in 1901 and rounded out his record at 86-7-7. Or, putting it another way, in his first 100 games as the leader of U-M's football fortunes, Yost had experienced defeat *only seven* times.

Entering the big game, both teams were 2-0-0. Michigan had scored 34 and 55 points against Case and Michigan State; OSU had scored 55 and 34 points against Otterbein and Denison.

59

The Detroit News

MICHIGAN ENDS RELATION WITH O. S. U., WINNING

A full house was on hand at Columbus in 1912 for the "last" UM-OSU football game. (Photo courtesy of Michigan Athletic Department)

"Good-Bye Michigan," Makes Ohio State Sad

The Columbus Dispatch

Midway through the initial period, State's Campbell Graf fumbled at his 45-yard line and Michigan's James Craig, without breaking stride, scooped up the bouncing ball and streaked for a touchdown. George Patterson added the point-after to give U-M a 7-0 lead. (In 1912, there were three big rule changes that are still in effect today. Touchdowns went from five to six points, a fourth down was added, and the playing field was reduced from 110 to 100 yards.)

The score remained 7-0 until the fourth quarter when Michigan, after receiving a punt at the Ohio 47-yard line, went on to score in seven plays. Craig rambled for 25, then five, then eight and a first down at the Bucks' nine. George Thomson took it to the five, Ernest Hughitt got nothing, and Thomson tore down to the one. It was fourth down. The ball was given to Thomson again and the big fullback responded with a touchdown. Patterson's placement was perfect and the final 14-0 score had been posted.

"Yost's warriors might have become disheartened and played an even more ragged game than they did. What put courage into them was that almost from the start of the game they were working under a lead," reported the *News*. "Coach John Richards (OSU) made many substitutions, and perhaps erred in generalship, as he sent 25 men into the game. . . .When he put his best men back in the fourth quarter, they could not stop Michigan. . . . Yost, on the other hand, made few substitutions and most of those late."

The Wolverines finished their 1912 schedule with a loss to Syracuse, a win over South Dakota, a loss to Penn and a win over Cornell. The Buckeyes thumped Cincinnati, Case, Oberlin and Ohio Wesleyan but lost to Penn State and Michigan State. The OSU-MSU game was the first meeting of the two teams on the gridiron, and it would be the last for another 39 years – the first season of W. W. Hayes as coach at Columbus.

As the University of Michigan and Ohio State University seemingly ended their rivalry, the Wolverines had clearly been dominant, winning twelve, losing none and settling for ties twice. The point total was even more one-sided – 355-21, an average score of 25.3 to 1.5.

Perhaps it was this overwhelming dominance by Michigan, coupled with OSU's entry into the "Big Nine", that caused so many observers and writers in 1912 to ignore a future resumption of the series. It was written off as ancient history, with no suggestion or even hope expressed that at some future time, the two schools would be football opponents again.

TIMEOUT

MICHIGAN RE-ENTERS THE CONFERENCE

Michigan ended its 10-year period as an athletic independent when on June 9, 1917, the school officially re-entered the Western Conference. With Ohio State and Michigan as the two newest members, the Conference truly became the Big Ten for the first time.

The principle reasons for Michigan's defection from the Conference following the 1908 season had included the following:

1. The reduction of the number of football games to only five.

2. Freshmen and graduate students were ineligible for varsity competition, which of course, limited an athlete to just three years of eligibility.

3. The abolishment of athletic training tables and living quarters.

A concerted campaign had been underway for months – by U-M students and numerous alumni associations throughout the State – to convince their university to rejoin the Conference. Upon Michigan receiving an official invitation, the University Board of Regents voted unanimously to accept.

The big decision also made possible the renewal of the Michigan-Ohio State rivalry, and for many, that was all the reason needed.

1918

RIVALRY REBORN

Ohio State was coming off two consecutive Conference championships and, ordinarily, hope and excitement for another big season would be running rampant. But this was no ordinary time. It was 1918 and World War I dragged on. It was a time when America's football hero's "big game" was in Europe – on the *real* battlefield.

When OSU Coach John Wilce whistled his squad together for the first time in the fall of '18, he found not one single letterman from his title teams of the two previous years. His 1917 roster of 37 players had been reduced to only 15, mostly sophomores from the previous year's freshman team and incoming freshmen.

The outlook for Coach Fielding Yost at Michigan was not much brighter. His squad of 21 players included 14 freshmen, six sophomores and one junior – and only five who had logged playing time the previous year.

In September, 1918, the Big Ten Conference suspended its activities as a controlling body and tendered that authority to the War Department to carry out the function of controlling all athletic activities, both intercollegiate and intramural. The Government allowed any member of the Students' Army Training Corps to participate in varsity competition regardless of class standing, thus making freshmen eligible. Among the War Department's restrictions was a rule permitting each team only one overnight trip during the season.

The Buckeyes blanked Ohio Wesleyan 41-0 and Denison 34-0. The Wolverines topped Case 33-0, Chicago 13-0, Syracuse 15-0 and Michigan State 21-6. That brought the season to Saturday, November 30, 1918, and time for the renewal of the Michigan-Ohio State football series.

It was the first time the two rivals would meet as members of the same Conference, and this was another factor adding spark to a rivalry that really needed no additional spark.

They hadn't faced each other since 1912. Michigan had struck up some heated competition with a few teams from the East, namely Penn, Cornell, Harvard and Syracuse. The Eastern boys more than held their own (8-6-1 advantage) against Coach Yost and his Midwestern storm troopers. However, the Wolverines still came through with an impressive overall record of 31-11-1 during the period.

It took no time at all for membership in the Big Nine to get Ohio State all fired-up and ready to go. In just three years after joining up, the Buckeyes were undisputed champions of the Conference in 1916. OSU liked it so much they repeated as champs the following year and the Scarlet and Gray recorded a 29-5-3 record during the five-year absence of Michigan from their schedule.

As the big day dawned, the Buckeyes' big following was ecstatic. Their warriors were riding a 20-game unbeaten streak and had lost just one time in their last 28 gridiron dates.

Excitement ran high in Columbus that day. Just three weeks before, a war had ended. All became quiet on the Western Front on November 11, and World War I was history. That, along with the big game with Michigan, had the city upside down.

But when the sun set that frigid Saturday afternoon, absolutely nothing had changed. Michigan beat Ohio State with two fourth quarter touchdowns, 14-0 – the same final score that had shown on the scoreboard the last time they met.

Woe betide the Buckeyes.

"The periods went scoreless more because Michigan played indifferent football, went into the Ohio line without snap and generally appeared too confident of victory. It was when the first half ended scoreless and the minutes of the third quarter drew to a close that the Wolverines awoke," wrote Harry LeDoc of the *Detroit News*.

Midway in the final period, a fabulous punt led to Michigan's first touchdown. With the ball at U-M's 25, Frank Steketee got off a booming kick that sailed over the head of OSU's R. E. Rife. The

MICHIGAN DEFEATS O. S. U. SCORING ON GOETZ'S FEAT AND STEKETEE'S TRUE PEG

Tackle Blocks Punt Behind Ohio State Goal Line, Falls on Ball; Forward Pass Brings Other Touchdown; All Scoring in Last Period.

Detroit News

ball struck the turf and started bouncing end-over-end-over-end and finally rolled dead way back at the Buckeye two-yard line. (From where Steketee was standing, he actually kicked the ball 85 yards.)

Three plays netted nothing and Rife was in punt formation behind his own goal line. Back went the snap and in went a vicious Michigan charge, led by its big left tackle, Angus Goetz. Rife slammed the kick against the chest of Goetz and the ball ricocheted into the corner of the endzone. Within a split second there was a mass of humanity in desperate pursuit of the pigskin. Goetz was there first. He pounced on the prize. Touchdown, Michigan. Steketee sent through a successful conversion and the score was 7-0.

Ohio took the ensuing kickoff and marched to the Michigan 38 but stalled. The Wolverines answered with another long punt that sent OSU back to its own 14. Rife's short punt put U-M in good shape at Ohio's 35. Aided by a 15-yard penalty, Michigan reached the 10-yard line and Steketee tossed a pass to Robert Dunne for a touchdown. Steketee converted. Ball game.

The win concluded a perfect 5-0-0 season for Michigan and a share of the Big Ten title. Ohio followed up with a 56-0 crushing of Case before falling to Illinois and Wisconsin, and in just one year OSU went from 1.000 to .000 in the Conference.

The Buckeyes still had not beaten Michigan.

1919

GAME 16

VOODOO VANISHES

"ANN ARBOR, MICH., OCT. 25 – Charles 'Chic' Harley, the premier football player certainly of the Western Conference, if not of the entire country, became a captain of achievement here today, rather than nominal leadership, when 25,000 football fans, gathered from the plains and valleys of two states, watched this superman of the moleskin lead an attack with all the dash of an old-time cavalry chieftain, that resulted in a 13-3 victory for the Scarlet and Gray. In support of this favorite son were a dozen other men who were in the fray at various times during the four quarters, and who had the inspiration to follow as nearly as possible their gallant leadership. When it all ended and the October sun was sinking in its setting of gold, the crowd went its way slowly, but on the lips of thousands was praise for Harley."

So read the lead of H. A. Miller's story, appearing on the front page of the *Columbus Sunday Dispatch* the day following the most glorious Ohio State football victory ever in 1919.

It was a feat requiring 22 years (16 games) to accomplish, but the Ohio State Buckeyes had *finally* beaten the Michigan Wolverines. And as Miller wrote, the score was 13-3, in a game played on Ferry Field.

The Bucks blocked a punt in the first quarter for one touchdown, later surrendered a field goal and the first half ended 7-3. State put the game away midway through the third period on a long touchdown run by Harley and held off the Wolverines the remainder of the afternoon to preserve and gain the gigantic triumph, possibly the biggest in OSU's football history.

WIN NO. 1 OVER MICHIGAN

The history-making Ohio State football team.
1st row – Clarence McDonald, James Flowers, Robert Spiers, Dean
Trott, Ferdinand Holtkamp, Charles "Chic" Harley, Andrew
Nemeck, Lloyd Pixley, Iolas Huffman, William Slyker and Cyril
Myers.
2nd row – L. W. St. John, Director of Athletics, Robert Weaver, Don
Wiper, Constantine Farcasin, Richard Cott, F. L. Schweitzer,
Gaylord Stinchcomb, Frank Willaman, Harry Bliss, Thomas
Davies, Charles Taylor, Harold Wiper, and Coach John Wilce.
3rd row – Foote, manager, Oliver Matheny, Robert Wieche, Mark
Fuller, Max Friedman, E. G. Gurney, trainer, Neil Gilliam, E. Y.
Johnson, Kenneth Ewart, Frederick Bell, E. L. Johnson and Kime,
manager. (Photo courtesy of OSU Photo Archives.)

The Columbus Sunday Dispatch.

HARLEY-LED BUCKEYE GRIDIRON WARRIORS BRING BACK TO COLUMBUS TOWN THAT LONG-COVETED WOLVERINE SCALP; PRESIDENT CALLS ON COAL MINERS TO RESCIND STRIKE ORDER

TWENTY-FIVE THOUSAND FANS WATCH OHIO STATE STALWARTS HUMBLE THEIR ANCIENT FOE

Detroit News

OHIO STATE SCORES FIRST VICTORY OVER WOLVERINES

Score of 13 to 3 Indicates Exactly Relative Merits of Teams; State Superior in Every Department.

Both teams went into the game with perfect records – unbeaten, untied and unscored upon. Michigan had rapped Case 34-0 and Michigan State 26-0. Ohio had drilled Ohio Wesleyan 38-0, Cincinnati 46-0 and Kentucky 49-0.

Michigan's Robert Dunne kicked off to Gaylord Stinchcomb and the historic game was underway. Stinchcomb was belted hard by the on-rushing defenders, the ball flew from his grasp and Archie Weston recovered for Michigan at the Buckeye 20-yard line.

"Gloom". . . ."Doom". . . ."Here we go again". . . ."Wait'll next year". . . ."Why didn't I stay home. . . ." had to be among the immediate (and quieter) reactions on Ohio State's side of the stadium in that awful moment.

Michigan's right end, Harold Rye, suffered a broken leg on the kickoff and when play was finally resumed, the Wolverines couldn't move and early disaster for OSU was avoided. Following two exchanges of punts, the Buckeyes drove to the U-M 20 and missed a field goal try. Michigan took over and a fumble brought up fourth-and-16 back at its 14-yard line. Clifford Sparks was standing in punt formation near the goal line but Russell Meyers raced in, blocked it, and at the end of a mad scramble, Ohio's James Flowers had the ball and the Buckeyes had six points. Harley's conversion made it seven.

Late in the second period, Michigan's Sparks kicked a 37-yard field goal and at intermission OSU held on to a slim four-point lead.

Michigan received the second-half kickoff and eventually punted to Ohio's 10. Harley kicked back and the Wolverines started at the OSU 42. On fourth-and-two from the 34, a pass was incomplete and the Buckeyes were holding on for dear life.

In just two lightning-fast plays, State covered the 66 yards for a TD. Stinchcomb darted for a 24-yard gain, and Harley shot the remaining 42. With 7:30 remaining in the third period, Ohio State led 13-3. It stayed that way as Harley's conversion attempt went awry.

From that point on, the game settled into a flurry of Michigan passes, most of them incomplete, and Ohio runs for sparse yardage, plus plenty of punts.

Ohio State had defeated Michigan.

Coach Yost had a long-standing custom of never visiting an opponent's locker room after a game. However, on this day, he

CHARLES W. "CHIC" HARLEY

Hometown hero "Chic" Harley, of Columbus, led the Buckeyes to a 13-3, first-ever victory over Michigan in 1919 at Ann Arbor. (Photo courtesy of OSU Photo Archives.)

The Columbus Sunday Dispatch.

COLUMBUS, OHIO, SUNDAY, OCTOBER 26, 1919.

All the News and Gossip of the Sporting World

WA-HO--WA-HO--RIP-ZIP--BA-ZO--I-YELL--I-YELL--O-HI-O

XODUS OF JOYFUL STATE ROOTERS STARTS FROM ANN ARBOR SOON AFTER GREAT VICTORY ACHIEVED

PECIAL TRAINS AND MACHINES BRING HAPPY FANS BACK HOME

HARLEY-LED WARRIORS BRING HOME LONG-COVETED MICHIGAN SCALP

CHIC RUNS TRUE TO FORM IN WIN

Superior Team Gallantly in First Victory of Buckeyes Over Wolverines

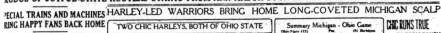

TWO CHIC HARLEYS, BOTH OF OHIO STATE

SYRACUSE GOES DOWN IN DEFEAT

Washington and Jefferson Springs Surprise in East by Winning 13 to 0.

CHICAGO ESTABLISHES ITSELF AS CHAMPIONSHIP CONTENDER

Maroons Bury the Crippled Northwestern Eleven Under an Avalanche of Touchdowns and Triumph 41 to 0—Quarterback Graham Is Shining Light at Bang.

Summary Michigan - Ohio Game

YALE RECOVERS AND BEATS TUFTS

Old Eli Has Little Trouble in Winning From Bay State Team 27 to 0.

Harvard Wins Easy Contest

Crimson Has Little Trouble in Taking Contest From Virginia by Superior Work

DELAWARE PLAYER IS BADLY INJURED

Statistics Show Superiority of Ohio State Machine

DETAILS OF HOW CHIC HARLEY AND COMPANY PLEASED THOUSANDS OF OHIO FOOTBALL FANS AT ANN ARBOR

FIRST PERIOD

SECOND PERIOD

THIRD PERIOD

broke his rule. Yost went to the Ohio State dressing quarters and made a brief speech.

"The gruff old warrior's words were few and were burdened with a sting of defeat, but spoken with an earnestness that left no doubt as to their sincerity," wrote Miller. "After congratulating Dr. Wilce (OSU coach), Yost said to the team: 'You deserve your victory; you fought brilliantly. You boys gave a grand exhibition of football strategy and while I am sorry, dreadfully sorry, that we lost, I want to congratulate you. And you, Mr. Harley, I believe are one of the finest little machines I have ever seen. Again, I want to congratulate Ohio State.'"

In Coach Yost's wildest dreams, though, he wouldn't have suspected what waited down the road for his 1919 team. Perhaps he did. He beat Northwestern 16-13 but the Wolverines then dropped their remaining three games – 13-0 to Chicago, 29-7 to Illinois and 34-7 to Minnesota – and a final 3-4-0 record. It was the first losing season for Yost in this his 23rd year of coaching and it represented Michigan's first losing autumn in 28 years.

Three straight defeats by a Michigan football team? What was the collegiate athletic world coming to?

Ohio State blanked Purdue and Wisconsin to set up a Big Ten championship showdown with Illinois on November 22 at Columbus. The Illini kicked a 27-yard field goal with only eight seconds left in the game for a 9-7 victory and the 1919 Conference title.

While there was some temporary disappointment over the loss of the Big Ten crown, it was, in the year ahead, completely overshadowed by the exultation of Buckeye fans everywhere. They could and did have their first-ever victory over hated Michigan to celebrate, to savor, and to celebrate and savor again and again.

1920

A WIN STREAK OF 2

For the third straight year a touchdown on a blocked punt proved decisive in the Ohio State-Michigan game and in 1920 it was the Buckeyes who got the score in the fourth quarter for a 14-7 win at Columbus on November 6. The tight victory kept Coach John Wilce and his Scarlets unbeaten and on track for a possible Big Ten championship.

OSU had warmed up for its league matches with hefty shutout wins over Ohio Wesleyan (55-0) and Oberlin (37-0). Then Purdue (17-0), Wisconsin (13-7) and Chicago (7-6) fell.

Michigan was next.

The Wolverines had clipped Case and Michigan State by identical 35-0 scores before losing to Illinois 7-6. After a 21-14 win over Tulane, U-M was ready for "The Big One."

Ohio State was next.

Early in the second quarter of a scoreless game, Michigan reached OSU's five-yard line where it was first-and-goal. The Bucks put on a classic goal line stand and held. Unable to punch out a first down deep in its own territory, Ohio called upon Harry Workman to punt from the endzone.

Robert Dunne, standing on the Buckeye 34, called for a fair catch. Ohio's Noel Workman, roaring down the field, did not see the fair catch signal and blasted full-speed into Dunne. That cost Ohio 15 big ones and the official stepped it off down to the 19-yard line. Frank Steketee advanced it to the 17, Ed Usher to the 14 and then to the seven, first down. Jack Dunn blasted for four yards and on the next play he scored. Steketee's kick was good and U-M led 7-0.

Later in the second period, Harry Workman kicked Michigan into trouble at the four-yard line. The Wolverines punted right back and Harry Workman returned 13 yards to the 34. On second down, a Harry Workman-to-Noel Workman passing combination worked beautifully for a 31-yard gain down to Michigan's three. It took the Bucks four bucks into the line before Herbert Henderson finally plunged in from the two. Harry Workman's conversion tied the count at 7-7.

The game moved on and, very late in the third quarter, Ohio missed a field goal from the 35. A Wolverine tried to run the kick back but was dropped just two yards outside his own endzone. Time was called to swap ends of the field as the contest moved into the final period. It was first down but Coach Yost, in an abundance of caution, decided he didn't want his boys playing around with the football in such a dangerous area, and ordered Steketee to kick it out.

Ohio team captain and left tackle, Iolas Huffman, had other ideas. Huffman stormed through the line, slammed the kick to earth and fell on it for the touchdown – and margin of victory. Gaylord Stinchcomb kicked good and it was 14-7.

Ohio State had beaten Michigan again! And ole Iolas was a hero.

In their final two games the Wolverines blanked Chicago 14-0 and Minnesota 3-0 to post a 5-2-0 season.

The Buckeyes had only one game remaining and it was against Illinois at Champaign, where a win would lock up another undisputed Conference crown. With time for just one play, with the score tied 0-0, and the line of scrimmage at exactly midfield, Harry Workman unleashed a desperation heave. As the ball was airborne, the gun sounded to end the game. Russell Myers streaked under Workman's pass, caught it and scored. Ohio State won 7-0 to cap a 7-0-0 season and the Buckeyes were Big Ten champs for the third time since they had joined the Conference five years ago.

It was now Ohio's turn to sing, "California, Here I Come." The Rose Bowl invited OSU to play a fabulous University of California team that would not lose a game until 1925. The Buckeyes enjoyed their first visit to Pasadena, but the game itself was a big letdown. Final score: Bears 28, Bucks 0.

Six months later (June 2, 1921), the Conference governing

body adopted a policy of no post-season games (bowls) in the future. Iowa was asked to play in the Rose Bowl after the '21 season and appealed to the Conference to reconsider – but to no avail. It would be 26 years before a Big Ten team would go bowling again.

1921

GAME 18

GET ON THE BALL, BOYS

"As the soft shadows of a brilliant October day threw a cloak of dull gold over Ferry Field, and more than 40,000 spectators slowly started towards the exits, a band of 100 pieces, in blue top-coats and flaring scarlet caps and led by a drum major who apparently had tumbled out of a nursery book, proudly tramped about Michigan's playground playing Ohio State's fight airs. Picturesque and dramatic was this final scene, all made possible by a ball bounding free of Michigan hands," was the game-ending description of H. G. Salsinger of the *Detroit News*.

The bouncing ball that Salsinger remembered had been observed early in the second quarter and became, no doubt, the game's pivotal element. Standing near his own goal line, Michigan's Frank Steketee got off a hurried punt that hit the ground and was bouncing along in the vicinity of U-M's 40-yard line. Of the Michigan players who rushed down to cover the kick, none touched the ball that would have "downed" it. As the punt covering corps nonchalantly watched the pigskin roll, Ohio's Johnny Stuart zipped between the defenders, scooped up the ball, and took off. "Michigan's eleven, startled, stood bewildered just long enough to put Stuart past the outstretched arms of the tardy tacklers," reported Salsinger.

The big play gave the Buckeyes all the points needed on this particular day but just in case, they added another touchdown in the fourth quarter and made it three in a row over the Wolverines, 14-0. The game was played on October 23 and the 40,000 fans on hand was the largest crowd yet to see a Michigan football

The Wolverines opened the season with the school's 300th grid game, a 44-0 rout of Mt. Union College. At this point, the all-time record stood at 231-57-12 for a winning percentage of .790. Then Case fell 65-0, Michigan State by 30-0, and it was invasion time by Ohio State.

The Buckeyes had opened up with a 28-0 win over Ohio Wesleyan. Oberlin was next on the schedule. Oberlin was to provide a game-type scrimmage to sharpen OSU for Minnesota. A classic "breather," as it were. Just five years before, the Bucks had obliterated Oberlin, 128-0. But in 1921, Oberlin "obliterated" Ohio State, 7-6, in a ground-shaking shocker that could easily have qualified as the biggest upset of the season. But it wasn't to be. Rather, Centre College's 6-0 super surprise of mighty Harvard at Cambridge became the top football story of 1921, a distinction later confirmed in 1950 when sportswriters dubbed it the "upset of the half-century."

OSU rebounded with a 27-0 win over Minnesota and braced for the Michigan encounter.

In a drive highlighted by Harry Kipke's 32-yard run in the first quarter, Michigan reached Ohio's 10-yard line but had to settle for a field goal try by Steketee, who missed the mark by just inches. From then on the contest developed into one of short plunges and numerous punts. That was the character of the game when OSU's Stuart darted in and grabbed the Michigan punt for the game's first score.

After Stuart's heads-up touchdown play, Lloyd Pixley converted for a 7-0 score. "Ohio State, having gained an advantage of seven points, gathered momentum in her attack and swept over Michigan through the remainder of the game," said the *News*.

The score remained 7-0 until late in the third period when another breakdown in Michigan's kicking game led to the Buckeyes' clinching touchdown. Standing at his own five-yard line, Steketee's punt was partially blocked and Ohio took over at the Wolverine's 28-yard line. Five plays later the ball was on the one as the quarter came to a close.

"As the teams changed goals, the Ohio State coaches poured fresh men on the field for a final smash at the Michigan line," said the *News*. Michigan held on the first smash but Charles Taylor crashed over for the score on the second. Pixley's kick was good. Fourteen-to-nothing.

"Michigan's line lacked charge, and against the superior weight and strength of Ohio State's was overpowered. . . .In the second half the Buckeyes' drive became more intense and Michigan went down before the onslaught. . . .Ohio followers came on special trains and 500 automobiles, there were many well-dressed women but not typical football enthusiasts for the most part. . . . Michigan's cheerleaders, who have been successful in handling the

77

PART 4
Sport, Automobiles, Financial, Real Estate,

NET PAID CIRCULATION LAST SUNDAY
241,236.
90,000 MORE

The Detroit News

"ALWAYS IN THE LEAD"

SUNDAY, OCTOBER 23, 1921.

"ALWAYS IN THE LEAD"

MEN OF WILCE ECLIPSE CONFERENCE HOPES OF YOSTMEN, 14 TO 0

Ohio State Brought Her Western Conference Champions to Ferry Field, Conquering Michigan in the First "Big Ten" Battle of Wolverine's Season. Here Are Some of the Buckeyes.

| Tarey | Doig | Isabel | Weaver | Cott | Huffman | Trott | Myers | Workman | Pixley |

| U. of D. . . . . . 28 | Yale . . . . . . 14 | Chicago . . . . . 9 | Northwestern . . 38 | Wisconsin . . . 20 | O. S. U. . . . . 14 |
| Boston . . . . . 0 | Army . . . . . . 0 | Princeton . . . . 0 | Saginaw Eastern . .10 | Illinois . . . . . 0 | Michigan . . . . . 0 |

Note a portion of the big crowd shown in the newspaper photograph. The attendance was 40,000 in the first Michigan-Ohio State game played at the new Ferry Field in Ann Arbor. Also notice the interesting headline declaring OSU coach John Wilce eclipsing UM coach Fielding Yost.

crowds of 28,000 present at the 'big games,' had no such success today. They seemed lost. . . . The big crowd was too much for them," were among observations of the *News*.

Michigan went on to defeat Illinois and Minnesota but were tied by Wisconsin. The Buckeyes, after blanking Chicago and Purdue, had only a below-par Illinois team to beat to gain a share (with Iowa) of the Conference championship. The Illini were winless (0-3) in league play and had yet to score a point when they travelled to Columbus. But, for the third year in a row, the OSU-Illinois game turned into a classic duel. Illinois won 7-0. The Bucks had surrendered only two touchdowns all season, and both resulted in defeats – 7-6 and 7-0.

Michigan finished 5-1-1; Ohio State 5-2-0.

1922

NEW STADIUM, OLD STORY

It was a grand and glorious Homecoming Day in Columbus that October 21. Michigan's football team was in town. Everybody had come from everywhere. It was also Dedication Day for Ohio State University's magnificent new football stadium – a massive, horseshoe-shaped structure whose major dimensions, in 1922, were staggering. The fortress-like monster rose a third-of-a-football field in height, stretched two-and-a-half football fields in length, and was two football fields wide. Permanent seating capacity was 62,110 with temporary seating on Dedication Day of another 10,000. For the game, all 72,000-plus seats were filled.

"COLUMBUS DISCOVERED AMERICA, THE STADIUM WILL HELP AMERICA DISCOVER COLUMBUS," read a big banner on one of the parade floats. By mid-morning, it seemed as though most of America had already discovered Columbus. The parking lots began to fill. The stands were swelling with people. The 700 ushers required to handle a full house had their hands full.

The big place was seething with excitement. After all, it was a Michigan-Ohio State weekend, new stadium or not, and the Buckeyes had not lost to their Ann Arbor rivals since 1918.

But there was to be no Scarlet and Gray victory party after this one. The Wolverines, led by the great play of halfback Harry Kipke, went back to their old series ways and completely shut the Buckeyes down, 19-0.

OSU entered the game with unimpressive shutouts over Ohio Wesleyan (5-0) and Oberlin (14-0). U-M beat Case 48-0 and was held to a scoreless tie by Vanderbilt.

Top photo: "X" marks the spot — the spot of the future Ohio Stadium.

Bottom photo: By the flood-swollen Olentangy River in early spring of 1922, steel is up and Ohio Stadium's horseshoe configuration is dramatically defined. The stadium was built in only 13 months at a cost of $1.4 million — 80 per cent of which was covered by donations from just over 13,000 people. (Photos courtesy of OSU Photo Archives)

With a new stadium, Dedication Day and Michigan in town, football was definitely front page news on the day of the 1922 game.

With all of the pre-game formalities and hoopla finally finished, Ohio's Lloyd Pixley kicked off to Douglas Robey and the game was on. The Wolverines knocked out two first downs before punting to the Bucks' 20-yard line. Ohio punted; Michigan punted. Ohio punted again, and the boot was partially blocked. U-M took over at the OSU 38. After an incomplete pass, Kipke ripped off a 13-yard gain. Irwin Uteritz went for three, Robey for three, and Kipke for two, to bring up a fourth-and-two situation at the Buckeye 17. Wanting a quick score, Coach Fielding Yost sent in Paul Goebel, and Goebel produced the points – three of them – with a field goal.

An Ohio error late in the second quarter led to the visitor's second set of points. With the scrimmage line at OSU's 35, the snap from center went to the wrong back, bounced off his shoulder to the ground and Angus Goetz recovered for Michigan at the 26. On second down from the same spot, right halfback Robey started a sweep right, stopped suddenly, and threw the ball back across the field to Kipke. Technically, it was a lateral. Kipke waltzed untouched into the endzone for the touchdown. Goebel's conversion was good and it was 10-0.

"When Ohio State was ten points behind, (Harry) Workman began calling for forward passes. He passed recklessly and also passed with poor judgment, considering the kind of defense Michigan showed against this passing attack," observed H. G. Salsinger of the *Detroit News*.

81

SOUVENIR
DEDICATION
PROGRAM

MICHIGAN
VERSUS
OHIO STATE

Sat. Oct. 21, 1922

50 CENTS

THE DISPATCH RECEIVES THE FULL REPORT OF THE ASSOCIATED PRESS

The Columbus Sunday Dispatch.

COLUMBUS, OHIO, SUNDAY, OCTOBER 22, 1922.   VOL. LII. NO. 114.   PRICE TEN CENTS

OHIO'S GREAT STADIUM IS DEDICATED
MICHIGAN AVENGES DEFEAT OF 1921

Thousands Thrilled by Magnificent Spectacle

RECORDED BY THE CAMERA'S EYE AT THE
OHIO-MICHIGAN GAME SATURDAY

Where to Find Dispatch
Features Today

**BUCKEYES BATTLE
IN VAIN AGAINST
SUPERIOR TEAM**

Early in the third period, Kipke tallied his second touchdown of the day when he intercepted a pass and went 38 yards. Goebel missed the conversion and the score stayed at 16-0. Later in the quarter, Ohio moved down to Michigan's 14 where it was first down. A run of one yard and three straight incomplete passes shattered any hopes of a Buckeye comeback.

In the final period, another interception by Kipke, his third of the afternoon, set up Michigan's final score. He picked this one off at the Ohio 25 and, when things stalled, took it upon himself to get something out of it – and he did – with a drop-kick field goal to finish the scoring for the day, but not the drama.

As the previous year's game at Ann Arbor ended, the Ohio band and fans raced onto the field, paraded around and blared forth playing and singing fight songs – a display that did not in any way set well with the Michigan students and alumni. Many of those Michigan students and alumni didn't forget.

"As the referee's whistle blew ending the game, the Michigan band broke from its section and started across the field. . . .'The Victors' was played and the band and thousands of Michigan rooters paraded across the virgin turf of the stadium while thousands of other spectators that saw today's game stood mutely in the aisles against the dull gray background, watching the triumphant march of the victors," reported Salsinger.

He also wrote, "The powerful Ohio State backs, who were depended on to crash the Michigan line, failed. . . .Ohio State's indi-

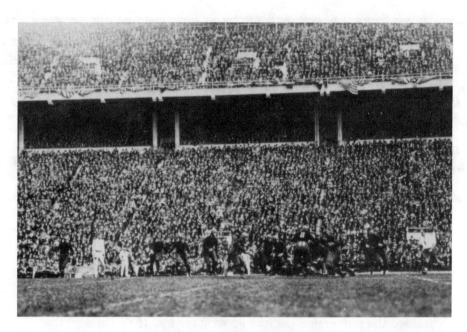

The new plant was packed.

Michigan halfback Harry Kipke scored on a 26-yard run, a 38-yard interception and kicked a 37-yard field goal to lead his team's 19-0 victory in 1922. He would later become head coach at UM.

vidual players fell shy of the standard claimed for them. . . .Michigan won because Michigan knew more football than Ohio State."

In four remaining games, OSU managed only 24 points and lost to Minnesota, Chicago and Iowa, before edging Illinois, 6-3. The Bucks' final 3-4-0 record was the team's first losing season in 24 years.

Michigan had come back. The Wolverines bopped Illinois, Michigan State, Wisconsin and Minnesota to end with a 6-0-1 record and a piece of the Big Ten title along with Iowa and Chicago.

Breaking a three-game losing streak to Ohio State, the Maize and Blue increased their series lead to 14-3-2.

1923

GAME 20

YOST WITH THE MOST – AGAIN

Coach Fielding Yost had his Michigan Wolverines back on track and into a full-stride "Hurry Up" gait in 1923. There were seven major college teams with perfect records that year and Michigan was among this elite group. But down at Columbus, the grid scene offered nothing for Buckeye fans to get excited about.

U-M had blanked Case 36-0 and broken Vanderbilt's 21-game unbeaten streak, 3-0. OSU earned a 24-7 victory over Ohio Wesleyan and were tied by Colgate, 23-23.

"Ohio State ascended to football glory by way of their air attack and Ohio State has remained among the front elevens through her ability to carry on in forward passing," reported the *Detroit News* on game day. But, in the October 20 meeting at Ann Arbor, it was Michigan that exploited the passing game to perfection, and the air game led to a 23-0 bombing of the Bucks as Irwin Uteritz threw touchdown passes of 25 and 32 yards. The final figures would show the Wolverines passing for 152 yards and Ohio State a scant 46.

The main feature of a scoreless first quarter was a remarkable punt by Harry Kipke. Standing on his own goal and with a strong wind to his back, the Michigan star pounded the pigskin all the way to Ohio's 15-yard line – an 85-yard bomber. The kick got U-M out of a hole and, judging by later developments, gave the team a shot of confidence that sustained them for the rest of the game.

The underdog Buckeyes played tough Michigan to a standoff until just before intermission when the Wolverines broke on top. Starting from the OSU 46 after receiving a punt, quarterback

Uteritz went to work with a 22-yard completion to Kipke. Five plays later from the Ohio seven, where it was fourth-and-four, Coach Yost inserted his kicker, Jack Blott, and Blott booted a field goal. It was Michigan's 14th in the series; and it was a 3-0 ball game.

On Michigan's first possession of the second half, the Wolverines drove down to the 12-yard line where Ohio held and Blott narrowly missed kicking another field goal. Later in the period, a blocked punt led to Michigan's first touchdown. Taking over at their own 47 after the big defensive play, Uteritz and Louis Curran combined for a 37-yard pass completion to Ohio's 16. A behind-the-line pass play lost nine yards back to the 25, but Uteritz came right back with a touchdown toss to Herbert Steger. Blott added the point for a 10-0 lead. It was the sixth consecutive game in the series that had produced a blocked punt.

Early in the final period, Uteritz and his aerial attack yielded another touchdown. On third-and-six from the Buckeye 36, Uteritz swung a short one out to Kipke, and Kipke made a beautiful run into the endzone. Blott's kick made it 17-0.

As the game was drawing to a close, Steger intercepted a pass at OSU's 41 and Michigan finished off the weary Buckeyes with a nine-play ground attack that ended with Steger's eight-yard smash for a touchdown on fourth down. The Wolverines tried to pass for the conversion but failed. Final: 23-0.

The afternoon had been a long one for the Buckeyes.

It is interesting that 1923 marked the first time newspapers carried a box of complete game statistics, commonly referred to today as the "yardstick." The figures showed that Michigan gained 98 yards "through the line" and 18 yards "around the end." Total yards for the day (rushing and passing) was: Michigan 257, Ohio State 118.

The Bucks lost to Iowa, topped Denison and Purdue, but dropped their two final games to Chicago and Illinois for a disappointing 3-4-1 season.

Michigan won its last five games to post its second straight undefeated season, with no losses in the last 18 games. It is unfortunate that there couldn't be a Michigan-Illinois matchup in 1923. Both teams finished 8-0-0 to become co-champions of the Big Ten.

Following the season, Yost announced his decision to retire as coach in order to devote full-time to the athletic directorship, a position he had taken in 1921. It would not be a lasting retirement.

Against non-Conference foes in 1923, the Big Ten had an impressive 22-3-2 record.

1924

FRUSTRATION ENDS IN VICTORY

In the decade world-renowned as the "Golden Age of Sports," the year 1924 saw the birth of two of football's most time-honored legends.

Michigan opened the season with a 55-0 stomping of Miami (Ohio), before edging Michigan State, 7-0. That brought the season to Saturday, October 18. Michigan, having not lost a game in three years, was at Champaign to play Illinois; Notre Dame was at New York City to play Army.

The Irish won, 13-7. "Outlined against a blue-gray sky, the Four Horsemen rode again today. . . ." wrote Grantland Rice of the *New York Herald Tribune*. The Four Horsemen were born.

During the same moments, a time zone to the West, a junior running back named Harold Grange was making peewees of a powerful Michigan team with the most incredible exhibition one man has ever staged in one college football game.

Grange returned the opening kick-off 95 yards for a touchdown. Next came a 67-yard streak; then one of 56 yards; another for 44 – all for touchdowns, all in the first quarter. Just like that, the score was 27-0. After resting in the second quarter, Grange returned in the last half and scored on a 12-yard run, later ran 40 yards to Michigan's 18, from where he threw a touchdown pass. Grange accounted for all six touchdowns as Illinois won, 39-14. And remember, Grange's seemingly impossible feat came against a great Michigan team – a team that hadn't lost in 20 games and a team that had surrendered only nine touchdowns in the last 31 outings.

"The Galloping Ghost" became a household word.

This was the first year of George Little as head coach at Michigan. Little had been an assistant under Yost, and his team rebounded admirably from the Grange devastation with wins over Wisconsin, Minnesota and Northwestern by a combined 61-0 score. Ohio State was next on the schedule.

Even though the Buckeyes had scored only four touchdowns in six games leading up to their encounter with Michigan, there was only one loss. OSU edged Purdue 7-0, played Iowa to a scoreless tie, topped Ohio Wesleyan 10-0, tied Chicago 3-3, came out all even against Wooster 7-7, before losing 12-7 to Indiana. The Bucks were 2-1-3.

Michigan was 5-1-0 and it marked only the third time in series history (21 games) that Ohio State had to face a Wolverine team that was *not* undefeated.

A paid attendance of 68,284 jammed Ohio Stadium to watch the two rivals square off for the 21st time. OSU scored in the first minute of play and held on until the fourth quarter, when the relentless Wolverines rallied for two touchdowns and a field goal to swing an exciting 16-6 battle in their favor.

Michigan quarterback Benny Friedman threw 20 passes in the game. "It was the best exhibition of passing and the worst exhibition of receiving that we have ever seen since the introduction of the forward pass," said the *Detroit News*. Eight of Friedman's passes were dropped and the errors kept the Wolverines in trouble throughout the first three quarters of the game.

Ohio returned the opening kickoff only to the 18. The game's first scrimmage play netted nothing. Bill Hunt then shot for 20 yards. On the third play, Hunt threw a pass to Harold Cunningham just beyond the line of scrimmage. Cunningham snaked through the secondary defenders and suddenly there was nothing between him and the goal. A 62-yard touchdown! The Hunt-to-Cunningham pass play entered the record books as the longest in the series. It was a record that would not be broken for 37 years. The conversion was missed and the underdog Buckeyes had a quick 6-0 lead.

The gigantic stadium rocked.

Early in the second quarter, Bierman threw his first "touchdown pass," dropped cleanly at the OSU five-yard line. The Bucks took over but had to punt. A hurried Bill Jenkins kicked only a nine-yarder and Michigan got the ball at Ohio's 32. Friedman threw another perfect pass, this one to the eight. It too was dropped.

HUNT-TO-CUNNINGHAM

Bill Hunt (L) and Harold Cunningham teamed-up on a 62-yard touchdown pass play for OSU's only score in 16-6 loss to Michigan in 1924. It would stand as the series' longest TD pass until 1961. (Photos courtesy of OSU Photo Archives.)

Moments later, Michigan got the ball again when Harry Hawkins intercepted a pass at Ohio's 37. Once again, Friedman was on target, but once again a certain touchdown pass slipped through his receiver's fingers. "Here, Friedman threw his headgear away in disgust," the *News* reported.

Friedman's next five passes were incomplete (two dropped) and his passing stats at halftime read zero-for-12.

Ohio continued to hold, and the game moved to late in the third period with the score still 6-0. Starting at his own 49 after a punt, Michigan's F. A. Rockwell swept left end for 27 yards to Ohio's 24. A Friedman-to-Rockwell pass gained nine. "Then Michigan tried her best-known and beloved play, almost the oldest play in Michigan football catechism, known far and wide between the two oceans as the 'Statute of Liberty' play," reported the *News*.

Friedman dropped back to pass and cocked his arm. Steger came around, took the ball and ran nine yards down to the six as the third quarter came to a close. When play was resumed, Rockwell blasted for four yards as the Buckeyes tried desperately but in vain to protect their narrow margin. On the next play, Phillip Marion burst through the line and tumbled into the endzone for a touchdown. Rockwell's conversion was good. Frustrated all afternoon, the Wolverines had finally taken the lead, 7-6.

Later in the quarter, Ohio's Ollie Klee fumbled a punt that was recovered by Michigan's Harold Steel at the Buckeye 38. Marion went for four. Friedman then connected on a pass to Rockwell at the Ohio 10-yard line, but two Buckeyes slammed Rockwell causing a fumble recovered by Klee for OSU. On first down, Rockwell got the ball back when he picked off a pass at the Buckeye 32. On fourth down from the 10, Rockwell kicked a field goal to make the score 10-6.

With time running out, Hunt fooled the Wolverine defense with a 56-yard run from punt formation to put the ball down at the 19. On second down, Edliff Slaughter, a U-M guard and the biggest man on the squad, intercepted a pass in the endzone and hoofed it all the way back to Ohio's 40. Friedman found Bill Flora open for a pass that was good for 24 yards to the 16. Friedman's three runs gained nine to the OSU seven-yard line. On a run off a fake field goal try, Michigan got a first down. Two plays later, Rockwell scored with a minute left in the game. The conversion was blocked.

The wild afternoon of football had produced a total of 11 pass interceptions – six of them by Michigan.

91

Both Michigan and Ohio State lost their one remaining game; the Wolverines 9-2 to Iowa, the Buckeyes 7-0 to Illinois.

After 21 encounters, Michigan was way out front, 16-3-2, and had outscored the Buckeyes 437-68.

The 1924 encounter was the first Michigan-Ohio State game to be broadcast on radio. WWJ in Detroit, the first radio station in the world to broadcast regularly scheduled daily programs (August 20, 1920), carried the game "live" from Ann Arbor. The announcer was E.L. "Ty" Tyson. Just three weeks before (October 25), WWJ aired the first football game as Michigan defeated Wisconsin 21-0 at Ferry Field in Ann Arbor.

E.L. "Ty" Tyson, right, and Doc Holland formed the Michigan football broadcast team. Tyson was the play-by-play announcer of the first Michigan-Ohio State game to be aired on radio. The game was carried "live" by WWJ, Detroit. (Photo courtesy of WWJ.)

1925

THE BUCKEYES
WERE BLUE

Fielding Yost's itchy britches to get back among the troops got the best of him. After one year behind the desk as athletic director, "Hurry Up" decided that he wanted to return to his old job as head coach. So, he just re-hired himself. George Little, the one-year man, was out.

The Yostmen won their first five games of the season, amassing 108 points to zero for opponents Michigan State, Indiana, Wisconsin, Illinois (including Red Grange) and Navy. In the sixth game of the campaign, Northwestern managed only a field goal, but it was enough for a 3-2 win in the rain and mud at Chicago. It was one of the season's biggest upsets.

Ohio State was 4-1-1. There had been a tie with Chicago, a loss to Iowa and victories over Ohio Wesleyan, Columbia, Wooster and Indiana. It was now time to go to Ann Arbor.

Michigan won again. The final of this one was 10-0, played on November 14 in the final game of the series at Ferry Field.

Even though the Buckeyes held Michigan to a relatively close score, they never came close to scoring and spent the entire afternoon warding off repeated Wolverine threats.

H. G. Salsinger of the *Detroit News* wrote, "The statistics reveal Michigan's superiority on attack but this superiority existed between the two 15-yard lines. Inside this territory, Michigan was powerless."

The game statistics bear out Salsinger's observations. The Wolverines galloped around for 15 first downs and 260 total yards; OSU managed just one first down and 72 yards.

Rev. J. Snell's Thrilling Story
"THE FIREBUG"
In Today's Boys' and Girls' Magazine

The Detroit News

PART 4 | Sporting News and Financial

"ALWAYS IN THE LEAD" • • •

SUNDAY, NOVEMBER 15, 1925.

"A NEWS IN EVERY HOME"

| Michigan . . . 10 | Princeton . . . 25 | Dartmouth . . 33 | Harvard . . . . . 3 | Minnesota . . 33 | Wisconsin . . . 21 | W. & J. . . . . . 7 |
| Ohio State . . 0 | Yale . . . . 12 | Chicago . . . . 7 | Brown . . . . . . 0 | Iowa . . . . 0 | Mich. State . . 10 | U. of D. . . . . . 0 |

OHIO'S VERSATILE PASS DEFENSE BOTHERS, BUT MICHIGAN WINS

When Passes Failed "Bo" Molenda Had Little Difficulty Crashing Through Ohio State's Front Line

Early in the game, Benny Friedman was off target on a 37-yard field goal, and Ohio took the ball at its own 20. U-M's Bill Flora broke through on punt formation and blocked the kick. Even though OSU's Myers Clark recovered the ball, under a brand new rule it automatically became Michigan's ball on downs. Previously, a blocked punt had been "anybody's ball."

On this particular blocked kick, Michigan took over at the State one-yard line. Yost moved his left tackle, big Tom Edwards, to fullback and on two straight smashes into the line by Big Tom, the Wolverines were still short – by six inches. Exit Edwards, enter John Molenda, the regular fullback. Molenda crashed the line and he, too, was shy – by six inches. Molenda was handed the leather again and finally made it. Friedman's conversion made it 7-0.

In the second quarter, the Wolves drove to the Ohio 15 but were stopped. On first down, Benny Oosterbaan, who later would become head coach at Michigan, intercepted a pass at the Buckeye 17. On fourth-and-18, Friedman, standing on the 38-yard line, kicked a field goal and the scoring was concluded for another year even though Michigan camped in Ohio State territory for the remainder of the game.

The Maize and Blue blanked Minnesota the following week to capture the Big Ten championship. The overall record was 7-1-0 and the season's scoreboard showed Michigan had outscored its opposition by a 227-3 margin. However, those three points surrendered by the Wolverines led to the team's only defeat.

Ohio State lost to Illinois for a 4-3-1 alumni-griping season. The old grads and other OSU fans were also unhappy with their 3-17-2 record against Michigan.

1926

GAME 23

IDENTICAL, ALMOST

By mid-morning, one knew this would be the warmest day of the month. The sun was bright, the sky was clear. There was still plenty of nip in the air, but that meant only that it would be a perfect day for football.

Columbus was literally bursting at the seams. All hotel accommodations had been gone for months. Thousands upon thousands had secured rooms in outlying towns. And here they came from every direction. The entire region was enmeshed in one massive traffic snarl.

Ultimate destination: Ohio Stadium. Ultimate aim: The Michigan-Ohio State football game. By noon, well over 100,000 people had found the place. Not only was the Columbus Police Department out in full force, but also soldiers from nearby Ft. Hayes. The extra security force was to prevent feared storming of the gates. It had happened at last year's OSU-Illinois game when 5,000 crashed through and entered the stadium.

Hundreds had camped overnight at the General Admission gate, where 2,000 tickets went on sale at 10 o'clock the morning of the game.

The OSU band arrived early to serenade. Later, a cloth banner was unfurled stretching the entire length of the football field. In huge red letters, it read simply: "BEAT MICHIGAN!"

By now the place was packed. The official attendance was announced as 90,411. It was also reported that an estimated 15,000 were left outside clamoring for tickets. A very unfortunate incident took place just before kickoff. An "air bomb" launched from outside the stadium shot up and over the high walls, fell into the crowd and exploded. Several spectators were injured and had to be rushed to the hospital.

The Buckeyes entered the big game with a perfect 6-0-0 record; Michigan was 5-1-0, suffering only a 10-0 loss to a powerful Navy team that was on its way to an unbeaten season.

The game those 90,411 fans witnessed in Columbus that November 13 turned out to be a 17-16 Michigan victory. The final score, however, was just part of the story. If ever any football game deserved to be labeled a classic, this was it.

Ohio won the toss and received. Louis Gilbert kicked off to Fred Grim. After three punts, the Wolverines were backed up to their 12-yard line. Gilbert fumbled on first down and Robin Bell recovered for Ohio at the 11. Three plays gained but five yards and Myers Clark came on to kick a field goal for a 3-0 Buckeye lead.

Later in the first quarter, the fired-up Bucks stopped a fourth-and-one gamble by Michigan at the OSU 40-yard line and scored in three quick plays. Grim broke through the line for a 19-yard gain to the Wolverine 41. Bell then threw a long pass that Clark caught at the five before being belted out of bounds just one yard shy of the goal. Martin Karow blew in for a touchdown to become the first Big Ten player to score a TD against Michigan in two years. Clark kicked the conversion and after only 12 minutes into the game, Ohio State was in command, 10-0.

The hometown crowd was going wild.

On their second series of downs after the OSU score, the Wolves marched 46 yards to Ohio's 18 where Benny Friedman missed a field goal. The Buckeyes had to punt out – to Michigan's 37-yard line. Two runs gained four yards before Gilbert completed a pass to Friedman for 14 yards to Ohio's 45. Friedman fired one deep to Bennie Oosterbaan who made a spectacular, leaping stab at the Buckeye 11. Two plays later, Friedman went to Oosterbaan again. Touchdown Michigan! Friedman kicked good and the Wolverines were right back in the fight.

After more punt-trading, Michigan tied the game with a minute left before intermission. It was a Friedman 42-yard field goal.

Halftime: Ohio State 10, Michigan 10.

The second half rocked along with no serious threats until the Wolverines got a tremendous break on the last play of the third period. Gilbert sent a low, line-drive punt that hit at the OSU five-yard line. Elmer Marek, back to field the kick, apparently thought

Middle-West's Greatest Crowd Watches Game

Ninety Thousand in Ohio Stadium; Soldiers, Police Keep Back Mob; Air Bomb Injures Spectators.

The Detroit News

Everybody loves a winner, and everybody in Ohio tried to get in to see the undefeated Buckeyes battle Michigan in 1926. Those who did had an exciting time, but the Ohioans came away disappointed.

the ball would bound into the endzone. It didn't. The safetyman was forced to play the ball. Two Wolverines smashed into Marek, one high and one low, and the ball squirted free. Raymond Baer fell on it at the six-yard line. Baer wore blue.

Three plunges at the Buckeye defense left Michigan a yard short. On fourth down, Friedman retreated to pass, was rushed hard, and threw the ball to a covered Leo Hoffman in the endzone. Hoffman out-fought three red-shirted defenders and caught the football. It was a touchdown. Friedman kicked the point-after and the Yostmen had scratched back to take a 17-10 lead.

After the kickoff and an exchange of punts, the Bucks started from their own 31-yard line and quickly marched goalward, mostly by air. It was Bell-to-Clark for 23 yards to the U-M 46; Bell-to-Karow to the 37; Karow to the 34; Bell-to-Karow to the 19; Byron Eby-to-Bell to the 15; Eby to the 10, and Karow to the seven. From there, Eby swept left end for a touchdown. The stadium was hysterical with delight. Clark, a drop-kicker, took a direct snap from center. In charged the Michigan ends – Oosterbaan from the left and Bill Flora from the right – Clark was forced to hurry his kick. The ball shot through the uprights, but lower than the cross-bar. The score remained 17-16.

The Ohio rooters were crushed.

The Buckeyes got one more shot, but from the 50-yard line Hunt's pass was intercepted by Friedman at the 38. Three plays

A portion of the reported 90,411 fans who jammed Ohio Stadium for the 1926 game. (Photo courtesy of OSU Photo Archives)

later, the game ended and the huge majority of the great throng filed silently from the stadium.

The game statistics, as the score, were close. Each team picked up nine first downs; Ohio led in rushing yards, 95-93; Michigan led in passing yards, 96-91, and total yards, 189-186. U-M completed six of 14 passes; OSU five of nine. The two teams punted the pigskin a total of 22 times (12 by the Buckeyes) for just over 1,000 yards.

The similarities of the two teams continued. The following week, Michigan edged Minnesota 7-6; Ohio edged Illinois 7-6. Michigan finished with a 7-1-0 record; Ohio finished with a 7-1-0 record. For the season, Michigan outscored its eight opponents by 153 points (191-38); Ohio outscored its eight opponents by 153 points (196-43).

About the only difference between Ohio State and Michigan in 1926 was that the Wolverines shared the Big Ten title with Northwestern, both with perfect Conference records. There was another slight difference – the one point in the head-to-head meeting of the two teams.

The win by the Wolverines widened their margin over the Buckeyes to 18-3-2.

1927

GAME 24

OOSTERBAAN & GILBERT

The crush on Ann Arbor was something the quiet college community had never before experienced. If Ohio State could have a new stadium, then the University of Michigan could have one also. Michigan did get one, and it was Dedication Day for the Wolverines' huge new football bowl.

With limited hotel accommodations available in Ann Arbor, the roads had to take the load. And all roads leading to Ann Arbor were jammed to a virtual standstill. From the air it looked as though giant black snakes were invading the town from all directions.

Fans streamed in from Detroit, Flint, Battle Creek and Lansing. They were also coming from other surrounding communities such as Moscow and Cement City, Brooklyn and Maybee, Fairfield, Litchfield, Plainfield and hundreds of other towns throughout the State. Not to mention an enemy influx from Ohio. The traffic had state troopers and the local police force scratching their heads in bewilderment.

At least 87,000 people struggled their way into town, found a parking nook and went to the stadium. No doubt there was at least one among those thousands to wish he had brought along the piano or bureau or dining room table – where the tickets had been left behind.

"But, honey, I thought you brought the tickets!"

"No, Duncan, I washed your clothes, ironed that silly-looking shirt you have on, arranged for Mother to keep the children,

OHIO STATE
UNIVERSITY VS
UNIVERSITY of MICHIGAN
ANN ARBOR - OCTOBER 22, 1927
OFFICIAL PROGRAM - FIFTY CENTS

got up at four o'clock this morning, prepared this picnic, cooked breakfast, dragged you out of bed at six, cleaned the house because Mother was coming, and went to get Mother, all so we could leave at seven like you said you wanted to. *You* were supposed to bring the tickets, Duncan, *dear*."

Then there is always at least one nervous soul who leaves his automobile engine running. With 87,000 hopped-up football fans at the same place at the same time, anything can happen, and usually does.

Even though the Ohio State game was the official dedication game, Michigan had already played twice in its new plant. Ohio Wesleyan christened it on October 1 before an official paid attendance of 17,483. However, high school students from all over the State were invited as guests of the University to attend the game, and that swelled the on-hand attendance to around 50,000. U-M won 33-0. The next week, 27,864 showed up for a 21-0 win over Michigan State. Then came another shutout, 14-0 against Wisconsin at Madison.

Ohio went North with wins over Wittenberg and Iowa, and a loss to Northwestern.

It was Saturday, October 22, and the huge crowd was expecting a duplicate of last year's thriller at Columbus. The 1927 game wasn't a classic, but the feats of two of its performers were classic.

Michigan scored three touchdowns; Ohio State scored none. Benny Oosterbaan (an end) threw three passes, Louis Gilbert (a halfback) caught all three – all three for touchdowns. Gilbert also kicked three conversions as the Maize and Blue boxed the Buckeyes with still another defeat. Final score: Oosterbaan/Gilbert 21, OSU 0.

In 1927, for the third straight year, Benny Oosterbaan was named to the All-America team (as an end).

Statistically, it was a strange game. Subtract Michigan's three touchdown plays and the Wolverines managed only 93 yards for the afternoon. The final figures showed OSU a 10-4 leader in first downs, while the total yardage went to Michigan, 191-163.

Midway through the second period, the Wolverines had worked their way to Ohio's 45-yard line, where it was second-and-20. Oosterbaan, who could throw the football a country mile, moved from end to the backfield, took the snap from center and let one fly. Gilbert, streaking down the sidelines, snagged the ball on the run and scored.

Seven-to-nothing.

More than 600 neighborhood
stations in Detroit take
News want ads—One near you.

PART 4 } SPORTING NEWS

354,000 SUNDAY CIRCULATION

The Detroit News

SUNDAY, OCTOBER 23, 1927.

'Oosterbaan-to-Gilbert' (Three Times) Defeats Ohio For Michigan

Illinois Beats Northwestern by Point; Minnesota Swamps Iowa

Wolverines Overcome Hoodoo of Dedication

How the Largest Crowd in Michigan's History Appeared When the New Stadium Was Dedicated

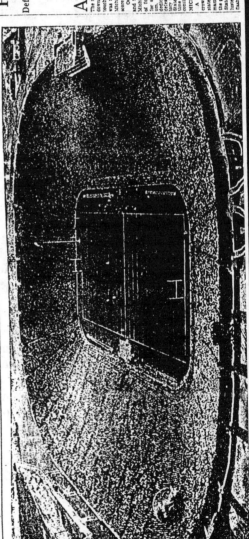

Defense Stiffens When Buckeyes Near Goal;
Largest Crowd in State's History
Watches 21 to 0 Triumph.

By H. G. SALSINGER

ANN ARBOR, Oct. 22.—Benny Oosterbaan, Michigan's All-America end, threw a foot ball three times this afternoon and Louis Gilbert, the weaving halfback, caught each of the three passes.

The result of the three braves and the three catches was a goal at each performance and when each was of the touchdown and direct for Michigan defense stiffened when stiffening is most needed. Ohio State was kept scoreless and Michigan won her sixth consecutive victory over the Buckeyes. The score, as you may have guessed, was 21 to 0.

Oosterbaan and Gilbert reversed the expected order of passing today and their perfect execution enabled Michigan to smash a surviving law of foot ball which provides defeat for any team dedicating its stadium. Michigan helped Ohio State dedicate her stadium in 1922, and cracked her 19 to 0, the first victory for a Michigan team over Ohio State in four years. Since that time Michigan's success has been continuous.

MICHIGAN'S LARGEST CROWD.

A brilliant day and the largest crowd that ever saw a game in this state attended the dedication of the much new foot ball theater. But the game, unlike the Michigan-Ohio State battle of a year ago, lacked luster. There were only momentary flashes, only momentary thrills. The

THE LINEUPS

Just after intermission, Gilbert returned a punt 21 yards to the OSU 40. On first down, the ball went back to quarterback Leo Hoffman. Oosterbaan, from his end position, swung around and was given the ball by Hoffman on what appeared to be an ordinary end-around play. But it wasn't. Oosterbaan stopped, spotted Gilbert downfield and pegged it deep. Gilbert grabbed the ball at the two-yard line, tore away from two Buckeyes and fell across the goal.

Fourteen-to-nothing.

Touchdown No. 3 came late in the game. Ohio was backed up to its own goal and punted out to the 35. Four plays later the Wolverines were at the eight, but a penalty set them back to the 13. Again, Oosterbaan went behind the line, took the snap and dumped a short pass off to Gilbert who raced over for the score.

Twenty-one-to-nothing.

That about sums up the 1927 OSU-Michigan football game.

Ohio's main threat came after the ensuing kickoff. In eight plays the Buckeyes reached Michigan's eight-yard line where a fourth-down pass was incomplete. Two plays later the game was history. It would be a long time before followers of both teams would forget the Oosterbaan-Gilbert passing combination that worked so well that day in Ann Arbor. The triumph gave the Wolverines a 19-3-2 series difference. In points scored, the tally was 485-86.

Each team had four games remaining on 1927 schedules and each came out with a 2-2 split. U-M was 6-2-0 for the season and the Buckeyes were 4-4-0. To say that OSU alumni were disenchanted with their school's football program would be a gross understatement.

MICHIGAN'S BENNIE OOSTERBAAN

Earned three "M" football letters (1925-26-27) as an end and also made All-American *all three years. Even though an end, strangely enough, he still shares the record (with Tom Harmon) for most touchdown passes THROWN in the Ohio State series — four. He also made All-American in basketball and All-Big Ten in baseball, winning nine letters. Oosterbaan would become head football coach at Michigan 21 years later (1948).*

1928

GAME 25

BUCKS AX HEX

It was Saturday, October 6, the opening day for Big Ten football. At Columbus, the Buckeyes posted all-time win No. 200 at the expense of Wittenberg, 41-0. Meanwhile, at Ann Arbor, there was turmoil. On the eve of the first game, the Wolverines didn't have a coach. Actually, they had two – Elton Wierman and Fielding Yost. But, having two coaches is like having none. At the last minute it was decided that Wierman, who had played under Yost, would coach the team in 1928. The confused situation could have easily been the cause for Michigan to lose a season opener for the first time in 40 years. Ohio Wesleyan pulled the big surprise, 17-7.

The fabulous coaching career of Fielding Yost had finally and officially come to a close.

The following week, Ohio State won again and Michigan lost again. It was now time for "The Big One." With Michigan's 0-2-0 record, the 1928 game has the distinction of being the only one in the history of the series in which one of the teams entered the contest without a victory.

OSU was riding a dreadful six-game losing streak to Michigan, but the Scarlet and Gray finally broke the Wolverines' whammy with a 19-7 win before 72,723 onlookers at Columbus on October 20.

The hometown fans really enjoyed this one. Their Buckeyes blasted out 13 first downs and held Michigan to only one; and the winner's 157 total yards were 107 more than U-M could manage against a tough OSU defense.

105

DR. JOHN W. WILCE – OSU COACH, 1913-28

Ohio snapped a scoreless game eight minutes after the kick-off. Taking a punt at the Michigan 44-yard line, the Buckeyes tallied in six plays. On third-and-three, Charles Coffee went 14 yards to the U-M 23. Coffee then lost seven, but got 14 back on the next play and the scrimmage line was the 16. Alan Holman ran wide before passing to end Wes Fesler. Fesler got his finger tips on the ball and was giving a good juggling act while on the run. He finally gained control of the ball but stumbled in doing so and fell at the Michigan three-yard line. Before a defender could reach him, Fesler frantically crawled on his stomach the remaining "three longest yards" for a touchdown. Fred Barratt's conversion was wide, but Ohio was on top 6-0. Wes Fesler would become coach at Ohio State 19 years later.

The Wolverines retaliated with a wild, wild touchdown to take the lead. Michigan's John Totske drove a punt that hit at the Ohio 16 and started bounding towards the endzone. Coffee was in no position to field the ball so he let it roll, thinking it would go beyond the goal line. Two Michigan linemen (one of them Leo Draveling) were closing in fast. To prevent them from grounding the ball near the goal, Coffee threw himself at the opposing players. They roared into Coffee, knocking him head-over-heels backwards and Coffee's head hit the ball and knocked it into the endzone. It was now a "live" ball.

By now, OSU's Holman, who had come across the field to the rescue, fell on the ball in the endzone, but he couldn't corral it. Draveling dived at the ball and got his hands on it just one foot inside the back line of the endzone, but the ball squirted from his mad grasp out of the field of play. The officials ruled that Draveling had possession long enough for a touchdown. Ohio State vehemently disagreed. Joe Gembis' point-after was perfect and Michigan led, 7-6.

"Michigan had secured the traditional Michigan break and took advantage of it. That has been the way of Michigan teams for years," reported the *Detroit News*.

Late in the second quarter Ohio regained the lead. Michigan punted to the OSU 45. Five straight carries by Byron Eby gained 24 yards down to the 21. On a "student body right" call, everyone went in that direction except Eby. He went left and pranced unmolested into the endzone with the ball. Once again, Barratt missed the conversion. OSU 12, U-M 7.

The Buckeyes put Michigan to rest by scoring again late in the game on a seven-play, 60-yard drive capped by a 27-yard

Columbus was packed with people for the 1928 Michigan game, and the outcome put them in a mood to celebrate.

touchdown pass from Holman to Coffee. Barratt finally kicked a good one and the Buckeyes had their fourth win over Michigan after 19 losses and two ties.

Disaster had set in at Michigan. A week later the Wolverines lost again, 7-0 at Wisconsin. Counting from the tail end of the previous season, that made five defeats in a row, something that had not happened to the Wolverines in 45 years. Three three-point wins (3-0 over Illinois, 3-0 over Michigan State, 10-7 over Iowa) and a 6-6 tie with Navy followed and a final 3-4-1 record.

The Buckeyes, playing the remainder of their schedule on "Cloud Nine," beat Indiana, tied Princeton, lost to Iowa, beat Muskingum, and lost to Illinois. The agitation that had surfaced among Ohio State alums after the last two seasons was somewhat soothed by the win over Michigan, but with the poor finish and a 5-2-1 record, the general feeling was that the unrest was still present.

As things turned out, the Michigan-Minnesota game two years earlier had been the 243rd and last of the coaching career of Fielding Yost.

ꞏnday Dispatch.

The World at Your Door	This Section
Dispatch Want Ads ꞏIiring Results	Local & Telegraph News. Editorial Page. Comment on Week's Events.

ꞏ1, 1928.

PRICE TEN CENTS

ꞏENGEANCE

CELEBRATION

ꞏempt to ꞏkeep up ꞏith ꞏ of the crowd that pulled, hauled and ꞏta way about the floor, came beꞏK for more ꞏeet was a mad mass of The hotel lobbies were ꞏto overflowing. They ꞏer for a moment and ꞏtors would ꞏump a new ꞏn the lobby.

"Locomotives" and other Ohio State jeⱡⱡs were answered by "Fight the Team," with many a voice out of key
One female ꞏhoopee artiⱡt at one of the hotels, who giggled suspiciously, sighting "Ethel" across the lobby, yelled "Oh Ethel, I've lost the party. Ain't that funny." ꞏhe then went into
(Continued on Page Six.)

WEAK MICHIGAN TEAM NOT EASILY DOWNED, HOWEVFR, DESPITE 19 TO 7 SCORE

Yost's phenomenal career as gridmaster spanned 29 years (25 at Michigan) and his all-time record was 196-35-12 for a winning percentage of .831. His Michigan teams were 165-29-10, .833, and outscored the opposition 5855-800 for an average score per game of 28-4. He won (or shared) 10 Big Ten championships and had eight unbeaten teams. His only losing season was in 1919 when U-M went 3-4-0. Ohio State was more than glad to see Yost move to the athletic directorship on a full time basis; the Buckeyes were able to solve the mysteries of the man only three times on the football field, while losing to him 16 times (one tie). Under Yost, Michigan outscored OSU, 414-78.

Maybe the most impressive statistical aspect of "Hurry Up's" record was the fact that of his 25 teams at Michigan, 17 combined for an unbelievable 122-9-8 record.

Fielding Harris Yost would later become a member of football's Hall of Fame.

Another coach's career changed directions in 1928. Dr. John Wilce, who had tendered his resignation six months before, stepped down as coach at Ohio State after 14 years. His record of 78-33-9 (.688) made him OSU's all-time winningest coach and Dr. Wilce's mark would stand for 33 years. He was 4-7-0 against Michigan.

109

1929

GAME 26

"BLACK SATURDAY" FOR MICHIGAN

The Buckeyes led 7-0.

In the second quarter, Michigan was fourth-and-one at the OSU four-yard line. In the third quarter, Michigan was second-and-eight at the OSU 19. Early in the fourth quarter, Michigan was first down at the OSU 11. With time running out, Michigan was fourth-and-one at the OSU six.

The Buckeyes won 7-0.

In one of the grandest exhibitions of "hold that line" in Ohio State football history, the Buckeyes held on all afternoon and sweated out a tough win over Michigan in a game that had the huge Ann Arbor crowd climbing the walls at the end.

The Buckeyes' new head coach was Sam Willaman, who had played at OSU in 1911-12-13, all years when Michigan and Ohio State were not on each other's schedule. Willaman left Columbus for his first taste of the Michigan rivalry with a team with wins over Wittenberg (19-0) and Iowa (7-6).

Michigan scheduled a doubleheader as its opener and the Wolverines copped two games in one day – 39-0 over Albion and 16-6 over Mount Union. A 17-0 victory over Michigan State followed but Purdue administered a 30-16 pounding in the first meeting with the Boilermakers since 1900.

"Nearly 90,000 saw the game," reported the *Detroit News*. "The crowd started arriving at the stadium before noon. One hour before the game the seats were more than half filled. . . .Special trains had been arriving all morning. More than 20,000 came from Ohio. Hundreds came by automobile and nearly every car that arrived in town was decorated. . . .Ohio State brought her band. It is so large that it all but requires a special train to carry it around the country. . . .It was announced in the press box that Michigan's backfield today averaged 189 pounds, the heaviest that has ever represented Michigan. . . .Half an hour before the game the field was filled with football players and the cheering sections got into action. . . .Gov. Fred W. Green attended the game as the guest of Michigan athletic director Fielding Yost, occupying a box near midfield."

Ohio State kicked off to open the 26th game of the series that October 19 and the Buckeyes kept Michigan backed deep in its own territory throughout the first quarter. On the first play of the second period, U-M's James Simrall, standing eight yards deep in his own endzone, was rushed hard and sliced a punt that put the Bucks in business at the 23-yard line. On third down from the 22, quarterback Alan Holman drilled a perfect pass caught by Wes Fesler at the five and carried quickly in for a touchdown. Fred Barratt converted. The scoring was over for the day, but the excitement had hardly begun.

Soon afterwards, Michigan's Roy Hudson intercepted a pass and returned it 27 yards to the Ohio 36. J. Truskowski completed a pass to Joe Gembis for 13 yards. Needing one yard on fourth down, Gembis got the first down by a whisker at the Buckeye 13. Three smashes into the line netted nine yards. After the fourth smash, the Wolverines were still short, and the ball went over.

Glee reined on the Scarlett's side of the stadium.

Early in the third quarter, Michigan found itself with good field position after a short Ohio punt. Starting at the OSU 26, Bill Heston ripped off 15 yards and Gembis gained two more to the nine. Heston took the ball again. He was hit hard by Samuel Selby and fumbled. Selby recovered for the Bucks at the 11.

Ohio State went on offense but it was tough going. By now, the Wolverines had shut the door. The only weapon left for the Buckeyes was their defense. They were to have more opportunities to put it to the test.

For example, early in the final period, Heston broke loose for a 40-yard dash to the OSU 27. Three plays got eight yards. On fourth down, the Buckeye line held again.

But the best for OSU fans was yet to come. With just minutes remaining to be played, Ohio punted the Wolves back to their own 33-yard line and seemingly had the game safely tucked away. The Wolverines had other ideas. Three runs were good for 17 yards and a first down at midfield. Heston gained nine to the 41. Michigan's screaming faithfuls were ready to settle for a tie in this one and were roaring their warriors goalward.

Truskowski backtracked to pass, spotted the speedy Heston and hit him for a big 26-yard pickup to Ohio's 15-yard line. Two line plunges picked up three yards to the 12. Heston hit for six more to the six. Fourth down, one to go.

Michigan broke from the huddle snarling. The grim, determined and weary defensivemen moved in tight. All of the "nearly 90,000" were on their feet and bellowing. Quarterback Simrall shouted out the signals. The two lines collided and the ball carrier sought an opening in the heap of humanity. A big pile up. "Did he make it? Did he make it? Did he make it?" It was the question of the moment. The stadium was beserk.

After the bodies on the field were untangled, the officials sized up the critical situation. No! He did *not* make it! The belligerent Buckeye defense had held once again.

Ohio State took possession with time for only one play. It was mercifully brief, and the game ended. A second straight Ohio State victory over Michigan went into the books.

The game statistics showed that the Wolverines got more first downs, 11-5, and more total offensive yards, 229-140. But the biggest numbers of the day were the seven and the zero.

Just as so many times in previous years, after Ohio State played Michigan, Buckeye football fortunes took a nosedive for the remainder of the season. They won only one more, lost three and had a tie for a final 4-3-1 record.

Was there some basis that OSU tended to "call it a year" after the Michigan game? A check of the records reveals a startling fact. In the 26 years of the Ohio State-Michigan series, the Bucks' total record going *into* the big game was 83-9-10 (.862). The record *after* the Michigan game plunged to only .593 (120-79-15). Sure, the schedule had its effects; like meeting tougher competition later in the season. But a drop from .862 to .593?

The Wolverines followed up by losing 14-0 to Illinois. Next, in a game that received a tremendous national press buildup, Harvard made its first football trip ever into the Midwest. In a thrilling contest, Michigan beat the Eastern rivals, 14-12. In four previous games against Harvard, a true powerhouse of the era, U-M had not only been winless, but also scoreless. Michigan finished the season with a victory over Minnesota and a tie with Iowa for a 5-3-1 record.

Wes Fesler, a future OSU head coach, scored the only TD in the 1929 game on a pass from Alan Holman, as the Bucks got a much-needed victory.

As for the Ohio State-Michigan series, the count was 19-5-2 and the Wolverines' scoring lead was 492-110.

Michigan's "Black Saturday" of frustration against OSU in 1929 preceded by six days a historic event whose consequences far overshadowed concern about winning and losing college football games. On Friday, October 25, panic struck the Nation and the world as the bottom dropped out of the high-flying stock market.

It was "Black Friday," a day of lost fortunes. The Great Depression that was to plague the United States in the coming decade was officially set in motion.

113

1930

GAME 27

HARRY NEWMAN......13
OHIO STATE.................0

The romantic decade of the 1920s was history. It was a decade tagged as "The Roaring Twenties" and "The Golden Age of Sports," among others. The 1930s wouldn't be so lucky.

The Michigan football team got off to a fine start in the new decade with an unbeaten season and another Big Ten championship, the team's 12th football title (won or shared) – twice as many as Illinois and Minnesota, who each owned six crowns. Ohio State had three first-place trophies and every member, except Indiana, had captured at least one championship.

For the second straight season, Michigan opened with a doubleheader sweep, this time over Denison (33-0) and Eastern Michigan (7-0). Michigan State held the Wolverines to a scoreless tie and Purdue fell 14-13. Ohio State reeled off two straight shutouts, over Mount Union and Indiana, before Northwestern became a 19-2 spoiler.

A bitter cold October 18 arrived and time for the 27th collision between the two old rivals. Michigan was to be the winner, 13-0, before 68,359 frigid fans at Columbus.

The Buckeyes never had a chance.

Just before halftime of a scoreless game, Michigan began a drive from its own 46 after taking a punt. On first down, quarterback Harry Newman faded back to pass, had what seemed like an eternity, and heaved a long one down the right sideline. Teammate James Simrall grabbed the pass at about the OSU 20 and broke away from a red-shirted defender. Simrall was forced to reverse his field, got hemmed-up, and reversed his direction again. He was now being chased by Lewis Hinchman and Robert Horn. Hinchman caught Simrall at the five, and rode him down – but not until the two had reached the Buckeye one-yard line. On the next play, Newman took a direct snap, hesitated for a moment

114

Movie Stars in Caricature!
Look for the "LAUGHING GALLERY"
Starting in Next Sunday's News

The Detroit News

THE HOME NEWSPAPER

PART 4

SPORTS NEWS
REAL ESTATE
FINANCIAL

SUNDAY, OCTOBER 19, 1930

FOR BEST RESULTS—NEWS WANT ADS

Michigan Conquers O. S. U., 13-0—Michigan State Beats Colgate, 14-7

Notre Dame . . 21	Army 6	Northwestern . . 32	Yale 21	Wisconsin . . . 27	Cornell 12
Carnegie Tech . . 6	Harvard 0	Illinois 0	Brown 0	Pennsylvania . . 0	Princeton . . . 7

Glenna Collett Wins Third Straight Women's National Crown, 6 and 5

Ohio State's Horseshoe Stadium From The Detroit News Airplan and Action Pictures of Game Rushed From Columbus to Detroit

60-YARD RUN STIRS 12,000

HARRY NEWMAN REPEATS STUFF

while the two lines crunched together, and with a good running start, leaped up and over for a touchdown. Newman also added the conversion, and with only one minute left on the first-half clock, favored Michigan had a hard-earned 7-0 lead.

The Wolverines kicked off to start the third quarter, immediately forced a punt which was fumbled, and recovered at the OSU 45. On third down from the 40, Hinchman passed complete to Clare Wheeler for 21 yards to the Ohio 19. Two running plays got five. From the 14-yard line, Newman shot untouched through the middle of the Ohio line, and rambled in for his second touchdown of the game. His conversion attempt was blocked.

Michigan 13, Ohio State 0.

In this game, final statistics were deceiving. Even though the Buckeyes never seriously threatened, they outgained Michigan in total yards, 272-224, and recorded more first downs, 13-6. But the score went in Michigan's favor for the 20th time in the series. Ohio State had five victories and two games had been ties.

After a scoreless duel with Wisconsin, OSU defeated Navy, Pittsburgh and Illinois to wrap up a 5-2-1 season. Michigan topped Illinois, Harvard, Minnesota and Chicago for an 8-0-1 finish – the team's 16th undefeated season – and a share of the Conference championship with Northwestern.

115

1931

GAME 28

UPSET SPECIAL

Michigan opened the season with a doubleheader triumph over Central Michigan (27-0) and Eastern Michigan (34-0) in the third and last of the opening day twin bills at Ann Arbor. It had never been a box office success, as crowds averaged only 14,100 in the three years.

After a 13-7 win over Chicago, U-M had a 15-game unbeaten streak working as Ohio State loomed on the horizon. The Buckeyes were 1-1-0 following a 67-6 smashing of Cincinnati and a 26-21 loss to Vanderbilt.

In a tremendous upset, OSU took advantage of a few breaks and socked the Wolverines 20-7 before 58,026 at Ann Arbor on October 17. Only fifty-eight thousand at an Ohio State-Michigan game? Considering the economic circumstances of the day, that kind of turnout was a mighty tribute to the appeal of the rivalry.

John Heston received OSU's opening kickoff, fumbled, and Martin Varner recovered for the Scarlets at the 24. The Wolverines held. Later in the period, Heston fumbled again and this one led to trouble. Ohio recovered on the Michigan 30 and went to work. William Carroll went to the 25; Lewis Hinchman to the 19; Mike Vuchinich to the 17, and Hinchman to the 10. Carroll skirted left end for a touchdown. Robert Haubrich converted and Ohio made its 7-0 lead look easy.

"Michigan did not appear entirely to have snapped out of the listlessness that characterized its performance against Chicago," observed Tod Rockwell of the *Detroit Free Press*.

116

William Carroll, a hometown boy from Columbus, scores his first of two touchdowns in Buckeyes' 20-7 upset of Michigan in 1931. (Courtesy of OSU Photo Archives)

The Buckeyes reciprocated Michigan's generosity and late in the period lost the ball on a fumble at their own 17. It was to lead to the Wolverines tying the game. U-M got down to the Buckeye five, but couldn't punch it over. OSU punted out to the 41. Stalled, Michigan punted back down to the one. Ohio chose to kick it out on first down. Michigan's right end, Ivan Williamson, stormed through and blocked the kick by Carl Cramer. Williamson also recovered the ball – Michigan touchdown. DuVal Goldsmith's kick knotted the count at 7-7.

Williamson's great effort made the sixth time in series history that a punt had been blocked and recovered for a touchdown. Michigan turned the trick in 1905, 1911 and 1918; Ohio State in 1919 and 1920.

Just before halftime, a march by the Wolverines penetrated to the OSU 16-yard line but another fumble killed the threat.

The Bucks took the second-half kickoff and promptly scored the decisive points. Helped along by more sloppy Michigan play,

BUCKS UPSET TRADITIONAL FOE

including four penalties, OSU reached the enemy 45. Carroll went to the 39; Cramer to the 34; Cramer to the 27, and Cramer to the 24. Cramer then switched to the passing game and completed a 10-yarder to Sidney Gillman to the 14. Hinchman carried to the seven and then got a first down at the two. It took three plays, but Carroll crashed over for the score to propel OSU into a 13-7 advantage. Haubrich missed the conversion.

Late in the game the Buckeyes were assured of their upset victory when Cramer returned a punt 45 yards for a touchdown. Louis Peppe, the third player to handle the point-after responsibility, kicked good and Ohio had a big 13-point cushion with just over five minutes left in the game.

Michigan took the ensuing kickoff and, sparked by three Newman pass completions of 30, 21 and 15 yards, reached Ohio's four-yard line. Four plays later they were still at the four. It was all over. After such a lackluster performance, Michigan's hopes for a second straight Big Ten championship looked dismal.

The Buckeyes were flying high. But not for long. A week later, Northwestern brought them back to reality, 10-0. Four straight shutout wins over Indiana, Navy, Wisconsin and Illinois followed before a season-ending setback to Minnesota. The 6-3-0 record, however, included wins over Michigan and Illinois, marking the first season ever that the Buckeyes beat both of its biggest rivals.

Michigan regrouped. The Wolverines rebounded from the OSU loss and blanked Illinois, Princeton, Indiana and Minnesota by an aggregate 84-0 score. In between, U-M also shutout Michigan State but had to settle for a second straight scoreless tie with the Spartans.

That brought the season to November 28 and the final Saturday. Northwestern was 5-0-0 in the Conference and had to play Purdue (4-1-0). Michigan (4-1-0) met Wisconsin (3-2-0). The Wolverines zeroed the Badgers 16-0 and the Boilermakers bounced the Wildcats 7-0. That threw the 1931 Big Ten title race into a final three-way tie. Michigan, Northwestern and Purdue all ended with 5-1-0 records.

After losing to the Buckeyes, Michigan did not allow its remaining six opponents a single point.

1932

GAME 29

"BROTHER, CAN YOU SPARE A DIME?"

In the five previous Michigan-Ohio State games, the average attendance was 74,200. The 1932 match in Columbus attracted a paltry 19,500. Actually, the game "attracted" many thousands more, but that's the number that showed up for the game – or had the money to pay for a ticket to show up for the game.

"Hey, George, are you going to the game Saturday?"

"Are you crazy, Ralph? Hell, no, I'm not going to the game. I've got to see if I can find some work. Are you going?"

"Yeah!"

"Really? Where'd you get the money?"

"I got a job sweeping the stadium after the game. They said we could watch the last half from the endzone."

"Can you get me on? You know, I'm an alumnus and I haven't missed a home game since 1926, until this year."

"I doubt if I can be of any help, but I'll try."

"Try. I need the money, plus I want to see that game."

A similar conversation could have taken place any where in the country. It was 1932 and America was in the depths of the Great Depression.

Michigan's 300th all-time football victory had come in the 1932 season opener, 26-0 over Michigan State. Another win was registered a week later against Northwestern, 15-6. Ohio State was next in line and the Wolverines were hoping for No. 302. The Buckeyes were waiting for Michigan's trip with a 1-0-1 record, having disposed of Ohio Wesleyan, 34-7, and battled Indiana to a 7-7 draw.

119

MICHIGAN ALL-AMERICAN QB HARRY NEWMAN

Against the Buckeyes in 1930 at Columbus, he scored all of his team's points in a 13-0 victory. Returning to Columbus in 1932, he accounted for all of his team's points in a 14-0 win by throwing two touchdown passes and kicking both conversions. (Photo courtesy of Michigan Athletic Department)

A Buckeye (white jersey) trying to snag a pass or make a great interception in the 1932 game at Columbus. The photographer might have positioned this angle to include the "full" part of the stadium crowd, as the attendance was less than 20,00 that day.

OSU ran all over Michigan and outgained them in total yards, 206-132. But the Wolverines got what they went to Columbus to get – No. 302. The score was 14-0.

The only touchdown Michigan needed came in the first three minutes of the game. After the first series, U-M punted Ohio into trouble back at the five-yard line. A hurried kick from his own endzone by Carl Cramer went out of bounds at the Buckeye 28.

The Wolves hopped on the opportunity, mixing good running and passing to reach the 10-yard line. Harry Newman then tossed a short pass to John Regeczi and it was a quick touchdown. Newman's conversion made it 7-0.

In the second quarter, William Carroll tried to run from punt formation on fourth-and-two at midfield. Nobody on the Michigan side was fooled and Carroll was nailed for no gain. U-M wasted no time. After a couple of plays, Newman threw a long aerial to Ivan Williamson who gathered in the ball at the seven-yard line and raced in for the 46-yard TD play. Newman's kick was good and Michigan had a 14-0 lead.

"Until the second Michigan touchdown the Buckeyes acted as though Newman and his friends were some uncanny kind of a combination that couldn't be stopped. They appeared to be a much befuddled ball team. But following Williamson's brilliant catch, the Buckeyes came to life and smeared the Michigan team from one end of the field to the other – but couldn't score," reported Tod Rockwell of the *Detroit Free Press*.

To illustrate Rockwell's point, Ohio State moved inside Michigan's 10-yard line a total of five times, and came away with an empty bag on each occasion.

And while Michigan was recording No. 302, Ohio State was absorbing No. 21 – the 21st defeat at the hands of the Wolverines in this the 29th renewal of the series. U-M had now outscored Ohio in the autumn wars, 526-130.

Michigan Coach Harry Kipke and his team finished out the season by beating Illinois, Princeton, Indiana, Chicago and Minnesota by a total score of 68-7. It all added up to an 8-0-0 performance and Michigan joined Southern California and Colgate in major college ranks as the only teams to finish with perfect records. It was also good enough for a third straight Big Ten championship.

Ohio State was to suffer no further losses, either. There were back-to-back ties with Pittsburgh and Wisconsin, and victories over Northwestern, Pennsylvania and Illinois for a final 4-1-3 record.

1933

NATIONAL CHAMPIONS

It was not until 1936 that the *Associated Press* began its system of national team rankings. There were, however, other ratings that were considered "official." The one that probably carried the most prestige was the "Dickinson System," originated by Dr. Frank Dickinson, a professor at the University of Illinois.

Obviously, because Ohio State and Michigan played early in the season it couldn't be predicted that their game would determine the Big Ten championship. Nor for that matter, the national championship. But in 1933, that's the way it was.

OSU started the season by giving rude treatment to two visiting Southern teams. The Bucks bombed Virginia 75-0 and took Vanderbilt 20-0. U-M defeated Michigan State 20-6, Cornell 40-0 and the Wolverines had not lost a game since the Buckeyes beat them three years ago.

October 21 rolled around and once again it was time for the two Midwest rivals to settle their differences. On paper, there didn't seem to be much difference, but on the field, where the games are played, there proved to be a vast difference, at least on this particular day.

Michigan won 13-0 in the school's 400th football game. The contest was played in Michigan's mammoth bowl before a mammoth crowd. The newspapers reported an attendance of 93,506, but it was later confirmed by U-M athletic officials that the actual paid admissions totaled "only" 84,403.

The powerful Maize and Blue gained 205 total yards; Ohio only 70. The Buckeyes were never in the game, and never got within striking distance of the enemy goal line.

"As the game progressed the Michigan thrusts became more severe and Ohio wilted," reported Tod Rockwell of the *Detroit Free Press*. "The Wolverines dented the Buckeyes' fighting line in the first period, cracked it wide open for a touchdown in the second, bent it badly in the third period and swept through for the second touchdown in the final two minutes of the game."

The first touchdown came after Michigan received a punt at the 50-yard line. A John Regeczi to John Heston pass netted nine. Regeczi, Heston and Herman Everhardus then took turns running with the ball and advanced it down to the 15-yard line. After Everhardus gained three, Authur Renner pitched one to Heston that resulted in a seven-yard gain to the five. On second down from the three, Renner faked a lateral to Heston, kept the ball and darted in for the score. Mike Savage's conversion try was no good and the Wolverines led, 6-0.

With Ohio desperately trying to pass its way up field deep into the fourth quarter, Charles Bernard intercepted a Carl Cramer pass at the Bucks' 24. Staying on the ground, Michigan muscled out its final score. Renner powered to the 19; Russell Oliver to the 13; Heston to the eight; Fred Petoskey to the two; Everhardus to the one, and Everhardus for the touchdown. Savage made good this kick for the final 13-0 score.

Would Michigan's victory voodooism over Ohio State ever vanish? The series spread now reached 22-6-2 and the Maize and Blue's scoring bulge was 539-130 for a game average of approximately 18-4.

Another *Free Press* reporter, M. F. Drukenbrod, was at the game and a few of his colorful first-person comments are worth recalling. For example: "College spirit ran rampant. I saw a sample of it in the stands. Two old grads trying to get a nip at the same time out of the same bottle. . . .Michigan's squad is racing across the field. What a gang. And here comes Ohio. Zowie, what bulk!. . . The rival captains meet near midfield and shake hands. They chat for a few seconds, maybe about a date tonight with a couple of nifties. . . .What a run. I tell you these college boys can go. . . .They play for fun, like fun they do, in these Ohio-Michigan games. Such bumping. . . .An Ohioan still may get away for a touchdown, but we doubt it. You can't bend a stone wall. . . .Dusk is gathering over the playing field. No story of a football game is complete without mention of the dusk or lengthening shadows."

The Buckeyes bounced back from the Michigan disaster and

SPORTS | FINANCIAL

The Detroit Free Press

103rd Year. No. 171 | Sunday, October 22, 1933 | Free Press Want Ads Bring Best Results

Michigan Decisively Outplays Ohio State and Wins, 13-0

Gophers Down Pitt, 7-3 — Skibos Beat Notre Dame, 7-0 — Army Downs Illini, 6-0

Here's the Mighty Host of 93,508 at Ann Arbor, the Largest Crowd That Ever Saw a Western Conference Game

Depression or not, Ohio State meant box office appeal at Ann Arbor. Michigan's 16-game unbeaten streak may have had something to do with it, but for the other four UM home games that season, attendance averaged less than 31,000. Note that the Skibos beat Notre Dame, 7-0. Who were the Skibos? Carnegie Tech. What is a Skibo? It's the name of a castle in Scotland owned by the school's founder, Andrew Carnegie.

defeated Indiana, Pennsylvania, Wisconsin and Illinois. The Wolverines continued onward, besting Chicago and Iowa, playing a scoreless tie with Minnesota and taking Northwestern.

Under prevailing rules, a tie did not count in Conference standings. This gave Minnesota, with an odd 2-0-4 league record (4-0-4 overall), a share of the Big Ten championship with Michigan and its 5-0-1 record. Ohio State, at 4-1-0, took third place.

Dr. Dickinson's system said that Michigan had the best team in the Nation in 1933. And who could argue with the man or the system. The Wolverines were riding a 22-game unbeaten streak and in the last four years had racked up a 31-1-3 record – its lone loss being to Ohio State. The five closest contenders for the '33 national title were Princeton, Pittsburgh, the Buckeyes, Army and Southern Cal.

A name associated with the 1933 Michigan-Ohio State game deserves special mention. John Heston, a Michigan senior, was the third of his family to play against the Buckeyes. His father, Bill Heston, was an All-American and scored five touchdowns against OSU over four seasons, 1901-04. Bill Heston, Jr. played in the 1929-30 series games, and John participated in the 1931-32-33 games. In the nine games in which the Hestons played against Ohio State, their Michigan teams won seven and lost two.

1934

GAME 31

EUPHORIA-PLUS

An event Ohio State University boosters all over the nation — and world — had long awaited finally unfolded. It was a 37-year wait. Thirty-seven long years. But finally OSU was able to do a big number over the arch rival Michigan Wolverines on the football field.

Final score: Ohio State 34, Michigan 0.

The big day was Saturday, November 18, 1934, and the happy Homecoming crowd of 68,678 rocked long and loud.

One more time....Ohio State 34, Michigan 0.

The smashing defeat of the hated Wolverines was complete, as revealed by these statistics: OSU led in first downs 24-3 and in total yards 460-40. Including kickoff and punt returns, the Buckeyes raced up and down the gridiron for 638 yards, UM only 86.

In addition, the big numbers were piled up against the defending national champions. But at game time, Michigan's status and stature of a year ago was meaningless. Gone from last year's powerhouse were 19 lettermen and Coach Harry Kipke's '34 squad of 46 players was loaded with 26 sophomores.

The Wolverines' fall from the ranks of the mighty was witnessed from the outset of the season with its first loss (16-0) to Michigan State since 1915. Chicago then got in more licks with a 27-0 drubbing. UM recovered to top Georgia Tech 9-2, but that was it. "Mighty Michigan" did not win another game all fall. Illinois, Minnesota and Wisconsin blasted the Blue by a combined score of 51-6. The Buckeyes were next in line and they anxiously awaited their turn with big steel-tipped belts ready to rap.

The entire Big Ten, in fact, was relishing Michigan's sudden and complete collapse. Here was a team that had taken four straight conference championships and 15 titles overall. Nobody else was even close. In their years as part of the Big Ten family, the boys from Ann Arbor had compiled a 94-24-6 (.782) record in the league.

Nobody likes a bully. And the conference felt UM had been a bully much too long.

While Michigan was experiencing its problems, the Buckeyes had lost only to Illinois (14-13) and had beaten Indiana, Colgate, Northwestern, Western Reserve and Chicago by a weighty average score of 38-3.

GERALD R. FORD

The future President of the United States was voted the Most Valuable Player on Michigan's 1934 team and played in the East-West Shrine game in San Francisco. In 1933, injuries drastically limited his playing time. (Photo courtesy of Michigan Athletic Department.)

OHIO STATE ROUTS MICHIGAN BY 34-0

68,000 See Buckeyes Score Their Most Decisive Victory Over Rivals.

LOSERS ARE BEWILDERED

Completely Crushed by Dazzling Attack That Yields Red and Gray 638 Yards.

That famed Michigan jinx, nemesis of Ohio State grid teams since the turn of the century, was buried far beneath the cleat-torn sod of the Buckeye gridiron Saturday as the Wolverines, baffled by Coach Francis Schmidt's intricate offense, went down to a 34-to-0 defeat, the most humiliating ever handed an Ann Arbor eleven by the Scarlet and Gray. — The New York Times.

In the thrashing of UM, Ohio had a 13-0 halftime lead resulting from short plunges by Dick Heekin and Damon Wetzel in the first and second quarters.

But the underdog Wolverines hung on and, going into the final period, still trailed by just 13, before the home team pushed across three more touchdowns.

Frank Antenucci recovered teammate Jack Smith's fumble that bounded into the endzone. Next came a 60-yard TD pass play from Frank Fisch to Merle Wendt, then a Tippy Dye-to-Frank Cumiskey scoring pass of 20 yards. Regis Monahan kicked three conversions and Sam Busich one.

As the game ended, down went the goal posts at each end of the stadium.

The Bucks went on to blast Iowa 40-7 and posted a 7-1-0 season mark. And since it included an honest-to-goodness trouncing of Michigan, it was the kind of season OSU alumni and fans could relish and cherish — for at least one year.

Michigan lost again, 13-6 to Northwestern, to conclude its most disastrous season ever: one win, seven losses and a mere three touchdowns scored.

National champions one year, 1-7-0 the next year.

Minnesota replaced the Wolverines as the Big Ten kingpin. OSU was second, followed by Illinois and Purdue. UM was 10th.

Playing center for Michigan in that 1934 game against Ohio State was a senior named Gerald R. Ford, who won two "M" football letters.

He would later become President of the United States.

127

1935

GAME 32

OSU EYED ND, NOT UM

Pre-season reports pegged Ohio State as one of the top teams in the Nation and in Ohioland there were serious expectations that the Buckeyes would bring home a national championship.

The Bucks broke from the gate with a 19-6 win over Kentucky and followed that up with an 85-7 slaughter of Drake. Then came two Conference triumphs, 28-7 over Northwestern and 28-6 over Indiana. That brought the season to November 2 and unbeaten Notre Dame went to Columbus amid thunderous fanfare. It was the first-ever meeting between the two teams and the big game fired the imagination of the whole Nation. The press was there from everywhere. The Irish were 5-0-0; the Buckeyes 4-0-0.

The game matched the buildup.

OSU led 13-0 in the fourth quarter. Notre Dame scored two touchdowns (the latter with just over two minutes left to play) but missed both conversions and still trailed 13-12. Ohio recovered an on-sides kick but fumbled from punt formation at midfield. With 32 seconds remaining, the Irish completed a desperation pass for a touchdown and an 18-13 victory.

The whole State of Ohio was in a state of shock.

Meanwhile, Michigan had lost its opener to Michigan State but then reeled off consecutive wins over Indiana, Wisconsin, Columbia and Pennsylvania. OSU won its next two over Chicago and Illinois; U-M lost its next two to Illinois and Minnesota. The Gophers' victory was by a score of 40-0 and remains the second worst defeat in Michigan's proud football history.

The tradition of Ohio State and Michigan meeting as the final game of the season had its beginning in 1935. The Bucks were 6-1-0; the Wolves 4-3-0.

During game-week, Ohio developed an obsession to beat Michigan by a wider margin than Minnesota had managed. That meant, of course, a spread of more than 40 points. The Buckeyes scored enough touchdowns to accomplish their mission, but missed four conversions and had to "settle" for a 38-0 triumph. The game was played on an extremely cold afternoon at Ann Arbor before 53,322 who braved the miserable weather conditions.

The Bucks hopped on their underdog opponents with two first-quarter touchdowns and in general had an easy and thoroughly enjoyable afternoon on their hosts' own playground.

With eight minutes left in period one, Ohio scored when Richard Heekin rammed over from a yard out. Sam Busich's conversion was good and it was 7-0. However, Busich would have his kicking problems for the rest of the game.

On the ensuing kickoff, Michigan couldn't get anywhere and punted. Fielding the kick was William (Tippy) Dye at his own 35-yard line and Dye streaked 65 yards for a touchdown. "A half dozen Michigan men had a shot at him but it was like hitting a shadow. Tippy just shook them off by sheer speed," wrote Tod Rockwell of the *Detroit Free Press*. Dye's jaunt became the first punt returned for a touchdown in the series. Busich missed the conversion and OSU now led 13-0.

A few minutes before intermission, Matt Patenelli tossed an eight-yard touchdown pass to John Bettridge to cap a quick 66-yard drive that had started with the recovery of a Wolverine fumble. Busich missed again and the score was 19-0.

The only third period score came on Authur Boucher's two-yard plunge. After Busich missed still another conversion, and with the score 25-0, the Buckeye rooters realized that it would take three touchdowns in the final period to get their more-than-40-point victory.

Early in the final period, the Bucks put on a razzle-dazzle show for another touchdown. First, Nick Wasylik completed a short pass to Busich. Busich got hemmed up and lateraled to James McDonald. McDonald got hemmed up and lateraled to Wasylik, who had followed the play closely after initiating it. Wasylik scored to complete the fancy play that took a lot of time but covered only 23 yards. It was, in effect, a triple flea-flicker, but there was no report that it was a planned play. Again, Busich missed the PAT. Score: 31-0.

129

PART TWO
SPORTS   AUTOS
MARKETS

Chicago Sunday Tribune
THE WORLD'S GREATEST NEWSPAPER

NOVEMBER 24, 1935.

9 PARTS

A ★

OHIO, MINNESOTA WIN; BIG TEN CHAMPIONS

Heekin later scored his second touchdown of the game and Busich got back into the kicking groove, but too late. The Buckeyes had their second straight shutout over Michigan, and the second straight by a wide margin.

When the whistle blew an end to the game, post-game activity on the field got underway and a big portion of the crowd stayed around to watch, despite the bad weather.

Rockwell described it: "But the Buckeye-Wolverine battle wasn't over. Buck fans rushed onto the gridiron to uproot the north goal posts. A merry battle of first class fisticuffs between some hundreds of Bucks and Wolverines took place. Right well did the boys swing despite heavy overcoats. The Bucks, cagy these last few years, worked up a gang at the south end of the field and in a twinkling had uprooted the posts there. It was great fun for an hour after the game and served to entertain many unwilling to join the traffic rush immediately adjacent to the stadium."

As for the game statistics, OSU was way out front in first downs 20-5; in yards rushing 295-12; in yards passing 152-73, and in total yards 447-85. As the figures show, the game was not really as close as the 38-0 score. There was no report on the outcome of the "first class fisticuffs."

Ohio State and Minnesota shared the Big Ten title with matching 5-0-0 records, but the Gophers, riding a 24-game unbeaten streak, were declared national champions. The Bucks' loss to Notre Dame had definitely cost them the chance to chant "We're No. 1." For the third year in a row, OSU finished with a 7-1-0 record. Michigan, after getting off to a 4-1-0 start, lost its last three games by a total score of 0-81 and a final 4-4-0 record for the year.

Rounding out the nation's top five teams in 1935 were SMU, TCU, Princeton and OSU. Notre Dame lost 14-7 to Northwestern the week after its clash with Ohio State, was later tied by Army and dropped from contention for national honors.

Even though Ohioans didn't get their hoped-for national championship, there was a consolation prize that they were glad to have – 38-0.

Michigan's series lead was now, 22-8-2.

1936

GAME 33

3 STRAIGHT!

Michigan picked up in 1936 where it had left off in 1935 – losing. First Michigan State, then Indiana and then Minnesota beat up on the battered Wolverines to push the losing streak to six games. The humiliating ordeal ended with a 13-0 win over Columbia but resumed immediately as Illinois, Pennsylvania and Northwestern got in their punches. OSU was next. Coach Harry Kipke and his boys were 1-6-0 and had scored only 36 points.

The Buckeyes opened up in 1936 with a 60-0 blitz of New York University. Then they dropped a pair – 6-0 to Pittsburgh and 14-13 to Northwestern, before edging Indiana 7-0. Then came a big date with Notre Dame at South Bend. Before the biggest crowd (50,017) to attend a game at ND at that time, the Irish held OSU on the 12-yard line in the closing minutes of the rain-soaked game to salvage a 7-2 victory. There has not been an Ohio State-Notre Dame game since. The Bucks rebounded to defeat Chicago and Illinois and prepared for Michigan with a record of 4-3-0.

For the third straight year, "The Big One" went to Ohio State. A Homecoming crowd of 56,202 watched and cheered a 21-0 victory at Columbus. The last quarter was played in a downpour but it was reported that very few of the happy Buckeyes left the stadium early.

Michigan started the game as though it meant business and the horrors of a possible upset gripped the large turnout of OSU fans. Taking the opening kickoff, the Wolverines muscled through the tough Ohio defense that, despite three losses, had yielded only four touchdowns all season. U-M moved all the way to OSU's three-

Buckeye Tippy Dye (50) has already released this 14-yard TD pass to a wide-open Frank Cumiskey for a 6-0 lead in the 1936 game at Columbus. (Photo courtesy of OSU Photo Archives)

The Columbus Sunday Dispatch

CENTRAL OHIO'S ONLY SUNDAY NEWSPAPER

CLASSIFIED ADS—

SUNDAY, NOVEMBER 22, 1936.

C—1

BUCKS BEAT MICHIGAN, 21 TO 0, IN FINAL

Third In Row Is Registered Second Time

Notre Dame Breaks Northwestern's Clean Slate

DYE TO BOOTH PASS SETS OFF BRILLIANT AERIAL ATTACK FOR BUCKEYES

Irish Display Faultless Style Against Purple

yard line but couldn't push the ball over. Hopes of pulling off a big surprise vanished, and Ohio fans breathed easier.

Early in the second quarter, the OSU offense got cranked up and mainly on the passing of Tippy Dye, drove 76 yards for a touchdown – the final 14 coming on a completion to Frank Cumiskey. Michigan blocked the first of all three Ohio conversion attempts. During the course of the game, Michigan would also block two field goal tries. Also during the course of the game, Dye would complete 11 passes in 18 attempts for 143 yards.

The underdog Wolves "hung in there" and held the score to the one touchdown difference until midway of the third quarter. Ohio started a drive from its own 31. From the U-M 31, John Rabb took a shovel pass from Dye at the line of scrimmage, reversed his field and scooted for a touchdown and a 12-0 advantage. Later in the same period, Dye got off a 47-yard punt return, all the way down to Michigan's three. The Wolverine defense became stubborn here and Bill Booth booted a field goal to increase his team's lead to 15-0.

In the final quarter, a short Michigan punt gave OSU the ball at the Wolverine 34. The running of Booth and Frank Antenucci led a swift drive to the 10, and Nick Wasylik scored the game's final touchdown on a sweep around left end.

Ohio led in first downs 18-5, and total yards 341-117, to make their shutout victory complete. Michigan had suffered through its second 1-7-0 season in the past three years. The Buckeyes' odd season ended with five wins, all by shutouts, and three losses, even though the team surrendered only 27 points.

With three straight series victories, Ohio State's deficit had been reduced to 22-9-2. In the point parade, Michigan had 539, OSU 223.

1937

GAME 34

SAME WINNER,
SAME SCORE

After the 1937 game was entered into the record book, the series scoreboard for the past four years showed: Ohio State 114, Michigan 0. Furthermore, the Buckeyes had outgained their hapless rivals 1533 yards to only 283, and led in first downs, 71-17 in the four lopsided games.

In freezing temperatures at Ann Arbor before 65,000 heavily-bundled fans, OSU won again, 21-0, as Michigan reached Buckeye territory only once and was held to three yards rushing and 41 passing. Last year's game (also a 21-0 score) ended in a hard rain; this one in a heavy snowfall.

Going in, the Bucks were 5-2-0, having beaten TCU, Purdue, Northwestern, Chicago and Illinois. The TCU game was OSU's 400th. The losses were to Southern California (13-12) and Indiana (10-0).

Michigan opened up by losing three straight – to Michigan State, Northwestern and Minnesota. Adding these setbacks to the four in a row at the end of the 1936 season added up to seven straight. Never before, and never since, has a Michigan football team experienced such a streak. It ended as Coach Harry Kipke and his troops got their act together and reeled off four wins in a row, beating Iowa, Illinois, Chicago and Pennsylvania, for a 4-3-0 record.

The game's first score, a safety, came on the first play of the second quarter. A great Michigan goal line stand had held the Bucks at bay on the three-yard line. On first down, Norm Purueker attempted to run from punt formation but OSU's Charles Ream wasn't fooled and slammed Purueker to the ground behind the goal. Ohio 2, Michigan 0.

Just before halftime, the visitors made it 9-0. James Miller intercepted a Stark Ritchie pass and returned it 29 yards before lateraling to Nick Wasylik who got seven more yards out of the play to put the ball on the Wolverine 33. Miller immediately teamed-up with Nick Nordi for a pass completion to the four-yard line. Three plays later, Miller ripped into and through the right side of the line for a touchdown. Jim McDonald converted with 30 seconds left before intermission.

Late in the third quarter, another pass interception led to another quick Buckeye score. Wasylik picked this one off and returned it six yards to the U-M 44. On first down, Wasylik hit Miller with a pass at the 15 and Miller made the rest on his own. The conversion was no good but Ohio was comfortably on top 15-0.

In the final period, U-M got off a poor punt – four yards poor – that sliced out of bounds at its 29. Wasylik and his passing arm were at it again. He was on target to Nardi for a 13-yard gain. Four plays later from the four, Wasylik was on the money once more to Nardi for a touchdown. The PAT try was again missed. In the last 10 attempts at conversions against Michigan, OSU kickers had been successful only three times.

Final score: 21-0.

As Harry Kipke walked off the frozen turf that November 20, it would be his last game as head coach at Michigan. Kipke had held the position for nine years and left behind a 46-26-4 (.632) record. He won a national championship in 1932 and four Big Ten crowns. However, in the last four years, Kipke's teams had fallen on hard times as indicated by a 10-22-0 record. During one 14-game stretch, beginning in 1935 and extending into 1937, the Wolverines won only one game.

The series now stood 22-10-2, Michigan; points scored, 539-244, Michigan. The Wolverines had absorbed four defeats in a row by OSU. Despite the gloom, there was reason to hope for better days. A new coach was in the immediate future, and there was the promise of help from a reported "phenom" on the freshman squad.

1938

GAME 35

A FAMINE ENDS,
A FAMINE BEGINS

Michigan's new head coach was Herbert Orrin Crisler. Nobody called him "Herb" or "Orr" or "H.O." He was known as "Fritz" – Fritz Crisler.

It was also the first year of varsity play for Thomas Dudley Harmon. Harmon would later become a two-time All-American and a Heisman Trophy winner. He would make the cover of *Life* magazine and would become one of college football's all-time popular "Saturday Heros."

Another first in 1938 was the now-famous Maize and Blue "winged helmet" that Michigan football teams still wear. Crisler brought the design with him from Princeton.

And still another first: the first time in five years for Michigan to defeat Ohio State. The result, by an 18-0 score, was the most welcome of all the firsts.

"Today's triumph was so welcome to those fans who have followed Michigan closely in the last five years that many of the exuberant ones in attendance tore up a Buckeye goal post in a wild melee after the game," wrote Tod Rockwell of the *Detroit Free Press*.

Crisler had played his football at the University of Chicago under Amos Alonzo Stagg in 1917 and 1919. He was in the armed forces in 1918. At Chicago he won nine letters in football, baseball and basketball. He attended medical school at Chicago in 1920-21 before joining Stagg as an assistant coach in 1922, where he remained until 1929. Crisler began his career as a head coach the following year at Minnesota. After two seasons with the Golden

Gophers (1930-31) he moved to Princeton for six seasons, 1932-37. It was then on to Ann Arbor.

His first game at Michigan resulted in the Wolverines' first win (14-0) over intrastate rival Michigan State in five years. After a 45-7 runaway over Chicago came his first and only defeat of the season, 7-6 to Minnesota. In the fourth game, Yale led 13-2 at the half but U-M rallied for a 15-13 triumph. Then came victories over Illinois 14-0, and Pennsylvania 19-13, before a scoreless duel with Northwestern. Crisler was 5-1-1 with Ohio State in front of him.

Coach Francis Schmidt, in his fifth year at OSU, had experienced a seesaw season. There was an opening win over Indiana, a loss to Southern California for the second straight year, a scoreless tie with Northwestern, wins over Chicago and New York University, a loss to Purdue, and a victory over Illinois. It all added up to a 4-2-1 record and Michigan was next.

On paper, the teams were virtually even. Michigan had outscored its opponents by 73 points (113-40); the Buckeyes topped their foes by 72 points (119-47).

They met at Columbus on November 19 before 67,534 screaming fans. More than 10,000 were Michigan rooters who had made their way into Buckeye Country – eager for revenge.

Harmon was just what Michigan had hoped he would be – too much for Ohio State.

Early in the game, OSU drove to first down at the U-M 20 but could get no further. Later in the quarter, the Wolverines got a break and cashed it in. It was a bad pitch on a lateral and Michigan's Wally Hook pounced on it at the OSU 17. A gain of seven yards by Paul Kromer and a pickup of four more in two carries by Hook got a first down at the six. Harmon got one, Kromer four, and Harmon the final yard for a touchdown – Michigan's first against Ohio State since 1933. U-M was to miss all three of its conversion tries this day, and the score was 6-0.

The two teams sparred back and forth for the next two periods and the Wolverines gamely held on to their slim six-point lead. A highlight of the third quarter was a 78-yard punt by OSU's Mike Kabealo. The kick traveled from his own two, where he was standing, all the way to Michigan's 20.

On the last play of the third period, Harmon intercepted a pass thrown by James Sexton to set up Michigan's second touchdown. Harmon returned the pass 12 yards to Ohio's 41-yard line. Then Harmon passed 23 yards to Edward Frutig. Howard

U. of M. Ends Famine Against O.S.U. With 18-0 Victory

OOPPPS! A fumble at Ohio Stadium in 1938. Identifiable players include John Nicholson (67), Francis Smith (18), Jack Myer (77), James Langhurst (8), John Brennan (65), John Seigle (62), Edward Phillips (21), Paul Kromer (83) and Ralph Heikkinen (36). This was the first year that Michigan wore its now-famous "winged helmets." (Photo courtesy of Michigan Athletic Department)

Mehaffey ripped through for 13 more yards and suddenly the Buckeyes found themselves backed to their own five-yard line. Harmon's touchdown burst was cancelled by a five-yard offsides penalty and the ball moved back to the 10. Harmon threw incomplete. Kromer recovered his own fumble at the 15. On third-and-goal, Harmon hit an all-alone Frutig with a strike in the endzone for a 12-0 lead.

As the game wound down and the Buckeyes became more desperate, Louis Levine made Michigan's third interception of the day at the Ohio 44. Two plays later and it was 18-0. Norm Purucker hit for seven yards and Fred Trosko broke loose for the final 37 and the TD.

The winners led in first downs 10-9, total yards 269-109, and penalty yards 45-5. Of the last 13 touchdowns scored in the series, only three had been successfully converted.

After the 1938 game, Michigan's series lead was 23-10-2. The point spread, after several years of shrinkage, stretched to 557-244.

1939

GAME 36

A HOLLOW TITLE

There were 50 seconds left in the game and the score was tied, 14-14. Michigan was on Ohio State's 24-yard line. It was fourth down and goal-to-go as the determined Bucks had pushed them back from their six. Fred Trosko knelt at the 32-yard line and Tom Harmon was set to try a game-winning field goal. Center Archie Kodros sent back a perfect snap. Trosko placed the ball down. Harmon approached and swung through his right foot. He missed the ball. Completely. But that was the plan. Trosko was sprinting to the left. And Trosko had the football. The Buckeyes had been badly faked. Trosko turned goalward and kept going until he scored the winning touchdown. Harmon converted.

Michigan 21, Ohio State 14.

If ever one young man went from the game's goat to the game's hero, it was Fred Trosko that day in 1939.

The game was played at Ann Arbor under a frigid gray sky and the crowd of 80,227 went absolutely hysterical over the final outcome – most with glee; the rest with bitter frustration, especially after seeing their team blow a 14-point lead.

Ohio State's season started with shutout wins over Missouri and Northwestern. Then came a big test at Minneapolis against powerful Minnesota – Big Ten champions for the past two years and losers of only five games in the last six years. The Bucks won, 23-20. While OSU was still thinking about its big victory of the previous week, Cornell sneaked into Columbus and pulled off (what was thought at the time) a stunning 23-14 upset even after Ohio jumped on top 14-0. Cornell and Texas A&M were the only

Michigan Beats Ohio, 21-14, on Last-Minute Touchdown, but Bucks Take Undisputed Big Ten Title as Iowa Is Tied

Wolverines' Great Rally Erases a 14-Point Deficit

80,227 See Harmon Lead Attack; Trosko Dashes 32 Yards for Winning Score on Fake

teams in the Nation with perfect records that year, and the Ivy League's Big Red had a final No. 4 ranking by the AP pollsters.

Upset or not, the Bucks got mad. Until the Michigan game they would yield no more points, clobbering Indiana, Chicago and Illinois by a combined score of 106-0.

The Buckeyes were ranked No. 6 in the country.

Michigan was cruising along with a 4-0-0 record after wiping out Michigan State, Iowa, Chicago and Yale by an average score of 40-7. Something then happened. Illinois pulled off a 16-7 shocker and Minnesota continued its jinx over the Wolverines with a 20-7 victory. A close 19-17 decision of Pennsylvania followed. This Michigan team, Tom Harmon or no Tom Harmon, just didn't seem to be one that could keep pace with the hot Buckeyes.

And for the first ten minutes of the game, Michigan didn't. The Ohioans jumped off to a quick two-touchdown lead but the underdog Wolverines scratched back all afternoon to capture the classic struggle.

Ohio State kicked off to open the series' 36th game that November 25. After an exchange of punts, OSU's James Strausbaugh intercepted a Trosko pass and returned it 29 yards to the Michigan 26. Three running plays gained only eight yards, a field goal try was short, and U-M took over at the 20-yard line. Troska fumbled on first down and Vic Marino recovered for OSU at the line of scrimmage. Frank Zadworney, Don Scott and Strausbaugh blasted down to the eight, where it was first-and-goal. On fourth down from the five, Scott passed to Marino deep into the endzone for a touchdown. A fancy shift at the line made left guard Marino

140

Final Sports
The Detroit News
Final Sports
SUNDAY, NOVEMBER 26, 1939
THE HOME NEWSPAPER

| Michigan . . 21 | Cornell . . 26 | N'thwestern 7 | Minnesota . 23 | Purdue . . 7 | Duquesne . 22 | Yale . . . . 20 | USC . . . . 20 | U. D. High . 40 | Mich. St. 18 |
| Ohio St. . . 14 | Penn . . . . 0 | Iowa . . . . 7 | Wisconsin . 6 | Indiana . . 6 | Carnegie T. 7 | Harvard . . 7 | Notre D'me 12 | High. Park . 13 | Temple . . . |

80,227 See Michigan Beat O.S.U. in Last 40 Seconds

Harmon as He Scored His Touchdown, Photographed Close Up and by Long-Range Camera

Trosko Scores Winning Touchdown on Old Fake

Wolverines, Behind 14 to 0, score in Last Three Periods to Win Major Grid Drama of the 1939 Season, 21 to 14

By H. G. SALSINGER

ANN ARBOR, Mich. Nov. 25—

an end, and eligible as a pass receiver. Scott kicked the point and the favored Bucks led 7-0 after seven minutes of play.

Three minutes later, it was 14-0. And it was another Trusko mistake that led to the second quick score. John Hallabrin intercepted a long pass by Trusko at the Ohio 27 and ran it back 43 yards, was cornered, and lateraled to Scott, who went 10 more yards to the Wolverine 20. Three plays netted only two yards but on fourth down, Scott shot his second scoring pass, this one to Frank Clair. Scott converted and with five minutes left in the first quarter, Trusko had thrown two interceptions, fumbled once, and the mistakes had directly staked the Buckeyes to what looked to be an insurmountable 14-0 lead.

The Maize and Blue settled down and began their gritty comeback. Midway through the second period, Harmon and Joe Rogers teamed-up with a 44-yard aerial strike to Ohio's seven. On third down from the four, Harmon cooly hit end Forest Evashevski for a touchdown. Harmon's conversion was perfect and the score was 14-7.

Like Michigan in the first half, OSU played give-a-way in the second half. And like OSU in the first half, Michigan took advantage of the gifts.

Early in the third quarter, Scott fumbled and Ralph Fritz recovered for U-M at the Buckeye 35. Tom Harmon was now cranked up. He immediately rifled a pass to Rogers for a 19-yard advance down to the 16. Harmon then swept around the right side – touchdown. Michigan was still a point shy but Harmon took care of that, too, with his extra-point kick and Ohio State was now "behind," 14-14.

141

The Bucks took the ensuing kickoff and a 57-yard burst by Strausbaugh triggered a fast drive to Michigan's 11-yard line. Hallabrin fumbled. Bob Westfall recovered—Michigan's ball.

A punting duel developed and the game-clock kept ticking away the time. With just over three minutes left, OSU had a possible game-winning march working that had reached Michigan's 38-yard line.

Fumble!

Westfall was at the right place again; he made his second giant recovery of the second half. Westfall's defensive heroics were still not over, though.

Thomas Dudley Harmon went to work again. His slashing runs and pinpoint passing led the Wolverines to Ohio's six-yard line. The desperate Bucks shoved them back to the 24 and it became fourth down and game-to-go. Coach Fritz Crisler then sent in sophomore Bob Ingalls with a play. The play was a fake field goal. And the play worked for a touchdown.

The Buckeyes wouldn't quit. Taking the kickoff, they quickly drove to midfield. With just ten seconds left, Scott pegged a long pass that sailed into the endzone. As the football spiraled through the air there was still hope for OSU. But there was that man Bob Westfall again. The sophomore from Ann Arbor intercepted. The ball game was over. All emotions had been spent.

Both teams registered 11 first downs. Ohio led in net rushing yards 170-107; Michigan led in passing yards 146-36, and in total yards 253-206. The Wolverines were penalized 20 yards, OSU none.

If there could be any such thing as a consolation prize for Buckeyes following their bitter loss to Michigan, it came in the news that Northwestern (with only a 3-4-0 record) tied heavily-favored Iowa 7-7 to give Ohio State the Big Ten crown outright.

But it was an un-celebrated championship.

This was the last year of the "Big Ten," for a while anyway. The University of Chicago, a charter member of the association, had won only 11 Conference games in the past 14 years, and withdrew from further competition. The Maroons captured six Conference championships, the last one in 1924. It was now back to the "Big Nine" and would remain that way until 1953.

In the decade of the 1930's, Ohio State posted a 57-19-5 (.735) record; Michigan 53-26-4 (.663). In their personal conflicts on the football field, the rivals split 5-5, played before a total paid attendance figure of 624,206. The crowds in Ann Arbor averaged 68,800; in Columbus 56,100.

The major news in the college football world in late November, 1939, centered around the big bowl matchups. The Rose Bowl had Tennessee (ranked No. 2) against Southern California (3rd); the Sugar Bowl had Texas A&M (1st) versus Tulane (5th); the Orange Bowl invited Missouri (6th) and Georgia Tech, while the Cotton Bowl had a strange pairing by today's Cotton standards—Boston College and Clemson.

That same week, though, the news from other parts of the world was getting grim. A Polish luxury liner was sunk in the North Sea by German mines; Russia bombed Helsinki and the Red Army roared into Finland, and British and German fleets were striking up some heavy naval shoot-outs.

World War II was heating up.

1940

GAME 37

A HERO LEAVES
IN HIGH STYLE

See Tom run. See Tom throw. See Tom kick. See Tom do everything. It was Saturday, November 23, 1940, and the great Tom Harmon's 24th and final game as a collegian. The place was Ohio Stadium and 73,648 rain-drenched fans sat and watched in amazement. Harmon, the two-time All-America, put on a one-man show and about the only thing the OSU players could do was stand around and also watch.

On Harmon's tally-sheet that rainy afternoon some four decades ago were these entries:

- Scored three touchdowns.
- Passed for two touchdowns.
- Kicked four conversions.
- Personally scored 22 points.
- Carried the ball 25 times.
- Gained 139 yards rushing.
- Threw 22 passes.
- Completed 11 for 151 yards.
- Ran and passed for 290 yards.
- Punted three times for a 50.0-yard average.
- Returned three punts for 81 yards.
- Accounted for 371 yards.
- Played 59 minutes of the game.

Final score: Michigan 40, Ohio State 0.

144

"OLD 98" ON THE GO AGAINST OHIO

The top photograph shows Tom Harmon harrassing the Ohio State defense in 21-14 win at Ann Arbor in 1939. A year later at Columbus (bottom photo), Harmon is once again being chased by Buckeye defenders. In both pictures, OSU's No. 33, tackle Charles Maag, is after "Old 98." In three games against Ohio State, Harmon scored five touchdowns, passed for four more, kicked seven conversions, and rushed and passed for 618 yards. His 37 points is still a series record. (Photos courtesy of Michigan Athletic Department.)

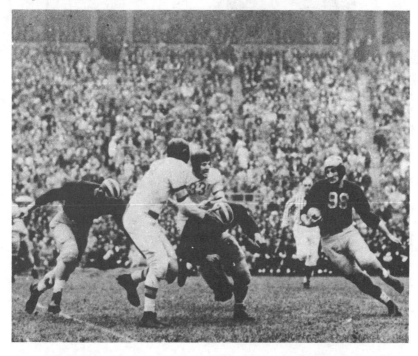

*THE BUCKEYES ENTER OHIO STADIUM
FOR THE 1940 GAME WITH MICHIGAN*

The Wolverines entered the 37th series renewal with a 6-1-0 record and a No. 6 national ranking. They opened the season in Berkeley, California, hopped aboard a United Air Lines' DC-3 and went West to become the first University of Michigan football team to fly — in an airplane. If the final score of the game was any indication — Michigan 41, California 0 — then the trip was a big success both in the air and on the ground.

Coach Fritz Crisler's boys proceeded to handle Michigan State 21-14, Harvard 26-0, Illinois 28-0 and Pennsylvania 14-0. Once again, though, the time came to face those mean ole Gophers from Minnesota, and the Gophers did indeed beat Michigan again, 7-6. The defeat definitely cost the Wolverines the Big Nine title and, more than likely, a national championship, as Minnesota went on to win the country's top spot in the final AP poll. Michigan rebounded with a 20-13 thumping of Northwestern and it was Ohio State next.

The Buckeyes were surviving, but that's about all. After beating Pittsburgh and Purdue, they lost three straight games — to Northwestern, Minnesota and Cornell — before recovering with victories over Indiana and Illinois. With OSU's 4-3-0 record, the prospects of Harmon and Michigan held no great attraction for the coaching staff or the players in Columbus.

After the kickoff, Ohio held on for the first nine minutes of play, until Harmon scored from the seven-yard line to cap an 80-yard drive. The Wolverines scored again just 69 seconds later. Paul Kromer took a Buckeye punt at his own 19 and raced all the way — 81 yards — for a touchdown. At that time, it was the third longest run in the series. Harmon's conversion made it 13-0.

A 77-yard march in the second quarter ended with a 17-yard pass from Harmon to Forest Evashevski. Harmon kicked the point and it was 20-0 at halftime.

The next touchdown was the culmination of another 77-yard drive with the final 16 coming on a Harmon-to-Ed Frutig scoring strike. "By this time nobody was thinking about the eventual outcome. Everybody was thinking about Harmon. So Mr. Harmon gave the boys and girls what they wanted," wrote John Sabo of the *Detroit Free Press*.

Another third quarter score came on Harmon's 18-yard run to conclude a 52-yard series. With 38 seconds left in the game, Harmon got his hands on the football for the last time in his college career. That last play resulted in an eight-yard touchdown, his 33rd for U-M in three seasons. Harmon also added the conversion.

COACH FRANCIS SCHMIDT

Coached at Ohio State for seven years (1934-40) and was 4-3-0 against Michigan. Behind Coach Schmidt is a pair of Michigan football pants (also note the pants on his key chain). Schmidt formed a club of OSU boosters, called the "Michigan's Pants Club". The club's slogan — "Michigan puts on its pants the same way we do." (Photo courtesy of OSU Photo Archives.)

PAUL KROMER

This Michigan halfback, from Lorain, Ohio, returned a punt 81 yards for a touchdown against the Buckeyes in the 1940 game at Columbus. (Photo courtesy of Michigan Athletic Department.)

PART TWO
SPORTS   MARKETS

Chicago Sunday Tribune
THE WORLD'S GREATEST NEWSPAPER
NOVEMBER 24, 1940.

3 TRIBUNE

MICHIGAN WINS, 40-0; N. U. 20, NOTRE DAME 0

MINNESOTA DEFEATS WISCONSIN, 22-13; IOWA, INDIANA TRIUMPH

HARMON SCORES 3 TOUCHDOWNS AGAINST OHIO

DECEPTION, A TIMELY BLOCK, A SPEEDY N, U. TOUCHDOWN JAUNT

NORTHWESTERN 20
NOTRE DAME 0

CLAWSON LEADS WILDCATS WITH 2 TOUCHDOWNS

"When Tom Harmon left the field after his third touchdown dash of the day, the whole crowd, friend and foe alike, stood up and cheered," wrote Sabo. "As Harmon left, the Michigan section of the stands emptied. Ten thousand Michigan rooters mobbed Harmon and formed a guard of honor to escort him to the locker room."

Harmon's glory days as America's No. 1 "Saturday Hero" were over. His remaining official football act was to accept the Heisman Trophy.

With three straight victories over Ohio State, the Wolverines now held a 25-10-2 series lead. The scoring was: Michigan 618, Buckeyes 258.

Ohio State was more than anxious for Harmon to get-on with whatever he was going to get-on with. In Harmon's three games against the Bucks, he scored five touchdowns, passed for another four, kicked seven conversions and his 37-point total is still a series record.

Other figures Harmon compiled against OSU included: 266 yards rushing, 64 carries (4.2 average); 26 pass completions (in 47 tries) for 352 yards and 618 tandem offensive yards – 238 yards *more* than the entire Ohio State team gained during the same three games. Perhaps the most impressive figure of all is that in the three games, Harmon missed only three minutes of action. Compared to today's football generation, one that cut its teeth on separate teams for offense and defense, Harmon's performance defies true appreciation.

After the 40-0 final score had been posted in 1940, one had to flip the pages of Ohio State's record book all the way back to 1905 to find a beating as bad. Ironically, that was a 40-0 loss to Michi-

*About the only thing OSU coaches and players could
do in 1940 was huddle around and watch Harmon....*

gan in a game highlighted by the 113-yard run by Alfred Barlow.
In the same game, a fellow by the name of Tom Hammond scored
14 of Michigan's points by kicking.

The "Harmon" game was the last for Francis Schmidt as
coach at OSU. Schmidt had been at the helm for six seasons and
he resigned under pressure just one year after winning a Big Ten
crown. Schmidt's record was 39-16-1 and 4-3-0 versus Michigan.

The Wolverines, 7-1-0, finished the season with a No. 3
national ranking behind Minnesota and Stanford. Tennessee and
Boston College rounded out the top five.

1941

GAME 38

BOTH ARE 20-20 LOSERS

In football, tie games usually produce mixed emotions. One side feels it has lost, while the other side is overjoyed to have escaped without a loss. Not so in the 1941 fracas between Michigan and Ohio State; both teams blew enough chances for victory to qualify as bona fide losers after butting to a 20-20 draw.

The Wolverines and Buckeyes galloped up and down the gridiron all afternoon and had the 85,733 fans gathered at Ann Arbor roaring from start to finish. At halftime, the score was 7-7; after three quarters, 14-14. Both teams scored in the final period and both teams failed on the conversion. In between the touchdowns, there were 34 first downs and 680 total offensive yards.

This was Paul Brown's first year as head coach at OSU. The *Associated Press* reported, "A 'Draft Brown' movement which started a couple of minutes after Francis Schmidt had resigned the head coaching job December 16 (1940) swept the Massillon High School miracle man into the vacant berth. . . .Never in the history of Buckeye athletics has a man received the state-wide support of fans, alumni and other coaches as did Brown. . . .With practically everyone in Ohio on the Brown band-wagon, the athletic board's unanimous decision today was a mere formality."

With such a mandate, Brown was fully expected to start immediately performing miracles.

His first game was a 12-7 win over a tough Missouri team and would be the Tigers' only loss of the regular season. Then came a 33-0 drubbing of Southern Cal – a gigantic upset. The big win brought out 15,000 cheering fans to greet the Buckeyes when they stepped off the train on their return from Los Angeles. Brown was already performing miracles and good things continued to happen when the Bucks got a 16-14 victory over Purdue. Then Northwestern went to Columbus and knocked the miracle theory over by a 14-7 margin. But Brown got back on course with victories over Pittsburgh 21-14, Wisconsin 46-34 in a wild one, and Illinois 12-7.

Michigan had topped Michigan State, Iowa, Pittsburgh and Northwestern by a combined 79-14 score and was primed for another clash with powerful Minnesota. The Gophers won again, 7-0, to keep an eight-year jinx over the Wolverines alive. With Minnesota "out of the way," Michigan went back to its winning ways with shutout successes over Illinois and Columbia.

It was now time for the 38th Buckeye-Wolverine battle and both teams sported 6-1-0 records.

Weatherwise, it was a day that started out bright and sunny. But by game time, the sky had become heavily overcast, the temperature was plummeting and icy winds made conditions miserable for players and ticket holders.

Michigan kicked off and the exciting, back-and-forth affair was on. OSU came out ahead in an initial exchange of punts and, from midfield, went for a score. Jack Graf completed a short toss to Richard Fisher and the play gained 17 yards. On third down from the 28, Graf's pass to Sam Fox was good for 13 yards to the Michigan 15. Graf and Fisher, in three carries, got a first down at the four-yard line. Two smashes by Graf got the touchdown. John Hallabrin kicked the point and Ohio led 7-0.

In the second quarter, the Buckeyes drove to the U-M 20, but were hurled back to the 35, where the Wolverines took possession. Keyed by a 33-yard run by Robert Westfall, a Michigan drive of eight plays took the ball to Ohio's six, where it was fourth and one. OSU held.

This is one of several goal line plays in the 1941 game at Ann Arbor and exactly which one is difficult to determine. For certain, though, there's plenty of frantic action going on. Identifiable players are OSU's Robert Shaw (40), Leon Schoenbaum (82), Jack Graf (44), and UM's Al Wistert (11), Don Ingalls (66) and Phil Sharpe (85). (Photo courtesy of Michigan Athletic Department)

The Bucks punted out to their 47 and Michigan, in just four plays, was again at the six, this time with a first down. Once again the Wolverines failed; once again Ohio State succeeded.

As the first half neared its conclusion, OSU punted out again, this time only to the 42. Michigan would not be denied again. Paul White got loose around end for a 23-yard gain to the 19. Westfall blasted to the 12; Kuzma to the four; Westfall to the three; Kuzma to the two, and Kuzma for the touchdown. Bill Melzow converted and just 40 seconds before intermission, the score was even at 7-7.

The Buckeyes took the second-half kickoff, couldn't move and punted to Michigan's 35. The running of Kuzma and Westfall got a first down at the OSU 44. Paul White ran for eight yards and Kuzma for six to OSU's 30. Westfall went for 11 yards. After two running plays netted nothing, Kuzma hit a wide-open Harlin Fraumann in the endzone for a touchdown. Melzow's kick made it 14-7.

The Wolverines kicked off and here came the Buckeyes. Starting at their 20-yard line, they executed a 10-play march to make it

....Fifteen days after the 1941 Michigan-Ohio State football game

a tie game again. Fisher got 15, Graf nine and Tom Kinkade 11 to U-M's 45. Switching to the air, Graf threw to Leon Schoenbaum for 20 yards and to Bob Shaw for 13 more. It was first down at the 12. Three straight smashes by Graf left the ball two yards short of a first down at Michigan's four. Fisher got three and the first down, Kinkade got the touchdown, and Hallabrin got the conversion to put the score at 14-14.

Michigan took the ensuing kickoff and led by Westfall's 42-yard sprint, quickly reached the Buckeye four-yard line as the third period came to a close. After changing directions, the Wolverines couldn't punch it in.

Ohio took over and went 96 yards for the go-ahead touchdown. With Kinkade and Fisher running the ball, the Bucks banged out three straight first downs and reached the 48. Graf then threw a pass to Fisher who caught it on the run at the 30 and scored to complete a 52-yard play. Hallabrin's conversion was wide. OSU 20, U-M 14.

Michigan answered. Ohio's kickoff went out of bounds at the Wolverine 35. On first down, a penalty retreated the offense five yards. Then came precision clockwork – a Kuzma-to-George Ceithaml pass to the 50; White to the 37; Kuzma to the 28; Westfall to the 21; White to the 13; Kuzma to the 10; Kuzma to the five, and Westfall for the touchdown. Six minutes remained as Melzow got set to kick what could be the winning point. It, too, went wide. The score remained 20-20.

Ohio had something working late in the game but on a fourth-and-one at their own 45, Michigan halted the threat. There were a few more sparks, including the only punt of the second half, but the fireworks were spent.

Michigan led in first downs 19-15, total yards 375-303, and penalty yards 35-5. In the last four series games, U-M had been hit with 120 yards in penalties to only 30 for Ohio.

It was the series' third tie game and the first since the 1910 deadlock at 3-3 in Columbus. The series now stood 25-10-3, Michigan.

Even though both teams finished with identical 6-1-1 records, Michigan picked up a No. 5 final national ranking, while OSU was not listed among the top ten teams. Minnesota won the national championship again, followed by Duke, Notre Dame, Texas and then the Wolverines.

The 1941 Michigan-Ohio State game was played on Saturday, November 22. Two weeks and one day later, the Japanese sprung their game-plan on Pearl Harbor. World War II was on.

1942

MIRACLE COMPLETED

Coach Paul Brown didn't waste any time in performing the task that Ohio State University students, alumni and fans expected of him – a miracle. His 1942 Buckeyes beat Michigan, won the Big Nine title and added frosting supreme by winning the national championship.

When September, 1942, rolled around. the country's involvement in the war was about to reach its first full year and had not, as yet, substantially affected the collegiate football programs around the country. Drastic interruptions would come a year later.

OSU did not go undefeated, but neither did any other major team in the Nation. It was the first time in the 20th Century that all of the so-called major college teams lost at least one game.

The Buckeyes' road to gridiron glory began on September 27 in Columbus with a 59-0 stomping of Ft. Knox. Teams representing military installations would become common on college schedules over the next few years. Three more home games followed. OSU defeated Indiana 32-21 and Southern California 28-12. That brought the season to October 17. Iowa Pre-Flight, a Navy entry, entered the day rated No. 1 in the country but were sent reeling by a 28-0 upset by Notre Dame. Ohio State popped Purdue 26-0 and went atop the *Associated Press* polls. Georgia, featuring Heisman Trophy winner Frank Sinkwich (an Ohioan who almost enrolled at OSU) and sophomore flash Charley Trippi, was ranked second, followed by Alabama, Michigan, Illinois and Georgia Tech. The season progressed:

OCT. 24 – The Buckeyes remained No. 1 with a 20-6 win over Northwestern. Georgia and Alabama won to remain in the 2-3 positions, while Michigan and Illinois lost and fell from contention. Notre Dame, beating Illinois, moved into fourth place. Georgia Tech was fifth and Wisconsin sixth.

OCT. 31 – Ohio State lost to Wisconsin (17-7) at Madison and tumbled all the way to sixth. Georgia topped Alabama and moved into first place. Wisconsin's big win sent the Badgers to No. 2, while Georgia Tech advanced to third. Notre Dame stayed fourth, and Boston College moved into fifth place.

NOV. 7 – The Buckeyes pounded Pittsburgh 59-19 but for some astonishing reason the pollsters were not impressed and dropped OSU four notches – all the way to 10th. Georgia slaughtered Florida 75-0 to remain No. 1; Tech clobbered Kentucky 47-7 and moved up to second; Boston College toppled Temple 28-0 and placed third. Meanwhile, Michigan handled Harvard and moved to No. 6 behind Alabama, a 29-0 winner over South Carolina.

With ten teams ahead of Ohio State and only three weekends left in the season, a national championship seemed an absolute impossibility for Buckeye boosters. But in college football weird things can happen in three weeks and 1942 yielded one of the strangest finishes ever. Paul Brown needed a lot of foreign aid to perform his miracle – and he was to get it.

NOV. 14 – OSU poured it on Illinois 44-20 and this impressive showing jumped the Bucks all the way to fifth place. Meanwhile, two of the top five teams lost – Notre Dame to Michigan, and Alabama to Georgia Tech. With just two weeks remaining, the top five were Georgia, Georgia Tech, Boston College, Michigan and Ohio State.

NOV. 21 – Big news came out of both Columbus, Georgia and Columbus, Ohio. In the season's biggest shocker, Auburn upset Georgia 27-14. At the same time, OSU was beating Michigan 21-7. Boston College clipped Creighton 33-19 and the nation's sportswriters voted the B.C. Eagles No. 1. Georgia Tech stayed second with a 27-7 victory over Florida. Suddenly, the Buckeyes were in third place. Now, with only one game to go it was: Boston College, Georgia Tech and Ohio State.

In just two weeks time, Tech had eliminated Alabama; Auburn had eliminated Georgia; Michigan had eliminated Notre Dame, and OSU had eliminated Michigan.

NOV. 28 – This was the day. Ohio State did its part by winning – 42-12 over Iowa Pre-Flight, the team that had been in first

157

"All the News That's Fit to Print."

The New York Times.

LATE CITY EDITION

Section 1

VOL. XCII...No. 30,902.

NEW YORK, SUNDAY, NOVEMBER 22, 1942.

TEN CENTS

COFFEE SALES HALT AFTER WILD BUYING; A RUSH FOR BUTTER

Housewives Plead in Vain for Beverage on Eve of Week's Pre-Rationing Drought

STORES MAY CURB BUTTER

300,000 Eating Places in N. Y. Asked to Keep Records of Food Served in December

Dates of Rationing For Consumers

Explains Relief and Rehabilitation Work WW Cover Both Sen and Peace Period

LEAVES OFFICE ON DEC.

GASOLINE

COFFEE

FUEL OIL

LEHMAN FORECASTS YEARS OF SERVICE IN WAR-TORN LAND

WAR POWERS BILL GETS 'SAFEGUARDS'

House Subcommittee United in Voting Substitute for Administration Draft

Major Sports Results

FOOTBALL

ALLIED FORCES MOVING IN TO HIT THE AXIS AT BIZERTE AND TUNIS; R. A. F. AGAIN BOMBS TURIN PLANTS

'Peace' Cries Heard As King Visits Genoa

ITALY'S WORST RAID

One Flight Group Sends Down 54 Two-Ton High Explosives in Hour

BLASTS START HUGE FIRES

Hundreds of British Planes in Attack Battle Route Over France—Three Lost

U. S. TROOPS GAIN ON GUADALCANAL

Small Japanese Patrols and Advance Line in Fighting 5 Miles West of Airfield

FORTIFICATION CAPTURED BY AMERICANS

AXIS IS HEMMED IN

Net Tightens in Tunisia as Nazi Army Braces for Crucial Battle

FRENCH ATTACK GERMANS

Storm Defense Dugouts After Allies Capture Crossroads in Clash South of Paris

Ohio State Checks Michigan, 21-7, Before 71,896 for Big Ten Title

...ear Guard Battered By British Beyond Bengazi

CAIRO, Egypt, Nov. 21—The fall of Bengazi yesterday

RUSSIANS HOLD OFF NAZIS IN CAUCASUS

Germans Suffer New Losses in Effort to Revive Offensive—Stalingrad Blows Fail

MOSCOW, Sunday, Nov. 22—

War News Summarized

SUNDAY, NOVEMBER 22, 1942

Shake-Up in Standard Oil Follows Attacks on Reich Link; Teagle Out

French West Indies Quit Laval; Martinique in a New Pact With U.S.

WASHINGTON, Nov. 21—The

British Army Adopts Crusaders' Emblem

LONDON, Nov. 21—Great Britain has adopted the emblem of Crusaders' maltese, the cross and sword with the sword of St. George of England, as official announcement said tonight.

place six weeks earlier. But, No. 1 Boston College would need to lose to Holy Cross, which they did, by a score of 55-12. Now, No. 2 Georgia Tech would need to lose to Georgia – which they did, by a score of 34-0.

Thus, in one afternoon, the No. 1 and No. 2 ranked teams in the Nation were crushed by a total score of 89-12! The Ohio State Buckeyes, obviously, zoomed into first place – and into orbit. It was an incredible finish to a wild football season.

Ohio State had its national championship.

Looking back on that "Fall of '42," it seems appropriate that the season should have such a whirlwind finish. Bold frontpage headlines daily told the war's horrible news – cities literally leveled by devastating bombing raids. . . .huge ships going down in powerful sea battles. . . .entire squadrons of planes shot from the air. . . .invasions. . . .retreats. . . .thousands of American fighting men dying in North Africa, on Pacific islands such as Guadalcanal, and many other "over yonder" places.

It was to be football's "last hurrah" for a while. Every boy of age and physically fit, college student or not, in just a few months would be a "million miles" away participating, one way or an-other, in a war. Football, in a few years, would return to take its normal, crazy place in our society. But first, there was more im-portant business that had to be taken care of.

It was "Time-Out."

While Ohio State was waving its banner, Michigan, now "Harmonless," was also in the national rankings picture. The Wolverines opened up with back-to-back blanks of Great Lakes (9-0) and Michigan State (20-0). On October 10, U-M lost to Iowa Pre-Flight 26-14, marking the school's 100th all-time football defeat. It took 63 years and 472 games for Michigan to lose 100 – a grand record, indeed.

After a 34-16 victory over Northwestern, the Wolverines fell to the Minnesota "hex" for the ninth straight year, 16-14. No team had ever dominated Michigan in such a manner. The last Maize and Blue victory over the Gophers had been in 1932 (3-0). In 1933 there was a scoreless tie. From Michigan's viewpoint, the Little Brown Jug had been in Minnesota's possession for much too long.

The Wolves shook off the Minnesota setback and took Illinois 28-14, and Harvard 35-7 in the last game between the two schools. In a big game at South Bend, Michigan won 32-20, the most points any team had scored against Notre Dame since 1904.

The Big day arrived. Michigan was 6-2-0 and ranked No. 4; Ohio State was 7-1-0 and ranked No. 5. The weather was cold and

*The Wolverines' Bob Wiese plunges for a TD in the third period of the
1942 game at Columbus to pull his team to within seven points, but the
Buckeyes won, 21-7. (Photo courtesy of Michigan Athletic Department)*

rainy, the track slow and muddy. These conditions mattered little
to the 71,896 fans who showed up at Ohio Stadium to watch the
Buckeyes down Michigan for the first time since 1937. The score
was 21-7 as halfback Paul Sarringhaus threw three touchdown
passes, two to Les Horvath and the other to Bob Shaw.

A glance at the game statistics says that OSU was outplayed.
Possibly so, but with five turnovers and a blocked punt, the
Wolverines could reasonably be charged with an act of self-
destruction.

Early in the second period of a scoreless game, OSU's Charles
Csuri broke through and blocked Tom Kuzma's punt that bounded
out of bounds at the U-M 30-yard line. On first down, Sarringhaus
hit Horvath with a pass for 12 yards. A play later from the 15-yard
line, the same passing combination got Ohio on the scoreboard.
Eugene Fekete kicked the conversion to put OSU on a 7-0 cushion.

PART TWO		Chicago Sunday Tribune	TRIBUNE PHONE NUMBERS
Sports	Markets	THE WORLD'S GREATEST NEWSPAPER	

NOVEMBER 22, 1942.

WISCONSIN WINS, 20 TO 6; OHIO CLINCHES TITLE

NOTRE DAME WHIPS N. U.; GREAT LAKES ROUTS ILLINOIS, 6 TO 0

BADGERS BEAT GOPHERS AFTER TEN YEAR LAPSE

WISCONSIN TROTS OUT TRUSTY PASS PLAY TO HELP WHIP MINNESOTA

BUCKEYES TOP MICHIGAN, 21-7, BY AIR ATTACK

The third-ranked Buckeyes clinched the Big Ten title but would have to wait a week to for their national title — when No. 1 Boston College lost 55-12 to Holy Cross, and No. 2 Georgia Tech lost 34-0 to Georgia. Those unbelievable developments shot OSU to the topspot.

Coach Paul Brown led Ohio State to a national championship in 1942 and then entered the Armed Forces. Upon his return from the war, he marched to a new professional football team in Cleveland, rather than back to Columbus and the college game. It was a real blow to the Buckeyes. (Photo courtesy of OSU photo archives)

Michigan was in the game, and when the whistle blew to a close the first half, had the ball on the Buckeye one-yard line.

Late in the third quarter, OSU started on its 36-yard line after receiving a punt and scored in just three plays. From the 40, Sarringhaus faded deep, dodged Michigan's charging linemen, and "slung one." Shaw, streaking down the sideline, caught it at the 25 and tight-roped the boundary chalkmark for a 60-yard touchdown play. Fekete's conversion made the score 14-0.

Ohio's kickoff went out of bounds at U-M's 36 and the Wolverines got back in the ball game with a seven-play touchdown drive. Two passes, Paul White-to-Bob Chappuis for 26 yards, and Chappuis-to-George Ceithapel for 18 more, quickly got Michigan to Ohio's 20. Robert Wiese rammed for two; White for three; Wiese for three; Wiese for 11, and Wiese for one and the score. With just six seconds left in the quarter, James Brieske made the point for a 7-14 deficit.

Late in the game, Ohio reached the Wolverines' eight-yard line but missed a field goal. Michigan took over, fumbled on second down and Bob Jabbusch recovered for the Bucks at the 33. Sarringhaus and Horvath promptly made their second touchdown hook-up. Fekete again kicked true.

The losers led in first downs 17-9, yards rushing 155-140, yards passing 138-132, total yards 293-272, and penalty yards 25-5.

A victory over Michigan. . . .a Big Nine title. . . .a national championship. . . .what more could Buckeye fans ask for? They loved it. A man named Brown was man-of-the-year in the State of Ohio.

1943

GAME 40

MILITARY MIGHT – AND DID

It was wartime football. Some of the nation's colleges had teams that included Navy V-12 and other military trainees. For the military personnel, all eligibility rules were suspended and in some cases, seniors from the previous season found themselves back in intercollegiate competition, often with teams they had faced as opponents in the past. Other schools fielded what were called "civilian" teams, while many colleges dropped football altogether in 1943, including Alabama, Auburn, Tennessee, Baylor, Ole Miss, Boston College, Fordham and Kentucky.

Michigan was military; Ohio State was civilian.

Coach Paul Brown had only five members (all juniors) from his national championship team of a year before. He had no seniors or sophomores; but he did have 39 freshmen. This was Brown's raw material for a football team for the 1943 season.

There have been worse football teams. Ohio's first game was against powerful Iowa Pre-Flight and the Buckeyes lost 28-13 – their first defeat in a season opener since 1894. There was a 27-6 win over Missouri before four straight setbacks. Then came two straight wins, 46-6 over Pittsburgh and 29-26 over Illinois.

Meanwhile, at Ann Arbor, there was definitely not a manpower shortage. Coach Fritz Crisler's 52-man squad included 23 Marine trainees (were they known as "Wolvermarines"?) and 18 furnished by the Navy. Among that group were four lettermen from the University of Wisconsin, one from the University of Minnesota and four from last year's Michigan team.

Chicago Daily Tribune
THE WORLD'S GREATEST NEWSPAPER

3 CENTS PAY NO MORE!

FINAL

VOLUME CII—NO. 279 C.   MONDAY, NOVEMBER 22, 1943.—43 PAGES   PRICE THREE CENTS

NIMITZ STRIKES IN PACIFIC

TELL CHURCHILL NOT TO MEDDLE IN '44 ELECTION

Hint He Might Aid F.D.R. Assailed.

Farmers Rebel Against OPA Snoop Tricks

BY GAIL COMPTON.

300,000 SLASH IN GOVERNMENT PAY ROLL ASKED

Byrd Group Makes Second Demand.

FOLLOWING THE FOREIGN POLICY.

AMERICA'S FOREIGN POLICY?

JUST WHAT KIND OF FOREIGN POLICY DOES HE WANTS ME TO ADOPT?

OPA

Union Chiefs Score Tribune; Members Hail It for Exposé

BATTLE RAGES AS YANKS LAND ON MAKIN, TARAWA

War Summaries

Hold Beachheads After Shelling by Fleet.

Would Query High Staff on M'Arthur Aid

MICHIGAN DEFEATS OHIO STATE, 45-7
Wolverines Clinch Share in Title With 5 Touchdowns in Second Half

Navy Men Die in Plane Crash

KENNEY KEEPS A PROMISE—WITH SLIGHT CHANGES

STALLING IN WAR TO AID F.D.R. IN '44 FEARED BY BARSON

THE WEATHER

Tribune Features

LARGEST OF GILBERT ISLES

OCTOBER, 1943   930,000   THE CHICAGO TRIBUNE

The Wolverines creamed Camp Grant, Western Michigan, Northwestern, Minnesota, Illinois, Indiana and Wisconsin by an average score of 31-8. In between was a 35-12 loss to Notre Dame, also loaded with service talent. It brought U-M's all-time edge over the Irish to 8-2-0 and the two teams would not meet again for 35 years.

It was time for the 40th game of the series. Michigan was 7-1-0 and rated No. 3 in the nation; Ohio State was 3-5-0 and rated a huge underdog. With gasoline and tires strictly rationed, attendance at the game was held to "only" 45,000, about half the throng under normal circumstances in Ann Arbor, and they watched as Brown's fuzzy-cheeked youngsters played as tough a game as they were capable of playing. In the third quarter, the score was only 13-7, but Michigan's military might was just too much to handle and the game turned into a rout.

Final score: 45-7.

Considering the makeup of the teams, it didn't mean that much, but just for the record, the 45 points scored against OSU that November 20 was the most in one game since 1904.

The Wolverines knocked out 23 first downs to Ohio's two, and 531 total yards to 95 for the Buckeyes. The "big boys" were caught with 65 yards worth of penalties and the "kids" none.

Six different players scored Michigan's seven touchdowns. Bob Wiese got it started with a one-yard plunge to cap a 10-play, 40-yard march. The conversion was blocked by Gordon Appleby. Michigan, 6-0. It was 13-0 after the next possession with a 42-yard march in eight plays. Walter Dreyer bulled over from the two. Rex Wells' conversion was on target.

Michigan reached Ohio's 19, 25 and eight-yard lines in the second quarter but were held by the hustling young Bucks. Early in the third period, Bill Hackett blocked a punt and OSU took over at midfield. Three runs gained 14 yards before quarterback Ernest Parks, operating from the T-formation, kept the ball, turned the corner and scored on a beautiful 36-yard run. John Stungis kicked good and the underdogs were under by only a 13-7 score. It was at least a contest.

OSU kicked off and, after an exchange of punts, U-M went 60 yards in seven plays for its third touchdown. A 27-yard run by Earl Maves was the big gainer and Wiese scored his second touchdown of the game from the one. Wells' kick was perfect and it was now, 20-7.

The dam broke.

165

In the next 20 minutes of play, the Wolverines tallied four touchdowns. Bob Nussbaumer scored on a 30-yard run; a 10-yard pass from Jack Wink to Vince Mroz made it 32-7; Maves scored from eight yards out, and the final touchdown came on a 20-yard run by Don Lund. Only one of the last four conversions was successful and it was kicked by Elroy (Crazy Legs) Hirsch, who had been a star running back at Wisconsin, but was now attending Michigan, compliments of the Marines.

The win gave Michigan a 26-11-3 lead in the series and the Wolverines had 690 points to Ohio's 306.

Michigan's 1943 season produced its first Big Nine championship in 10 years and a No. 3 final rating in the AP poll behind Notre Dame, and Iowa Pre-Flight.

1944

WAR BABIES

World War II was raging in Europe and the Pacific. On the home front, colleges were still playing football but the game, for the most part, was just a shadow of its old self. Most of the rosters were made up of freshmen too young for the draft or players who could not meet military physical standards (4-Fs). The continuance of college football and major league baseball, despite acute manpower shortages and travel difficulties, were encouraged and tolerated for civilian and military morale reasons. There was also an element of a psychological ploy, as President Franklin Roosevelt wanted the enemy to know that America could fight a war on foreign soils and seas and at the same time, "play games" at home.

There were a few bona fide teams scattered around the country but none could remotely match the awesome Army team of 1944, featuring Glenn Davis, Doc Blanchard and a cast of other stars. "Mr. Outside" and "Mr. Inside" and the rest of the Black Knights averaged 56 points per game and smothered a good Notre Dame team (8-2-0) by a score of 59-0 – the all-time worst defeat in the proud grid history of the Irish.

The Ohio State team was all-civilian and its roster consisted of 31 freshmen and 12 upperclassmen. Even the head coach had gone into the service, Paul Brown having been commissioned by the Navy the previous April. Replacing the immensely-popular Brown was Carroll Widdoes, who had moved with Brown from Massillon High School to Columbus as an assistant.

THE WEATHER

THE ATLANTA CONSTITUTION
For 77 Years an Independent Georgia Newspaper, Georgia Owned and Georgia Edited

THE SOUTH'S STANDARD NEWSPAPER

ATLANTA 1½, GA. SUNDAY MORNING, NOVEMBER 26, 1944

Price Ten Cents

Patton Advances 7 Miles; Hodges Through Forest

Four Killed, 38 Hurt In Belgian Riot

Fighting in Brussels Flames as Marchers Protest Martial Rule

Subs Destroy 27 Jap Ships; Foe Loses 4th Leyte Convoy

New Air Raid Rocks Manila

POVERTY STILL LURKS

Atlanta Hearts Open For Opportunity Fund

PLAY, FIDDLE, PLAY!

Ill Atlantan C----
By S----

Buckeyes Take Big 10 Title

Horvath Leads Mates to 18-14 Comeback Win

SPORTS

THE ATLANTA CONSTITUTION • Sunday, Nov. 26, 1944

12-C • THE ATLANTA CONSTITUTION

Unbeaten Yale Deadlocked by Virginia, 6-6

Hartsfield, Peggy, Et Al. To Send U. S. S. Atlanta Into Action Dec. 3

HILLS WITH THRILLS

Tech-Irish Weather Flu-Perfect!

IN OTHER PAGES

AMERICANS IN REICH 'MINE' MILK IN CAVERNS 1,200 FEET BELOW GROUND

By the middle of the season, Michigan coach Fritz Crisler did not have a single player from his Big Nine championship team of 1943.

More than likely, both Widdoes and Crisler performed the most masterful coaching jobs of their respective careers in 1944. It was unthinkable in August that either team would finish among the nation's top ten, but each of them pulled it off.

Widdoes whipped his squad into a well-precisioned outfit that won all its games, captured the Big Nine championship, and was ranked No. 2 behind Army in the final *Associated Press* balloting. Widdoes' team was Ohio State's first to go unbeaten since 1917.

The Buckeyes started with a 54-0 mashing of Missouri and kept on marching, with wins over Iowa 34-0, Wisconsin 20-7, Great Lakes 26-6, Minnesota 34-14, Indiana 21-7, Pittsburgh 54-19 and Illinois 26-12. Michigan was next.

Crisler took his boys and matched OSU win-for-win. However, the Wolverines had an additional game on the schedule and that one game turned out to be a loss – 20-0 to Indiana. There were victories over Iowa Pre-Flight 12-7, Marquette 14-0, Minnesota 28-13, Northwestern 27-0, Purdue 40-14, Pennsylvania 41-19, Illinois 14-0 and Wisconsin 14-0. Ohio State was next, and the Wolverines would be challenged to stop the third highest scoring team in the Nation. The Buckeyes were averaging 34 points per game, topped only by Army and Tulsa.

Ohio State (8-0-0) vs. Michigan (8-1-0) in Columbus for the Conference championship, and 71,958 came out to witness one of the most thrilling games in the series. OSU, after trailing 7-6 and 14-12, finally won it, 18-14, when a controversial coaching decision late in the game backfired on the Wolverines.

The Buckeyes took the opening kickoff and went to Michigan's 39-yard line and stalled. After some kick-backs, OSU's great Leslie Horvath returned a punt 18 yards to his own 44. A ground-oriented attack reached Michigan's three, where it was fourth-and-one. Horvath bucked for two yards and a first down at the one. Michigan made the Bucks work for their one yard. On the third crack, Oliver Cline crashed over. With 1:42 left in the first quarter, Tom Keane missed the conversion, but the Buckeyes had a 6-0 lead.

As the game approached halftime, Michigan had not gotten past OSU's 45-yard line and the rugged Bucks seemingly had the game under complete control – until Ralph Chubb intercepted a Horvath pass and returned it 30 yards to Ohio's 25. The big break

Michigan Leads 7-6, 14-12

woke up the Wolverines and Ohio State would have a crisis on its hands for the rest of the afternoon.

Chubb carried four times for 24 yards down to the one-yard line. From there, Bill Culligan scored. Joe Ponsetto added the point-after and with just 22 seconds before intermission, Michigan had grabbed a 7-6 lead.

State was stunned.

The Wolverines came out snarling in the second half. Chubb returned the kickoff 30 yards to the 39. Donald Lund ripped off a 13-yard gain and Chubb followed with nine more and suddenly Michigan was at the Ohio 39. Wham! Lund fumbled on the next play and Gordon Appleby recovered for OSU.

Ohio punted. On third down from the U-M 25, Chubb fumbled and once again it was Appleby to the rescue with a recovery, this time at the 23. The stadium exploded with delight. In six plays the Bucks were on the one. Horvath scored. The conversion try was blocked and with 8:12 remaining in the third quarter, OSU had regained the lead, 12-7.

Early in the fourth quarter, Michigan fumbled away the ball again at its 37 and the Bucks reached the 16 but were stopped. The Wolverines took over and marched relentlessly down the field – all 84 yards – and scored. Culligan once again had the touchdown honors from one yard away. Ponsetto kicked good. Time remaining in the game was 8:12 and scrappy Michigan led again, 14-12.

Then came the big decision by Crisler that was second-guessed for years. Michigan gambled with an on-sides kick and the ball flew out of bounds at Ohio's 49-yard line. The Buckeyes had new life and began pounding away at the middle of Michigan's line. Nothing fancy, nothing cute. Just straight-ahead, power football. They kept the drive alive for over five minutes and had pushed to inside the Wolverines' one-yard line.

OSU'S LESLIE HORVATH
1944 HEISMAN TROPHY WINNER

Scored two touchdowns in Buckeyes' 18-14 win over the Wolverines that year. In the 1942 Ohio-Michigan game, Horvath's two touchdowns powered Bucks to 21-7 triumph. (Photo courtesy of OSU Photo Archives.)

171

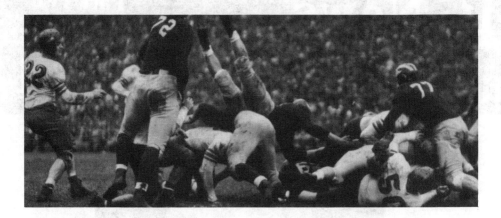

It's a topsy-turvy world, this annual Michigan-Ohio State thing. Action seen here in the 1944 game at Columbus includes Les Horvath (22), Clement Bauman (72), Milan Lazetich (77), Gordon Appleby (50) and a host of other arms and legs and rumps. (Photo courtesy of OSU Photo Archives)

Horvath hurdled the line and tumbled into the endzone for the game-winner. The conversion was missed again but it mattered not. With three minutes and six seconds to be played, OSU was again out front, 18-14.

No description of the screaming and hollering and stomping at Ohio Stadium would be adequate to convey the joy of the Buckeye loyalists.

A minute later, as Michigan took to the air in desperation, the Wolverines' doom was sealed as Dick Flanagan intercepted a Culligan pass. The Buckeyes had victory No. 12 over Michigan.

Ohio led in first downs 17-10 and rushed for 225 yards (led by Horvath's 104 in 33 carries) but did not complete a pass in four attempts. Michigan's total yards added up to 190.

The next day there were headlines and hot rumors that Ohio State would go to the Rose Bowl to meet Southern California. However, on Monday the Conference faculty directors met in Chicago and vetoed such nonsense. The Tennessee Vols were happy with the Big Nine vote. They went instead.

Even so, it was a great season for OSU. Leslie Horvath was later named the winner of the Heisman Trophy, beating out Glenn Davis of Army. Horvath became the second Heisman winner to play in the series – and OSU's first, following Tom Harmon who won it four years earlier.

Another big honor rolled in. Carroll Widdoes was named national Coach Of The Year.

Ohio State's final 9-0-0 record was good enough for a second place finish nationwide, while Michigan, 8-2-0, was voted eighth best. These were outstanding accomplishments when one considers the other teams to finish in the top ten that year: Army, Navy, Bainbridge Navy, Fourth Air Force, Iowa Pre-Flight, Randolph Field, plus Notre Dame and Southern California.

The next time Ohio State and Michigan would meet on the football field, World War II would be history.

1945

GAME 42

V-M DAY

German military leaders agreed to unconditional surrender on May 7; Japan's formal "we've had enough" was signed aboard the USS Missouri on September 2. The war was over.

But vestiges of wartime football remained.

Ohio State's roster was a hodgepodge. Fifteen were 17 years old, nine were 18, eight were 23 or older (including two who were 26). Nineteen other members were within those age ranges.

Michigan's 45-man squad was broken down as: 24 "civilians" (freshmen), 13 "Navy," (trainees), four "Marine" (trainees) and four "dischargees" (veterans).

The two teams met at Ann Arbor on November 24. Midway through the third period, struggling Michigan trailed 3-0. The Wolverines had not driven past the 50-yard line, had accumulated just over 100 yards in total offense, and were backed up to their own one-foot line by an Ohio punt. The Buckeyes had not exactly been running rampant, but they were in a great position to move in for the kill. . . .

Michigan won, 7-3.

Coach Paul Brown was gone for good from the Columbus scene. He turned "pro" and accepted a coaching offer from the Cleveland Browns of the new All-America Football Conference.

Ohio State, under the guidance of Carroll Widdoes, entered the game with a 7-1-0 record and was favored. The Bucks had lost only to Purdue (35-13) in the fourth game of the season, and had beaten their seven other opponents by an average score of 27-4 per game.

Michigan was 6-3-0. Its three defeats, however, were to three of the best teams in America – No. 1 Army (28-7), No. 3 Navy (33-7) and No. 4 Indiana (13-7).

A crowd of 85,132 crammed Michigan's bowl and watched as the 42nd game of the series unfolded. There was an added atmosphere of excitement in the air, due to relief from the pressures and worry of the war, and to gratitude that the game of football and other institutions of American society were on their way back to normalcy.

Midway through the first period, Michigan's Bob Nussbaumer recovered a fumble at OSU's 15-yard line. On first down, Howard Yerges dropped the ball and the Bucks recovered. That would be U-M's only play from scrimmage in Buckeyeland until the game-winning drive in the fourth quarter.

The half ended, 0-0.

Five minutes into the third quarter, OSU's Robin Priday intercepted a Pete Elliott pass at the Buckeye 42 to set the stage for the game's first score. Ollie Cline rushed for five yards and Harold Daugherty got a first down at Michigan's 47. A 35-yard pass play from Daugherty to Tom Watson put the ball at the 12. On fourth down from the 10, Max Schnittker kicked a field goal and it was 3-0.

Dan Dworsky fielded the subsequent kickoff at the goal line, dropped the ball, fumbled around with it and by the time he could get control, a bunch of Buckeyes roared in and belted him down inside the one-yard line. The play kept Michigan in hot water for the remainder of the third quarter. But they slowly gained yardage on each exchange of punts, and with 12 minutes left in the game had finally "backed" Ohio to its 25 with a kick. On successive plays, Michigan's defense plowed through and inflicted losses of six and five yards. On third down, OSU got off a punt into the wind that went out of bounds at its own 44.

With 11 minutes remaining, the winning drive started. Elliott threw incomplete once but came back with a big 25-yard strike to Henry Fonde at OSU's 19. Elliott got away for seven to the 12, then took it to the 10. On the next play Elliott was stacked up for no gain. It was fourth-and-one. The big crowd stood. This could, after all, be the ball game. Fonde got the call and Fonde got the first down with a five-yard smash. On the next play Ohio was offsides and the ball was placed at the one-yard line. (The rule differs slightly today). Fonde skirted end for the score. George Chiames' kick made it 7-3 and six minutes and 45 seconds remained for Ohio State to do something about it.

The "down" Buckeyes received the kickoff and worked it to their 41, but a fourth down pass was batted down. They got possession once more but Elliott intercepted a pass and Michigan was able to run out the clock.

The Wolverines had won.

The statistics were fairly even. Each team registered 11 first downs; Ohio led in total yards 188-170, while U-M's 15 yards in penalties were one more than had been assessed against OSU.

Michigan was 7-3-0 for the season and ranked No. 6. Ohio State was 7-2-0, but failed to crack the top ten.

The Wolverines' series win gave them a 27-12-3 lead; the Buckeyes were falling further behind.

A few weeks after the season, Carroll Widdoes asked OSU officials that he be relieved as head coach. He remained as an assistant under Paul Bixler. Both Bixler and Widdoes had come to OSU with Paul Brown in 1941. Widdoes' two-year record was a "respectable" 16-2-0.

In 1945, Indiana captured its first Western Conference championship and now all the league's members had won a title. With the "postwar era" to begin next year, Michigan had won (or shared) the most Conference championships, 16. Minnesota had 12; Ohio State seven; Illinois six; Northwestern six; Chicago five; Purdue four; Wisconsin four; Iowa three, and Indiana its one.

1946

NO CONTEST

WHO .... Michigan and Ohio State
WHAT .... Football Game
WHEN .... November 23, 1946
WHERE .... Columbus, Ohio
WINNER ...... Michigan

The score was 58-6 in a Wolverine scoring orgy that produced eight touchdowns, seven conversions and one field goal. No OSU football team had been so rudely embarrassed since 1902, when their Buckeye ancestors lost 0-86 – also to Michigan.

The Wolverines, with a 5-2-1 record, were favored over the 4-2-2 Bucks. But the pre-game point-spread was nowhere near a plus 50.

As in each of the past four seasons, the makeup of the team rosters was different and a direct reflection of the times. The freshmen and military trainees were out, and the veterans were in.

Ohio State had 65 military veterans on its 79-man squad; Michigan's 50-member roster listed 43 veterans. The Buckeyes had 37 lettermen; the Wolverines 39. The average age of the two teams was in excess of 21 years.

College football, in 1946, once again was no place for "kids."

Henry Fonde got the touchdown carnival started with a one-yard run after seven minutes of play. It continued: Bob Mann on a 16-yard pass from Bob Chappuis....Fonde on a 14-yard pass from Chappuis....Chappuis on a five-yard run....Halftime.... Mann on a 21-yard run....Paul White on a 32-yard pass from

U-M Wallops Bucks, but Illinois Wins Big 9 Title

Illini Breeze to 20-0 Edge over Wildcats

Northwestern Never Threatens Champions' Trip to Rose Bowl

BY BOB LATSHAW

UCLA Grabs Rose Bowl Berth

Cards Deal Teutons 21-13 Loss

OSU Slaughtered, 58-6, in Lost Cause

78,634 See Chappuis Set Record for Yardage; Even B Team Play

BY LYALL SMITH

Blocking Like This Paves Way for Wolverines' First Touchdown

THE DETROIT FREE PRESS

SPORTS

PART FOUR   SUNDAY, NOV. 24, 1946

Chappuis....Dick Rifenburg on a 40-yard pass from Bill Culligan....Culligan on a four-yard run....and a James Brieske field goal, plus seven Brieske conversions spread throughout the afternoon.

Ohio State scored late in the game on a 60-yard pass from Francis Doolittle to Rodney Swinehart. To add one last little touch of humiliation, Howard Yerges blocked the conversion.

The afternoon started out with 78,634 fans in the stands but the few who were left to see Ohio's long touchdown pass wore Maize and Blue. It was a sad Homecoming Day for the Buckeye faithful.

"The memory of today's game over dangerous Ohio, a team that beat Southern California by three touchdowns earlier this year, will endure forever," wrote Watson Spoelstra of the *Detroit News*.

The game statistics were what one might expect: First downs 22-4; yards rushing 200-47; yards passing 309-78, and total yards 509-125. All Michigan.

With Michigan's crushing defeat of OSU, the series lead widened to 28-12-3 in games, and to 769-333 in points.

For the first time in 26 years, a Western Conference team was allowed to play in a bowl game. It was the first year of the Rose Bowl pact with the Pacific Coast Conference (as it was then called). Illinois (7-2-0) carried the Big Nine banner to Pasadena and routed UCLA (10-0-0) by a score of 45-7 – to the complete dismay of the West Coast fans and especially the West Coast press.

178

1947

BACK TO THE ROSE BOWL

For the third straight year Ohio State had a new coach and for the third straight year it didn't matter to Michigan who was coaching. The Wolverines won again, 21-0, to put the finishing touches to a perfect 9-0-0 campaign that earned them a trip to the Rose Bowl.

Michigan buried its first four opponents – Michigan State 55-0, Stanford 49-13, Pittsburgh 69-0 and Northwestern 49-21. That output of 55 points per game was a hard pace to maintain, and the Wolverines slowed down slightly against Minnesota (13-6) and Illinois (14-7). After this "resting up," Michigan resumed the runaway pattern by blanking Indiana 35-0, and by thrashing Wisconsin 40-6. The latter win clinched the Big Nine championship.

The Buckeyes had a mean pack of Wolverines to deal with and were dreadfully short of weapons. First-year coach Wes Fesler, who played for OSU in 1928-29-30 and scored two touchdowns in the series, was hurting through the worst OSU season since 1897. The Scarlets had beaten Missouri 13-7, Northwestern 7-6, and tied Iowa 13-13. But on the other side of the ledger, Purdue, Southern California, Pittsburgh, Indiana and Illinois all beat up on the Bucks.

OSU entered Michigan Stadium with a 2-5-1 record and had scored the fewest number of points (60) in 23 years.

A rain that fell up until game time didn't seem to keep anybody from the ball park as 85,938 squeezed into the big bowl and watched Michigan manhandle the Buckeyes with no problem on

Fritz Crisler, who brought the famed "winged helmet" to Michigan, gave up coaching after the 1947 season to devote full time to serving as athletic director. During his 10-year tenure (1938-47), the Wolverines compiled a 71-16-3 (.806) record, including 7-2-1 against Ohio State. Crisler Arena on the UM campus is named for him.

the muddy field. Forget the modest score of 21-0. The Wolverines bashed out 24 first downs to Ohio's nine and totaled 449 offensive yards to the opposition's 174.

The game's first touchdown came with four minutes left in the first quarter when Chalmers (Bump) Elliott scored from the three to cap a 68-yard drive. Highlighting the snappy march was a 26-yard run by Bob Chappuis. and a Chappuis-to-Bob Mann 17-yard pass play to Ohio's three-yard line. After Elliott's touchdown, James Brieske's conversion made it 7-0.

Ohio held on and the first half ended with no additional scoring. In the third period, Michigan socked out an 80-yard march and Chappius scored from the two. After Brieske's point-after, it was 14-0 and U-M rooters could now rest a little easier.

With 11 minutes left in the 44th game of the series, the Wolves tallied a final touchdown on a short run by John Weisenburger. Brieske then kicked the 100th conversion of his college career.

All-American halfback Bob Chappuis (49) is on the loose early in the 1947 game at Ann Arbor. Giving chase are OSU's Jameson Crain (89) and Joseph Whisler (36). (Photo courtesy of Michigan Athletic Department)

Ohio should never have let Bob Chappuis escape the State. The Michigan junior from Toledo riddled the Buckeyes with 12 pass completions in 26 attempts for 217 yards, and ran for 90 more for a fabulous 307-yard afternoon.

OSU's final 2-6-1 record was the school's lowest since 1897.

The Wolverines went West with a 13-game win streak. After the Rose Bowl it was 14. They chewed Southern California into little pieces, 49-0, precisely the score of Michigan's last visit to the Rose Bowl 46 years earlier. It was also Fritz Crisler's last game as coach at U-M, and he departed with Coach of the Year honors. Crisler's 10-year record at Michigan was 71-16-3 (.805). He resigned the following spring to devote full time to being athletic director and named Bennie Oosterbaan as his successor. Oosterbaan was a three-time All-America (1925-26-27) at Michigan and since that time had been an assistant coach at U-M.

The 1947 season produced the best Michigan record since another 10-0-0 mark in 1904 and the Wolverines' 394 points were the most since 1905.

The Maize and Blue finished No. 2 behind Notre Dame in the final *Associated Press* poll taken at the end of the regular season. But after Michigan walloped Southern Cal in the Rose Bowl, the football public and many newspapers refused to accept the verdict. A Detroit paper canvassed sports editors from coast to coast, except in the State of Michigan, and the result was overwhelmingly in favor of the Wolverines. This prompted the AP to take another poll and in it U-M got top honors by a margin of almost 2-1.

United Press International (UPI), which did not have an official poll at that time, got into the act, and of all things, polled the Southern Cal players (who played against both teams). Twenty-two Trojans participated and voted 17-5 in favor of the Irish. (ND had defeated USC 38-7).

The controversy raged on and the *Atlanta Journal* even called for a "Super Bowl" match between the two teams to settle the issue. A clear-cut champion was never settled upon. Officially, the records of the AP list Notre Dame as national champions for 1947, with no asterisk or other acknowledgment of the post-Rose Bowl poll which Michigan captured.

ALL THE NEWS ALL THE TIME

Los Angeles Times

PART-A—PICTORIAL

VOL. LXVII   Ten Parts   C C   FRIDAY MORNING, JANUARY 2, 1948   Page A   PRICE 15 CENTS

GREAT THRONG SEES ROSE PARADE
Wolverines Wallop Troy in Rose Bowl, 49-0

JANUARY 1, 1902 — MICHIGAN...... 49, STANFORD..............0
JANUARY 1, 1948 — MICHIGAN...... 49, SOUTHERN CAL....0

MONDAY MORNING QUARTERBACK
Irish-Wolverine Super Bowl
Would Settle Individual Brawls

The Atlanta Journal — *January 5, 1948*
Long after the Rose Bowl game, the controversy over the nation's No. 1
team continued in headlines and stories all across the country. The
"Monday Morning Quarterback" of the Atlanta Journal *was Harry*
Mehre, former Notre Dame player and head coach at Georgia and Ole
Miss. Could it be that he was the first to use the name, "Super Bowl?"

1948

GAME 45

"ANYTHING YOU CAN DO, OSU, WE CAN TOO"

The story of Michigan's 1948 football season was, "undefeated, untied, undisputed champions. . . .and unable." Unable, that is, to play in the Rose Bowl. As Ohio State had done four years earlier, the Michigan Wolverines roared to the national championship and, in reaching the summit, had to chase down and overtake a gridiron giant, not once, but twice.

Michigan's exciting "Fall of '48" got underway on the fourth Saturday in September.

SEPT. 28 – U-M handed Michigan State its first defeat in an East Lansing home opener in 28 years with a hard-fought 13-7 victory. The Wolverines broke a 7-7 tie early in the fourth quarter on Tom Peterson's three-yard touchdown run, then held on to the disappointment of a record MSU crowd on hand to dedicate an enlarged Spartan Stadium. It was Michigan's 15th straight victory and the first *Associated Press* poll was a week away.

OCT. 2 – Oregon, the pre-season pick to win the Pacific Coast Conference, went to Ann Arbor with a hotshot quarterback named Norman Van Brocklin. Van's passing figures that day of 13-for-24 for 194 yards were impressive, but only second best. Michigan QB Charles Ortmann pitched for 217 yards on eight completions in 16 throws. Even though the Ducks came out ahead in yardage, 363-357, Michigan recorded second and third quarter touchdowns and repelled numerous Oregon threats to win 14-0. The first AP poll of the season was released the following Tuesday and Michigan was placed No. 7. Michigan supporters were enraged! After all, the Wolverines had reeled off 16 straight victories.

OCT. 9 – Purdue fell 40-0 at West Lafayette. U-M held the Boilermakers to only 36 yards rushing and 132 total yards and this one-sided win brought some attention. The second poll had North Carolina (and Charley "Choo-Choo" Justice) rated first, Notre Dame second, Northwestern third and Michigan in the fourth spot. Army and California were fifth and sixth.

OCT. 16 – In a big showdown between the No. 3 and No. 4-ranked teams at Ann Arbor, Michigan blanked Northwestern 28-0 by scoring three touchdowns in a three-and-a-half-minute span in the second half. It didn't matter that North Carolina beat N.C. State 14-0 or that Notre Dame popped Nebraska 44-13. The pollsters saw Michigan as the best and the Wolverines zoomed all the way to No. 1.

OCT. 23 – The No. 1 team went to Minneapolis and the No. 1 team was glad to get out of town still No. 1. Minnesota's tough Gophers led 7-0 in the second quarter and 14-13 in the third, but Dick Rifenburg scored with a 15-yard interception, and a 64-yard touchdown bomb from Ortmann to Leo Koceski got Michigan a 27-14 win to stay on top. It was the school's 400th all-time football triumph. Notre Dame defeated Iowa 27-12, North Carolina beat LSU 34-7, California blanked Washington 21-0 and Army dumped Cornell 26-7, and the top five teams remained the same.

OCT. 30– In a game that was rocking along 7-7 at Ann Arbor, Illinois' Dick Eddleman returned the second-half kickoff 94 yards for a touchdown that was called back for an offsides penalty. Michigan later moved in front 21-7 before the visitors pulled within 21-20, but a 39-yard scoring pass from Ortmann to Harry Allis in the fourth quarter sewed up a 28-20 game. Illinois, only 2-7-0 that year, outgained the winners 296-234. Everybody was out to knock off No. 1.

Michigan, unbeaten in 20 games, fell from the top. Notre Dame, unbeaten in 24 games, went to the top. The Wolverines definitely had their work cut out; they were now in the ring with the "Big Boy." The poll difference was only three points (1762-1759), but the Irish didn't care. They were back on top. The three other top teams also won: North Carolina 14-7 over Tennessee, Army 49-7 over VPI, and California 13-7 over Southern Cal.

The following Tuesday, Harry Truman pulled the year's biggest upset by beating Tom Dewey in the Presidential election. Michigan and Ohio could not even agree on a President, as Michigan went for Dewey, and Ohio for Truman.

NOV. 6 – Michigan 35, Navy 0 at Ann Arbor. It was the

winner's 21st straight win and the loser's 12th straight loss. Notre
Dame, although blasting Indiana 42-6 to keep its unbeaten streak
alive at 25, somehow fell to No. 2. The Wolverines were back on
top. North Carolina fell from contention after a 7-7 tie with
William and Mary, and with three weeks to go in the season, the
top five teams were Michigan, Notre Dame, Army, California and
Penn State.

NOV. 13– Michigan made Indiana its 22nd consecutive victim
by a 54-0 score. The Irish extended their unbeaten streak to 26
with a fourth-quarter touchdown to nudge Northwestern 12-7.
Now, the Wolverines had a big 231-point lead over Notre Dame
in the polls and a solid "We're No. 1." Army was third followed by
California, North Carolina and Penn State.

Meanwhile, Ohio State had beaten Missouri and Southern
California, lost to Iowa, beaten Indiana and Wisconsin, lost to
Northwestern, and beaten Pittsburgh and Illinois for a net 6-2-0
record. The Bucks were foaming at the mouth and fired sky-high
to knock Michigan out of a national championship.

NOV. 20 – Michigan vs. Ohio State at Columbus. One more
Wolverine win and the 1948 national championship would come
to rest in Ann Arbor.

Before 82,754 fans, the determined Buckeyes gave powerful
Michigan all it wanted and the Wolverines were more than happy
with a tough 13-3 win. The game's statistics reflect OSU's determination against the "best" team in the country. The Bucks got
more first downs, 11-9, and outgained the opposition, 203 yards
to 170.

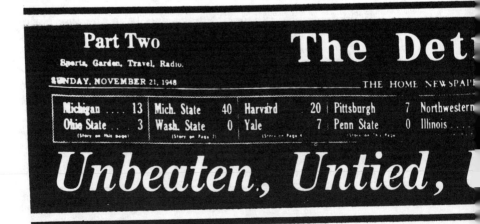

Part Two

Sports, Garden, Travel, Radio.

The Detr

SUNDAY, NOVEMBER 21, 1948

THE HOME NEWSPAPE

Michigan 13	Mich. State	40	Harvard	20	Pittsburgh	7	Northwestern
Ohio State .. 3	Wash. State	0	Yale	7	Penn State	0	Illinois ....
(Story on this page)	(Story on Page 2)		(Story on Page 4)		(Story on This Page)		

Unbeaten, Untied,

OSU scored first. Midway through the first period, the Bucks punted Michigan back to its 12-yard line. On first down, Peterson started a sweep and as he was hit tried to lateral to Ortmann, but the pitch was bad and Jack Lininger recovered for Ohio at the Wolverines' eight-yard line. Gerald Krall got nothing; an offsides penalty retreated the offense back to the 13; a pass was incomplete, and Hague kicked a field goal to give the Buckeyes a 3-0 lead.

In the second quarter, State drove to Michigan's 38, stalled and punted to the eight. An Ortmann pass was completed to Dick Rifenburg who collided with a game official and fumbled. Jimmy Clark recovered at the Michigan 22 and Ohio had another good opportunity. But the Wolverines meant business on this particular day and pushed the opposition back seven yards. This forced a punt that went out of bounds at the 10-yard line. Michigan's ball.

The 90 yards were covered in only five plays.

A pass interference call gave Michigan a first down at its own 43. Pete Elliott passed 13 yards to Ortmann at OSU's 44. On third-and-10, Ortmann hit Allis, who had gotten past the secondary, for a touchdown. Allis kicked the conversion and Michigan led 7-3.

It stayed that way until late in the fourth quarter when U-M put the game on ice. Starting from their own 38 after receiving a punt, Walter Teninga completed a 26-yard pass to Leo Koceski. Koceski was on the receiving end of another pass, this one from Elliott, for 13 more yards. Elliott then hit Rifenburg, good for 12 yards to the OSU 11. Koceski gained one, Teninga eight, and Peterson popped over from the two. The conversion was flubbed and the final score of 13-3 went down.

A week later, Notre Dame walloped Washington 46-0, and on December 4, the Irish scored with 35 seconds remaining to tie Southern Cal 14-14 and kept its unbeaten streak going at 28 straight.

In the season's final poll, the voters said Michigan was No. 1, Notre Dame No. 2, followed by North Carolina, California, Oklahoma, Army, Northwestern, Georgia, Oregon and SMU.

Because of the Big Nine's "no repeat" rule, Michigan was denied a Rose Bowl trip. Northwestern defeated Illinois 20-7 on the final Saturday to sew up second place and the bowl bid. The Wildcats' opposition was undefeated (10-0-0) California. The heavily-favored Golden Bears led 14-13 in the fourth quarter and had reached NU's 15. But the 'Cats held, took over and drove 85 yards for the winning touchdown with just over three minutes left in the game. The score was 20-14.

Michigan completed its second straight perfect season and had not lost since the fifth game of the 1946 season. It was the Wolverines' third "official" national championship (1932, 1933 and 1948) to go along with six other "unofficial" titles in 1901 through 1904, and in 1923 and 1947.

It had become a habit for Ohio State to go into the annual Michigan game with the Wolverines unbeaten (25 times). It was a habit about to be broken, and the Buckeyes would not have to face that situation again for 22 years.

1949

GAME 46

NOBODY LIKES A TIE? HA!

Even though Michigan and Ohio State entered their big game tied for the Big Nine lead with 4-1-0 records, it was not a battle for the Rose Bowl as such. The Wolverines were still locked out by a Conference rule that prohibited the same team from going to the bowl more than once in the first three years of the Big Nine-Pacific Coast Conference tie-up.

But for OSU, it was a different story. If the Buckeyes could beat Michigan, they'd go; if the Buckeyes tied, and if Minnesota could beat Northwestern the same day, the Buckeyes would still go.

After the first four weeks of the 1949 season, neither Michigan nor Ohio State gave much indication that they would later be playing for the Conference championship. The Wolverines were 2-2-0; the Buckeyes were 2-1-1.

The Wolverines opened up by edging Michigan State 7-3 and by belting Stanford 27-7. There had not been a loss on the football field by the Maize and Blue since October 26, 1946. The victory streak had reached 25 games and, like all streaks, was destined to end. Army did it, 21-7. The disappointed Wolves failed to recover in time for their next week's date with Northwestern and lost again, 21-20. It was the first time in 10 years that U-M lost games back-to-back.

OSU opened with a wild 35-34 win over Missouri and followed up by smothering Indiana 46-7. There was a 13-13 tie with Southern California and a shocking 27-0 loss to Minnestoa.

Michigan picked up the pieces and pinned Minnesota 14-7 while Ohio was dumping Wisconsin 21-0; Michigan blanked

Section **D**	SPORTS National, State and Local Amateur and Professional Events	**The Columbus Sunday Dispatch** OHIO'S GREATEST HOME NEWSPAPER	SPORTS Complete Football Scores, Pictures and Stories	Section **D**

COLUMBUS 16, OHIO   •••   SUNDAY, NOVEMBER 20, 1949   MAin 1234

STUDENTS, FACULTY, ALUMNI GET FIRST CRACK ($5.50) AT TICKETS FOR ROSE BOWL

ROLLICKING BUCKS SING 'CALIFORNIA HERE I COME'

Illinois 13-0 and Ohio beat Northwestern 24-7; Michigan popped Purdue 20-12 and Ohio got past Pittsburgh 14-10; Michigan defeated Indiana 20-7 and Ohio outscored Illinois 30-17.

OSU was 6-1-1 and ranked No. 7; U-M was 6-2-0 and ranked No. 5.

The Buckeyes tied Michigan (on a minor miracle), Minnesota defeated Northwestern, and the Roses belonged to Ohio State in 1949.

A minor miracle? Seven minutes remained in the game and Ohio was about to kick the conversion for a 7-7 tie. The boot was wide. But wait! Lying on the ground at the line of scrimmage was a flag. A penalty flag. A Michigan lineman was offsides and the Bucks had new life. Jimmy Hague, the kicker, got another chance also, and he made good this time to give Ohio State its "victorious" tie and the trip to Pasadena. The game was played before 97,239

The Columbus Sunday Dispatch

OHIO'S GREATEST HOME NEWSPAPER

COLUMBUS 16, OHIO   •••   SUNDAY, NOVEMBER 20, 1949   MAin 1234

Ohio Rooters Go Wild as Buckeyes Rally to Tie Michigan

BUCKS TIE WOLVES, SHARE TITLE; WIN ROSE BOWL BID

HOW THEY DID IT!

HOW WE DID IT!

The Detroit News
THE HOME NEWSPAPER FOR MORE THAN 74 YEARS · · · · · ·

Sports
Radio, Television, Financial, Fraternal
FOR BEST RESULTS . . . NEWS WANT ADS

Northwestern 9	Minnesota 14	Purdue 14	Notre Dame 28	California 33	Princeton 19	Pittsburgh 19	Oklahoma 28	Tennessee 6	Baylor 35
Illinois 7	Wisconsin 6	Indiana 6	Iowa 7	Stanford 14	Dartmouth 13	Penn State 0	Santa Clara 21	Kentucky 0	So. Methodist 26

7 | *Michigan Shares Title With OSU* | 7

California Qualifies to Face Buckeyes in Rose Bowl

at Ann Arbor, the largest crowd to see the two rivals square off up to that time.

Michigan scored early, on the second possession. OSU's Fred Morrison bobbled the snap from center on punt formation, couldn't get the kick away and the Wolverines took over at the enemy 44-yard line.

Quarterback Charles Ortmann opened the drive with an 11-yard pass to Harry Allis. Ortmann gained 10 more yards in two carries for another first down at the 23. Don Dufek drove for eight yards, then one. Ortmann was stopped cold. On fourth-and-one at the 14, Dufek rammed for three. Leo Koceski lost his footing and four yards. After two incomplete passes, it was fourth down at the 15. Walter Teninga faked a sweep to his right, leaped high and fired a perfect pass to Koceski in the corner of the end-

THE WEATHER
Windy and cold with
light snow
tonight.

Columbus Evening Dispatch
OHIO'S GREATEST HOME NEWSPAPER

VOL. 79, NO. 141 · · · · Telephone—MAin 1234   COLUMBUS 16, OHIO, MONDAY, NOVEMBER 21, 1949   40 PAGES   FIVE CENTS

NEW BUS FARE: 7 TICKETS FOR 50 CENTS

Court Sets Temporary Price; Nickel Ordinance Set Aside

(Continued on Page 5, Col. 1)

It's Official! OSU Goes to Rose Bowl

Bucks Unanimous
Choice of Big Ten
For Annual Classic

zone. Allis added the point-after. Michigan 7, Ohio State 0.

The Wolverines later reached Ohio's 22 and 18 but couldn't score as the first half ended with only one touchdown on the boards.

The Buckeyes came out storming to start the second half. They returned the kickoff to their 34 and in three plays were down to the U-M 14. Gerald Krall streaked 33 yards, Ralph Armstrong added nine, and Ray Hamilton hammered for 10 more. The Bucks were in great shape when disaster struck. Michigan's Charles Lentz intercepted a pass at the three-yard line and raced out to the 25. Michigan drove 64 yards but fizzled at the Bucks' 11.

Time ticked away and the scoreboard clock now showed 9:40 left to play. Michigan punted to sophomore Vic Janowicz who fielded the ball at his 36, dropped it, kicked it around, and finally recovered the bouncing ball himself back at the 20.

Here, Ohio State got off the canvas and drove for what amounted to 2,230 miles, the distance from Columbus to Los Angeles, for its "Rose Bowl Touchdown." Morrison burst through for 15 yards on first down. Krall got two, then 10 and a first down at the 47. Pandel Savic and Hamilton followed with Ohio's play of the game. Savic drilled a pass to Hamilton, who grabbed the ball at the Michigan 40 and raced goalward. He didn't quite make it, but he was close enough. Teninga bounced Hamilton out of bounds at the four-yard line. On the next play, Morrison struck to the one and then smashed over for the touchdown.

Hague missed the "California, Here We Come" kick. . . . Penalty flag. . . .Hague then got his kick. Seven minutes still remained, but this ball game was "over."

Nobody's ever satisfied with a tie? On November 19, 1949, Ohio State University and all of its football followers were deliriously happy with one. The entire State was upside down. It had, after all, been 29 years since their Buckeyes last went bowling. It was also the first time in five years not to be beaten by Michigan.

OSU registered more first downs than U-M, 14-11, but the total yardage figures went to the Wolverines, 288-231. For the second consecutive year it was a 10-0-0 University of California team awaiting the Big Nine's representative, and once again a heartbreaking defeat was suffered by the Golden Bears. OSU trailed 7-0 at the half and the third quarter ended 14-14. Late in the game, California flubbed a punt from its own 16, Ohio took over and Jimmy Hague kicked a game-winning, chip-shot field goal with less than two minutes left in the contest.

MIDWINTER NUMBER

Los Angeles Times

VOL. LXIX   IN SIX PARTS   PART A   C C   TUESDAY MORNING, JANUARY 3, 1950   244 PAGES   TWENTY-FIVE CENTS

OHIO STATE WINS BOWL GAME
Brilliant Rose Parade Awes Vast Throngs

The Buckeyes finished the season with a 7-1-2 record and a No. 6 national ranking. Michigan was 6-2-1 and got the No. 7 spot. Notre Dame, after its fourth straight undefeated season and with no losses in 38 games, won the 1949 national championship. Next came Oklahoma, California, Army and Rice, then the Buckeyes and Wolverines.

In the Michigan-Ohio State rivalry, the 1940's was the decade of the Wolverines. U-M won six, lost two and tied two and outscored the Bucks 232-85. Michigan also led in first downs 167-101; yards rushing 2100-1230; yards passing 1293-641, and total yards 3393-1871. The Wolves completed 84 of 195 passes (.431) while the Buckeyes completion percentage was only .298 (39-for 131). OSU's 38 turnovers were one more than by Michigan, and in penalty yards, U-M led 271-163. In the 1940s, Michigan's overall record was 74-15-3; Ohio State's 57-27-6. For their 10 dates, total attendance was 778,000 – 399,000 in Ann Arbor and 379,000 in Columbus.

After 46 Michigan-Ohio State games over a 52-year period, the Maize and Blue led 30-12-4 and held a point advantage of 810-343, or approximately 18-7 per game.

193

1950

DON'T BELIEVE IT IF YOU DON'T WANT TO

This is a true story, and here are the cold facts.

The Wolverines did not get a first down, gained only 27 yards rushing, were unable to complete any of their nine passes, and punted 24 times. Yet, they won the game.

In one of the freakiest football games *ever* played, the University of Michigan defeated Ohio State University. The score was 9-3 in a "game" played at Columbus on November 25, 1950. OSU faithful would like to forget the whole thing, but they can't; it was too nightmarish. The U-M people will never forget it even though hardly any were there to see it. They couldn't get to Columbus.

The day before the game the worst blizzard since 1913 paralyzed the Midwest, the Northeast and dipped as far South as Tennessee. Where it didn't snow, record-low temperatures gripped the entire Eastern half of the country.

"Those who could went on with the show, but Arctic blizzards stalled football, basketball and even hockey in various parts of the Nation," reported the *Associated Press*. The Pitt-Penn State game in Pittsburgh was postponed; at Knoxville, over 100 tons of snow were removed from the field for the Kentucky-Tennessee game; in Athens, Georgia, only 2,000 people braved windy, 12-degree temperatures for the Georgia-Furman game. All of the games in the East and Midwest were played on frozen fields and, in many cases, with snow on the ground or falling.

Until the big blizzard blew in on Friday, the sole topic of the sporting public around Columbus and elsewhere in Big Nine Country was: "Who is going to the Rose Bowl?" In possibly the

Empty seats at a Michigan-Ohio State football game are a sure sign of trouble somewhere. The trouble in 1950 was snow and ice. Headlines and photographs on the following pages complete the story of the worst weather disaster ever to affect a game in the series. (Photo courtesy of OSU Photo Archives.)

Absolutely the last word in
"THE SHOW MUST GO ON!"

most intriguing race in Western Conference history, four teams – Michigan, Ohio State, Wisconsin and Illinois – had a shot at the championship going into the season's final Saturday. The no-repeat rule knocked OSU from any bowl considerations, but there were all sorts of combinations of wins and losses and ties that could send the Wolverines, Badgers or Illini to California for New Year's.

But on Saturday morning, the sole topic of conversation was the weather. It couldn't be ignored, even on the day of Michigan vs. Ohio State.

The Buckeyes lost their season opener to SMU 32-27 before reeling off six straight wins (including an 83-21 smashing of Iowa), were averaging 39 points per game, and reached the No. 1 spot in the *Associated Press* poll – briefly – until Illinois knocked them off, 14-7.

By Michigan standards, the Wolverines were having a disastrous season. They lost to Michigan State; beat Dartmouth; lost to Army; beat Wisconsin; tied Minnesota; lost to Illinois, and beat Indiana and Northwestern.

The Buckeyes were 6-2-0 and the Wolverines 4-3-1 when the miserable day of their 47th meeting came. A total of 82,700 tickets had been sold for the game and, miracle of miracles, 50,503 made it through the turnstiles. It was, after all, Ohio State and Michigan. Just break out the foul-weather gear and supplies.

There was talk right up to the scheduled kickoff time about possibly postponing the game. The two athletic directors, Fritz Crisler of Michigan and Richard Larkins of Ohio State, made the decision to play after two lengthy discussions. They reasoned that if more than 50,000 people came out to see a ball game, it would be unfair to send them home.

By game time, the temperature was near zero and the snow was swirling about in the huge horseshoe, driven by 25-30 mile per hour winds whipping in from the Northwest. In other words, it was cold.

While officials were talking about play or no-play, several hundred workers struggled and suffered for almost two hours to remove the snow-packed tarpaulins covering the frozen field. A cheer went up as they finished and the announcement came that there would be a football game.

The game started only 30 minutes late. OSU kicked off and the afternoon of freak play was underway, with the Buckeyes jumping out to a quick lead. Michigan received and immediately punted. OSU couldn't move and Vic Janowicz, helped by the wind, got off a booming punt that rolled dead at the U-M six-yard line.

THE WEATHER

𝕮𝖔𝖑𝖚𝖒𝖇𝖚𝖘 𝕰𝖛𝖊𝖓𝖎𝖓𝖌 𝕯𝖎𝖘𝖕𝖆𝖙𝖈𝖍

OHIO'S GREATEST HOME NEWSPAPER

Associated Press
News, Features,
And Wirephotos

VOL. 80, NO. 148   Telephone—MAin 1234   COLUMBUS 16, OHIO, SATURDAY, NOVEMBER 25, 1950   14 PAGES   FIVE CENTS

OHIO PARALYZED BY BLIZZARD
Traffic Snarled, Trains, Buses Off Schedule

Michigan had to punt again and Ohio's Joe Campanella blocked it. Bob Momsen, whose brother Tony was playing for Michigan and would be heard from later in the game, recovered at the eight.

On first down, Janowicz got himself bottled up and kept retreating to avoid trouble, but in the process he got into more trouble. Hopelessly trapped in the snow back at the 29, he threw wildly and was called for intentionally grounding the ball. This cost OSU five more yards and the line of scrimmage was suddenly at the 34 – a 26-yard loss on one play! Janowicz got 13 of the lost yards back on a pass completion to Tom Watson, but that was all. Janowicz, standing at the 27, slammed a field goal through the blowing snow for three huge points and a 3-0 lead. Many observers felt the game had been won right there.

As play continued, neither team wanted the ball and just kept punting on first or second down. Michigan's Charles Ortmann finally got one out of bounds at the Ohio four. Janowicz went back to punt on first down but Michigan's right tackle, Al Wahl, blocked it. The ball shot out of the endzone for a safety. With 4:54 left in the first quarter, it was Ohio State 3, Michigan 2.

From that point on the Buckeyes stayed in deep trouble. Poor field position finally took its toll. Following the safety, OSU free-kicked from its own 20. On fourth-and-seven from its own 40, U-M's Ortmann punted to the Buckeye 14. Fourteen kick-backs later, Michigan won the game.

How much trouble did Ohio stay in? The facts are these: in the rest of the first half, the Bucks started from their own 10, 16, 15, 9, 14, 20 and 9. With just 47 seconds remaining before intermission, the Buckeyes were third-and-six at the 13-yard line and

The Columbus Sunday Dispatch
OHIO'S GREATEST HOME NEWSPAPER

Associated Press
News, Features,
And Wirephotos
International News Service

VOL. 80, NO. 149   ***   Telephone—MAin 1234   COLUMBUS 16, OHIO, SUNDAY, NOVEMBER 26, 1950   172 PAGES   PRICE

Nine-Inch Snow Sets Record; Blizzard Continues

Traffic Is Paralyzed By Storm

Winds To Lessen, Mercury Due to Rise a Little on Sunday.

WOLVES WIN ON BLOCKED KICKS

Big 10 Title Is Captured By Michigan

Blizzard Bowl

Michigan 27 0 0 0--9
Ohio State 3 0 0 0--3

SPECTATORS HUDDLE IN SNOW-FILLED SEATS ATOP C DECK IN FRONT OF PRESS BOX AS BUCKS AND WOLVES CLASH.

Worst Storm Since 1913 Sweeps Northern Ohio

Snow, Wind, Cold Leave Eight Dead; Business, Traffic Paralyzed. Tugboat Reaches Port. | Bad Storm Rips East Seaboard. | 'IF THE PEOPLE ARE UNHAPPY, IT'S MY FAULT,' DICK LARKINS ASSERTS

Part Two   **The Detroit News**   Sports

THE HOME NEWSPAPER FOR MORE THAN 77 YEARS

Miracle in Ice Bowl Puts 'M' in Rose Bowl

Janowicz was in punt formation. Tony Momsen blew in, blocked the kick and fell on it in the endzone. Touchdown! Harry Allis converted and the Wolverines led 9-3.

It was the eighth time in series history that a blocked punt had resulted in a score. It happened in the 1905, '11, '18, '19, '20 and '31 games, as well as twice in 1950.

As for the second half, Ohio got a big break on Michigan's first possession when Richard Anderson recovered a fumble at the Wolverines' 30-yard line. On third down from the 29, Oswald Clark intercepted a Janowicz pass and the threat passed. The remainder of the game saw punts, punts, punts and more punts. Plus, plenty of new snow. Newspaper accounts of the game reported that early in the fourth quarter it was impossible to see players on the field from the press area.

Two minutes before the game's end came the shocking news from Evanston that Northwestern had upset Illinois 14-7. This was the winning combination and the jubilant Wolverines became undisputed champions of the Big Nine and were going to the Rose Bowl, where it would be warmer. Wisconsin topped Minnesota 14-0, but Michigan's victory and the loss by Illinois were what counted.

The post-game scene in the winning dressing room was bedlam. Michigan coach Bennie Oosterbaan told the Press, "Imagine having a great team like Fesler (OSU coach Wes) had and then not being able to use it because of the conditions. Naturally, I'm happy to have won, but the conditions were such that it wasn't a fair test of football."

Fesler said, "You can't take a thing away from Michigan. We both faced the same conditions. I certainly agree with Bennie however, that it wasn't a test of gridiron skill."

For a consolation prize, OSU's Vic Janowicz was named to receive the Heisman Trophy in 1950. Kyle Rote of SMU was a distant second in the voting.

For the third consecutive year, the Big Nine Rose Bowl entry had to face an unbeaten University of California team, and for the third consecutive year a score late in the game did the Bears in. California led 6-0 with 5:37 remaining to be played. Michigan got a touchdown and PAT for a 7-6 lead. The Wolverines scored again when a Cal gamble backfired. Final: Michigan 14, California 6.

Since the two conferences agreed to their pact five years earlier, the combined records of the Coast teams going into the game

had been 46-1-2, compared to 34-8-3 for the Midwest visitors. But a PCC team was yet to win.

Michigan's down-the-stretch comeback in 1950 was phenomenal. As late as November 6, the Wolverines were a "losing" team with a 2-3-1 record, and had been outscored 75-73. Two months and four games later, Coach Oosterbaan and his charges had won the Big Nine and Rose Bowl championships, plus a No. 9 national ranking. These were achievements to savor, for it would be 14 years before another football title of any kind would come Michigan's way.

On the national scene, Oklahoma, Army, Texas, Tennessee and California were voted the top five teams in 1950.

As for the Wolverine-Buckeye wars, U-M now led 31-12-4. A new coach was coming to Columbus – a coach who would cut sharply into the Michigan winning margin, and who would become an institution in his own right.

Statistical highlights of one of the strangest games in college football history. The game was played in Columbus, Ohio, on Saturday, November 25, 1950.

	MICHIGAN	OHIO STATE
First Downs	0	3
Yards Rushing (Net)	27	16
Yards Passing	0	25
Total Yards Gained	27	41
Passing	0x9	3x18
Turnovers	1	3
No. of Punts*	24	21
Yards Penalized	25	30

*The two teams punted the ball almost 1,400 yards. Including all snaps of the ball, Michigan got off 71 plays, Ohio State 70.

The players who participated in that memorable "Snow Bowl"

MICHIGAN

Harry Allis .... End
Wesley Bradford .... Halfback
Oswald Clark .... End
Donald Dufek .... Fullback
Merritt Green .... End
Allen Jackson .... Guard
Thomas Johnson .... Tackle
Peter Kinyon .... Guard
Leo Koceski .... Halfback
Carl Kreager .... Center
Richard McWilliams ... Guard
Tony Momsen .... Center
Bill Ohlenroth .... Tackle
Don Oldham .... Halfback
Charles Ortmann .... Halfback
Russell Osterman .... End
Lowell Perry .... End
Bill Putich .... Quarterback
Ralph Straffon .... Fullback
Ralph Stribe .... Tackle
Robert Timm .... Guard
David Tinkham .... Fullback
Robert Wahl .... Tackle
James Wolter .... Guard

OHIO STATE

Richard Anderson .... End
John Blitz .... Guard
Fred Bruney .... Halfback
Joe Campanella .... Tackle
Tony Curcillo .... Quarterback
Robert Demmel .... Halfback
Richard Ellwood .... Quarterback
Lou Fischer .... Guard
Charles Gandee .... Fullback
Sherman Gandee .... End
Robert Grimes .... End
Ray Hamilton .... Halfback
Robert Heid .... Center
Vic Janowicz .... Halfback
Walter Klevay .... Halfback
Richard Logan .... Tackle
Jerry Manz .... Guard
Robert McCullough ..... Center
Robert Momsen .... Guard
Thor Ronemus .... Guard
Steve Ruzich .... Guard
Karl Sturtz .... Halfback
Bill Trautwein .... Tackle
Tom Watson .... End
Richard Widdoes .... Quarterback
Julius Wittman .... Tackle

With the infamous "Snow Bowl" only a fond memory, Coach Oosterbaan and his "M" men get a boisterous campus send-off to sunny southern California and the Rose Bowl. (Photo courtesy of Michigan Athletic Department)

MIDWINTER NUMBER

Los Angeles Times

| VOL. LXX | PART A | IN SIX PARTS | TUESDAY MORNING, JANUARY 2, 1951 | 240 PAGES | PRICE 35¢ |

SPECTACULAR ROSE PARADE THRILLS VAST THRONG
MICHIGAN RALLY BEATS CALIFORNIA IN BOWL, 14-6

1951

GAME 48

WOODY'S ARRIVAL

Three weeks after last year's infamous "Snow Bowl" in Columbus, Wes Fesler resigned as head coach at Ohio State. In January, OSU boosters began a concerted "We Want Brown Back" movement. Paul Brown did consider returning to the college game but decided that professional football was where he wanted to be. He stayed in Cleveland. The athletic board interviewed numerous candidates, including a dark horse whose name was Wayne Woodrow Hayes.

Hayes was hired.

The official signing came on February 18, 1951, just four days after his 38th birthday. Woody Hayes was born on Saint Valentine's Day.

Ohio State football, the Ohio State-Michigan football rivalry, and Big Ten football in general, would never be the same again, at least for the next three decades.

Woody Hayes was a Buckeye born and a Buckeye bred. He coached at two high schools and three colleges – all in Ohio. Upon graduation from Denison University, where he played tackle for three years, Hayes began his coaching career in 1935 as an assistant at Mingo Junction High School. After three years at MJHS, he became head coach at New Philadelphia High, where he stayed for three years before joining the Navy five months before the attack on Pearl Harbor in December 1941. He rose to the rank of lieutenant commander in the Navy and returned to civilian life in 1945. Hayes returned to his alma mater, Denison, as head coach for three years and moved on to Miami (Ohio) for two more

206

years. Hayes brought a 33-11-0 college coaching record with him to Columbus, where he became the 19th coach in OSU history and the fifth in the last 10 years.

Woody's first game at Ohio State resulted in a tough 7-0 win over SMU at Columbus on September 29. The following week his assignment was the No. 1-ranked team in the country – Michigan State, also at Columbus. The Buckeyes led 20-10 in the final period but MSU scored two quick touchdowns, the last one on a fourth-down, 27-yard pass. OSU lost that one, 24-20.

A 6-6 tie with Wisconsin and a 32-10 loss to Iowa followed and the Bucks were bungling along with a 1-2-1 record. Some outspoken alumni already were questioning Hayes' selection. A 47-21 trouncing of Iowa soothed the feelings for a while. The next three games saw a 3-0 win over Northwestern, an even closer win over Pittsburgh, 16-14, and an even closer match with Illinois – 0-0 – the only blemish on the Illini record that year. In one week, Woody would get his first *real* taste of "The Big One."

While Hayes was breaking-in at Ohio State (and Ohio State was breaking-in to Woody), coach Bennie Oosterbaan and his Michigan team were also having it rough. Very rough. The Wolverines lost to Michigan State 25-0 and then to Stanford 23-13. There were three straight wins; then three straight losses. Ohio State was 4-2-2; Michigan 3-5-0.

Opposing the weakest Michigan team in 15 years, the Buckeyes once again couldn't put it together when faced with the task of beating the Maize and Blue. U-M won a sloppily played, mostly dull 7-0 game before 95,000 fans and a national television audience of millions. The big crowd on November 24 at Ann Arbor welcomed the sunny, cool day, a dramatic improvement over last year's blizzard conditions.

By failing to score in the 1951 game, OSU could count a mere two touchdowns against Michigan in the last seven years.

The game statistics, along with the final score, suggest a close game. However, the listless Bucks' deepest penetration in the first half was to the Michigan 39-yard line. In the second half, they got no closer than the Wolverines' 24. Each team recorded 14 first downs and OSU led in total yards, 222-215. There were 12 turnovers in the game and Ohio led in that devastating department, 8-4. In addition to its lone touchdown, Michigan twice reached as deep as the Buckeye six but were stopped once by a fumble and once by an interception.

The "highlights" of the first quarter included Michigan's recovery of a Vic Janowicz fumble and a subsequent drive to the

*Woody Hayes became a part of the Columbus foot-
ball scene in 1951 and the Ohio State-Michigan
rivalry wouldn't be the same for the next 28 years.
(Photo courtesy of OSU Photo Archives.)*

OSU six-yard line, where Ted Toper threw an interception to George Russo. The period also produced an 11-yard Michigan punt and one for 10 yards by Ohio State.

The game's only score came on a 49-yard Michigan march in the second quarter after taking a punt. The drive included key pass completions of 14 and nine yards, both from Bill Putich to Toper. From the 11, Putich pitched one to Don ZanFagna, who leaped high in the air to make a circus catch. When he came down hard at the six, the ball popped free and Ohio recovered. But the officials said ZanFagna had retained possession until the play was dead, and it was still Michigan's ball.

"Ohio State" vehemently protested the call.

On the next play, "Ohio State" yelled even louder as Don Peterson scored on a sweep. There were claims of holding by more than one of the Michigan linemen. The score stood.

In just over one quarter of play, Woody Hayes had gotten into the spirit of the Buckeye-Wolverine rivalry.

Following the touchdown, Russ Rescorla converted to make it 7-0 and the scoreboard took a rest for the remainder of the afternoon.

Midway through the final period, OSU drove to Michigan's 24 but fumbled. They got the ball three more times but threw two interceptions and fumbled again. Late in the game, U-M got down to the Bucks' six, but dropped the ball. It didn't matter.

After 48 games in the series, Michigan now led 32-12-4 and had outscored Ohio State, 826-246. The Bucks' last victory was in 1944.

Unbeaten Illinois won the Big Nine championship and smothered Stanford 40-7 in the Rose Bowl for the Conference's sixth straight post-season victory. The Midwesterners had now scored 185 points to only 55 for the Pacific Coast Conference – an average score of 31-9 per game. The West Coast scribes showed signs of slipping into paranoia over the situation.

1952

GAME 49

U-M WAS SNIFFING ROSES

All of Ohio State's previous 12 wins over Michigan had been labeled "precious," to say the least. There had been so few. But the Buckeyes' 1952 series triumph had to be the sweetest by far up to that time. The Wolverines were on their way to a Big Nine championship and the Rose Bowl, but Woody Hayes and his troops ambushed their rivals in Columbus and inflicted a punishing 27-7 surprise.

What else could a Buckeye ask for? As one OSU booster put it, "It's more fun to knock those (expletive deleted) out of it than for us to win it!"

Scarlet and Gray fans, the vast majority of the 81,541 in attendance, roared and roared their uncontrollable delight.

Michigan and Wisconsin entered the season's final Saturday tied for the Conference lead, both with 4-1-0 records against Big Nine opponents. Purdue and Minnesota were hot on their heels at 3-1-1. Minnesota tied Wisconsin and had Michigan beaten OSU, all of the cookies would have belonged to the Wolverines. But it was not to be. While the two leaders were losing or getting tied in their finales, Purdue topped Indiana and slipped through the back door to tie the Badgers as co-champs. Wisconsin would get "the vote," and represented the Conference in the Rose Bowl.

Both Michigan and Ohio State came into their 49th meeting with 5-3-0 season records. The Maize had lost to Michigan State, Stanford and Illinois; the Scarlets to Purdue, Iowa and Pittsburgh. U-M was the betting favorite – anywhere from one to six or seven points, depending on the offeror's mood or condition. But even longer odds would have been vulnerable to eight (8) Michigan turnovers.

Ohio State turned its "B-B Boys" – Borton and Bruney – on Michigan that dank November 22. John Borton tossed three touchdown passes and scored one himself. Fred Bruney intercepted three Wolverine passes on a turf made soggy and slow by showers throughout the night.

At the start of the second quarter, the Bucks were on Michigan's six-yard line with a first down. Four straight smashes into the line netted only two yards and many were probably thinking, "Well, same old story. . . ." The Wolves punted out short – to their 26 – and this time OSU cashed in. Six plays advanced the ball down to the eight and Borton threw his first scoring pass, to Bob Joslin who made a great diving catch in the endzone between two defenders. Ohio had its first touchdown of the afternoon and only the third against Michigan in eight years. Thurlow Weed's kick was good for a 7-0 lead.

Exactly seven minutes later OSU had seven more points and a 14-0 advantage, again on a Borton-to-Joslin pass. This one was from 28 yards out to cap a seven-play, 60-yard drive following a Michigan turnover. Weed converted again.

With 19 seconds left in the first half, U-M reached OSU's 21-yard line but Bruney intercepted in the endzone to keep the Wolverines off the scoreboard.

Early in the second half, Ohio's Dick Doyle recovered a fumble by Ed Kress at the Michigan 20. In five plays the score climbed to 21-0. Borton, on a quarterback keeper, skipped in from the four for the score. Weed was on target again.

With just over eight minutes left in the game, George Jacoby picked off a Kress pass at the U-M 42. Six quick plays produced the touchdown as Borton hit Bob Grimes with a pass to cover the final 19 yards. The conversion was missed, but Ohio State had its first four-touchdown lead over Michigan in 17 years.

The Wolverines kept a whitewash off the record books with a score late in the game. Starting at the OSU 29, U-M pieced together a 10-play march ending with a two-yard TD run by Frank Howell. Russ Rescorla kicked the point and the 27-7 went up.

Both teams ran 68 plays and the Wolves led in first downs 14-12, and total yards 322-271, but hardly any team can overcome eight turnovers – even Michigan.

The "Fall of '52" was not a good year for Western Conference football. Only once before in the league's 56-year history had its teams lost more games to non-conference opponents than were

The "happy Buckeyes" shown in the Dispatch *photo are George Rosso (47), Marts Beekley (48), Dick Thomas (90), George Jacoby (73), Bill Vavroch (79), Capt. Bernie Skvarka (who missed the season due to an injury), Coach Hayes and Tony Curcillo (25).*

won. The 8-12-2 performance came in for much coffee break discussion and commentary by sports journalists around the U.S.

While the University of Michigan was left out in the football cold in 1952, the State of Michigan wasn't. Michigan State swept everything in sight and captured the end-of-season No. 1 spot in the AP ranking, and the title of national champions.

To underscore the unprecedented poor performance of the Big Nine in intersectional competition in 1952, Wisconsin had to go and lose in the Rose Bowl. Southern Cal came through to break the streak of six losses by Pacific Coast Conference teams. It was only a 7-0 victory but it was desperately needed therapy in the nick-of-time for West Coast sportswriters.

1953

GAME 50

COLOR THE GOLDEN
GAME MAIZE & BLUE

If there could be any such thing as a Michigan-Ohio State football game being played "just for fun," then the 1953 game was played just for that reason. No championship or Rose Bowl bid was on the line. In fact, not even a runnerup position was at stake.

But did that matter? Not at all! Over 20,000 Buckeyes made the trek from Columbus and the biggest crowd of the year – 90,126 – assembled at Ann Arbor on November 21 to see the big boys fight it out in the rivalry's Golden Anniversary game – the 50th meeting between the two old war horse teams.

The Bucks were 6-2-0 with losses to Illinois and Michigan State. Michigan broke fast from the September gate with four impressive wins in a row. Then the bottom fell out and the Wolverines lost three of their next four games.

Ohio State had two super running backs – Bob Watkins and a future Heisman Trophy winner, Howard "Hopalong" Cassidy. OSU's well-balanced offense had averaged 322 yards per game (195 rushing, 127 passing) and this, coupled with Michigan's miserable showing during the last half of the season, made the Buckeyes solid favorites to get two victories in a row over the Wolverines.

It didn't work out that way. Michigan stormed onto the field keyed to just the right pitch. Their 70,000 or so rooters were sky-high, too. If the Buckeyes didn't realize at that point that they were in trouble, they soon discovered the real truth. The visitors never had a chance and were literally run into the ground, by a 20-0 score, as the Wolves salvaged some revenge for the 20-point licking they had taken in Columbus last year.

Michigan did not allow OSU within 30 yards of its goal until the fourth quarter when the game was safely tucked away. On offense, the mean Wolves riddled Ohio's defense for 285 yards rushing and "threw-in" 19 more yards just for the heck of it.

Just as OSU had turned its "B-B Boys" (Borton and Bruney) on U-M last year, the Wolverines came back in 1953 with its own version of the "B's," only one better. Their "B-B-B Boys" – Balzhiser, Baldacci and Branoff– scored 14 of the game's 20 points.

U-M began its first scoring drive on the last play of the first quarter from the OSU 40. With Richard Balzhiser doing most of the running, the ball was advanced to the OSU one-yard line where it was first-and-goal. On second down, Balzhiser bulled over. Louis Baldacci added the conversion and underdog Michigan was on top 7-0.

Three minutes later Michigan scored again. Balzhiser intercepted a John Borton pass at the Buckeye 39 and Tony Branoff later scored from the six. Baldacci's conversion was off the mark and the half ended 13-0.

Near the end of the third quarter, Tad Stanford intercepted another Borton aerial at the line of scrimmage and returned it 13 yards to the OSU two. Danny Cline scored from there and Baldacci's kick gave U-M the 20th and final point.

In the fourth quarter, Ohio recovered a fumble at the Michigan 23 but were held for downs at the 16. The losers later got down to the 33 and 25 but were denied anything that would have been constructive.

Watkins and Cassidy rushed for over 1400 yards in 1953 but on this particular day, Michigan had their number. The Wolverines got 15 first downs, OSU 10, and the winners also led in total yards, 304-202, plus penalty yards, 74-10.

Ohio State wound up fourth in the Conference and Michigan's seventh place finish was its lowest in 17 years.

After 50 games of this great rivalry, the Wolverines led 33-13-4 and in total points, 853-373.

For the first time since 1939, the Western Conference was once again the "Big Ten." Michigan State had been officially accepted into the elite circle in 1949 but this was the Spartans' first year of eligibility for league honors. So, what did the brand new member do to impress their colleagues? Michigan State finished No. 3 in the Nation behind Maryland and Notre Dame and won a share of the Conference championship (with Illinois). Then the Spartans carried the proud old family crest to the Rose

214

Bowl and came from a 0-14 deficit to lick UCLA 28-20.

Actually, the Conference was well aware of this smart aleck new brother. The Spartans had beaten Michigan four years in a row and had also taken care of Ohio State the last two times they met. It was a high-riding period for MSU.

1954

BUCKEYES GO 99.67 YARDS, BAG A NATIONAL CROWN

This was a classic. A genuine classic. And the entire country saw it via the relatively new magic of black and white television. One of the participants, Ohio State, was not only atop the Big Ten standings, but was also rated No. 1 in the national polls. The other participant, Michigan, was not nearly as well off, but the winner still would automatically go to the Rose Bowl, giving the events of the day even more dramatic qualities.

Two minutes remained in the third quarter and the No. 1 ranked team in the country had been kicked around and ripped apart all afternoon, although the score was only 7-7. Michigan was first down at the Buckeye four. At that precise moment in the game, the Wolverines had 213 total yards, OSU only 69.

Three running plays produced almost four yards. It was fourth down and the Wolverines were on the one-foot line. The next play gained six inches which left Michigan six inches short. The TV announcers were telling their audiences, "This is a game of inches, folks."

The story immediately got more intriguing.

Ohio State took over and drove 99 yards, two feet and six inches in 11 plays to go out front. The Buckeyes scored again with just seconds left in the game for an incredible 21-7 victory, a Big Ten title, a trip to California for New Year's and a national championship – all because Michigan couldn't get four yards in four plays, or even one foot in one play.

Woody Hayes was in his fourth year at OSU and his dynamic presence was now being felt by the rest of the Conference. Michigan was squirming the most. The big season unfolded. . . .

SEPT. 25 – OSU 28, Indiana 0, at Columbus. It was the Buckeyes' season opener and win No. 1 gave them a ranking of No. 14. The top five teams after the second weekend of the season were Notre Dame, Oklahoma, Iowa, UCLA and Wisconsin.

OCT. 2 – OSU 21, California 13, at Columbus. The Bucks held a slim 14-13 lead in the fourth quarter before Howard "Hopalong" Cassady's interception set up an insurance touchdown that he scored himself. OSU cracked the top ten; they were voted 10th. Notre Dame lost to Purdue 27-14, Oklahoma topped TCU 21-16, Iowa mashed Montana 48-6, UCLA edged Maryland 12-7, and Wisconsin beat Michigan State 6-0. It was now the Sooners' turn to move to the front of the pack, followed by UCLA, Wisconsin, Iowa and Purdue as the Big Ten placed three teams in the top five.

OCT. 9 – OSU 40, Illinois 7, at Champaign. Ohio moved up six notches, all the way to fourth. The top five teams all had close calls, one way or the other. It was Oklahoma over Texas 14-7; UCLA over Washington 21-20; Wisconsin over Rice 13-7; Iowa under Michigan 13-14 and Purdue even with Duke 13-13. The ratings now read: Oklahoma, Wisconsin, UCLA, Ohio State and Purdue.

OCT. 16 – OSU 20, Iowa 14, at Columbus. In a real thriller, the Bucks drove 64 yards in the third quarter to break a 14-14 tie and then stopped the Hawkeyes on the five-yard line with 1:52 left to play. Oklahoma stayed No. 1 with a 65-0 clobbering of Kansas; Wisconsin remained No. 2 by beating Purdue 20-6; UCLA did not move from No. 3, despite a 72-0 slaughter of Stanford; OSU continued No. 4, and Ole Miss moved to No. 5.

OCT. 23 – OSU 31, Wisconsin 14, at Columbus. In a battle between the No. 2 Badgers and the No. 4 Buckeyes, Ohio trailed 7-3 until late in the third quarter when Cassady intercepted a pass and returned it 88 yards for a touchdown. Ohio scored three more touchdowns in the next nine minutes. And now it was "WE'RE NO. 1!" for Buckeye rooters. Oklahoma fell to No. 2 after an unimpressive 21-0 win over Kansas State. UCLA bombed Oregon 61-0 and remained No. 3. The Uclans had played one more game than OSU and were smothering the opposition by an average score of 44-7. The Bucks' games were averaging 28-10. Undoubtedly, the coaches of the country were impressed by the Bruins' high scores. In 1954, *United Press International* (UPI) entered the poll business by soliciting votes of a panel of coaches. UCLA topped their list.

For the remainder of the season, the race for No. 1 was reduced to choosing among the Buckeyes, Bruins and Boomer Sooners.

OCT. 30 – OSU 14, Northwestern 7, at Evanston. Ohio State escaped this near-disaster with a fourth period TD to snap a 7-7 tie. The struggle didn't go unnoticed by the pollsters who dropped OSU to second place. UCLA's 27-6 romp past California shot the Uclans to the top of both the AP and UPI polls. Oklahoma got by Colorado 13-6 and fell another step to third.

NOV. 6 – OSU 26, Pittsburgh 0, at Columbus. No problem, but the Bucks remained No. 2 as UCLA walloped Oregon 41-0 and Oklahoma dumped Iowa 40-0.

NOV. 13 – OSU 28, Purdue 6, at West Lafayette. UCLA had an open date and, for all practical purposes, it cost them the AP national championship. OSU was voted back on top by the writers and sportscasters. Oklahoma's 34-14 win over Missouri kept the Sooners third. The UPI poll listed UCLA-OSU-OU, 1-2-3.

While the exciting battle for No. 1 was going on in Buckeye-land, Michigan's football followers were watching grimly. The Wolverines opened with a 14-0 win over Washington but lost to Army 26-7. Two squeakers followed– 14-13 over Iowa and 7-0 over Northwestern. A 34-0 rout against Minnesota gave the surging Wolves a 4-1-0 record. But then came a stunning upset and at the same time a damaging Conference loss, 13-9, to an Indiana team that won only two other games that year. Coach Bennie Oosterbaan righted his listing ship with victories over Illinois 14-7, and Michigan State 33-7. It was U-M's first success against the Spartans since 1948.

NOV. 20 – Ohio State vs. Michigan. UCLA vs. Southern Cal. Oklahoma vs. Nebraska.

Football fever in Ohio had never been so red hot when that wet, cold November day arrived, and the 51st meeting with Michigan loomed. Inside the great horseshoe stadium were 82,348 screaming fanatics, every swinging one intoxicated with excitement. Thousands more were outside the high gray walls clamoring for a miracle, namely a little piece of cardboard bearing the words, "Admit One." As time ticked down to kickoff, and the last ticket had been gobbled up, the mass of disappointed fans scattered in all directions for the nearest TV sets.

By game time the steady drizzle that fell on the city all morning had stopped. Big tarpaulins that covered the playing area were all that prevented a mud battle.

Michigan returned the opening kickoff out to its 32-yard line and this classic duel was on. The Wolverines came out in a weird offensive formation that thoroughly confused the Bucks and kept them perplexed for a good portion of the game. The surprise was an unbalanced line that had just one player, a tackle, on the left side of the center. Anyway, on the game's first scrimmage play, Dan Cline burst for 27 yards to OSU's 41. Ten plays later the Wolves were fourth down at the enemy seven and on a razzle-dazzle with three players touching the ball, Cline scored. Ron Kramer kicked good. Underrated Michigan 7, undefeated Ohio State 0.

Michigan continued to dominate the game and in the second quarter staged an offensive drill that carried 78 yards to the Ohio 14. The "Series 500," as U-M called its special formation, bogged down and Kramer's field goal try sailed off harmlessly to the left.

Just before the halftime break, Ohio still had not moved past Michigan's 48 but a big break fell its way and the game was tied. Jack Gibbs, who was not even listed in OSU's football brochure, intercepted a James Maddock pass and streaked 45 yards down to the Wolverines' 10. A delay penalty cost the offense five yards, but Bill Leggitt promptly hit Fred Kriss with a touchdown pass. Thurlow Weed, the littlest man in a football uniform that day at 5-5 and 145 pounds, kicked the conversion for a 7-7 score.

At intermission, Michigan had run 40 plays to Ohio's 19 and was leading in first downs, 11-4. Even though the score was tied, the Buckeyes' side was worried sick.

Michigan kept applying the pressure and late in the third period marched 69 yards to OSU's 21. There, Fred Baer fumbled and Hubert Bobo recovered for the Bucks. Four plays later, however, Bobo's punt was partially blocked by Kramer. The ball shot straight up in the air and was fielded at the line of scrimmage by U-M end Tommy Maentz who returned to the Ohio 14.

When Michigan moved to a first-and-goal at the four-yard line, Ohio State's chances ranged from slim to none.

Fullback Dave Hill rammed it to the three. Cline crashed the line and came away with nothing. Hill hammered out three more yards down to the one-foot line. It was fourth down. Once again Hill got the call and slammed into the mass. But 248-pound Jim Parker and 200-pound Jim Reichenbach, together, slammed into the 188-pound Hill. The 448 pounds won. Dave Hill didn't make it. He was six inches shy. Literally. Six inches shy!

On a scale of 1 to 10, excitement in Ohio Stadium registered 11.

The Bucks took possession and quarterback Leggitt punched

WEATHER
Cloudy, cooler Sunday, high
45. Partly cloudy, cool
Monday, high 48.
(Weather Map on Page 10-D)

Columbus Sunday Dispatch

OHIO'S GREATEST HOME NEWSPAPER

SECTION A

ASSOCIATED PRESS NEWS
FEATURES, WIREPHOTOS
International News Service

VOL. 84, NO. 144   •••   Telephone—CApital 1-1234   COLUMBUS 16, OHIO, SUNDAY, NOVEMBER 21, 1954   214 PAGES   PRICE 15 CENTS

'CALIFORNIA, HERE WE COME'

Fighting Buckeyes Come From Behind To Victory Over Wolverines, 21 to 7

Tide of Battle Turns After Goal Line Stand

"THE DAY THEY TORE THE GOAL POSTS DOWN"

for three yards and then six as the third quarter came to a close. Everybody, including the players and coaches, welcomed a timeout to recapture some lost sanity. When play resumed, it was third-and-one at the nine and Leggitt pushed forward for two yards and a first down.

Boom!

Cassady burst through the left side of the line, sped past the secondary, angled back to the right and away Mr. Hopalong went . . . .25-30-35-40-45-50-45-40. . . .to be finally forced out of bounds at the Michigan 37.

Ohio State had clawed its way out of disaster.

It was Leggitt to the 32 and Bobo to the 24 and a first down. Bobo went to the 18, Leggitt to the 16, Leggitt to the 11 (another first down) and Leggitt to the nine. Leggitt then faded to his left and retreated back to the 20, spotted Carl Brubaker open and rifled a pass that was on target for a touchdown.

Pandemonium!

With 10:57 left in the game, Weed added another point and the score was, somehow, Ohio State 14, Michigan 7.

Stunned and shocked, the Wolverines couldn't get going against the wildman Buckeye defense. They had a chance with just over three minutes to go, after recovering an OSU fumble at their own 45. But two plays later, Cassady let his presence be known again with an interception of a long pass that was returned 13 yards to the Buckeye 39. Bobo's 24-yard dash sparked a quick drive to the one, and Cassady scored just 44 seconds from the end. Weed's conversion made it final and very much official, 21-7.

"Even the steel goalposts, solidly imbedded in massive chunks of concrete, came down," reported Lyall Smith of the *Detroit Free Press*. "Thousands of fans swept out onto the sodden grass and snakedanced through the Michigan band which was tooting away with vim, vigor and a leaden lump in its collective stomach. Downtown hotel managers hurriedly rushed every breakable, smashable item out of their lobbies as a football city started to quiver with an excitement which would carry every thing before it just as Ohio's gridders had done to nine straight opponents in this championship season."

The final stats showed Michigan leading in first downs 15-13, yards rushing 229-192, yards passing 74-58 and total yards 303-254. All but 93 of OSU's 254 yards came on the two fourth quarter scoring drives. Cassady was the leading ground gainer with 94 yards in 14 carries.

221

A Foot to Go, but Like 2,500 Miles to M

Ohio Marches 99 Yards, 2 Feet
Into the Rose Bowl

Detroit Free Press

The 1954 Buckeyes became only the second team in Western Conference history to win seven league games in one season. The University of Chicago had done it in 1905 and 1913.

The AP national champions – Ohio State. The UPI national champions – UCLA. And the two would meet in a college "Super Bowl" at Pasadena, right? Wrong. This was the first year of a "no repeat" rule adopted by the Pacific Coast Conference and UCLA had been to the Rose Bowl last year. Runnerup Southern Cal went instead and got roughed up by the Buckeyes, 20-7, in the rain and mud.

Ohio State finished 10-0-0 and had won its second national championship in the last 10 years. Buckeye fans of age will *never* forget their 1954 football team, the first OSU team to win as many as 10 games in one season.

1955

WILD AND CRAZY

As comedian Steve Martin would say, "This was a *wild* and *crazy* game."

Ohio State turned Howard "Hopalong" Cassady loose and the leading Heisman Trophy candidate keyed a 17-0 victory over the Wolverines before a then-record Michigan Stadium crowd of 97,369. For the Scarlets, it was their first win in Ann Arbor since 1937. It was Michigan's 600th all-time football game and only its 132nd loss.

Besides the final score and the absolute and complete shutdown by OSU of Michigan's offense, the highlight of this game came in the last two minutes of play. It was not determined what kind of record might have been established, but it had to be some kind of record.

Ohio had just scored a safety and led by the odd score of 11-0. It seemed, somehow, appropriate. Ron Kramer's "free kick" from the 20-yard line traveled a distance of one yard and the Buckeyes took possession on Michigan's 21. (A one-yard kickoff?). The following is a play-by-play account of the weird ending to that weird 1955 Michigan-Ohio State football game:

• Don Southerin gained eight yards. The play was nullified by offsetting penalties. First-and-10 at the 21.

• Cassady gained six. Second-and-four at the 15.

• Frank Ellwood gained six. But OSU was hit with a 15-yard personal foul penalty. Second-and-19 at the 30.

• Ellwood gained 10. Michigan was penalized to the six-yard

line, personal foul. First-and-goal.

- Before the next play could be run, Michigan was penalized again, this time for unsportsmanlike conduct. First-and-goal at the one.
- While OSU was in the huddle, the same penalty was called again against the Wolverines and two were ejected from the game. First-and-goal at the 18-inch line.
- Don Vicic scored the game's final touchdown. The conversion was flubbed.
- OSU kicked off and Ed Hickey returned it to his own 42. A personal foul penalty against Ohio put the ball at the Buckeye 43 – Michigan's only visit past midfield all day! First-and-10.
- Michigan completed a pass but offsetting personal foul penalties nullified the play. First-and-10.
- Terry Barr ran 11 yards. The play was called back on a Michigan holding penalty. First-and-22 at the U-M 45.
- OSU was penalized five yards for delay of the game when their fans roared onto the field. First-and-17 at the 50.
- Michigan threw an incomplete pass. Second-and-17 at the 50.
- Jim Van Pelt gained seven yards but the play was called back by a personal foul penalty. Second-and-32 at the 35.
- Michigan ran two more plays without "incident" and the game ended.

During all of this "foul play," the officiating crew was pelted with snow balls gathered from the remains of a three-inch snowfall, scraped into piles beyond the boundary lines. As the game ended, the fans took over and boisterous behavior was the order of the moment. Buckeye fans ripped down both goal posts and there were numerous "skirmishes" occurring on the playing area and along the snow-covered sidelines.

It was a wild finish to a wild afternoon of football.

Ohio State went to Ann Arbor with two losses—both outside the Conference (6-0 to Stanford, 20-14 to Duke). The Bucks were 6-2-0 overall and 5-0-0 in Big Ten play. Michigan was 7-1-0 and ranked No. 6 in the Nation. The lone loss was to Illinois, and the Wolverines were 4-1-0 in Conference action.

The 1955 game also had its Rose Bowl ramifications. The Buckeyes were locked out due to the "no repeat" rule. By winning, Michigan would automatically get the bid. A Michigan loss and the Wolverines' other big rival, Michigan State, would get the nod. As things turned out, U-M's own ineptness against OSU sent

HOWARD "HOPALONG" CASSADY

His 52-yard run in the fourth quarter set up the winning touchdown in the Buckeyes' incredible win over Michigan in 1954. Cassady would win the Heisman Trophy a year later. (Photo courtesy of OSU Photo Archives.)

MSU to the Rose Bowl. It was a galling experience for Michigan boosters from virtually every standpoint.

Midway through the second quarter, Cassady (29 yards) and Vicic (22 yards) paced a 70-yard drive to Michigan's seven where OSU had to settle for a field goal by Fred Criss. The half ended 3-0 and the Buckeyes had not let U-M any closer than 59 yards from their goal.

In the third period, Michigan once again stopped Ohio down close, this time at the eight. The Wolves punted out but OSU drove back for 52 yards in 10 plays and the game's first touchdown. Cassady scored on a two-yard plunge. The conversion was missed and the score was 9-0.

Paul Michael tackled Barr in the endzone for two points and the 11-0 lead as the game was drawing to a close. Kramer's one-yard kickoff followed and the "fun" began. On the game's final 15 plays, a total of 12 rules infractions were called (six on each team) and the officials mounted their own offensive show to the tune of 85 yards.

Columbus Sunday Dispatch

OHIO'S GREATEST HOME NEWSPAPER

SECTION A

VOL. 65, NO. 143 ••• Telephone—CApital 1-1234 COLUMBUS 16, OHIO, SUNDAY, NOVEMBER 20, 1955 212 Pages 15 Cents—Pay No More

Bucks Whitewash Michigan, 17-0; Win Big 10 Title

The final figures clearly show it was a Michigan day of futility and frustration on the football field. The Bucks led in first downs 20-5, and in total yards 337-109. In penalty yards, the losers led 70-60. Woody Hayes' "three yards and a cloud of dust" philosophy was beginning to surface in 1955. His Buckeyes threw three token passes against Michigan and completed one for four yards. That completion was the team's first successful pass play in three games. For the season, Woody's team averaged only six tosses and two completions for 18 yards per game. The running game, on the other hand, produced 278 yards per outing.

Despite two straight series setbacks, Michigan's lead over Ohio was still a comfortable 33-15-4 and the point differential was 860-411.

For Cassady, who would be the winner of the Heisman Trophy by an overwhelming vote total, it was the finish of a fabulous four-year career. Cassady gained 2466 yards rushing in 435 carries (5.7 average), caught 43 passes for 619 yards, returned 42 kickoffs of 681 yards (16.2), returned 35 punts for 340 yards (9.7), and ran back 10 intercepted passes for 210 yards. He also completed three passes in 13 attempts. It all added up to 4380 total yards. Furthermore, Cassady's 37 touchdowns set a Big Ten record that would stand for the next 20 years. He and his classmates were 3-1-0 against Michigan. *Sports Illustrated,* in its second year of publication in 1955, pictured Cassady on the cover of the October 24 issue.

The Buckeyes finished the season with a No. 5 national ranking behind Oklahoma, Michigan State, Maryland and UCLA.

Michigan's Rose Bowl gift to Michigan State resulted in a thrilling 17-14 Spartan victory over UCLA. State won on a 41-yard field goal with seconds left in the game as the Big Ten made it nine-out-of-ten against the PCC.

1956

GAME 53

MICHIGAN REMEMBERED

Four major college teams were slapped with NCAA probation for recruiting violations in 1956 and among the unfortunate four was Ohio State. Also grounded were California, Southern California and North Carolina State. The punishment periods varied, and OSU's was one year. The major effect of the probation was that should the Buckeyes win the Big Ten crown, as many expected them to do, they would be prohibited from representing the Conference in the Rose Bowl. Developments on the football field made it a moot issue.

Ohio started strong with resounding victories over Nebraska (34-7), Stanford (32-20), and Illinois (26-6). After a 7-6 loss to Penn State, OSU came back with three more wins, over Wisconsin 21-0, Northwestern 6-2, and Indiana 35-14. Then came a big showdown in Iowa City against league-leading Iowa. The Hawkeyes beat the Buckeyes 6-0 to break Ohio State's record-setting Conference win streak at 17. It is still a record.

Michigan and UCLA scheduled a first-ever meeting to open the season and the Wolverines walloped the Bruins 42-13. The next week, Michigan State visited at Ann Arbor and 101,001 packed the again-enlarged bowl. They saw the Spartans throw a 9-0 cloak over the Wolves. A 48-14 win over Army and a 34-20 conquest of Northwestern followed. Minnesota then caused the cancellation of any Rose Bowl reservations any Michigan hopefuls might have made. The tough Gophers, who lost only one game, won over the Wolverines, 20-7. Michigan bounced back and handed Iowa its lone defeat of the season 14-13, after trailing

13-0. A 49-26 warmup with Indiana came next and the Wolverines were more-than-ready for Ohio State. It was a game they had pointed to for a year. At Columbus, the Buckeyes were primed for their third straight win over Michigan, and their fourth in the past five years.

On paper the two teams were virtually even. Both had 6-2-0 records. OSU had outscored all opponents by 98 points; the Wolverines by 91. Michigan was averaging 336 yards per game (227 rushing, 109 passing), while the Buckeyes' average was 320 yards (286 rushing, 34 passing).

There was one big difference in 1956 and it wasn't on paper. The big difference was that Michigan remembered 1955 and the penalty-plagued, fight-infested fiasco with the Buckeyes in Ann Arbor. The Wolverines came out spittin' fire, scoring two quick touchdowns. Vicious defensive play thwarted Ohio's only serious threat, when the game was still very much in doubt, and Michigan walked away a 19-0 winner.

The game attracted 82,223 to Ohio Stadium and only the Michigan rooters had reason to jump around and yell to help them stay warm. The Buckeye faithfuls could do nothing but sit there and shiver in the 28-degree weather, made even more bitter by steady 15-20 mile per hour winds and nothing heartwarming on the field.

Ohio State won the toss and elected to go with the wind instead of the ball. The press (after the game) made a big deal over that decision, saying that Woody Hayes blew the game by not taking the ball first. For example, the *Detroit News* said, "Those who play with football fire get burned. In a strange gamble, Ohio State chose to kick off to Michigan today and that's where Ohio State lost to an aroused team."

Michigan took the opening kickoff and went 77 yards in a scoring drive that required 14 plays and almost six minutes. The touchdown came on a pass covering 21 yards. James Van Pelt threw to Terry Barr, who faked past one defender, broke what seemed like a sure tackle and raced down the sidelines for the big six. Ron Kramer's conversion was good for a 7-0 lead.

On the ensuing kickoff, Michigan's Tom Maentz streaked in and hit Jim Rosenboro with a bone-jarring tackle that separated him from the ball. Van Pelt recovered at the OSU 27. This time the Wolves couldn't make it pay off and had to punt. Rosenboro fumbled again and Barr fell on it at Ohio's nine. On fourth down from the three, Barr faded to pass, saw daylight and ran it in. The

PAT attempt was missed, but after only nine minutes of action, mean Michigan led, 13-0.

In the third period, the Buckeyes marched to the U-M two-yard line, but couldn't push it over. Was it the turning point of the game? A score here would have put OSU within striking distance, and with momentum. It was just another item for the agenda at coffee breaks for the next 12 months.

There were just over five minutes left to play when U-M's Jim Pace broke free for a 46-yard gain to the enemy 28. Jim Maddock then connected with Pace for a 24-yard aerial pickup to the four, and three plays later, Maddock scored. Kramer again missed the conversion but few, if any, Michigan fans cared.

Michigan showed its contempt for Ohio's passing game and, for the most part, stacked up a nine-man line to challenge the Bucks' rugged running reputation. Ohio State failed to take the bait and played its own game, attempting only four passes all day and completed one for a 10-yard gain.

"Today the Wolverines embarrassed Ohio enough that a chant began among Ohio loyalists: 'Good-bye, Wood-die. Good-bye, Wood-die,' " reported Harry Stapler of the *News*.

The Wolverines threw 21 times and completed 10 for 156 yards. They rushed for 127 more for a 283-yard game. OSU had 192 yards – 95 percent of it by running. First down totals were in favor of the winners, 14-12, as well as penalty yards, 25-10.

In the quiet of the Ohio dressing quarters, Hayes defended his pre-game decision to kick off. He told the reporters, "Choosing to kick off was not much of a gamble when we did it. The wind was at our backs and we figured it would equalize things even if Michigan did get first crack at the ball. The wind was blowing hard at game time and we figured our defense would hold them and then they couldn't get off a long punt into the headwind."

Michigan's big win pushed them into the season's top ten list for the first time in five years—seventh place in both the AP and UPI polls. Oklahoma, Tennessee and Iowa were the top powers of the year.

Iowa won its first Big Ten championship since 1922 and the Hawkeyes' trip to California was the school's first bowl venture in history. It was not wasted. Iowa continued the Midwest's hex over Coast rivals with a 35-19 win against Oregon State. The two teams had met earlier in the regular season and Iowa won, but by the narrowest of margins, 14-13.

1957

GAME 54

"WE'RE NO. 1 – AGAIN!"

It was a first class race for first place and the national inter-collegiate football championship in 1957. There was only one un-beaten major college team – Auburn. Seven others lost just one game, and one of them was Ohio State.

For the second time in four years, there was no concensus on a champion by both the *Associated Press* and *United Press International* polls. The AP named Auburn as best; the UPI picked the Buckeyes as the top team – perfect grist for keeping the topic of football and the question of "Who's *really* No. 1?" alive during the off season.

After the season's round of first games, OSU would have gladly settled for at least a share of the Nation's No. 1 tag. The Bucks lost to TCU 18-14 at Columbus as the Frogs scored a third quarter touchdown and hung on for the rest of the afternoon. A Buckeye national championship and a Rose Bowl bid seemed light years away that September 29.

But that was it. The Scarlet and Gray would not meet defeat again for 14 games. The ground-hoggin' Bucks got it together and outscored Washington 35-7, Illinois 21-7, Indiana 56-0, Wisconsin 16-13, Northwestern 47-6, Purdue 20-7, and Iowa 17-13. It was enough to push the Buckeyes to the top in both rankings. More importantly, they were ready for Michigan.

Reports coming out of Ann Arbor were not as sweet. Michigan topped Southern Cal 16-6 and Georgia 26-0, but lost to powerful Michigan State 35-6. The Wolverines then took care of North-western and Minnesota, were tied by Iowa, lost to Illinois, and defeated Indiana. The record was 5-2-1. Not bad, but not good for Michigan.

> "With sophomore Bob White hitting with devasting power, Ohio State ripped Michigan 31-14, before a sellout 101,001 crowd that warmed the 30-degree air with a flare of fist fights after the game," wrote Pete Waldmeir of the *Detroit News*.

More feuds? More fusses? More fights? More friction? It's amazing how an old rivalry such as this one *really* begins to heat up when the teams become "equal" down on the football field. Michigan's previous overpowering domination of the series was now being seriously challenged by Woody Hayes – and Wolverines everywhere knew it, and Wolverines everywhere didn't like it. Losing to Ohio State, in their estimation, was bad enough, but with Hayes as coach, it was an almost unbearable situation for Michigan grid lovers. Hayes himself had become the enemy.

Ohio State was averaging 338 yards per game (only 49 by passing) when they headed North for the 54th game of the series. The Wolverines' 301-yard average was more balanced – 188-113.

Michigan won the toss and elected to take the wind advantage and kick off. It was the same strategy that had brought so much flak to Woody in last year's game. It worked for Michigan. The Buckeyes couldn't move on their first series and punted into a stiff breeze to give U-M excellent field position at its own 46-yard line. On third-and-six, James Pace who, along with OSU's White, ran wild all day, ripped off a 23-yarder to the Bucks' 27. Three plays later from the 19, Pace made a beautiful, twisting run and lunged into the endzone with Fran Kremblas desperately hanging onto one leg. James Van Pelt added the conversion and after five minutes and 55 seconds, Michigan led 7-0.

Ohio lashed back. Returning the kickoff to the 30, the Bucks cranked up the ground game and in 13 plays had evened the score. Three times in the march there were critical third down possession plays. White twice took care of the situation with gains of 12 and eight yards, while Charles LeBeau cracked for eight on the other. LeBeau, on three straight carries, scored from the two. Don Sutherin converted to make it 7-7 with just over three minutes remaining in the first quarter.

With 2:22 showing on the clock before intermission, Sutherin kicked a 33-yard field goal for a 10-7 Ohio lead. It lasted only one minute and seven seconds. After returning the ensuing kickoff to the 25, and on third-and-one, Pace popped through and shot 41 yards to Ohio's 25. Van Pelt then drilled a pass down the

231

middle to Bradley Myers for a touchdown. Van Pelt's kick made it 14-10 and Ohio State had serious matters to discuss at halftime.

The Buckeyes received the second-half kickoff and, aided by a surprise 31-yard pass completion from Kremblas to Leo Brown, drove 58 yards for the go-ahead-to-stay touchdown. Bulldozing White did his share of the damage and LeBeau scored from the eight, his second touchdown of the game. Sutherin's kick made it 17-14 just four minutes into the quarter.

Michigan immediately marched to Ohio's 31 but White recovered a fumble to stop the surge. OSU took the ball and on a fourth-and-one situation at the U-M 48, gambled and got away with it as White crashed for three.

"I didn't send in that play," Woody told reporters after the game. "Kremblas called it himself. I'm afraid I would have been more conservative and punted."

From the Michigan 18, Kremblas swept around the right side and scored. It was 24-10 after another Sutherin conversion and 1:36 remained in the third quarter.

The determined Wolves wouldn't quit and drove to Ohio's 31 again. But again a fumble shattered hopes of getting back into the game. Pace had the ball stripped from his grasp by White, and James Houston fell on it.

With six minutes remaining in the game, Kremblas intercepted a stray pass from Stan Noskin and the Bucks pounded out 72 yards for the final score. Mike Cannavino tallied from the 13 and Sutherin added his fourth point-after. With 3:34 showing on the clock, the Ohio State fans streamed out to rip down the goal posts. Officials stopped the game and restored some order, but the groundwork had been laid for another post-game fracas.

"This time the goal post tuggers were frustrated. As darkness fell on Michigan Stadium, the steel posts embedded in concrete were still erect," wrote Watson Spoelstra of the *News*.

We're National Champs, Hayes Tells Poll Voters

The Detroit News

Columbus Sunday Dispatch

OHIO'S GREATEST HOME NEWSPAPER

VOL. 87, NO. 117   Phone — CApital 1-1231   COLUMBUS 16, OHIO, SUNDAY, NOVEMBER 24, 1957   254 Pages   20 Cents

EXCLUSIVE INTERVIEW WITH WILLIAM RANDOLPH HEARST

Khrushchev Offers U.S. Peaceful Coexistence

Bucks Slap Wolves For Big 10 Sweep

101,001 Watch White Spark 31-14 Victory

By BRAD WILLSON, Dispatch Sports Editor

ANN ARBOR, MICH. NOV. 23—(two lines completed)

Woody took the opportunity after the game to express his opinion on the subject of polls. "We're the national champions," he told reporters in the Ohio locker room. "It's a dirty crime if we don't get it. We played the toughest schedule. Those neighbors down the line (Michigan State) didn't play Iowa. Besides, they lost to Purdue and we beat Purdue. You can't win the national championship if you don't win your own schedule."

There was no mention of TCU.

Actually, in the race for No. 1, Michigan State wasn't Coach Hayes' "problem." At the moment he was claiming No. 1, another team was beating Florida State in Tallahassee by a score of 29-7. It was Auburn. When the votes surfaced a couple of days later, the AP and its panel of writers and broadcasters had Auburn on top. The following week Auburn stomped Alabama 40-0 and captured its half of the national championship by a landslide. Ohio State won the UPI coaches poll just as handily.

Of the seven major teams to lose only one game in 1957, it is ironic that all the defeats were by seven points or less. OSU lost 18-14 to TCU; Oklahoma lost 7-0 to Notre Dame; Navy lost 13-7 to North Carolina; Mississippi lost 12-7 to Arkansas; Michigan State lost 20-13 to Purdue; Iowa lost 17-13 to Ohio State, and N.C. State lost 7-6 to William and Mary.

Oklahoma, national champions for the last two years, saw its fabulous 47-game unbeaten streak go down the drain in 1957. On November 16 at Norman, Notre Dame scored with 3:50 left to play for a 7-0 victory. It was the Sooners' first defeat since the opening game in 1953. Who beat OU in that one? Notre Dame, 28-21. The Sooner streak was approaching the all-time collegiate record of 56, held by Michigan since around the turn of the century.

Back in Ann Arbor, Pace, with 167 yards in 23 carries, and White with 163 yards in 30 attempts, were workhorses of the day – along with all those big linemen who were opening the holes for them. Ohio State led in first downs 19-16, rushing yards 372-270, total yards 421-377 and penalty yards 12-6. Michigan passed for 107 yards (5-for-12), while the Bucks hit on three of nine passes for 49 yards – the season's per game average on the nose.

Ohio State went West to face a 7-3-0 Oregon team in the Rose Bowl and the Webfeet, a 19-point underdog, gave the Buckeyes all they could handle. Sutherin kicked a field goal early in the fourth quarter for the victory. Final score: OSU Bucks 10, OU Ducks 7. On the day, Oregon outgained Ohio 351-304. Still, it went into the record books as a win and the Big Ten's mastery over the Pacific Coast Conference continued. After 12 games with only one victory, West Coast fans and press were no longer in shock. For the Midwest teams to win a Rose Bowl had become a normal condition. A lot of pain, but not surprising.

As for the Michigan-Ohio State rivalry, the Buckeyes were gaining ever so slowly, but gaining nevertheless. The series now stood at 34-16-4.

1958

GAME 55

HEARTBREAK HOTEL

Michigan trailed Ohio State by six points. Forty seconds remained in the game and also in the coaching career of Bennie Oosterbaan. His Wolverines had the ball on OSU's four-yard line. It was fourth-and-one for a first down. The ball carrier blasted into the line and had the necessary yardage for a first down. But he fumbled. And the Buckeyes recovered.

Final score: Ohio State 20, Michigan 14.

The Wolverines lost despite leading in first downs 24-12, and total yards 376-252. The difference, long before that final fumble, was five other turnovers.

Adding even more frustration to the bitter and heartbreaking defeat was the fact that the Michigan team had dedicated this game to "The Old Coach" – Coach Oosterbaan. It was his 100th and final game at the U-M helm. He had announced his plans to resign earlier in the season.

The players did their fieldwork well. Had they been able to punch across that last-minute touchdown and win the game, it would have gone down as the greatest upset in the history of the series.

Entering the 55th game, Ohio State's record showed only one loss – good enough for a No. 7 national ranking. The Wolverines had won only twice and had already surrendered more points in one season than any team in Michigan's 79-year football history.

The Buckeyes had started the 1958 campaign with three tough, tight wins – 23-20 over SMU, 12-7 over Washington and 19-13 over Illinois. An easy 49-8 victory over Indiana followed, then a come-from-behind 7-7 tie with Wisconsin. Northwestern broke a 14-game OSU win streak the following week, 21-0. Purdue overcame a 14-point deficit to tie the Bucks 14-14. Then came a big upset as Ohio State shocked No. 1-ranked Iowa 38-28. It was to cost the Hawkeyes a national championship which ultimately went to LSU.

Michigan's season was mostly, well, dismal. They edged Southern Cal 20-19, tied Michigan State 12-12 and lost to Navy 20-14. Then came October 18 and a game against Northwestern at Evanston. The Wildcats won 55-24 and not since 1891 had a team run up such an obnoxious point total against the Wolverines on the football field. Cornell was the perpetrator then, 58-12.

Michigan captured its only other game in 1958 by the same score as the first – 20-19 over Minnesota. The three "I's" – Iowa, Illinois and Indiana – then took turns and dumped U-M by an aggregate score of 66-28. Iowa's win was its first over Michigan in 15 meetings since 1924.

Ohio State was 5-1-2 but out of the Conference race as Iowa already had locks on the Rose Bowl. Michigan was 2-5-1.

A crowd of 82,248 jammed Ohio Stadium on a crisp, sunny November 22 and watched the two teams put on a thrilling offensive show that had everybody wilted at the end. The crowd also witnessed one of the greatest passing exhibitions in Big Ten history. Michigan's Bob Ptacek completed 24 passes (a Conference record) in 35 attempts for 241 yards. Brad Myers caught 12 – one shy of the Conference record. In all, the game produced 36 first downs and 638 total yards.

Underdog Michigan meant business. They returned the opening kickoff out to the 17 and immediately went to work. On second down, Ptacek cranked up and hit Gary Prahst for a 15-yard gain. Ptacek rambled for 21 more. Al Julian burst for 10 and the Wolverines were at OSU's 37. It was Ptacek-to-Prahst for nine; Julian for two; an incomplete pass, Ptacek-to-Prahst for another nine; Julian for six; Julian for four; and once more the Ptacek-to-Prahst passing combo clicked – this time for a seven-yard touchdown. It was all-or-nothing in this one. U-M went for a two-point conversion but didn't get it. Just over five minutes had elapsed and Ohio State was shocked, 6-0.

Later in the quarter, the Bucks were backed up to their own two-yard line by a punt but kept their poise and worked it out far enough to punt to Michigan's 29. On the play, a clipping penalty suddenly pushed the Wolverines back to their 14. Moments later,

Ohio recovered a Ptacek fumble at the 23. On fourth-and-one from the 14, Jerry Fields passed to Charles LeBeau at U-M's nine. Three plays later, OSU was fourth down at the two. Michigan, determined to win this particular football game, held and took over.

But the Wolverines couldn't stand their own good fortune. Two plays later, Eugene Sisinyak fumbled back to OSU's Don Clark at the 11-yard line. Three plays later from the seven, LeBeau scored. The conversion failed. With 3:37 gone in the second period, the score was knotted 6-6.

The snarling Wolves came right back, bringing the ensuing kickoff out to the 22, and for a touchdown in only seven plays. Myers went to the 27; a Ptacek-to-Myers pass took it to the 34; Ptacek went to Myers again to the 43; Myers went to the 45; another Ptacek-to-Myers pass gained 11 to Ohio's 44; once again it was Ptacek-to-Myers for 12 yards to the 32. Ptacek switched to Prahst on his next aerial and it was complete for a touchdown. This time the two-point conversion try was good – Ptacek to Prahst. Michigan was whooping it up with a 14-6 lead and with 7:53 remaining in the first half.

After an exchange of punts, LeBeau fielded a Wolverine kick at his 15 and returned it 28 yards. Fields completed a pass to Clark at U-M's 41. Four plays later the Bucks were at the 15, Fields hit James Herbstreit for a touchdown. Fields' pass for two more points was incomplete and Michigan held on to a 14-12 lead at halftime.

The Wolverines came out strong in the third period. After taking the kickoff, and after seven Ptacek pass completions, U-M was knocking at Ohio's 17-yard line. The Buckeyes sensed they were in trouble and responded. The defense swarmed in on Ptacek and smacked him for a 10-yard loss. On the next play, he was rushed hard again, slipped and fell for a four-yard loss. He lost another yard on third down. A penalty cost the Wolves five more yards and suddenly it was fourth-and-a-mile back at the 37. The sizzling drive fizzled with a punt into the endzone.

That series of downs decided the game.

The Buckeyes, still responding to danger, took over and mounted an 11-play, 80-yard victory march. White, a 6-2, 210-pound fullback, blasted over from the six. Fields, on an option, kept the ball and swung into the endzone for two more points. Ohio State was out front for the first time, 20-14; and just over three minutes were left in the third quarter.

Neither team threatened again until the clock had ticked

FUMBLE!

*Ohio State led by six....UM was fourth-and-one at the Buckeye four....
00:40 showed on the clock....OSU's Dick Schafrath (71) belts the
football from Brad Myers, and Jerry Fields (24) recovers. Jerry
Bowsher (52) is also in on the play. Michigan lost, 20-14. (Photo
courtesy of OSU Photo Archives)*

down to four minutes. Then the late-game drama began to unfold.

From fairly deep in his own territory, LeBeau threw a pass that came very close to becoming an OSU disaster. Michigan's Gerald Smith picked it off and was tackled at the Buckeye 34. Once again the big stadium became very much alive.

Darrell Harper hit for eight yards to the 26. Myers gained three for a first down at the 23. Myers went to the 19, Harper to the 17 and Myers to the 13 and another first down. The clock showed 1:50. None of the 82,000-plus would sit. Harry Newman's sweep got a yard to the 12. Ptacek gained two yards to the 10, and a Ptacek-to-Myers pass netted six more to the four-yard line.

That brought up fourth-and-one and 40 seconds left to play.

The ball was given to Myers. He fumbled. "I can't understand how it happened," he later told Pete Waldmeir of the *Detroit News*. "I had both arms wrapped around the ball and I could see a hole opening up. I went for it. As I got there someone (OSU's Dick Schafrath) hit me. And at the same time, another guy pushed his fist into the ball. I could have died right there. . . ." Brad Myers was heartbroken.

Fields recovered the big fumble for the Buckeyes. Jerry Fields was ecstatic.

"The Michigan men staggered back toward their bench and saw Oosterbaan alone except for some fans who had burst through the police line and were patting his back. The players surged to him and hoisted him high. It was nothing planned. A season and a career had ended," reported Waldmeir.

Yes, a career had ended. Bennie Oosterbaan had just finished his 34th year at the University of Michigan. He had gone to Ann Arbor as a freshman in 1924, was a three-time All-American player and was an assistant under Wieman, Kipke and Crisler before becoming head coach in 1948. As a varsity player his record was 20-4-0, as an assistant 120-46-6, and as coach 63-33-4. In all three roles, he was involved in 296 games in which the Wolverines won 203, lost 83 and tied 10, for a winning percentage of .703.

Under Oosterbaan, the Wolverines won three Big Ten titles, one national championship and one Rose Bowl game. His teams finished in the top ten nationally a total of four times.

Iowa won another Rose Bowl for the Big Ten, amassing 516 yards and blasting California 38-12.

1959

GAME 56

"BRAGGIN' RIGHTS"

A year's worth of braggin' rights was all that was on the line in the 1959 Michigan-Ohio State encounter. Ohio State was 3-4-1 and Michigan 3-5-0. It was to be the only time in series history both teams came into the big game with losing records.

OSU edged Duke in the opener. The following week Southern Cal beat the Bucks 17-0 at Los Angeles in a game in which the AP reported that Woody Hayes took a swing at Bob Shafer, sports editor of the *Pasadena Independent*, but instead hit Bob's brother, Dick.

Ohio then lost to Illinois, beat Purdue, lost to Wisconsin, beat Michigan State, tied Indiana and lost to Iowa.

Michigan, under new Coach Chalmers (Bump) Elliott, who played for the Wolverines in 1946-47, experienced an up-and-down year. His first Michigan team lost to Missouri and Michigan State, beat Oregon State, lost to Northwestern, beat Minnesota, lost to Wisconsin, beat Illinois and lost to Indiana.

The Buckeyes' defense was giving up an average of only 11 points per game, but the offense was scoring only nine. Michigan was being beaten by 18-12 per game. OSU was made a one-point favorite.

Even with both teams being "losers," 90,093 cared enough about the game to show up in Ann Arbor on November 21 to watch Michigan win 23-14 and break a three-game losing streak to the Ohioans.

"The afternoon was enlivened by the antics of Coach Hayes. Most of the spectators were huddled in overcoats or blankets, or

240

both, but for a while Hayes paced the sidelines in his shirt sleeves. The temperature was in the low 40's. Hayes kicked a yard marker and threw a chair into the air in a show of irritation over the officiating. But he never encroached on the gridiron and no penalty was imposed. The officials apparently ignored his verbal blasts," reported Sam Green of the *Detroit News*.

Ohio's Jerry Fields fumbled the opening kickoff and Tom Jobson recovered for Michigan at the 26. It took the Wolves only three plays to score. Stan Noskin's pass to Darrell Harper picked up a quick 15. Harper's two-yard run got it to the nine and Noskin again went to Harper with a pass for a touchdown. Harper's conversion was good and just 70 seconds into the game, the score was 7-0 with Michigan out front.

Not to be outdone, Ohio scored just three minutes and 31 seconds later. After returning the kickoff to his own 45, Roger Detrick carried 11 times in a 12-play drive that reached Michigan's two-yard line. Quarterback Fields faked a handoff to Detrick and shot a quick pass into the endzone to Jim Houston. Dave Kilgore missed the conversion and the Wolverines still led, 7-6.

The score stayed that way until just two seconds remained in the first half as Noskin scored from the four to climax a frantic 11-play, 69-yard drive. Harper was on target again and Michigan upped its lead to 14-6.

In the third period, the Bucks went 72 yards to tie the game. Detrick scored from the one and Fields hit James Herbstreit for a two-point conversion and a 14-14 score.

Later in the same period, Michigan marched 64 yards for the winning touchdown. Al Julian had runs of nine, seven and 11 yards to lead the drive and Anthony Rio plunged over from the one. Harper's kick was wide and Michigan led 20-14.

The Wolverines put things out of reach with just over five minutes left in the game on Harper's 29-yard field goal. It was the first series field goal for the Wolverines in 13 years, as they took a 35-17-2 lead over Ohio State in the 62-year old rivalry.

Each team got 20 first downs, while Ohio led in total yards 358-296. There were only 20 yards stepped off in penalties – 10 against each team.

Overall, Ohio State had the best of it over Michigan in the decade of the 1950s. The Bucks played .712 football (63-24-5), while Michigan slipped to .588 (52-36-3). Against each other, however, the two teams were virtually even. They split 5-5 during that 10-year period and the Bucks scored just 13 more points, 133-120.

Sports Today

All-City Team

Title, Roses for Badgers!

It's Wisconsin, 11-7; 'Cats Stumble, 28-0

QB Hackbart Passes Gophers into Ground   **Illinois Gives Ray Eliot Royal Sendoff—a Win**

How Big Ten Ended

STILL TIE, 3-3

Happy Ending for U-M! Ohio State Upset, 23-14

Wings Can't Hold Horvath

Even in Detroit, Michigan's big upset of Ohio State in 1959 was overshadowed by ninth-ranked Wisconsin's 11-7 victory over Minnesota, sending them to Pasadena. "'Cats stumble, 28-0" was eighth-ranked Northwestern's stunning loss to unranked Illinois.

Other statistics were also close: Michigan led in first downs 137-135; OSU led in rushing yards 1849-1672; U-M led in passing yards 950-711, and total yards 2622-2560. The Wolverines threw 180 passes and completed 85 for a .472 percentage. Ohio was 57-for-125, .456. In penalty yards U-M led 442-251. Also on penalties, in the previous 20 years (1940-59), the Wolves had been hit for 713 penalty yards in games against the Buckeyes, and OSU only 414.

The average attendance at all games during the decade had been 85,100—94,500 in Ann Arbor and 75,800 in Columbus.

1960

M + F = "V"

The team that could stop Tom Matte and Bob Ferguson in 1960 could eliminate 77 percent of Ohio State's offense. Quarterback Matte, who went on to a distinguished career as a running back with the Baltimore Colts, and fullback Ferguson, were running and passing for an average of 263 yards per game when it came time to meet Michigan in the 57th renewal of the series. This super-duo had rushed for 1407 yards, and Matte had passed for 697. Their combined effort of 2104 yards was all but 636 of the Bucks' total offensive yardage at that point late in the season.

Not including seven punts against the Wolverines, OSU operated only 42 plays all afternoon – 41 by Matte and Ferguson. The stubborn U-M defense did more than its part, holding M&F well below their customary output, but the offense failed to materialize and the Buckeyes escaped with a 7-0 win before 83,107 at Columbus on November 19.

The game's only touchdown was scored by Ferguson on a 17-yard run early in the fourth quarter.

For what it's worth as a historical note, Michigan came out ahead in the statistical battle, leading in first downs 17-9, rushing yards 132-128, passing yards 86-40 and total yards 218-168. It was only the second time all season that the high-powered Buckeye offense (the Big Ten leader) was held to less than 300 yards. However, four Michigan turnovers destroyed an otherwise gutsy performance.

Ohio entered the game with a 6-2-0 record and were made a 10-point favorite. There were wins over SMU, Southern Cal,

Above: Buckeye Bob Ferguson scored the only touchdown in 7-0 win in the 1960 game at Columbus.
Below: OSU's Tom Matte (41) can't escape from near his own goal. Also shown are UM defenders Reid Bushong (48), Kenneth Tureaud (39), Robert Johnson (89) and Richard Syring (55).
(Photos courtesy of OSU Photo Archives)

Illinois, Wisconsin, Michigan State and Indiana by an average score of 28-5. However, Purdue upset the Bucks 24-21 in the third game of the season, and Iowa made them a 35-12 victim the week before the Michigan game.

The Wolverines were 5-3-0 with victories at the expense of Oregon, Duke, Northwestern, Illinois and Indiana. There were defeats by Michigan State, Minnesota and Wisconsin.

Except for Ferguson's scoring run, the game was a complete defensive standoff and prompted Bob Pille of the *Detroit Free Press* to write, "Michigan and Ohio State knocked a half-century off their ancient rivalry Saturday. . . .Pushing and shoving as they must have in football days of yore, they finally struggled to a Buckeye decision."

Michigan reached OSU's 11-yard line in the second quarter but missed a field goal. Other than that one spurt, the closest Michigan came to the Buckeyes' goal was 35 yards and that in the game's closing seconds. Even then, an interception killed the last hope for a possible 8-7 win. Ohio State didn't do much better, except for the one scoring drive. But that was enough.

Here is how it went: On the last play of the third quarter, Bob Klein returned a Michigan punt eight yards to U-M's 42-yard line. Matte gained five before turning the show over to Ferguson. Big Bob, in two cracks, got six yards and a first down at the 31. He then plowed through for 14 more to the 17. Sticking with a good thing, Matte handed off to the 6-0, 217-pound junior and Ferguson responded with a power-drive run of 17 yards and the TD. Ben Jones added the conversion and Ohio had its 7-0 lead – plus its fifth series win in the last seven years.

Back on November 5 at Ann Arbor, an all-time first occurred in Big Ten football – brothers opposed each other as head coaches and both were former Wolverines. Michigan defeated Illinois 8-7, and Bump Elliott had beaten brother Pete.

Also in 1960, Woody Hayes wrapped up his first decade as gridmaster at Columbus with a record of 64-21-5. (.738) He was 6-4-0 against Michigan. Woody's "three yards and a cloud of dust" offense had fully blossomed. In the first four years, his teams averaged 19 passes per game. In the next six years that figure dropped to only nine passes per game.

In 1960, the Buckeyes ended with a 7-2-0 record and a No. 8 national ranking. There was no Rose Bowl for OSU or Michigan. In that game, Washington won its second straight New Year's Day outing with a 17-7 triumph over Minnesota, already voted national champions in 1960.

1961

GAME 58

WOODY POURED IT
ON FOR OSU'S 400TH

In 1961 there was a mad scramble all fall for the national championship. At one time or another, five different teams held the No. 1 spot.

Ohio State had as good a shot at the title as anybody. They began the season in third place (behind Iowa and Mississippi) but wasted no time in squandering the opportunity. TCU went to Columbus for the season's opener and scored a fourth quarter touchdown to tie and stun heavily-favored OSU 7-7, and it marked the second time in four years that the Horned Frogs cost Woody Hayes a national championship. The Buckeyes eventually worked back up to No. 2 (where they finished), but the AP and UPI pollsters apparently could not forget that tie with TCU.

OSU bounced back from the disaster and plastered UCLA 13-3, Illinois 40-0, Northwestern 10-0, Wisconsin 30-21, Iowa 29-13, Indiana 16-7 and Oregon 22-12. After the Oregon game on November 18, Ohio moved into second place behind Alabama.

Iowa began the season as the No. 1 team but as the weekends passed, Mississippi replaced the Hawkeyes, Michigan State replaced the Rebels, Texas replaced the Spartans, and Alabama replaced the Longhorns late in the season after Texas lost 6-0 to, who else, but TCU.

Michigan's hopes for a big season were bolstered by the results of the first two games – 29-6 over UCLA and 38-8 over Army. But once again, the Wolverines couldn't get by Michigan State. The Spartans used a 28-0 victory at Ann Arbor to earn their turn

246

in the No. 1 spot. Coach Bump Elliott's boys then edged Purdue by two, before suffering a three-point setback to Minnesota. Duke, Illinois and Iowa followed and were no trouble for the Wolves.

OSU was 7-0-1, Michigan was 6-2-0 and once again it was time for "The Big One" as 80,444 gathered at Michigan Stadium for the 58th meeting between the two teams. It was the smallest crowd for a series game in Ann Arbor since the 1943 wartime game. There were some who suggested that Michigan fans had an inkling of what might happen and didn't care to be a part of it. More likely, the chance to see the game on television influenced a rash of "no-shows."

But the Buckeye boosters were there in force. A win over the Wolves and OSU would celebrate a Rose Bowl trip throughout the night in the "foreign territory" of Ann Arbor, Detroit and environs. "If we win," thought Buckeye boosters, "surely the OSU faculty will vote for us to go to the Rose Bowl."

As the fourth and final period got under way, the Buckeyes led 21-12. Fifteen minutes and 37 points later, the final score read: Ohio State 50, Michigan 20, for the Bucks' 400th all-time football victory.

It was a game offering a wide array of action and oddities.

Ohio received the opening kickoff. On the fifth play of the game from his own 43, quarterback Joe Sparma was hit as he was about to pass. The ball flew up and Michigan's John Walker intercepted at the 33. On fourth-and-one at the 24, the Wolverines were stopped and a big break had gone by the boards.

OSU punted to the Michigan 34. On third down, David Glinka's pass was batted into the air and picked off by Ohio's Sam Tidmore at the U-M 35. The Bucks lost five yards on a penalty. On third-and-four from the 29, All-America Bob Ferguson began his battering ram tactics and bolted to the 25, to the 19, and then over the goal line. Dick Van Raaphorst kicked his first of six conversions and it was 7-0 with 3:26 left in the first quarter.

The afternoon's offensive fireworks had begun.

Early in the second quarter, Glinka fumbled and Ray Kristolic recovered for Ohio at his own 45. Two plays later, Sparma completed a 30-yard pass to Ormonde Ricketts to Michigan's 19. Ferguson rammed it to the 16, to the three, to the one, and in for the touchdown and the score moved to 14-0.

The ensuing kickoff was historic. Michigan's David Raimey took it at the 10 and raced all the way – 90 yards – for a touchdown. It was the first kickoff in the series ever returned for a touch-

Columbus Sunday Dispatch

OHIO'S GREATEST HOME NEWSPAPER

VOL. 91, NO. 149   Phone—CApital 1-1234   COLUMBUS 16, OHIO, SUNDAY, NOVEMBER 26, 1961   262 Pages   ★★★★ X   20 Cents

OSU BLASTS WOLVES, 50-20; BADGERS TRIP MINNESOTA, 23-21

Buckeyes Win Big Ten Title

HARD TO BELIEVE!

Ohio State	7	14	0	29	—50
Michigan	0	6	6	8	—20

The Detroit Free Press

Sports

SUNDAY, NOVEMBER 26, 1961

Bucks Pour It On M, 50-20

Badgers Kick Out Gophers

Seventh Try Does It, 23-21

Ferguson Bulls for 4 TDs

OSU Clinches Big Ten Title

down. Counting all games and scores since 1897, it was the 378th time that one team or the other had kicked off. Raimey's run to glory was also the second longest scoring run in the series, bettered only by Alfred Barlow's 113-yard journey with a missed field goal in the 1905 game.

After the thrilling touchdown, and after the Michigan stands began to settle down, Glinka missed on a pass for a two-point conversion. With 10:49 remaining in the second period, the count was now 14-6, Ohio.

Zip. Zip. Zip. Zip. It took only four plays for the Buckeyes to get back on the scoreboard. Starting from the 20, three plays netted a first down at the 31. Then halfback Paul Warfield took a handoff, streaked around the right side and got loose for a 69-yard touchdown. This turned out to be the second longest touchdown run from scrimmage in series history, topped only by Bill Heston's 70-yard dash in 1902. In 1908, OSU's Millard Gibson scored on an 85-yard run, but his came off a fake punt, which some football purists insist is not a play from scrimmage. In any event, Warfield put the Bucks ahead 21-6 and that's the way the half ended. But the "Believe It Or Nots" were far from over.

Take the third quarter for example, when each team had only one possession, but only one score was made. Here's how it happened: Michigan returned the second-half kickoff to its 22-yard line and proceeded to keep the ball for 15 plays and eight minutes and 26 seconds. On fourth down from the OSU one, Bruce McLenna finally powered over for the score. A two-point conversion was missed again and the score was 21-12.

At this stage of the game, a 50-20 final score was unthinkable.

The Wolverines' drive was a thing of beauty. And it happened to Woody Hayes' team, supposedly the masters of that kind of football. As if inspired by the Michigan exhibition in ball control, OSU took over and used 16 plays and 7:11 of the clock on an 80-yard drive that actually covered 121 yards with allowance for two penalties. As the third quarter came to a close, the ball was on U-M's one-yard line. It took two smashes by Ferguson at the other end of the field before he made it. The fourth quarter was 37 seconds gone as the score mounted to 28-12.

On the next kickoff, McLenna almost went 100-plus yards but Ohio's Ron Houck made a saving tackle at the Michigan 42. Moments later, Houck intercepted a Glinka pass at his own 14 and returned it to the 21. After a loss of a yard, Sparma hit Klein with a pass at midfield and Klein streaked in for a touchdown – an 80-yard pass play for still another series record. The previous record of 62 yards was set in 1924 by OSU on a Bill Hunt-to-

249

In the 1961 game, quarterback Joe Sparma (L) threw a 30-yard pass to Robert Klein (R), who ran the remaining 50 to complete an 80-yard play–the longest pass play in series history. (Photos courtesy of OSU Photo Archives.)

Michigan's David Raimey scored on a 90-yard kickoff return in the 1961 game – the only kickoff returned for a touchdown in series history. (Photo courtesy of The Michiganensian.*)*

Harold Cunningham completion. Just under 10 minutes remained in the game and OSU now led 35-12.

On their next possession, the Wolverines were forced to punt and Warfield returned it 20 yards to Ohio's 49. On a quick five-play drive, Ferguson carried four times for 48 yards and the TD – his fourth of the game – and a 42-14 score. That 42 total represented the most points Ohio State had ever scored in a Michigan game.

The clock showed 4:45. It was still enough time for 16 more points. Michigan took the kickoff and went 55 yards in 10 plays with James Ward scoring from the one. Ward also added a two-point conversion. Ohio State 42, Wolverines 20.

Now just 34 seconds remained in the game, but still enough time for eight more Ohio points. On first down from the 20, Sparma heaved a bomb snagged on the run by Warfield who took it to the Wolverine 10. Even though by this time many of the Michigan rooters were snarled in traffic outside the stadium, enough were left to boom out the boos. They were furious at Woody for that last long pass. After an incomplete pass into the endzone, Sparma connected with Tidmore who took it at the five and fought his way over for another OSU touchdown five seconds from the end.

Hayes still wasn't satisfied. He wanted an even 50 – and he got it – when Sparma threw to Tidmore for a two-pointer to wrap it up.

Amid thunderous boos from Michigan's side, the game ended and spectators took to the gridiron looking for trouble. And at this particular moment, trouble was easy to find.

The following are excerpts from accounts of the reporters on the scene representing Columbus and Detroit newspapers: "Close the gates of mercy! It was 50-20 and would have been worse if the Buckeyes hadn't run out of time. . . .Hayes had Ohio regulars on the field to the very final moment. . . .At the final gun, rambunctious fans swarmed the field to start brawls which continued another half hour. . . .The big push surrounded the north goal posts where a mob assembled and fights abounded. Police eventually would break up one group and another would start somewhere else. . . .The handshaking ceremony at midfield was more brief than Hayes anticipated. . . .Hayes, a gregarious fat man, acted as if he wanted to throw his arms around Elliott. . . .It is doubtful that the two coaches were exchanging the fraternal Sigma Chi handshake both learned in their student days. . . . Woody tested his vision again. Yep, he still had 50/20 vision. . . . His players hoisted him to their shoulders. And that's the way Hayes left the field, waving his baseball cap to the crowd. . . .Not

251

only did the '61 Buckeyes devastate hated Michigan, but they did it so thoroughly and sensationally that their performance will rank high among all-timers."

Ferguson, who would reap his second All-America honor, led all rushers with 152 yards in 30 carries. The stellar performance capped a great career at Ohio State which saw him gain 2162 yards in 423 carries, averaging 5.1 yards per rush, with 26 touchdowns thrown in.

The Bucks literally buried Michigan statistically – leading in first downs 22-16, yards rushing 312-162, yards passing 200-109 and total yards 512-271. The 512 yards was the most in one game since Hayes' arrival at OSU 101 games ago, and the 200 yards gained by passing was tops since 1953. Against Michigan, Ohio was seven-for-10 in the passing game; the Wolverines 10-for-17. Once again, U-M was penalized more yards, 40-20.

While all the antics were going on in Ann Arbor, good things were also happening to the Buckeyes in Minneapolis, where Wisconsin shocked Minnesota 23-21 in a real thriller. The Gophers missed a two-point conversion in the last minute of play. This gave the Buckeyes the Big Ten championship outright, the school's 12th football title won or shared.

Undoubtedly, the pollsters were impressed with Ohio's slaughter of Michigan as the Bucks gained 44 points on idle Alabama. With only one game to go against Auburn, the Crimson Tide held a slim seven-point poll lead over OSU. Alabama proceeded to blank the Tigers 34-0 and wound up No. 1 in both polls.

Ohio State also missed out on the Rose Bowl. The powerful Faculty Council voted 28-25 against the school's football team going to the bowl. In 1961, there was no contract between the Big Ten and what had become the West Coast Big Five, a league consisting of California, Southern Cal, UCLA, Stanford and Washington. The four other members split from the conference.

Although there was some sentiment among the Rose Bowl people to invite Alabama, the move never materialized and Minnesota got the bid. The bowl's first choice clearly was Ohio State. The Gophers atoned for losing the previous year with a 21-3 victory over UCLA as the Big Ten increased its bowl whammy to 13-3-0 over the Coast entries.

Michigan's series lead over the Buckeyes had now been reduced to 35-19-4. The Wolverines had 950 points, Ohio State 533, for an average score of 16-9 per game.

1962

GAME 59

OHIO'LL TAKE IT

It was one of those years.

Ohio State started the season as the No. 1 ranked team in the Nation and finished no better than No. 4 in its own Conference. Michigan started the season tied for first place with every other team in the Conference and finished all alone dead last.

Both clubs would just as soon forget 1962, but Ohio can at least remember and smile for the simple reason that it brought another victory over Michigan. Those victories are always keepers.

This one was played in Columbus and the Buckeyes were waiting for U-M's arrival with a 5-3-0 record. They had beaten North Carolina, Illinois, Wisconsin, Indiana and Oregon, and lost to UCLA, Northwestern and Iowa.

Michigan went visiting with a miserable 2-6-0 showing that included wins over Army and Illinois, and defeats by Nebraska, Michigan State (again), Purdue, Minnesota, Wisconsin and Iowa. In the three-game run against the Spartans, Boilermakers and Gophers, Michigan failed to score. It had not happened to a Wolverine football team in 27 years—three straight whitewashes.

The visiting team from Ann Arbor walked onto the field with a betting handicap of 19-plus points. According to the people who figure such odds, this was the biggest underdog role Michigan had played in series history.

"With Woody Hayes calling the plays, the Buckeyes tromped on Michigan just the way they've been tromping on people for years – with pure, simple, bone-shattering, teeth-jarring power ....it was no game....Michigan knew what was coming on

'Dull' Bucks Put U-M Through Grinder, 28-0

Detroit Free Press

DID HE SCORE?

From all indications, no. It looks as though Michigan's 180-pound Tom Prichard (21) had stopped Ohio State's 220-pound fullback Robert Butts (34) just inches short of the goal in the 1962 game at Columbus. Other identifiable players are UM's Bill Dodd (38), John Yanz (81), Dave Kurtz (63) and Bob Timberlake (28); OSU's Daryl Sanders (76) and Ormonde Ricketts (83). The Buckeyes won, 28-0. (Photo courtesy of OSU Photo Archives)

almost every play – a fullback smash – but was helpless to do anything about it," wrote Joe Falls of the *Detroit Free Press*.

For the second straight year Woody sicked his big fullback on the Wolverines and this time the Buckeyes came away a 28-0 winner.

Last year it was 6-0, 217-pound Bob Ferguson (30 carries, 152 yards); this year it was 6-0, 209-pound Dave Francis (31 carries, 186 yards).

"It was pretty dull, not at all what you'd expect from a Michigan-Ohio State game. It was devoid of any drama (ever see anybody cheer a wrecking crew at work?) and the 82,349 were hardly stirred by the might of Ohio State," reported Falls.

Even though the score was only 7-0 at the half, the final outcome never seemed to be in doubt. Michigan did not get past OSU's 21-yard line.

In the first quarter, the Bucks traveled 52 yards in eight plays and Francis carried all eight times, scoring from the one. Charles Mamula made good the first of four conversions. . . .7-0.

Soon after intermission, Ohio State drove 65 yards in 13 plays. During this possession, Paul Warfield gained 10 yards on one play; the other 55 yards and 12 plays were the direct responsibility of Francis. He scored from the three, for a 14-0 lead.

Early in the final period, Robert Butts tallied from the two to conclude another 52-yard march. Later in the game, Francis got free on what would have been a 59-yard TD run, but he stumbled – apparently from sheer exhaustion – and finally fell to the ground at the Michigan six. Hayes replaced his fallen star with another 209-pound fullback, David Katterhenrich. The fresh Katterhenrich ripped through the weary Wolverine defense for a touchdown in one play.

"It was a sad finale for the 11 Michigan seniors and it was sad, too, for the people who sponsored the telecast. . . .The Bucks would have carried Hayes off the field when it was over but, well, Woody's no lightweight. He looks almost like a fullback," said reporter Falls.

Francis, a senior, had carried the ball only 14 times in his previous two varsity seasons, but in 1962 he was called upon 119 times, and gained 624 yards, a 5.2 yard per play average.

In defeating Michigan for the seventh time in the last nine years, OSU ran 70 plays to only 47 for the Wolverines. The Buckeyes also led in first downs 19-9 and in total yards 337-142. U-M was penalized 10 yards, Hayes' team zero.

The series was still very much in favor of Michigan – 35-20-4.

Wisconsin captured the Big Ten championship and in the Rose Bowl trailed national champion Southern Cal 42-14 early in the fourth quarter. Suddenly, Badger quarterback Ron VanderKelen went white hot and almost pulled the game out with a phenomenal aerial exhibition before bowing, 42-37. In the game, VanderKelen completed 33 of 48 passes for 401 yards. The Trojan victory was good for West Coast morale, and the Wisconsin rally served to wake up TV viewers and help sponsors get their money's worth.

1963

GAME 60

"NO GAME TODAY"

The rifle shots rang out at noon Friday in Dallas and President John F. Kennedy was dead. There would be no Michigan-Ohio State football game at Ann Arbor the following day as originally planned.

In the initial Friday confusion of *everything, everywhere*, the decision was made by officials of both schools to play the game. However, by early Saturday morning, when the full impact of what had happened registered, Michigan's president, Harlan Hatcher, announced the postponement of the game for one week.

"Our main job all morning has been to head-off special trains and buses bringing fans from Ohio and around the State of Michigan," Hatcher told the press.

A few fans, maybe a hundred or two, showed up at the ball grounds. Some were seen quietly picnicking near the stadium. A few even strolled through the open gates and past the simple "No Game Today" signs that had been posted. Any elaboration in the message would have been superfluous. The people wandered aimlessly inside the mammoth 101,001-seat bowl. There was nothing else to do. They, along with the entire Nation, were in shock. College football that weekend, including scores of traditional rivalries that normally inspired intense passion, was virtually forgotten.

The following Saturday, the game was on. Before 65,577 wind-swept, snow-covered empty seats — the most empty seats for a Michigan-Ohio State football game since the depression year of 1932 — the Buckeyes rallied from a 10-point deficit to defeat the

FORECAST
By U.S. Weather Bureau
Mild, cloudy, rain, low tonight
55. Saturday rain, windy, colder, high 60.
(Vap and data on Page 3A)

Columbus Evening Dispatch

OHIO'S GREATEST HOME NEWSPAPER

FIVE STAR
★ ★ ★ ★ ★
STREET FINAL

VOL. 93, NO. 145   Phone—CApital 1-1231   COLUMBUS, OHIO 43216, FRIDAY, NOVEMBER 22, 1963   60 Pages   ✦✦✦✦ X   Copyright 1963 The Dispatch Printing Co.   7 Cents

JFK IS DEAD

Sniper Hits President In Motor Car

DALLAS, Tex. ☞—President John F. Kennedy, 35th President of the United States, was shot to death Friday by a hidden assassin armed with a high-powered rifle.

Kennedy, 46, lived about an hour after a sniper cut him down as his limousine left downtown Dallas.

Automatically, the mantle of the presidency fell to Vice President Lyndon B. Johnson, a native Texan who had been riding two cars behind the Chief Executive.

There was no immediate word on when Johnson would take the oath of office.

Asst. Presidential Press Secretary Malcolm Kilduff said Johnson was not hit. The new President previously had been reported wounded.

Kennedy died at Parkland Hospital, where his bullet-pierced body had been taken in a frantic but futile effort to save his life.

Governor Is Also Wounded

Lying wounded at the same hospital was Governor John Connally of Texas, who was cut down by the same fusillade that ended the life of the youngest man ever elected to the presidency.

Connally and his wife had been riding with the Presi-

PRESIDENT JOHN F. KENNEDY

JUST BEFORE KENNEDY SHOT—President John F. Kennedy, riding in motorcade approximately one minute before he was shot in Dallas. In the car riding with him are Mrs. Kennedy and Gov. and Mrs. John Connally of Texas.—(AP Wirephoto)

'Terrible' Sums

BULLETINS

Wolverines. It was the fourth straight OSU victory, and it turned out to be one of the most exciting games in series history.

The afternoon's activities were televised regionally and this, along with the uncomfortable weather conditions, contributed to the big no-show factor. The house count was a low, low 34,424.

Ohio State went into the game with a 4-3-1 record and had outscored its opposition by a scant 96-92 margin. Michigan was even all the way around, with three wins, three losses, two ties, 117 points scored and 117 points surrendered.

U-M won the first battle which lasted 21 minutes, 10-0, while OSU won the final battle of 39 minutes, 14-0 – and the war, 14-10.

The Bucks received the opening kickoff and the 60th collision between the two arch rivals had begun. On second down, Matt Snell was cracked hard by Joe O'Donnell, fumbled, and John Clancy recovered for Michigan at the Ohio 27. (This was the same Matt Snell who, five years later, was to co-star with Joe Namath in the Jets' 16-7 Super Bowl victory over Baltimore, in one of pro football's historic surprises.)

Michigan could get only a field goal as a result of Snell's fumble. The Wolves got down to the six-yard line, were shoved back, and had to be content with a 28-yard three-pointer by Bob Timberlake.

Ohio couldn't get on track and in the second quarter had punted to Michigan's 37. The home team turned the opportunity into another score. On a big third down play with four to go, Mel Anthony shot for 27 to the Bucks' 30. Timberlake, trapped on a pass play, got away for 15 to OSU's 15. Anthony carried three straight times to get the ball down to the four. John Bowser rammed for two and finally Dick Rindfuss came on for the TD. Timberlake kicked good and with nine minutes remaining in the half, Michigan's portion of the stadium warmed considerably when the "10-0" figures flashed on the big scoreboard.

Late in the period the cold Buckeyes had not yet crossed their own 40. But finally, something got them going and they put together a drive of 64 yards to the U-M six where it was fourth down. Quarterback Don Unverferth went to his great receiver, Paul Warfield, in the endzone. Warfield leaped, gathered in the ball, and landed hard on the turf. The impact separated ball and receiver.

"Incomplete pass," ruled the officials. The man in charge of Ohio State football took exception to the ruling and appealed.

"Hayes, outfitted in his customary short-sleeved shirt and not wearing a jacket despite the cold, raced 40 yards down the side-

Bitter weather has never kept fans from a Michigan-Ohio State football game — and it didn't in 1963. Instead, it was the death of a President. Even after a week's postponement, people were just in no mood for football. With plenty of empty seats as a backdrop at Ann Arbor, UM's Bob Timberlake kicks a 28-yard field goal in the first period for a 3-0 lead, but the Buckeyes won the game, 14-10. The holder is Forest Evashevski, Jr., whose father scored touchdowns in the 1939-40 games, both on passes from Tom Harmon. Other players shown are Melvin Anthony (37), Dwight Kelley (53), Arnold Chonko (23) and William Yearby (75). (Photo courtesy of Michigan Athletic Department)

lines to bellow that Warfield had possession long enough. The officials merely walked away," reported Jerry Green of the *Detroit News*. Appeal denied.

The Wolverines took over and punted out to their 44-yard line and there were just 56 seconds left in the first half. Unverferth went again to his favorite target – Warfield – for a nine-yard pass completion at the 35. On the next play, Unverferth went to his right, while his left halfback shot past two defenders down the left sideline. Unverferth stopped and fired a long pass into the endzone. The left halfback, Warfield, made a fantastic diving catch, landed on his back and somehow held onto the football. Touchdown. Dick Van Raaphorst added the conversion and with 41 seconds showing on the first-half clock, the Buckeyes had climbed back into the game, 10-7.

Neither team put any serious burden on the other's defense in the third quarter and the minutes kept blinking away in the cold and darkening atmosphere.

Early in the final period, OSU received a punt at its 24 and slowly started goalward. Three plays. . . .six plays. . . .nine plays . . . .12 plays. . . .14 plays. . . .and the Buckeyes were at Michigan's five-yard line. Unverferth scored on a quarterback keeper. Van Raaphorst's conversion was perfect and Ohio finally had the lead, 14-10, with 7:30 left to play. The few thousand OSU followers who made the trip to Ann Arbor went wild.

Both groups, however, still had thrills in store – the Maize and Blue boosters from their offense; the Scarlet and Gray rooters from their defense.

Slightly over three minutes remained as Michigan began a march of 54 yards to bring them to third-and-goal at Ohio's six. The Wolverines had two more shots and plenty of time – 1:46 – to get the job done. Timberlake threw into the endzone but three Buckeyes were there to knock the ball away.

Fourth down, game-to-go.

Timberlake retreated into the pocket and had lots of time as OSU flooded the endzone with defenders. Tom Kiehfuss, a sophomore from Cincinnati, came up with a big play to save the game for Ohio State. Timberlake spotted Craig Kirby, who had worked free in the corner of the endzone, and rifled a pass his way. At the last possible moment, Kiehfuss streaked in and ticked the ball with his fingertips. Kirby, for a split second, lost sight of it. The ball hit him in the chest and fell harmlessly to the ground.

By that slim a margin, Ohio State had won the game.

PAUL WARFIELD

The only Buckeye to score touchdowns in three different games against Michigan (1961-62-63). (Photo courtesy of OSU Photo Archives)

The Dispatch SPORTS pages

OHIO'S GREATEST HOME NEWSPAPER

BUSINESS, CLASSIFIED.

Week's Range of New York Stocks

COLUMBUS, SUNDAY, DEC. 1, 1963.   PAGE 33B.

BUCKS WHIP MICHIGAN IN FINALE

In Paul Warfield's last game as a collegian, the future Cleveland Brown and Miami Dolphin great caught five passes for 76 yards. Ohio bettered Michigan in first downs 17-14, and in total yards 297-223. The Wolverines were penalized 30 yards, one more than OSU.

Even though Michigan's series bulge was still 14 games (35-21-4), the rivalry in the last 38 years had come out all even. Since 1925, both teams had whipped the other 18 times and there were two ties. The scoring in that period was also amazingly close – 513-507, Michigan. Coach Hayes' own record was 9-4-0 against "that team up North."

In 1963, Ohio State finished in a tie with Michigan State for second place in the Big Ten, while Michigan matched marks with Purdue and Northwestern for fourth. In the past six years, the Wolverines' record was 22-29-3 – the worst six-year period in the team's history.

Illinois won the Big Ten title in 1963 and went on to defeat Washington in the Rose Bowl, 17-7.

1964

GAME 61

A BATTLE FOR THE BOWL

Ohio State was 5-0-0 in the Conference; Michigan 5-1-0. Their meeting in 1964 would give the winner the Big Ten championship outright, as well as the Rose Bowl invitation. No ifs, ands or buts about this one. It was to be a biggie.

The Buckeyes had won seven and lost one overall, losing only to Penn State 27-0 at Columbus in a shocking upset seven weeks into the season. Penn State had already lost four times, and apparently were too lightly regarded by OSU. The Wolverines were also 7-1-0, with the lone loss to Purdue, 21-20. In that game, Michigan committed five turnovers and also suffered 89 yards in penalties.

U-M was ranked No. 5 in the country; OSU No. 7. For the first time in several years the game assumed national significance and attracted national attention.

The day was November 21 and the thermometer hovered at 20 degrees and a 20 mile per hour wind that whipped through Ohio Stadium had the 84,685 fans bundled up and huddled together as so many sheep in a pasture. It didn't help much. Hardly anything happened in the game to warm the spirits of the home team fans, either. Michigan went to Columbus and won it all, 10-0. Or, was it "Ohio" 10, Ohio State 0? That's another story.

It was a happy day indeed for the lovers of the Maize and Blue. They hadn't enjoyed a victory over OSU since 1959 and it had been 14 long years since the last opportunity to live it up in California on New Year's Eve.

264

OSU won the toss and elected to take the wind. Michigan got nowhere and punted; Ohio punted; Michigan punted; Ohio punted; Michigan punted; Ohio punted. Almost 22 minutes of the game had been "kicked away."

Michigan broke the monotony with a fumble and the Buckeyes had the first break of the game. But nothing came of it even though the bobble was recovered at the U-M 29. Four plays later, Dan Porretta's field goal try was way short.

Michigan punted again and the Bucks got back to the 25, but again were stymied on a fourth-and-two plunge with 3:25 left in the first half. It was enough time, however, for the Wolves to get a big break. They took full advantage of it and scored the game's only touchdown.

With 64 seconds remaining before intermission and the scrimmage line at the Michigan 40, Stan Kemp punted and the wind had his long, high kick doing funny things. Robert Rein decided to field the ball instead of "letting it go." Rein dropped it and U-M's John Henderson pounced on the prize at the Buckeye 20-yard line.

On second down from the 17, Bob Timberlake threw complete at the five to James Detwiler who took it in. Timberlake kicked the conversion and Michigan took a 7-0 lead into the welcome warmth of the dressing room.

"Icy. Polar bears should have played in this one. It was so bad in the South endzone – the open end of the horseshoe – that a large number of fans didn't bother coming back for the second half," reported Bob Pille of the *Detroit News*.

In the third quarter, with 2:39 left, Michigan got down to Ohio's 14 after recovering a fumble back at the 44, but could get no further and Timberlake's field goal attempt was wide.

Keyed by Richard Volk's 25-yard punt return, U-M was quickly back in business at the Buckeye 25 and in three plays had penetrated to the nine as the third quarter ended. Two plays later, Timberlake kicked a short field goal to make it 10-0.

The Bucks stormed down the field after receiving the next kickoff. The 46-yard drive got as far as the Michigan 21 but Volk killed it with an interception at the eight. Ohio State got the ball three more times, but the drives were halted at the Michigan 37, 28 and 44, respectively.

Back to the Ohio vs. Ohio State story. Several Buckeye natives who had been persuaded to attend the University of Michigan did most of the damage to the Buckeyes. Henderson, from Dayton, recovered the fumble that led to the 17-yard TD pass from Timber-

MICHIGAN BEATS OHIO FOR BIG 10 TITLE

Notre Dame Jars Iowa, 28-0, for No.9

TURNS FUMBLE INTO SCORE, CHOKES OFF BUCKEYES 10-0

66-YD. PASS PLAY, HUARTE TO SNOW, SPARKS IRISH TRIUMPH

At the End of the Long Road—Cheers and Roses

lake, from Franklin, to Detwiler, from Toledo. Timberlake also kicked the conversion and a field goal as "Ohio" scored all of Michigan's points. Also, Volk, whose 25-yard punt return set up Timberlake's field goal, and who intercepted two passes, was from Wauseen, Ohio. It was a classic example of "native sons" returning to show their stuff to the home crowd.

It was just too cold for either team to accumulate impressive statistics. OSU led in first downs 10-9; U-M led in rushing yards 115-103; OSU led in passing yards 77-45, and in total yards 180-160. The two teams completed only 10 of 30 passes and there was a total of nine fumbles. Michigan led in penalty yards 36-25. In the last 12 games in the series, the Wolves suffered almost twice as many penalty yards as Ohio State − 442 yards to 228.

Michigan went West New Year's to face another OSU team − Oregon State University. Sparked by an 84-yard touchdown run in the second quarter by Mel Anthony, the Wolverines smothered the Beavers by a score of 34-7, giving the Big Ten a 15-4-0 Rose Bowl advantage over West Coast opponents.

For the first time in 15 years, *both* Michigan and Ohio State finished in the Nation's top ten. The Wolverines were voted No. 4 behind Alabama, Arkansas and Notre Dame; the Buckeyes wound up in the No. 9 slot.

1965

GAME 62

AN INSTANT HERO

The outcome of the 1965 Michigan-Ohio State game left a lot of people scratching their heads. Michigan people couldn't figure how they lost; Ohio people couldn't figure how they won. It was, by any standard, a weird game. But in retrospect, it was an appropriate finale for both teams, because both teams had experienced weird seasons.

In its first two games, Michigan gained 755 yards and needed every one of them in 31-24 and 10-7 victories over North Carolina and California, respectively. Georgia kicked three field goals for the difference in a 16-7 win, and Michigan State beat up on the Wolverines 24-7. U-M had beaten MSU only once in the past 10 years and three times in 16 years.

Two heartbreakers followed. Purdue's Bob Griese booted a 35-yard field goal with 55 seconds remaining to give the Boilermakers a 17-15 triumph. The next week, Michigan missed on a two-point conversion with 82 seconds left and lost 14-13 to Minnesota. The Wolverines relieved their frustrations the following week against Wisconsin with the biggest point binge in 12 years, 50-14. Then came a 23-3 win over Illinois. Northwestern came on to snap the two-game winning streak, 34-22.

Even though the Wolverines were piling up yardage at a 336 per game clip, they had only four games in the win column to show for it.

Ohio State, after losing 14-3 to North Carolina, edged Washington 23-21 with a field goal with 59 seconds left to play. Then came a 28-14 victory over Illinois and a 32-7 drubbing by

Michigan State. On back-to-back weekends, the Spartans showed their 1965 class by whipping both Michigan and Ohio State by a composite score of 56-14. The Buckeyes resumed by taking Wisconsin, 20-10, and then resorted to a late field goal again, this one with 77 seconds showing on the clock, to slip past Minnesota 11-10. OSU went on to topple Indiana 17-10, and Iowa 38-0.

Ohio State was 6-2-0; Michigan 4-5-0.

The Buckeyes came out ahead in a 9-7 thriller when Bob Funk booted a field goal with just 75 seconds remaining in the game as 77,733 looked on under gray skies in Ann Arbor. Funk's winning kick capped a long OSU drive that started back in Buckeye territory at the nine, and stalled at Michigan's 11.

The Wolverines led in total yards 335-261, accepted three OSU turnovers, reached the Bucks' six-yard line not only once, but twice, and the 16 and 18-yard lines on other occasions, but got no points on any of the four threats. For that matter, Ohio State crossed the midfield stripe only three times all afternoon. The difference was that the Buckeyes cashed for points twice and won.

The Bucks took an early lead on a five-yard pass from Don Unverferth to Bill Anders to conclude a 76-yard drive. Funk missed his first conversion of the season and the score was 6-0. Ohio didn't come close to scoring until the winning field goal.

In the second quarter, the Wolverines went 71 yards, all on the ground, to OSU's six but were held. Moments later, Mike Bass intercepted a Buckeye pass and returned it 10 yards to the Ohio 15. Three straight carries by fullback Dave Fisher got the ball to the two-yard line and it was Fisher again for the touchdown. Dick Sygar's conversion gave Michigan a 7-6 lead with 3:14 left before intermission.

The Buckeyes took the ensuing kickoff and worked their way out to the 41 but fumbled and Rick Volk recovered for U-M. This led to the Wolves' trip as far as the 16.

Early in the third quarter, Michigan knocked out a 70-yard march and was first-and-goal at Ohio's six. Visions of the game in the "W" column danced before Wolverine eyes. The Buckeye defense, however, had other visions. Three plays later the ball was still on the six. Sygar missed a field goal. Another field goal by Sygar was off-target in the final period. This was when Michigan faced a fourth-and-two situation at the Ohio 18.

As the clock wound down, the Wolverines' 7-6 lead seemed secure despite the missed scoring opportunities. OSU had lacked offensive punch throughout the afternoon. At 7:30 on the game

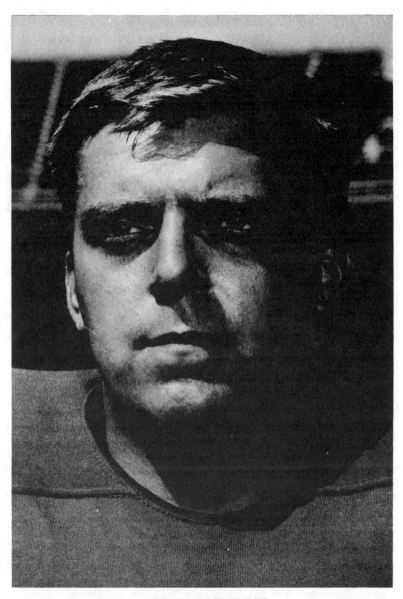

OSU'S BOB FUNK

His 28-yard field goal in the last 75 seconds of the game toppled Michigan 9-7 at Ann Arbor in 1965. Funk's FG accuracy that year also edged Washington 23-21 with 59 seconds left, and Minnesota 11-10 with 77 seconds remaining. (Photo courtesy of OSU Photo Archives.)

clock, U-M punted the Bucks into a hole at the nine-yard line and Michigan was certain Ohio State was safely put away for another year.

On fourth-and-two at their own 16, OSU went for broke and Will Sanders rammed for a first down to keep the drive alive. Ten plays later the Bucks were camped on the U-M 11 and only 1:15 remained in the game. It was fourth down and kicker Funk came onto the field. This was the ball game and the screaming thousands knew it. Funk, a goat all day because of his missed conversion in the first quarter, slammed the ball through the uprights for a 9-7 lead. Instant hero again. Funk had hit on last gasp field goals to provide the winning margin in three OSU games in the season.

Even though there was just over a minute left in the game, Michigan didn't hoist the white flag. The ensuing kickoff gave the Wolverines the ball at their own 33. John Gabler completed three passes to Jack Clancey for a 40-yard advance to the OSU 27. With six seconds to go, Michigan sent in Paul D'Erame, the 5-10, 212-pound kickoff specialist for a last ditch, desperation field goal attempt. It would have been a 44-yard shot but it fell short.

Woody Hayes had finished his 15th season at Ohio State and compiled a record of 97-33-7, .733, including 10 wins over Michigan.

The scramble for the national championship that year rivaled the 1942 season's mad finish when the Buckeyes captured the title. In 1965, Michigan State (No. 1), Nebraska (No. 2), and Arkansas (No. 3) all finished the regular season with 10-0-0 records. The *Associated Press*, for the first time, decided to wait until after the bowl results to bestow the crown. Arkansas lost 14-7 to LSU in the Cotton Bowl, Michigan State lost 14-12 to UCLA in the Rose Bowl and Nebraska lost 39-28 to Alabama in the Orange Bowl. The Crimson Tide slipped into the final No. 1 slot. Meanwhile, the UPI title went to Michigan State.

1966

THE "TRANSISTOR BOWL"

For the first time since 1897, when Michigan and Ohio State began playing football games against each other, their meeting was not to be the day's most important event—athletic or otherwise—occurring within the borders of the two states.

It was November 19 and the Wolverines were in Columbus. It's just as well, because back in Michigan, about 250 miles away in East Lansing, Michigan State (9-0-0) was hosting Notre Dame (8-0-0). Had the Buckeyes played in Ann Arbor, the best that could have happened is that "The Big One" would be ignored.

In terms of buildup in the national media, the 1966 Irish-Spartan clash might very well have been the "biggest" regular season college football game ever played. Bigger even than the Notre Dame-Army encounter at Yankee Stadium in 1946, a game in which there were over a million requests for tickets. And just as that earlier "Game of the Century" failed to live up to its billing (a scoreless tie), neither did the dream game in East Lansing.

All over America, sportswriters took on the added job of entertainment critic and blasted both teams and their coaches for a dull 10-10 tie that no one, it seemed, tried as hard to win as to keep from losing. In an age when television dramas of every description had conditioned the American public to expect exciting, happy or even sad resolutions of every conflict, a tie football game was an unforgivable insult.

Jack Saylor of the *Detroit Free Press* was in Columbus. Saylor dubbed the 63rd game in the Michigan-Ohio State series

Detroit Free Press

Inside This Section . . .
The Inside of Sports   Page 6
Racing Results   Page 7
Michigan Outdoors   Page 8
Want Ads   Pages 9-20

Detroit Free Press

Sports — Want Ads

SECTION C

SUNDAY, NOVEMBER 20, 1966

10 to 10

Why?

ND Rally Catches Spartans

BY HAL McCOY

Parseghian, Daugherty—Both look like they're No. 2

'Conservative' Irish Irk Spartans

BY JACK BERRY

St. Ambrose Is Goodfellow Champ, 33-19

BY HAL SCHRAM

Irish stew as Spartans' Regis Cavender (25) Storms in for TD

MSU—Irish Highlights

But Detroit Falls, 7-2

Wings 'Platoon' Goalies on Hawks

CHICAGO

Flowery Words for Purdue

BY JACK SAYLOR

U-M, Detwiler Roll over Bucks, 17-3

That infamous tie in 1966 between Ara's Irish and Duffy's Spartans sent Michigan-Ohio State to the bottom of the sports page — even in Detroit.

the "Transistor Bowl." Saylor wrote, "It was attended by 83,403 radios, accompanied by people with two eyes on the action here and one ear tuned to 'that other' game in East Lansing."

And except that it was Michigan vs. Ohio State, the game in Columbus had little going for it.

The Wolverines opened the 1966 season by blasting Oregon State, 41-0. The next week, Ohio State got underway against TCU and won, 14-7, while Michigan took California, 17-0. The Wolverines then dropped three in a row—to North Carolina, Michigan State and Purdue. Not to be outdone, the Buckeyes kept pace by losing to Washington, Illinois and Michigan State.

Michigan rebounded with three victories while OSU won two of its next three games. The Wolverines were 5-4-0; the Buckeyes 4-4-0.

U-M dominated the first quarter, driving to Ohio's 13,18 and seven-yard lines. The last penetration resulted in a Dick Sygar field goal with 2:57 remaining in the period.

Midway through the second quarter, the Buckeyes banged out a 53-yard march that was halted at the Wolves' nine. Gary Cairns booted a field goal for a matching three points.

After receiving the subsequent kickoff, Michigan moved out front to stay. Keyed by 34 and 13-yard pass plays from quarterback Dick Vidmer to Jack Clancy, the nation's leading pass receiver that year, the visitors went 66 yards in nine plays, capped by Jim Detwiler's seven-yard TD burst. Sygar's PAT was perfect and with 1:11 before the half, U-M was in front 10-3.

Coach Bump Elliott's boys put the game away with another touchdown in the third quarter when Vidmer and Clayton Wilhite collaborated on a 23-yard scoring pass. Another Sygar conversion completed the scoring at 17-3, Michigan.

In the fourth quarter, Ohio State had a first-and-goal at the nine but the determined Wolverine defense held tight, as they did a few minutes later at the 18.

Both teams racked up the yardage. Michigan led in first downs 21-20, yards rushing 272-146 and total yards 382-268. OSU completed 11 of 29 passes for 122 yards; Michigan's air game resulted in six-for-15 for 110 yards. Penalty yards? U-M once again led in that category, 89-38. Detwiler rammed the Ohio line for 140 yards in 20 carries, while Vidmer accounted for all of the Wolverines passing yardage.

Coach Woody Hayes' "cloud of dust" offense was losing some of its dust and luster. In 1966, the Buckeyes averaged 22 passes per game and in the last four seasons had thrown a total of 699 passes and completed 338 for 3864 yards. That made up 43 percent of the team's total yardage. How times change.

Michigan State won its second straight Big Ten title, but because of "the rule" (no-repeat), had to watch the Rose Bowl on television. Runner-up Purdue, with an 8-2-0 record (losses to Notre Dame and Michigan State), represented the Conference instead.

In a surprise and controversial move, the Rose Bowl committee selected Southern Cal as the host team. UCLA raised bedlam over the choice. The Uclans had beaten USC 14-7 and finished 9-1-0 overall, losing only to Washington. Meanwhile, the Trojans had dropped three of its last four games, including a 0-51 humiliation to Notre Dame, but got the nod because of their 4-1-0 Conference record, which was one-half game better than UCLA's 3-1-0 mark.

Purdue won the game 14-13 when the Trojans missed on a two-point conversion play with just over two minutes left to play.

Notre Dame won the national championship and Michigan State settled for second. Alabama, Georgia and UCLA rounded out the top five teams in 1966.

1967

GAME 64

1,000 TO 600

The Big Ten treated fans to a thrilling three-way race for the championship in 1967 but neither Michigan nor Ohio State were among the contenders. When the day arrived for the 64th meeting of the old foes, the Buckeyes stood fourth in the Conference and the Wolverines were one notch lower.

Except for Michigan reaching a milestone victory, and Ohio State beating Michigan, the season for both teams was, more or less, a washout.

Six weeks into the '67 campaign, the two teams combined could count only three wins—OSU was 2-3-0; U-M 1-5-0. At that point, however, both struggled from the canvas and KO'ed the next three opponents.

Michigan opened the season with a 10-7 win over Duke before losing to California, Navy, Michigan State, Indiana and Minnesota. The horrendous five-game losing streak was snapped in a 7-3 squeaker over Northwestern in a game the press played up as Michigan's 500th all-time football victory. It was, however, No. 499. The 500th came a week later at Champaign, by a 21-14 score against Illinois. A 27-14 triumph over Wisconsin was next and the Wolverines were on their way to No. 600, and 4-5-0 on the season.

For only the ninth time in the history of Ohio State football, the Buckeyes lost a season opener. Arizona did it 14-7. Victories over Oregon, Northwestern, Michigan State, Wisconsin and Iowa followed, interspersed with losses to Purdue and Illinois, and the Buckeyes were 5-3-0.

Against Michigan, the Bucks scored three touchdowns in the first 22 minutes of the game and held on for a 24-14 success at Ann Arbor before 64,411 and a regional television audience.

OSU took the opening kickoff and quickly went 79 yards for a score as Randy Hubbard bolted for the final 22. Gary Cairns' conversion was good and it was 7-0. On the Bucks' next possession the score became 14-0. Hubbard broke away for a 25-yard run to Michigan's 39 and six plays later Hubbard scored again, this time from the 12. Cairns converted.

The Wolves halted Ohio's next surge but the Bucks scored again on their fourth possession. A seven-play, 47-yard drive ended when quarterback Bill Long sneaked over from inside the one-yard line. With eight minutes still left in the first half and the score 21-0, a rout seemed imminent. OSU moved in again, to the 17-yard line, but missed a field goal.

Taking over at the 20, Michigan came to life and went 80 yards in eight plays for a touchdown. Dennis Brown's pass to Jim Berline covered the final 13 yards. When Berline crossed the goal, Michigan's point total in games against Ohio State reached the 1,000 mark. Frank Titas made it 1,001 by kicking the conversion with less than a minute to play in the first half. OSU was comfortably in front, 21-7.

Pointwise, it was a day of milestones in the series. For Ohio State, when Hubbard scored his second touchdown in the first quarter, the Buckeyes reached 600 points in games against Michigan. Cairns' conversion made it 601.

The scoreless third quarter was highlighted by a great Wolverine goal line stand, stopping the Bucks only six inches from still another touchdown.

In the final period, Brown pitched his second TD pass of the game, this one to John Gabler with 7:30 left to play. Titas tacked on the PAT and suddenly the Wolverines had gotten within striking distance at 21-14.

Anxious to close the gap, Michigan tried an on-sides kick. It failed to work and the Buckeyes took over at their own 46. Now the Wolverines had two enemies—the opposition and the clock. The opposition proceeded to use up five minutes of the clock with a ground-pounding drive to the 18-yard line. OSU stalled there but Cairns came on and booted a field goal with just over two minutes remaining in the game. The final of 24-14 was posted.

Even though OSU jumped off to a quick 21-0 lead, the final outcome of this game, more than likely, boiled down to the turnover score — Michigan 4, Ohio State 0.

The Bucks led in first downs 18-17, rushing yards 283-128 and total yards 328-307. The Wolverines completed 17 passes (24 attempts) for 179 yards, but an interception and three lost fumbles kept the team bogged down in its comeback attempt. Ohio was five-for-six in passing for 45 yards. For the eighth straight year, Michigan was penalized more yards in the annual battle, this time 34-8.

After 64 games, the Wolverines' series lead was 37-23-4.

As the final Saturday of the Big Ten season dawned, Purdue led the Conference with a perfect 6-0-0 record. Indiana and Minnesota, both with 5-1-0 records, were close behind. By dusk, Minnesota had topped Wisconsin and Indiana had stunned the Boilermakers. Out of the three-way tie the Hoosiers came up with the "Go West" signal and took the school's first bowl trip. The Trojans of Southern Cal, armed with O.J. Simpson, were perfect hosts—until kickoff time in the Rose Bowl. USC won 14-3.

1968

GAME 65

AGAIN. AND OSU JUST LOVED IT!

Seven seasons ago, Ohio State had mutilated Michigan, 50-20. In 1968, OSU slammed the Wolverines again, this time by a 50-14 score. The two games presented many similarities. For example, both times the Buckeyes scored 29 second-half points after leading by just one touchdown; both times an OSU fullback scored four touchdowns; both times the winners scored late in the game; both times Woody Hayes ordered a two-point conversion attempt, and both times the playing field after the game was the scene of boisterous behavior.

The 1961 game was not crucial. This one, in contrast, was for *everything*—the Big Ten crown, the Rose Bowl and a possible national championship.

Michigan was especially incensed over the two-point conversion attempts in the two runaway games. To put it more bluntly, Michigan was as mad as hell. Because of the Wolverines' year-long sour mood, the Buckeyes had a day of reckoning coming. But not yet.

When the AP and UPI pollsters were asked to cast their ballots in early September, none of them paid any attention to the Buckeyes or Wolverines. However, when November 23 rolled around and time for the two teams to settle their differences on the gridiron, instead of with talk and the written word, the Ohioans were ranked No. 2 in the Nation, and Michigan No. 4.

Michigan's surprise season started on September 21; Ohio's fabulous football fall a week later. Here are the schedules and results:

OHIO STATE (8-0-0)		MICHIGAN (8-1-0)	
Open	—	California	7-21
SMU	35-14	Duke	31-10
Oregon	21- 6	Navy	32- 9
Purdue	13- 0	Mich. St.	28-14
N'western	45-21	Indiana	27-22
Illinois	31-24	Minnesota	33-20
Mich. St.	25-20	N'western	35- 0
Wisconsin	43- 8	Illinois	36- 0
Iowa	33-27	Wisconsin	34- 9
Average	31-15	Average	29-12

The steamrolling Buckeyes were gouging out an average of 447 yards per game (292/155, rush/pass) and the Wolverines were averaging 405 yards (237/168).

A record-setting Ohio Stadium crowd of 85,371 turned the place into a sardine can of humanity and the partisan mass roared and roared with every one of Ohio's 88 plays, 467 yards and 50 points. They were in glory as they watched their Buckeyes run up the score. It was only the fifth time in history that a Michigan team had surrendered as many as 50 points in one game.

Back in Ann Arbor, over 10,000 fans jammed the University Events Building on the Michigan campus to watch the game on closed circuit television. Admission was $3.00 a head. It was a cheering, foot-stomping and singing crowd, and when Ron Johnson crashed over from the one-yard line in the first quarter to give the Wolverines a 7-0 lead, the building rocked.

Johnson also had a 39-yard dash in that early drive and there was a 21-yard pass from Dennis Brown to Jim Mandich as Michigan went 80 yards in nine plays after taking over following a missed field goal by Ohio State.

Larry Zelina returned the ensuing kickoff 52 yards to the Michigan 32. At the 23, a fumble momentarily halted the Bucks. U-M had to punt into the wind and OSU got it 45 yards out. The Buckeyes quickly moved in and fullback Jim Otis banged over from the five for his first of four touchdowns for the afternoon. Jim Roman's conversion was good and the score was 7-7. Roman would later add four more conversions and a field goal.

Detroit Free Press
Sports–Want Ads
SUNDAY, NOVEMBER 24, 1968

SECTION C

In This Section
The Inside of Sports Page 8
Outdoors with Opre Page 10
Want Ads Pages 11-22

Goodby, Title and Roses!
U-M Mauled, 50-14

BY JACK SAYLOR
Free Press Sports Writer

MSU:
Happy Finish

Spartans KO Cats, 31-11

BY JERF SILVESTER

EVANSTON —

Did Woody Pour It On? Bump: No

BY JOE FALLS
Free Press Sports Writer

It Takes 50 Points to 'Satisfy' Woody

BY JACK BERRY
Free Press Sports Writer

Wings Rip Leafs, 5-2

Last Shot Nips Pistons

Final Big Ten Standings

JIM OTIS

*Rammed for four touchdowns against
Michigan in Buckeyes' 50-14 rout. (Photo
courtesy of OSU Photo Archives.)*

As the second quarter got under way, OSU quarterback Rex Kern sneaked over from the five and it was 14-7. Later in the period, Michigan tied the score as Billy Harris recovered Mike Polaski's fumble at the Buckeye 28. Eight plays later, Johnson powered over from the one and after the PAT it was 14-14.

Ohio took the kickoff and used 17 plays to cover 86 yards. Otis got the final yard with just seconds remaining in the first half. Halftime: Buckeyes 21, Michigan 14, and obviously nothing had been decided yet.

In the third quarter, Zelina tallied on a six-yard run that capped a 72-yard OSU drive. Roman missed the point-after and the scoreboard read 27-14.

Michigan went right back to the Ohio 14-yard line but a holding penalty scrambled the march. The teams then traded an interception and a punt each as the game entered the fourth quarter and disaster came looking for the Wolverines.

Roman kicked a 22-yard field goal for a 30-14 advantage. Doug Adams quickly intercepted a pass at U-M's 31 and, helped along by a 15-yard personal foul penalty, Kern scored from inside the five-yard line for a 37-14 lead with 10 minutes still left to play.

OK, honey, let's see, that's a loaf of bread, a dozen eggs, a quart of milk....

The Dispatch
PAGE 1-31 ..... SUN. NOV. 24, 1968

SPORTS SECTION   SECTION B

Outdoor Features,
Vital Statistics,
Classified Ads

Bury Michigan, 50-14 for Title, Rose Bowl

BUCKEYES WIN IT ALL - - - BIG

On Ohio's next possession, Ray Gilliam ran 50 yards to the Michigan five to set up Otis' third touchdown. With 3:30 remaining, the count became 44-14.

"I've gotten to the point now where 50 points and nothing less is a satisfying margin the way college football teams play today and pass and score," Hayes told Jack Berry of the *Detroit Free Press* after the game.

So, Woody went out and got his 50.

Art Burton immediately picked off a pass at the Michigan 11. It was third-and-one at the two-yard line and reserve fullback Paul Huff not only failed to get the touchdown, but also the first down. Hayes quickly got Otis back into the lineup and the big fullback barreled into the endzone. That brought the score to 50-14.

Woody ordered a two-point conversion. It failed.

"When U-M quarterback Don Moorhead was rolled out of bounds in the final minute, the fists flew. Some more were directed at the Wolverines as they left the field, but most of the mob contented themselves with tearing down the goalposts....It looked as if a wholesale war might break out," reported the *Free Press*.

"So carried away were the fans by not only the glorious triumph but also the resounding margin that thousands swarmed onto the field at the finish, enveloped Coach Hayes and the Buckeye players, ripped down the goal posts at both ends of the field, surrounded the magnificent OSU marching band when it completed a post-game victory jam session by doing a script Ohio, and the many more thousands still in the stands literally rocked the giant horseshoe with foot-stomping, hand-clapping and hoarsevoiced cheering," wrote Paul Hornung of the *Columbus Dispatch*.

It was the first time in six years that the home team had won a Michigan-Ohio State football game.

CHALMERS "BUMP" ELLIOTT
The 1968 game against OSU was the last in
his 10-year coaching career at Michigan.
Bump was an All-America at Michigan in
1947 and his brother, Pete, made All-America
there in 1948. (Photo courtesy of Michigan
Athletic Department.)

Meanwhile, back on the campus in Ann Arbor, the mood
wasn't nearly so festive. "Just before the score hit 50-14, the crowd
was as silent as a concrete wall. A small voice echoed through the
darkness: 'We're No. 1.' Nobody laughed," typed Wells Twombly,
who was there for the *Free Press*.

Ohio led in first downs 28-17 and total yards 467-311. The Bucks' passing game was six-for-nine (46 yards) while U-M completed 14 of 24 passes for 171 yards. The Wolverines were penalized 43 yards—six more than the opposition. Otis was the day's big offensive weapon with 143 yards in 34 carries.

"In the moment of despair, Bump Elliott wore a warm smile. He was a gentleman to the end—to the bitter end. If he was angered at Woody Hayes for pouring it on in the final moments of Saturday's 50-14 romp, Elliott wasn't showing it," Joe Falls of the *Free Press* reported.

And that's the way Bump Elliott went out. It was his last game as coach at Michigan. Elliott's 10-year, 95-game record was 51-42-2 and his Wolverines had won the Big Ten championship and Rose Bowl in 1964.

On the day OSU was ripping Michigan apart, Southern Cal defeated UCLA 28-16 to remain No. 1 in the polls. A week later, however, Notre Dame came from behind to gain a historic 21-21 tie with the Trojans, and Ohio State went to the Rose Bowl as the top-ranked team in the country. The opponent, USC, was No. 2.

Although the Trojans kicked a field goal and Heisman Trophy winner O.J. Simpson streaked for an 80-yard TD to give his team a 10-0 lead in the second quarter, the powerful Bucks kept their poise and came back to take a 27-16 victory and the 1968 national championship—Hayes' third in 18 seasons.

A perfect 10-0-0 season, including a 50-14 victory over Michigan, a Rose Bowl triumph and a No. 1 national ranking in both the AP and UPI polls. For Buckeyes everywhere, 1968 was a vintage year.

The season also was the beginning of an incredible 10-year streak in which only OSU or Michigan would win or share the Big Ten football title.

With nine Buckeye victories over Michigan in the past 12 years, the Wolverines' series lead had been sliced to 37-24-4, and the point total to 1022-661.

Buckeye boosters couldn't care less about Michigan's soreness over the 50-14 score (and the two-point conversion attempt) in 1968. Michigan had put the timber to OSU in the past, too. For example, 86-0 in 1902, and 58-6 in 1946. So, all's fair in love and war, and especially in the Ohio State-Michigan football rivalry.

1969

GAME 66

PUPIL MASTERS TEACH

By mid-November, the 1969 Ohio State Buckeyes were being hailed in the national media as one of the all-time great college football teams. The journalists were using such terms as "unbeatable," "invincible," and "awesome," just to name a few, in describing the Bucks.

The power-packed Ohio team entered the Michigan game with 22 straight victories and for the season had averaged 46 points and 512 yards per game. The pre-season polls had Woody Hayes' 19th edition rated No. 1 and OSU proceeded to bury everybody in the way. Victims included, TCU 62-0, Washington 41-14, Michigan State 54-21, Minnesota 34-7, Illinois 41-0, Northwestern 35-7, Wisconsin 62-7 and Purdue 42-14.

This team played football like a runaway freight train and held a firm grip on the country's top position.

Glenn (Bo) Schembechler, a transplanted Buckeye, was in his first year as head coach at Michigan. Schembechler played high school football at Barberton, Ohio, and was an All-State lineman. His college playing days were spent at Miami of Ohio, where he played for Woody Hayes. He later received a master's degree from Ohio State and was an assistant coach on Hayes' staff. Schembechler then held assistant jobs at Presbyterian College in South Carolina, Bowling Green in Kentucky and at Northwestern before becoming head coach at his alma mater Miami in 1963. His six-year record there was an impressive 40-17-3—good enough to get Michigan's attention.

It took Schembechler, Michigan's 14th coach, but only the eighth since 1901, just five games to get his Wolverine team on the go. Michigan blasted Vanderbilt (42-14) and Washington (45-7), were blasted by Missouri (40-17) before beating Purdue (31-20) and losing to Michigan State (23-12). The record was 3-2-0.

Schembechler then shifted his team into overdrive and ran roughshod over Minnesota, Wisconsin, Illinois and Iowa by an average score of 45-6 per game.

When it came time to get eyeball-to-eyeball with Ohio State, the Wolverines were 7-2-0, averaging 36 points per outing and placed 12th in both the national polls. Despite the record and recent strong surge, Michigan was made an official 17-point underdog.

When the oddsmakers were calculating the differences between the two teams for their 1969 battle, someone apparently forgot about a small incident that occurred in the 1968 game—namely the late-game, two-point conversion try by OSU. Michigan had not forgotten that decision by Hayes with the score already 50-14, and even after a year, the Wolverines were still furious. As game time neared, the fury got more acute.

So Michigan came to take its fury out on the Buckeyes, and that they did, with an electrifying 24-12 upset before a record Michigan Stadium throng of 103,588, plus a national television audience of millions, on this cold, gray November 22 afternoon.

The place was absolutely cuckoo. All afternoon.

All of the scoring took place in the first half. In the second half, a supercharged Wolverine defense shut down the Bucks' powerful, ground-hoggin' offense. For the day, the U-M defense produced seven OSU turnovers to give the ball back to their offensive teammates. Six were pass interceptions and one a fumble recovery.

There wasn't too much defense by either team in the first two quarters of action. Ohio received the opening kickoff and on the game's first scrimmage play, Rex Kern ripped off a 25-yard gain and Jim Otis followed with seven more to spark a quick drive to the Michigan 10. The Wolverines held and handwriting began to appear on the wall. U-M punted and Larry Zelina returned it 36 yards to the Wolverine 16. Kern threw to Stan White for a 13-yard advance. Two plays later, Otis powered in for the touchdown. White missed the conversion, but Ohio was on top, 6-0.

Undaunted, Michigan marched right back. Glenn Doughty returned the ensuing kickoff 30 yards to the U-M 45. Quarterback Don Moorhead's three pass completions, two to Jim Mandich for 16

Above: Jan White scores on a 22-yard pass from Rex Kern in second quarter to give OSU a short-lived 12-7 lead in the 1969 game at Ann Arbor. Chasing White is Brian Healey (24), while Bruce Jankowski trails the play.

Below: UM's Garvie Craw (48) plunges over for a 13-12 lead. Others shown are Mark Debevc (83), Mike Sensibaugh (3), Bob Baumgartner (60) and Jim Mandich (88). (Photos courtesy of Michigan Athletic Department)

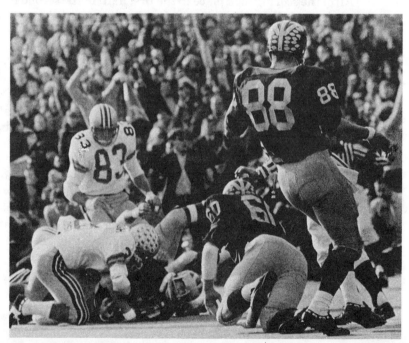

California, Here We Come
U-M 24, OSU 12

yards and one to Mike Oldham for eight yards, plus a John Gable run of 11 yards, keyed an eight-play drive to OSU's seven. Moorhead then broke for six yards and Garvie Craw crashed over on the next play. Frank Titas tacked on the point-after and with 3:35 left in the first quarter, the Wolverines led 7-6—the first time all season the Buckeyes had been on the short end of the score.

But it didn't bother the Bucks as they answered promptly with another touchdown. Kern hit White with a 28-yard pass and then a 22-yard strike for the score. White's conversion was good but Michigan was penalized half-the-distance and Ohio elected to go for two points. From the 54-inch line, Kern wanted to pass but he was sacked by Mike Kelly. Eight seconds into the second quarter and Ohio State had regained the lead, 12-7.

The Wolverines, to their credit, never broke stride. Doughty got off another good kickoff return, this time 31 yards to his own 42. Moorhead passed to Billy Harris for nine to the Ohio 49. Gabler carried it to the 42, a Moorhead-to-Mandich pass got it to the 33, and Billy Taylor got away on a beautiful broken-field run of 28 yards to the OSU five. Craw blasted to the one and then for the touchdown. Titas' kick was perfect and with 11:54 remaining in the second period, the Wolverines led 14-12.

The place was rocking.

One minute and 44 seconds later, Michigan had another touchdown. The Bucks couldn't move, punted, and Barry Pierson fielded the kick at the 37 and raced 60 yards before being over-hauled at the OSU three. Two plays later, Moorhead sneaked over from the two. A Titas conversion upped the score to 21-12.

Michigan Stadium rocked even harder.

The "invincible" Buckeyes were in deep trouble. After some punt exchanges, U-M got the ball at its own 20 and went for still another score. On third-and-eight from the Ohio 33, Moorhead hit Mandich with a pass to the eight. It was Moorhead-to-Mandich

289

*Michigan's Bob Baumgartner (60), Jack Harping (71), and Dan Dierdorf (72)
open things up for John Gabler (18) in the 1969 classic. Defenders include
Don Lamka (19), David Whitfield (88) and Mark Debevc (83).*

*A victory ride for Bo Schembechler after Michigan's shocking 24-12 upset of
the No. 1-rated Buckeyes in 1969. (Photo courtesy of Michigan Athletic Department.)*

again for a touchdown, but Michigan was slapped with a motion penalty and eventually settled for a 25-yard field goal by Tim Killian. With 1:15 remaining in the first half, the score was Michigan 24, Ohio State 12, and that's the way it ended.

Pierson intercepted three passes and Tom Curtis two to lead the hopped-up Wolverine defense in the second half. The defensive line shut off Ohio's powerful option play and forced them into a passing game, which spelled doom for the Buckeyes.

As the final gun sounded, "millions" of deliriously happy Wolverine fans swarmed onto the field as the Michigan marching band boomed out "Hail To The Victors." The field was still jammed long after the two teams had retreated to the dressing rooms, and the crushed OSU fans had retreated to wherever they could get away from it all.

Pupil had beaten teacher—Bo had beaten Woody. It was reported that the Michigan dressing quarters thundered with excitement.

The victory was the Wolverines' 517th on the gridiron and, more than likely, the sweetest ever. It was Ohio State's 198th defeat and no doubt one of the most bitter and heartbreaking. The Buckeyes trooped back to Columbus and called it a season; Michigan, Conference co-champs with the Bucks, took the Rose Bowl trip.

Statistics in the 1969 classic suggest a much closer game than the outcome. Michigan led in first downs 21-20 and total yards 374-373. OSU completed only 10 of 28 passes (155 yards) and threw six into the hands of Wolverine defenders. Moorhead connected on 10 passes (20 attempts) for 108 yards and six went to Mandich for 78 yards. For the 10th straight year, the Wolverines were hit with more penalty yards—37-5.

Michigan went West to face Southern Cal in the Rose Bowl. A few hours before kickoff, Schembechler suffered a heart attack and was rushed to the hospital where he was not even allowed to listen to the game. Stunned, the Wolverines lost their first Rose Bowl game, 10-3.

Bo, however, would be back.

The final AP poll placed the Buckeyes fourth behind Texas, Penn State and USC. The Wolverines were ninth.

In the decade of the 1960s, Ohio State had dominated the series. The Bucks won seven of the 10 series games and posted an overall record of 68-21-2, (.758). The Wolverines were 54-40-2, (.577).

*How sad, to see such sadness on the face of this
pretty Ohio State cheerleader. But Michigan won,
24-12. (Photo courtesy of* The Makio.*)*

Statistical breakdown of the series, 1960-69

	OHIO STATE	MICHIGAN
First downs	182	159
Yards rushing	2271	1726
Yards passing	920	997
Total yards gained	3191	2723
Passes attempted	159	167
Passes completed	73	87
Passes had intercepted	15	12
Fumbles lost	10	10
Total turnovers	25	22
Number of punts	39	47
Total plays	684	647
Yards penalized	185	369

Points scored: OSU 197, U-M 116. The total attendance for the 10 games was 779,248. The five games at Columbus averaged 83,800 and the five at Ann Arbor averaged 72,100.

(NOTE: In the last 30 years, 1940-69, Michigan had been penalized 1082 yards in the series, Ohio State only 599.)

1970

GAME 67

REVENGE

All talk all week was football in Ohio, Michigan and through-out Big Ten country. The two Midwest powerhouses were about to come together for the 67th time and both teams had perfect records. The Wolverines were 9-0-0 and ranked fourth by AP and fifth by UPI; the Buckeyes were 8-0-0 and ranked fourth by UPI and fifth by AP.

All talk all week was football, and specifically about how these season records to date would figure in the outcome of the big game.

MICHIGAN		OHIO STATE	
Arizona	20- 9	Open	—
Washington	17- 3	Texas A&M	56-13
Texas A&M	14-10	Duke	34-10
Purdue	29- 0	Michigan State	29- 0
Michigan State	34-20	Minnesota	28- 8
Minnesota	39-13	Illinois	48-20
Wisconsin	29-15	Northwestern	24-10
Illinois	42- 0	Wisconsin	24- 7
Iowa	55- 0	Purdue	10- 7
Average	31- 8	Average	32- 9

Webster's defines the word *revenge* as: *To inflict harm in re-turn for (an injury, etc.) .... Desire to take vengeance.* Revenge is a great motivator in the game of football. In last year's game, Michigan had the motivation and proceeded to inflict harm upon

294

OSU's perfect record and injury to their pride. In 1970, the force was on Ohio State's side and the Bucks used it to bring the Wolverines to their knees.

Ohio State won the battle of the unbeatens, 20-9, before 87,331 spectators in Columbus. The victory gave the high-riding Buckeyes a 42-1-0 record in the last two and a half seasons, plus other soul-warming goodies.

"This was our biggest victory," Woody Hayes told newsmen after the game. "It was the biggest because it makes up for what happened to us last year. The players were hurt. They promised me all along they were going to play their greatest game today — and they did. Going to the Rose Bowl wasn't the main thought on their minds — it was avenging last year's loss."

Jim Stillwagon, OSU guard, said, "We had a little debt to pay before we left Ohio State." Cornerback Jack Tatum put it this way: "It feels better beating Michigan than going to the Rose Bowl." Doug Adams, a linebacker, commented, "I've been thinking about Michigan every morning when I get up for a whole year." Quarterback Rex Kern added, "It was the dedication of the seniors. We didn't want to feel like we did last year."

Just as OSU was doomed going into the 1969 game, U-M never had a chance in 1970.

Michigan's Lance Scheffler received the opening kickoff and was doing just fine on the return until he stumbled. While trying to regain his balance, in stormed a Buckeye suicide squadman. Bingo! The ball flew from Scheffler's grasp into the arms of Ohio's Harry Howard who was downed at the Wolverine 26-yard line. On second down, Kern connected with Bruce Jankowski for 11 yards to the 13. Three plays produced just four yards and the Bucks were ready to take three points at this stage in the game and called upon Fred Schram to get them a field goal, which he did. It was a quick 3-0 lead for Ohio State and Ohio Stadium roared approval.

As the second period got underway, Michigan's Dana Coin tied the game three-all with 31 yard field goal, set up by Jim Betts' interception and 25-yard return to the Buckeyes' 18.

Except for a big break in the Bucks' favor, the first half probably would have ended in a tie. But it didn't. Late in the period, Michigan's Paul Staroba got off a booming 71-yard punt that would have had Ohio starting at its own 18. However, while the ball was in flight, a face-mask infraction was called. It was an unusual penalty in such a situation but it served to nullify the long punt.

Gen. W. W. Hayes' plotting against Michigan gets the full attention of his troops at Columbus in 1970. The plotting paid off – the Buckeyes won, 20-9. (Photo courtesy of OSU Photo Archives.)

Staroba's second punt went only to U-M's 47. OSU worked it to the 25 and Kern, on third-and-11, fired a perfect pass to Jankowski for a touchdown. Schram added the conversion and the home team was on top 10-3 at halftime.

After receiving the second-half kickoff, Ohio got off a short punt to midfield and the Wolverines took over and took it in for a touchdown. Don Moorhead hit Staroba for a 12-yard advance to the 38. Fritz Seyferth's two rushes netted 14 yards and Moorhead found Glenn Doughty for nine more to the 15. On third down from the 13, Moorhead threw a strike to Staroba in the corner of the endzone. Touchdown. Tim Anderson, a defensive back, shot in from the right side and blocked Coin's conversion. The Buckeyes still led, 10-9.

The Wolverines continued to dominate the game but couldn't get any points on the board. Early in the fourth quarter, Ohio took over on its own 27 after a punt. The powerful Buckeye offense, which had averaged 403 yards per game in the season, finally got in gear. Leo Hayden, on four straight carries, advanced the ball to the 50. Richard Galbos went to the 45, John Brockington to the 41, then to the 37. Hayden carried to the 34 and the 27. Kern then went to the pass, and completed one to Jan White for 16 yards to the U-M 11. Once again the Wolverines got tough down close and forced a Schram field goal of 27 yards. Ohio now led, 13-9.

After receiving the kickoff, Michigan came out throwing. But White intercepted a Moorhead pass at the Wolverine 24 and raced it down to the nine. Two plays later from the four, Hayden skirted around the right side for the touchdown that put the game away. Schram kicked good for a 20-9 score.

Now, the Buckeye rooters could start thinking about California and the Rose Bowl.

With 4:58 left to play, the Wolverines recovered a fumbled punt at midfield and moved to the 23. On fourth down a perfect pass was dropped at the 13-yard line and there went U-M's last chance for a comeback victory.

The win was Ohio's 25th of the series against 38 for Michigan (four ties). The Wolverines led in scoring 1057-693, an average of 16-10 per game.

The big difference in the 1970 game was Ohio's ability to stop Michigan's strong running game. The Wolves came in averaging 274 yards rushing but were held to a paltry 37. Moorhead did manage 118 yards passing (12-for-26) but it couldn't compare with the Buckeyes' 329 total yards of offense. The Wolverines were penalized 48 yards, Ohio 31.

Record 87,331 See Bucks Stomp Wolves, 20-9

FORECAST
By National Weather Service Sunday, winds, chance of rain. High near 50, low in 20s

Columbus Sunday Dispatch

OHIO'S GREATEST HOME NEWSPAPER

VOL. 100, NO. 145 — COLUMBUS, OHIO 43216, SUNDAY, NOVEMBER 22, 1970

SECTION A

Associated Press News, Wirephotos, United Press International and Chicago Daily News Service

200 Pages — 20 Sections — 25 Cents

Game's Spirit Bubbles Over

An Editorial

Buckeyes Are No. 1

The entire Central Ohio community extends hearty congratulations to The Ohio State University football team and coaching staff for its magnificent victory over the Wolverines of the University of Michigan and for a major Big 10 championship.

Ohio Fugitive Shot to Death

Hayden carried 28 times for 118 yards and Brockington gained 79 yards in 27 attempts, as these two running backs combined for all but 10 of OSU's running plays. The winners led in first downs 18-10.

What a difference a year makes. The happy Buckeye players were creating bedlam in their quarters.

Michigan's side was subdued. "The players dressed in silence and filed out quietly. None of them uttered a word. They didn't have to. The expressions on their faces said it all," wrote Joe Falls of the *Detroit Free Press*.

Ohio State was ready for Stanford (8-3-0) in the Rose Bowl—but not for Jim Plunkett. The Heisman Trophy winner completed 20 of 30 passes for 265 yards to lead his team to a 27-17 upset victory. Ohio trailed 10-0 in the first quarter but rallied for a 17-13 lead going into the final period. Punkett rallied his forces for two touchdowns and the win.

The final AP poll placed OSU fifth and Michigan ninth. Texas, the regular season champion, lost to Notre Dame in the Cotton Bowl, while Nebraska defeated LSU in the Orange Bowl. The Huskers got the No. 1 honor.

This was Coach Hayes' 20th season at OSU and his record stood at 134-43-7, .747. Against Michigan, he was 13-7-0.

298

1971

THE GONG SHOW

The Big Ten championship and Rose Bowl representative had already been decided when the Buckeyes went to Ann Arbor for the 68th game of the series. Michigan, with a perfect record, had picked up all the marbles. Still, the 6-3-0 Bucks were primed and more than willing to send the Wolverines to California with a defeat.

U-M had taken care of Northwestern 21-6, Virginia 56-0, UCLA 38-0, Navy 46-0, Michigan State 24-13, Illinois 35-6, Minnesota 35-7, Indiana 61-7, Iowa 63-7 and Purdue 20-17. It all added up to an average score of 40-6 and a No. 3 ranking behind Big Eight powers Nebraska and Oklahoma.

After a 52-21 romp past Iowa in the season's opener, OSU lost its 200th all-time football game, 20-14 to Colorado at Columbus. The Bucks then whipped California, Illinois, Indiana, Wisconsin and Minnesota before losing to Michigan State and Northwestern. Despite the three setbacks, both the AP and UPI polls had ranked the Buckeyes ninth.

Once again it was time for the Buckeye-Wolverine classic. The game turned out to be thrilling and entertaining for Michigan; heartbreaking and disgusting for Ohio State. U-M put on a gritty 72-yard drive deep into the fourth quarter and scored with just 2:07 left to play for a tough 10-7 victory in front of 104,016 wet, shivering fans. The afternoon's weatherman brought hail, rain, and sunshine. But it stayed frigid.

Whew! U-M 10, OSU 7

Woody Throws Tantrum Before 104,016

Detroit Free Press

SECTION

Sports D

Sunday, November 21, 1971

BY CURT SYLVESTER
Free Press Sports Writer

ANN ARBOR — It wasn't Woody Hayes' ball game but it was Woody who told the story best.

There he was, the reigning monarch of Ohio State football . . . storming on the field . . . screaming at the officials . . . scattering the yard markers . . . suffering in total frustration.

For the second time in three years, the dreaded enemy — the University of Michigan — had ruined his whole season in a single half game.

The Wolverines, unbeaten and third-ranked in the nation, left their mistakes behind them . . . yards in the closing minutes . . . Hayes and the Buckeyes, 16-7, before a two . . . crowd of 104,016 wet and shivering fans in Michigan Stadium.

IT MAY NOT rank with that earth-shaking

upset the Wolverines pulled here two years ago but what greater reward can a Michigan team have — a perfect season, a Big Ten Title, a Rose Bowl coming up and Woody seething on the sidelines.

The victory was the 11th without a loss for the season, marking the first time since 1948 that a Michigan team has completed its schedule without a loss.

And for Ohio State, hoping to spoil all that Michigan had worked for in one fatal afternoon, fell for the third straight time and finished the season with a 6-4 record . . . and a heartbreaking loss.

It was a 21-yard run by senior tailback Billy Taylor, with a devastating block by fullback Fritz Seyferth, that gave Michigan its only touchdown of the afternoon, with just two min-

utes and seven seconds left to play.

That TD, plus a second-quarter field goal by Dana Coin was all the Wolverines could muster against the rugged OSU defense but thank in the equally impressive Michigan defense, it was just enough.

"WE'RE TICKLED," said Michigan Coach Bo Schembechler in 'a throng of reporters. "We're really pleased. It has been a great season for us.

"People start to take shots at you and some times they can get to you, but they didn't get us in the first 11 games. I'll tell you, 11-0 isn't bad."

Very few of those 11 victories have been spread among so many game heroes as this last one, against the bitter foes from Ohio State.

There was Taylor, who forced himself to forget about two first-half fumbles and kept going for the winning run.

Please turn to Page 7D, Col. 1

Oh, My ...Woody Was Mad!

"This is the biggest One," (U-M) players shout after victory — Story Page 7D.

BY JACK SAYLOR
Free Press Sports Writer

ANN ARBOR — Woody Hayes was the perfect subject for a magazine cover Saturday . . . Mad Magazine.

Wayne Woodrow was mad . . . oh, my, was he mad!

Hayes' Buckeyes had been beaten by Michigan and the Ohio State coach was livid over a pass interception by the Wolverines' Tom Darden on which B. W. felt the rights of his conference had been infringed upon.

It seems Mr. Hayes used so much about the play at the time that he didn't feel like rehashing it after the game.

Writers fought their way across the field to the Ohio State clubhouse, fending off the better part of 104,016 claustrophobic fans along the way in camp on Woody's doormat.

It was not, as it developed a welcome mat.

WOODY LET the gentlemen of the press cool their heels outside for 35 minutes, while he presumably cooled his own inside.

The writers stood, bulleted about by the outpouring crowd and their ears hammering from repeated choruses of "Goodby, Woody, We're Glad to See You Go."

The only man admitted to the Ohio dressing room from the milling mob was Gov. John Gilligan of Ohio, proving Woody

Please turn to Page 7D, Col. 3

Woody Hayes screamed at an official, got socked with a 15-yard penalty, then ripped the cover (arrow) from a sideline marker.

In the Hayes' Era at Ohio State, at least in Michigan, Woody himself sometimes got as much, if not more, headline attention than his teams — 1971 was one of those times. But the Ol' Boy loved it all....

Woody Hayes went into orbit near the end. Although the officials finally "gonged" him, Woody refused to leave the stage and kept his act going.

"It wasn't Woody Hayes' ball game but it was Woody who told the story best," wrote Curt Sylvester of the *Detroit Free Press*. "There he was, the reigning monarch of Ohio State football, storming on the field, screaming at the officials, scattering the yard markers, suffering in total frustration."

"For the second time in three years, the dreaded enemy—the University of Michigan—had ruined his whole season . . . . It may not rank with that earth-shaking upset the Wolverines pulled here two years ago but what greater reward can a Michigan team have—a perfect season, a Big Ten title, a Rose Bowl coming up and Woody seething on the sidelines."

In the first half, Michigan had three good opportunities to make points but went out at intermission with only a 3-0 lead. Dana Coin had kicked a 28-yard field goal with five minutes left.

In the third period, Ohio's Tom Campana shocked the huge crowd with a beautiful 85-yard punt return for a touchdown — the longest TD punt return in the series (and would remain the longest for 20 years). Fred Schram's conversion made it 7-3 and there were rumblings of a tremendous upset.

Larry Cipa, reserve Michigan quarterback, had replaced injured Tom Slade earlier in the game and nothing seemed to work for the trailing Wolverines. Things were bleak, indeed.

With just over seven minutes left to play, Michigan received a punt at its own 28. On third-and-three, Billy Taylor burst for a big eight-yard gain and a first down at the 43. Another third down situation arose, this time with five yards to go and U-M surprised everybody, including the Buckeye defense, as Cipa threw a 22-yard pass to David Rather for another first down at Ohio's 32. Moments later, it was third down again, this time at the 23. OSU stacked up Taylor for no gain. On fourth-and-inches, the ball was given to Fritz Seyferth who leaped for two yards and a first down at the 21. Taylor, who had lost two fumbles in the first half, then scored the winning touchdown with just over two minutes remaining in the contest. Without a devastating block by Seyferth, though, there would not have been a 21-yard touchdown run. Seyferth wiped out cornerback Tom Campana to spring Taylor loose for his jaunt into the "land of milk and honey." Coin kicked good to make it 10-7, Michigan.

With just 1:25 left, and OSU trying desperation passes, U-M's Tom Darden seemed to go up the back of Dick Wakefield, Ohio's intended receiver, and intercepted the ball at the Michigan 32. Hayes thought surely there should have been an interference call. He was certain of it, in fact.

"Hayes charged onto the field, bumping officials and screaming at the top of his lungs," reported Sylvester. "All he got for his efforts was an unsportsmanlike penalty and 15 yards for Michigan.

"Hayes had to be restrained and led from the field by two of his players and one of his assistant coaches."

With just moments left in the game, the Wolverines were more than content to just run out the clock.

"When Cipa fell on the ball two straight plays and an official detected an Ohio State defender pummeling him in the pile, OSU got another 15-yard penalty and once again Woody cut loose," wrote Sylvester.

BILLY TAYLOR

His 21-yard touchdown run in the fourth quarter brought Michigan a 10-7 victory over OSU in 1971. (Photo courtesy of Michigan Athletic Department.)

"This time, Hayes grabbed the downs markers and tried to break it. He shot it javelin style onto the field. Then he headed for the first down marker and ripped off the bright orange plastic encasement, shredding it.

"The crowd went into near hysterics at Hayes' wild antics. After the game Woody rushed onto the field again and shouted at another official. He was then swallowed up by the masses that flooded the floor of the field while pulling down both goal posts."

Joe Falls of the *Free Press* reported, "For absolute frenzy, this one topped them all. Hayes was a raging madman at the end. . . . Maybe he had good reason. It'll be interesting to find out what the films show on Tom Darden's interception. Did he climb all over the Ohio receiver's back? Did Darden interfere?"

Woody, obviously, leaned to the theory that there had been interference.

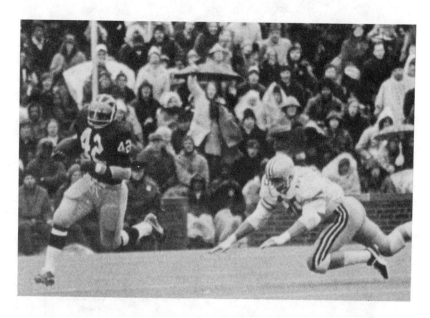

THE WINNING TOUCHDOWN!

This was the play that sent Woody Hayes into orbit in '71 — UM's Tom Dardin (35) going up-and-over and almost knocking the helmet off of Dick Wakefield, the intended receiver. (Photo courtesy of OSU Photo Archives)

TOM CAMPANA

Returned a punt 85 yards for a touchdown in 10-7 loss to Michigan in 1971. It was the series' longest TD run since 1908 and still ranks as the fourth longest. (Photo courtesy of OSU Department of Photography and Cinema.)

Michigan's defense cut off everything Ohio tried. The Bucks came into the game averaging 344 yards per game (237 rushing, 107 passing), but managed a mere 78 ground yards and just 60 by air. The winning Wolverines were way out front in first downs 20-7, and total yards 335-138. For the first time since 1957, the Buckeyes were penalized more yards than Michigan in their annual feud—64-49. The two 15-yarders late in the game, called against Coach Hayes, helped Michigan shed the long and unflattering streak.

The victory upped Michigan's series lead to 39-25-4 and its scoreboard advantage to 1065-700.

For the second year in a row, an unbeaten Big Ten champ faced an 8-3-0 Stanford team in the Rose Bowl and the Cardinals pulled another shocker, this time over Michigan in a 13-12 thriller. Stanford marched 64 yards to the Wolverines' 14-yard line and kicked a field goal with only 22 seconds remaining in the game.

Michigan's final standing in the national polls was fourth (UPI) and sixth (AP). Nebraska won the national championship for the second year in a row.

1972

A DEFENSIVE MIRACLE

Michigan was 10-0-0 and Ohio State 8-1-0 as the two sister institutions of the Big Ten prepared for their annual reunion. This reference to relationship, of course, is merely an acknowledgement of their respective memberships in the same sponsoring body. In no other respect could this reunion be thought of as a coming together of loving and long-separated kinfolk, hugging and kissing and breaking bread in peaceful harmony.

For example, what self-respecting family would have a reunion only to extract revenge. Reunion, as applied to a Michigan-Ohio State football game, simply means a coming together to resume hostilities, and to be as harmonious as possible so as to be more effective in breaking bones.

"Revenge—sweet revenge. Woody and his Buckeyes got it Saturday. But, man-oh-man, did they have to work for it. A whole year's steaming and stewing over last year's loss to Michigan. . .a whole year's plotting and retribution. . .a whole year's anger and determination," wrote Curt Sylvester of the *Detroit Free Press*.

The score was 14-11. The game was much closer than that. Ohio State won on two dramatic goal line miracles. Michigan ran 12 plays inside OSU's six-yard line, and eight times inside the three, but walked away with only one touchdown and a crushing defeat that cost the Wolverines an undisputed Conference crown and a trip to the Rose Bowl. Ohio State went instead.

The Wolverines had brushed aside UCLA, Tulane, Navy, Illinois, Minnesota, Indiana and Iowa by an average score of 32-4. In much closer games, they also beat Northwestern (7-0), Michigan

State (10-7) and Purdue (9-6) enroute to their perfect season and a No. 3 national ranking behind Southern Cal and Alabama.

OSU lost its only game eight weeks into the season, 19-12, to Michigan State, but walloped eight other opponents by an aggregate score of 237-99. It was the school's first 10-game regular season schedule in 30 years.

The Buckeyes, a six-point underdog, were ready for the invasion of their Northern foes with an eighth place national ranking. Just over 87,000 crammed Ohio Stadium on a dark, rainy November 25 and found themselves completely drained emotionally by the time the afternoon's drama concluded some two hours after kickoff. A national television audience also looked on and shared the excitement.

Michigan led in first downs 21-10, total yards 344-192 and operated 83 plays to only 44 for OSU. Still, they lost.

"Is there anyone in the house now who does not believe in the mystical powers of Wayne Woodrow Hayes? The Fat Man did it again, Saturday. Boy, did he do it! He took the second best team on the field and came out first best with it . . . You just don't come to Columbus for the big games and push the Fat Man around. He always seems to think of something," reported Joe Falls of the *Free Press*.

On this particular day, Coach Hayes "thinked" defense, and particularly the defense of his own team's goal line from close in.

Trailing 7-3 in the second quarter, the Wolverines had a first-and-goal opportunity at OSU's one-yard line. The defense denied a score. Early in the final period, with the score 14-11, the Buckeyes stood their ground again. Michigan was first-and-goal from the five; second-and-goal from the four; third-and-goal from the two, and fourth-and-goal from just inches away. The few inches never came and the old stadium shook all the way down to its 50-year-old foundation.

In the first quarter, U-M got to OSU's 22-yard line but a penalty stopped the drive. Later there was a penetration to the 27 and a missed long field goal try. A minute into the second period, Mike Lantry kicked a 35-yard field goal for a 3-0 Wolverine lead. It was short-lived as the Buckeyes fought back to go up 7-3 when freshman Archie Griffin gained 10 and 18 yards to set up Harold Henson's one-yard plunge. Blair Conway converted and the first half ended with the Buckeyes leading by four points.

Ohio State took the second-half kickoff and quickly made it 14-3. Aided by a five-yard penalty that resulted in a first down at the OSU 33, quarterback Greg Hare, on a second-and-six play,

307

Interesting headlines from the 1972 game. In Michigan (Detroit) it was Michigan losing it. In Ohio (Columbus) it was Ohio taking it.

rolled to the right on an option, darted back in and went 33 yards to the Wolverines' 30. Griffin broke through the right side and scored standing up. Conway kicked good again.

Michigan came right back. Chuck Heater returned the kickoff 41 yards to his own 43 and the desperate Wolves slammed down to OSU's five. It took four plays to cover the distance before fullback Ed Shuttlesworth finally scored from the one-foot line. Dennis Franklin tossed a pass to Clint Haslerig for two more big points and with 4:43 remaining in the third quarter, Michigan had pulled to within a field goal of the Big Ten title and the Rose Bowl.

Early in the fourth period, U-M's Randy Logan intercepted a Hare pass to put the Wolverines in great shape at Ohio's 29-yard line. They worked it to the five and a first down. Harry Banks swept end for one yard to the four. Banks hit for two more to the two. It was Banks again driving to within inches of the goal. In fact, it was so close that Michigan's side argued that he did indeed cross the line. But the officials said no.

That brought up fourth down. Nine minutes were left to play and a field goal here would have tied the score and possibly "won it all" for Michigan. "No, I didn't go for the one-yard field goal because I thought we could score from there. We should have scored from there," Bo Schembechler told reporters after the game.

Franklin's quarterback sneak failed.

The Bucks were still not out of the woods by any means. Operating from their own endzone, they punched it forward just enough to give punter Gary Lago a little kicking room. Lago lifted one out to the OSU 37. The raging Buckeye defense held firm—even pushed the Wolverines back a yard—and took possession. Griffin's 15-yard run and another 15 on a personal foul penalty against frustrated Michigan moved Ohio to the Wolverines' 32, where it was first down. However, Michigan wouldn't buckle and forced a long field goal try by Conway which was missed.

Michigan took over at the 20-yard line with exactly 80 yards to go and with exactly 80 seconds left to get there.

They wouldn't quit. A third-and-10 pass from Franklin to Bo Rather gained nine and Shuttleworth's plunge got a first down. After an incompletion, Franklin connected on two straight passes to Rather for 15 and 14 yards and another first down at Ohio's 41.

Time: 34 seconds.

Franklin was trapped on the next play but got back to the line of scrimmage. No time-outs were left so there was a hurried lineup and a quick out-of-bounds pass to stop the clock—at 00:13.

Good things are happening to the Buckeyes against Michigan at Columbus in 1972. (Photo courtesy of The Makio.*)*

Michigan had one more down but the crazed Buckeye rooters, who had been gathering around sidelines, exploded onto the playing field and reduced the wooden goal posts to splinters. OSU had removed the steel goal posts for this particular game and replaced them with the wooden "tear-away" models.

Under Coach Hayes' leadership, the crowd was coaxed off the field. During the melee, Hayes suffered a pulled leg muscle.

When Michigan finally got a chance at the last play, Franklin retreated to throw long. Tackle George Hasenohrl, the biggest man on the combined squads at 262 pounds, blasted in and Franklin never had a chance. Ball game. With no goal posts, what would have happened had Michigan gotton within field goal range? OSU officials, out of an abundance of experience, had foreseen that eventuality and had an extra set of wooden uprights available for immediate installation.

It was now Ohio State's ball with six seconds left to play. Once again the crowd swarmed all over the field and once again General Hayes (limping this time) came out to get the celebrants back. Order was restored and the official signaled for the clock to start. . . . five. . . .four. . . .three. . . .two. . . .one. . . .00:00. The game was officially over and the throng officially engulfed the gridiron.

The Buckeyes had recorded one of their all-time great football triumphs.

The defense didn't score any of the 14 points, but it was nevertheless a victory attributable directly to that unit, led by the great play of tackles George Hasenohrl and Pete Cusick and linebackers Randy Gradishar and Rick Middleton.

OSU moved to No. 3, U-M dropped to No. 8.

The 37 days between victory over Michigan and a Rose Bowl date with No. 1-ranked Southern Cal proved to be not enough time for the Buckeyes to return to earth. They surrendered the most points in one game in 26 years and lost to the awesome Trojans 42-17. The OSU record of 9-2-0 added up the most games played in one season by an Ohio State football team since 1905.

Hard times had fallen on Big Ten teams on New Year's Day as this was the Conference's fourth straight defeat, and fifth setback in six years. The Midwesterners still led, though, 17-10-0.

Even though clobbered by USC, the Buckeyes could brag, for at least a year, over the gallant victory past Michigan to keep the Wolverines out of Pasadena. The 75-year, 69-game series now stood 39-26-4, Michigan.

1973

GAME 70

THE SCORE? 6-4

It was one of the most drama-filled weekends in Big Ten history, and even had some cloak and dagger dimensions.

Ohio State (9-0-0) was ranked No. 1 in the nation; Michigan (10-0-0) was rated No. 4. With the "no-repeat" rule abolished two years earlier, the winner would go to the Rose Bowl.

Here is how the two powers stacked up for their 1973 collision:

OHIO STATE		MICHIGAN	
Minnesota	56- 7	Iowa	31- 7
Open	—	Stanford	47-10
TCU	37- 3	Navy	14- 0
Washington St	27- 3	Oregon	24- 0
Wisconsin	24- 0	Michigan St	31- 0
Indiana	37- 7	Wisconsin	35- 6
Northwestern	60- 0	Minnesota	34- 7
Illinois	30- 0	Indiana	49-13
Michigan St	35- 0	Illinois	21- 6
Iowa	55-13	Purdue	34- 9
Average	40- 4	Average	32- 6

The Buckeyes were ruled a solid favorite, but the way things had been going, this was Michigan's turn to get "revenge." At Ann Arbor, a record mass of 105,223 sat in cold, drizzly weather, while millions more all across the land watched on television from the coziness of living rooms, dens, taverns, motel, hotel and hospital rooms, as well as at places of work.

312

The Wolverines took their turn and had their revenge. Not by winning, but beating the odds with a 10-10 tie which left the two teams still tied for the Big Ten championship. The next day, Wayne Duke, commissioner of the Conference, took a telephone vote of the athletic directors to select the Rose Bowl representative. Don Canham, Michigan AD, told newsmen, "I can't imagine anyone going against Michigan. Frankly, I think the vote will be 9-1 in our favor."

Joe Falls of the *Detroit Free Press* wrote, "It has to be Michigan. Any other vote by the Big Ten athletic directors would be an injustice."

The coaches? Bo Schembechler was jovial (for Bo) with the press after the game, which meant he thought his team would get the vote. Even Woody Hayes was inclined to believe Michigan would get the nod, simply because OSU had gone the previous year.

But back to the game. OSU won the first half 10-0; U-M won the second half 10-0.

After a first quarter of the two heavyweights just sparring around, by the second period, they were loose. Sophomore Archie Griffin carried six times for 59 yards to spark a drive down to Michigan's 14-yard line, but OSU was forced to settle for a 31-yard field goal by Blair Conway.

Michigan's Gil Chapman returned the ensuing kickoff 72 yards to Ohio's 28. A clipping penalty, however, retreated the Wolverines back to their own 12—a 60-yard difference. The Bucks forced a punt, took possession at U-M's 46, and Griffin's 41 yards in five carries set up freshman Pete Johnson's five-yard touchdown blast. After Conway's conversion, Ohio State had what seemed to be an insurmountable 10-0 lead. The Buckeye defensive unit was one that had surrendered only four touchdowns all season.

The Wolverines took the second-half kickoff and went to Ohio's 22 before Neil Colzie intercepted a Franklin pass in the endzone. Later in the period, OSU drove to Michigan's 42 where it was fourth-and-two. Quarterback Cornelius Greene tried to make the yardage. He was short.

"That play wasn't called from our bench. . . .It was supposed to be an option with Archie (Griffin) carrying," said Hayes after the game.

If any play deserved to be called the turning point of the contest, that had been it.

Michigan, buoyed by the course of the game and with good

M Ties—Who Goes to Bowl?

QB Franklin Hurt After Rally Catches OSU, 10-10

Glum Woody Leans to U-M

Sorry, U-M... Ohio State Going To Rose Bowl

TV REPORT GAVE FALSE HOPE

U-M Players Very Bitter

Bo 'Very Bitter'

field position, moved to the Buckeye 13. Mike Lantry finally got the Wolves on the scoreboard with a 30-yard field goal on the second play of the final period. Ohio State 10, Michigan 3.

The Wolverines scored again, quickly. On the next possession, after a short punt came out to only the OSU 49, Franklin got on target. The big one was for 31 yards to Paul Seal for a first down at the 20. Three plays later, it was fourth-and-a-foot at the 10. Franklin faked a handoff to fullback Ed Shuttlesworth, kept the ball himself, cut inside Ohio's defensive end, and shot for the touchdown. Lantry's conversion made it 10-10 and Michigan Stadium became a deafening madhouse.

With just over two minutes remaining in the game, Franklin was hit hard as he let go a pass, fell on his right shoulder and broke a collar bone. As Franklin walked slowly off the field, Michigan's Rose Bowl hopes also suffered damage. Backup quarterback Larry Cipa came on. On fourth-and-two at the Ohio 40-yard line, Lantry, standing at the 48, slammed a long field goal try that had the distance but was off target by just inches. It came ever so close.

Ohio started at its own 20 with 1:01 to play and on first down U-M's Tom Drake intercepted a Greg Hare pass at the Buckeye 33 to give the Wolverines another shot. With the game down to 24 seconds, Lantry missed on a 44-yard field goal attempt and the struggle was over.

Ohio State 10, Michigan 10—the first tie in the series since the 7-7 knot in 1949.

On Sunday, the vote was announced from Conference headquarters in Chicago and to the surprise of practically everyone, it went in favor of Ohio State, 6-4. Less than 24 hours after the final gun on the gridiron, the Buckeyes had another turn at the revenge game. According to the *Free Press,* Ohio State got the votes of Illinois, Michigan State, Wisconsin, Purdue, Northwestern, and its own; Michigan was supported by Indiana, Iowa and Minnesota.

The news from Chicago threw the entire State of Michigan into a rage and uproar. It was reported that the broken collar bone suffered by Franklin had been a prime factor in the vote. After four straight Rose Bowl defeats, the Big Ten AD's were anxious for a win and picked a healthier team.

Schembechler was furious.

The game statistics went to Michigan—more first downs, 16-9, and more total yards 303-234. The Wolverines completed seven of 12 passes while Ohio was zero-for-four. Penalty yards? Michigan kept up the tradition by leading in that department as well, 37-0. Since 1940 (34 games), officials had stepped off 1256 yards in penalties against the Wolverines and only 729 against the Buckeyes.

Griffin and Shuttlesworth were the big offensive threats in the 1973 game. Griffin netted 163 yards in 30 carries; Shuttlesworth gained 116 yards in 27 attempts.

There wasn't any doubt that the athletic directors wanted the "most representative team" to carry the banner of the Big Ten to the Rose Bowl. In their judgement, it was Ohio State. They made a great choice. The Buckeyes doubled up on Southern Cal (9-1-1) by a 42-21 score to finish the season with a 10-0-1 record. Ohio State also copped the runner-up position for national honors. Notre Dame, by edging Alabama 24-23 in the Sugar Bowl, got the Irish No. 1. Oklahoma, the Crimson Tide and Penn State followed. Michigan, 10-0-1, stayed home during the Holiday Season as the No. 6 team in the country.

Never before had Michigan and Ohio State combined for 20 football wins in one season.

1974

KLABAN GOT HIS KICKS FROM THE WHOLE THING

Michigan was ranked No. 3 in the Nation with a perfect 10-0-0 record. Ohio State was the fourth-ranked team in the country with a 9-1-0 showing.

Here's the route the two teams took on the way to their 71st annual shootout:

MICHIGAN		OHIO STATE	
Iowa	24- 7	Minnesota	34-19
Colorado	31- 0	Oregon State	51-10
Navy	52- 0	SMU	28- 9
Stanford	27-16	Washington St	42- 7
Michigan St	21- 7	Wisconsin	52- 7
Wisconsin	24-20	Indiana	49- 9
Minnesota	49- 0	Northwestern	55- 7
Indiana	21- 7	Illinois	49- 7
Illinois	14- 6	Michigan St	13-16
Purdue	51- 0	Iowa	35-10
Average	31- 6	Average	41-10

The two giants collided. And what a ball game!

The scoreboard clock had blinked down to 18 seconds. Unbeaten Michigan trailed by two points and the desperate Wolverines called time out. The 88,000 or so souls crammed into Ohio Stadium were on their feet. Some were squealing and screaming, some were stomping around crazily and some stared numbly and silently into space. It was, more than likely, too late for prayer, but many were trying it, just in case.

317

The old place was a seething madhouse.

With the clock still suspended at 00:18, kicker Mike Lantry, a Vietnam veteran, and holder Tom Drake were setting themselves up back at the 23-yard line. This was it. This one was for *everything*. Not only would a field goal mean a Michigan victory over Ohio State, which in itself would be enough, but also a perfect regular season, an undisputed Big Ten title, an automatic bid to the Rose Bowl, and a possible national championship. All rode on this one play for the Wolverines. It was quite a load.

Somehow, it seems cruel that so much should ride on one play in one college football game; that so much pressure be heaped upon the shoulders of 11 young men, or in this case, on one Mike Lantry.

The official's whistle blew to resume action. The big linemen were down in position. Time seemed to stop. Back went the snap from center. Drake spotted the ball and Lantry's left foot slammed into it. The kick had plenty of distance as it sailed towards the uprights.

The Michigan players signaled "GOOD!" And the scant crowd of 4,000 Wolverine ticket-holders who had made the trip went wild. The Ohio players signaled "NO GOOD!" The officials signaled nothing. It was, at that moment, "TOO CLOSE TO CALL!" For an eternity of maybe six to eight seconds, the huge crowd agonized in suspense. Finally, it was officially signaled "NO GOOD!" The kick was wide to the left—reportedly by a mere 18 inches—and it was Ohio State's turn to explode. And they did. All 84-odd thousand.

In this the 292nd game in the 52-year history of Ohio Stadium, it was undeniably one of the most electrifying moments of the famous old horseshoe.

All of Ohio was in orbit. Buckeyes not at the game performed victory dances in front, around, and probably even a few on top of their television sets. Meanwhile, Wolverine faithfuls were crushed. Their team had just suffered the second straight "defeat" to OSU on a missed field goal late in the game and, in both cases, it was the only blot on the season's record.

In postgame comments to the news media, both Bo Schembechler and Woody Hayes had nothing but praise for Mike Lantry.

Schembechler: "He's a helluva kid. You can't blame Lantry. He has kicked more extra points and more field goals for Michigan than anybody in the history of the school. It wasn't his fault. We lost with our mistakes and should have already had won the game."

318

Hayes: "I hate to see that happen to a kid like that because he served his country in Vietnam. I have to feel that over the years and even in the game today, that the Man upstairs has looked after us."

Hayes, it should be noted, had suffered a heart attack the previous June. However, he was back among the gridiron wars in September.

There's still another "kicker" in the story of the 1974 game—a kicker named Tom Klaban, who just 10 years earlier had escaped with his family from behind the Iron Curtain in East Germany.

Michigan led 10-0 after the first 10 minutes of the game. Slowly Ohio State began a comeback. Ever so slowly. The Buckeyes did not score a touchdown, and in fact never came close to scoring one. It could have been because the Bucks were up against the No. 1 defensive team in the nation.

Klaban, however, took care of the points by booming four field goals, totaling 160 yards, to give OSU a 12-10 edge over the Wolverines.

Just two weeks before, the Buckeyes had been ranked No. 1 in the polls, but Michigan State pulled a stunner by scoring two touchdowns in the fourth quarter on runs of 44 and 88 yards for a shocking 16-13 upset. To add even more insult to injury, OSU was on MSU's one-yard line when the game ended.

Ohio State's season opener was against Minnesota at Minneapolis, and it marked the Buckeyes' first opener on the road since way back in 1894.

Against Michigan, the Bucks received the opening kickoff and amazed everybody by throwing on the first two plays—both incomplete. OSU punted. On U-M's fourth play, Dennis Franklin completed a 42-yard touchdown pass to Gil Chapman. Lantry converted for a quick 7-0 lead.

Ohio drove to Michigan's 33, but Steve Strinko intercepted a Cornelius Greene pass at the 26. Twelve plays later, the Wolves were on the enemy 20, fourth-and-eighth. Lantry booted a 37-yard field goal with 4:57 on the clock for a 10-0 advantage.

"If Buckeye followers were subdued when Michigan moved downfield in the last seconds and apparently had snatched victory from defeat, it was nothing to the hush that settled over the stadium in the first 10 minutes," wrote Paul Hornung of the *Columbus Dispatch*.

On the first play of the second quarter, Klaban swung into action with a 47-yarder after a 50-yard drive stalled at the Michigan 29.

Score: 10-3.

Bucks' Toe Beats Bo, 12-10

Klaban's Four Field Goals Victory Margin, Ohio, Michigan Share Title; Bowl Pick ???

OSU's Tim Fox (12) flies high — and in vain — trying to block Mike Lantry's 37-yard field goal in the first quarter that gave UM a 10-0 lead in the 1974 thriller at Columbus. Others shown are Rob Lytle (25), Greg DenBoer (84) and Kenneth Thompson (9). (Photo courtesy of Michigan Athletic Department)

320

Nine minutes and six seconds later, Klaban kicked a 25-yard field goal after Bruce Elia intercepted a pass at Michigan's 44.

Score: 10-6.

Ohio's next possession began at its 20-yard line and bogged at the U-M 25. Klaban came on for his third three-pointer, a 43-yarder, with just two seconds left in the first half.

Score: 10-9.

Five minutes into the third quarter, Klaban kicked what proved to be the game-winning points with a 45-yard field goal.

Score: 12-10.

Michigan was a long way from folding in this one, and kept applying pressure to Ohio's rugged defense which was itself the sixth best in the Nation against scoring. The Wolverines got down to the 39, but Neil Colzie intercepted a Franklin pass. Later, U-M was on Ohio's 30 with a first down, but wound up two yards farther out and Lantry's 49-yard field goal try was short.

With 1:50 left to play, Ohio State fans went into a tizzy when Nick Bounamici sacked Franklin for a 10-yard loss on third down to force a Michigan punt. OSU elected not to field the ball and watched as it rolled dead at the Buckeye 25.

"That's the old ball game," thought Buckeye boosters. But it wasn't the old ball game. Not quite. The Bucks were playing super-cautious just to avoid a fumble. The caution, however, combined with Michigan's judicious use of its time-outs, brought up a fourth-and-13 situation and the necessity to give the ball back to the Wolverines. Tom Sklademy got off a 32-yard kick to Michigan's 46.

Time: 00:57. Situation: Tense.

On first down, Franklin drilled a 23-yard pass to Jim Smith to the Buckeye 31 and put U-M within field goal range. After an incomplete pass, Ron Lytle ran a draw play for 10 more yards down to the 21.

Time: 00:39. Situation: More tense.

Lytle smashed for five more yards to the 16. Schembechler called time and got his field goal unit onto the field.

Time: 00:18. Situation: The tension peaked as the officials delayed their signal. Then, no one was tense anymore.

"The shock of defeat was in Schembechler's eyes as he started speaking to the writers. His voice was on the verge of breaking. But then, as he went on he seemed to grow angry as the thoughts of the day settled in his mind," wrote Joe Falls of the *Detroit Free Press*. " 'I'd like for you to show me any other team in the country which could come in here (Ohio Stadium) and keep that team out of the endzone. This was a tremendous accomplishment,' " Schembechler told Falls and the other newsmen.

TOM KLABAN

*Supplied all of the Buckeyes' points with field goals
of 47, 25, 43 and 45 yards in 12-10 win in 1974. (Photo
courtesy of OSU Photo Archives.)*

U-M Booted Out of Bowl?

Bucks' 4 FGs Win, 12-10; Vote Due Today

HE DOESN'T WANT TO GET INVOLVED IN ANY CONTROVERSY

'Lantry's FG Try Looked Good to Me'---Bo

HAD SOME UNEASY MOMENTS ON VOTE, HE ADMITS

'We Got It Because We Earned It'---Woody

Curt Sylvester of the *Free Press* wrote, " 'This was a classic example of a game that was decided by great kicking,' Hayes said in a soft-purring, cat-like way he has of speaking when he knows he just swallowed the canary."

OSU tailback Archie Griffin, who won the Heisman Trophy in 1974, led all rushers with 111 yards in 23 carries. Michigan was out front in first downs 18-14, and total yards 291-253. Each team netted 195 ground yards, while the Wolverines completed five of 14 passes for 96 yards and OSU three of six for only 58 yards. For a change, the Bucks were penalized more yards, 25-16.

The Conference athletic directors met in Chicago the next day but there was no suspense as to which team would get the Rose Bowl ticket. It would be Ohio State University. For the third straight year the Rose Bowl had a matchup of OSU vs. Southern Cal. In Pasadena, the Buckeyes led 17-10 with just over two minutes remaining and had USC backed up to its own 17-yard line. But lightning struck. With only seconds remaining, the Trojans scored on a 38-yard pass, and then completed a two-point conversion for an unbelievable 18-17 victory.

The Bucks finished the season with a 10-2-0 record and a No. 4 ranking. Only once before had an OSU football team played 12 games in one season and that was 69 years ago. Michigan finished 10-1-0 and got the No. 3 slot behind Oklahoma and Southern Cal.

THE ELLIOTTS OF MICHIGAN

These four Elliotts combined for 12 games over a 9-year period against Ohio State. The top photograph shows Bump (left) and Pete. Both made All-American — Bump in '47 and Pete in '48. The bottom photo are Pete's sons, Bruce (left) and Dave in their playing days at Michigan. Pete played against OSU in 1945-46-47-48; Bump in 1946-47; Bruce in 1969-70-71, and Dave in 1971-73-74. The four Elliott earned 12 "M" football letters and were 6-2-1 versus the Buckeyes. (Photos courtesy of Michigan Athletic Department)

Over the past three seasons (1972-73-74), the top six teams in the country and their regular season records had been: Alabama 32-1-0; Oklahoma 31-1-1; Michigan 30-2-1; Southern Cal 29-2-2; Ohio State 28-2-1, and Penn State, 29-3-0. Fate decreed that of the six, Michigan had no bowl trips to reward their success, while all the others played in post-season games in all three years.

1975

GAME 72

"I HATE YOU!
I HATE YOU!
I HATE YOU!"

Total exasperation. That's what Michigan's fandom felt following the 1975 game against the despised Woody Hayes and his dreaded Buckeye football team. Total exasperation.

Over the last six years, Michigan's combined record going into the OSU game had been 57-0-2. It undoubtedly failed to intimidate the Ohioans who lost only once to the Wolverines during the span.

A few days before the 72nd battle of the series, the *Associated Press* reported, "Woody Hayes loves the intense hate that Michigan fans show for him. 'It doesn't hurt my feelings at all,' said Hayes. 'It's the greatest compliment I could have. They (Michigan) couldn't beat me with two Michigan coaches. So they had to come down here and take a coach (Bo Schembechler) that I trained. And they haven't beaten me with him yet. Bo and I are a lot alike. We're both lefthanded, we've both had heart attacks and we both have such wonderful dispositions.' "

From the above quote it would appear that in the heat of the interview, Coach Hayes momentarily forgot the outcome of Ohio State-Michigan in 1969 and 1971, games won by the Wolverines under the coaching of Schembechler.

To say that the 1975 game was a "big one" fails to do justice to the situation. Ohio State was 10-0-0 and ranked No. 1 in the Nation. Michigan was also unbeaten, but had suffered two early-season ties to non-Conference foes for an 8-0-2 autumn showing and a No. 5 rating.

Such credentials upon entering this annual gridiron carnival has become almost routine.

The records:

OHIO STATE (10-0-0)		MICHIGAN (8-0-2)	
Michigan State	21- 0	Wisconsin	23- 6
Penn State	17- 9	Stanford	19-19
North Carolina	32- 7	Baylor	14-14
UCLA	41-20	Missouri	31- 7
Iowa	49- 0	Michigan State	16- 6
Wisconsin	56- 0	Northwestern	69- 0
Purdue	35- 6	Indiana	55- 7
Indiana	24-14	Minnesota	28-21
Illinois	40- 3	Purdue	28- 0
Minnesota	38- 6	Illinois	21-15
Average	35- 7	Average	30-10

The Conference records for both teams were 7-0-0 and once again the winner would capture the Big Ten title and go to the Rose Bowl. There was, however, for the first time, a consolation prize for the loser. It was a trip to Miami to play in the Orange Bowl. Oklahoma had already won the Orange bid and it's difficult to determine whether meeting the Sooners would be any kind of prize, consolation or otherwise.

Woody and his Bucks continued their whammy over Michigan by scoring two touchdowns within 59 seconds late into the fourth quarter to win again, 21-14, before 105,543 at Ann Arbor, an all-time record attendance for a college football game at that time.

The Buckeyes took a 7-0 lead over Michigan 10 minutes into the game with a 63-yard drive that ended with a seven-yard pass from Cornelius Greene to Pete Johnson. Tom Klaban, the hero of the 1974 game, converted.

That was it, offensively, for OSU for awhile. The Buckeyes would not get another first down until midway through the fourth quarter.

Schembechler and his coaching staff had put in a special play for the game and in the second period it worked for a touchdown. Freshman quarterback Rick Leach hit on a 30-yard pass to Keith

DISPATCH SPORTS

Bo Left Holding The Bag (Of Oranges)

Buckeyes Win Crown, Roses

★★★   ★★★   ★★★

Late Interception, TD Beat Michigan, 21-14

ARCHIE GRIFFIN

The only two-time Heisman Trophy winner in history. In four games against Michigan, he rushed for 395 yards in 91 carries (4.3 average). (Photo courtesy of OSU photo archives.)

Detroit Free Press

Bucks' Whirlwind Finish Ruins U-M Rose Bowl Dreams, 21-14

Johnson, and the strong running of Gordon Bell highlighted a Michigan march to the Ohio 11. Then came the "special" play—a halfback pass from Bell to wingback Jim Smith. Bobby Wood converted and it was a 7-7 ball game.

There would be no more scoring until a little over seven minutes from the end of the game—when 21 points more were to be put on the board.

With just over nine minutes left, OSU punted from its own endzone and Michigan took over at the Bucks' 43. Leach completed passes to Smith for nine and 11 yards, and there was running help from Rob Lytle to reach the one-yard line. Leach drove over for the score and Wood converted. With 7:11 showing on the clock, Michigan had grabbed a 14-7 lead over a Buckeye football team that seemed lifeless.

"At this moment with Michigan Stadium in a complete uproar and the Wolverine players mobbing their 18-year-old quarterback in the endzone, it seemed as though the Buckeyes had been exposed as one of the real hoaxes in many a season. They seemed to be nothing more than a figment of W. W. Hayes' imagination. . . .It would be Michigan, MIGHTY Michigan, in Pasadena and Woody, heh, heh, heh, drinking the dregs from the Orange Bowl in Miami," wrote Joe Falls of the *Detroit Free Press*.

Michigan kicked off. From his own 35-yard line, quarterback Greene went back to pass, couldn't find an open receiver, got trapped, tried to escape, was cut off from both sides, and retreated even further. It was the hounds chasing the rabbit. Suddenly, Greene found himself hemmed into the briar patch of his own endzone.

"Oh, how sad the Buckeyes looked" wrote Falls. "For now was their senior quarterback Cornelius Green, fleeing for his life in the endzone, retreating 35 yards from scrimmage, and throwing one of those panic passes that makes everyone rooting for the other team laugh in delight."

The Buckeyes and Greene had escaped disaster.

It became third-and-10, still at the 35. The record throng was wild. Greene quieted them, to some extent, with a 17-yard pass completion to Brian Baschnagel and a first down at the Michigan 48. OSU still had life. It was then Greene to Leonard Willis and Greene to Willis again to the 28. Archie Griffin crashed through for 11 yards. Greene, on a keeper, dashed for 12 more, all the way to the five. Five plays and five first downs had the Wolverines defense dizzy and the Wolverine fans astonished and concerned.

Three plays later, huge Pete Johnson, 6-1, 248 pounds, pounded into the endzone to make it 14-13 with 3:08 to play. Klaban cooly converted—14-14. Except for a few thousand loud Buckeyes, the big crowd sat stunned and silent.

Ohio State kicked off and Michigan came out throwing. They had to. There would be no Rose Bowl vote this year. The Conference athletic directors had devised a new formula to determine the representative, and for Michigan to win the right to go West for the holidays, they had to win the game. A tie would send them South to Miami.

On first down, Leach fired away. It was intercepted. OSU's Ray Griffin—brother and teammate of Archie Griffin—picked off the pass and "the other" Griffin streaked 29 yards to the Michigan three. Johnson immediately plowed over for the touchdown, his 25th of the season, with just 2:09 remaining in the contest. Klaban kicked good.

Buckeyes 21, Wolverines 14. Unbelievable.

A fourth down desperation pass by Leach was intercepted by Craig Cassady and Ohio State had successfully defended its lofty No. 1 rating.

"The Fat Man was beautiful. Just beautiful. No stomping around. No raging up and down the sidelines. No throwing yard markers, pushing people around or slugging players," typed Falls. "He just stood there, the sweet old man that he is, and held himself together like he had never done before in this long, emotional series.

"That's the Fat Man for you. He is always thinking of something new to do to his friends from Michigan. This time he did it with his poise. Imagine that. Poise. Whoever thought Woody Hayes knew a trait existed? But there he was, as calm as a cigar store Indian, sending in the plays that would turn this whole game around and bring his Ohio State team back from the brink of disaster. The Buckeyes were through. Or at least they should have been. Michigan had it. The Wolverines had it all. It was right there for them.

"Do you know what turned it around? It was the poise of W. W. Hayes, who held himself together and so the players held themselves together. They didn't panic. They didn't rattle. They could have folded up, but they didn't. And so it's hail to the victors. Hail to Ohio State, the champions of the West."

Fall's story continued, "Woody always seems to come up with the big play at the right time. Or Bo fails to deliver the big play at the right time. As much as anyone may pooh-pooh the idea, there

330

PETE JOHNSON

OSU'S massive fullback (6-1, 248 lbs.) scored all three touchdowns as a late rally got the Buckeyes a 21-14 win in 1975. (Photo courtesy of OSU Department of Photography and Cinema.)

is a psyche involved when these two men tangle with each other.

"What can be done about it? The only answer seems to be keep trying. . .and wait for the Fat Man to retire.

"They do retire their people at 65, don't they? Imagine if W. W. Hayes stayed around until he was 80? The Michigan team might have to add a psychiatrist to its staff."

Nobody realized it at the time, but when a happy Woody Hayes walked off the field at Ann Arbor that November 22, not only had he experienced his last victory over Michigan, but he had also seen the last touchdown that his Buckeye teams would ever score against the Wolverines.

Michigan got more first downs (19-12), doubled the Bucks in rushing yards (248-124), outpassed OSU (113-84) and led in total offense (361-208). The Wolves also led in penalty yards, 15-10. U-M's defense stopped Griffin (46 yards in 19 carries), the first time he had been held for less than 100 yards in 31 games.

Ohio State went to the Rose Bowl for the fourth year in a row. The No. 1-ranked Bucks went to meet UCLA (8-2-1), a team they blasted 41-20 back on October 4 at Los Angeles. OSU led 3-0 at halftime and were just 30 playing minutes away from the 1975 national championship. However, the Bruins rallied for a shocking 23-10 upset.

Ohio's loss opened the door for second-ranked Oklahoma to capture the title with a win over Michigan later that night in Miami. The Sooners did, with a 14-6 victory. It was the first time in history that a Big Ten team had played in any bowl game except the Rose. (Michigan State lost 6-0 to Auburn in the 1938 Orange Bowl, before the Spartans had come into the Conference.)

The AP's final top five teams were Oklahoma, Arizona State, Alabama, Ohio State and UCLA. Michigan was No. 8 on the list.

Archie Griffin won the Heisman Trophy again in 1975 to become the first two-time winner of the award. In Griffin's great four-year career, he got his hands on the football 982 times and gained 6559 yards, an average of 6.7 yards per touch of the pigskin.

Griffin rushed for 5589 yards in 924 carries (6.0 average), caught 30 passes for 350 yards and returned 28 kickoffs for 620 yards. Against Michigan, he rushed for 395 yards in 91 attempts. During his stay at Columbus, the Buckeyes racked up a 40-5-1 record. Their regular season record was 39-1-1—the lone loss to Michigan State and the one tie to Michigan.

So great was Griffin's fame and admiration that automobiles

all over Ohio were decked out with bumper stickers reading: "Thank You, Mrs. Griffin."

After 25 years, Hayes' record against the Wolverines had climbed to 18-6-1, but Michigan still led, 39-28-5.

And they did – 21-14.

1976

THE DRAGON BEHEADED

In the mid-1970s, it would have been most difficult to convince the current crop of Michigan football fans that it took Ohio State 22 years (16 games) to chalk up its first victory in the series, and that after the first 24 games, the Buckeyes had won only three.

"So what?," would be the response. "All I know is that we haven't beaten them in four years, and only eight times since ole Woody became coach down there 25 years ago."

To add even more salt to the Wolverines' wounded pride about the four previous series games is to reflect on how Michigan completely out-played the Bucks in every phase of the game—except scoring. The four-game totals showed Michigan with more first downs, 74-45, and more yards in both rushing and passing that added up to a 1299-887 margin. But all Michigan had to show for this statistical dominance was one devastating tie and three ruinous defeats.

In the spring of 1976, Bo Schembechler had had open-heart surgery, but by August was back on the job. Upon his return, Bo found that the pre-season polls had his Wolverines ranked No 1 in the land by an overwhelming margin. And for the first two months of the season, Michigan vindicated the judgment of the pollsters who had bestowed the high honor.

Michigan opened the season with a "close" 13-point win over Wisconsin (40-27), before blasting Stanford 51-0, Navy 70-14, Wake Forest 31-0, Michigan State 42-10, Northwestern 38-7, Indiana 35-0 and Minnesota 45-0. That's outscoring the opposition at a clip of 44-7 per game.

But in the ninth game of the season at West Lafayette, Purdue's "Spoilermakers," with only a 3-5-0 record and a defense that had already surrendered 199 points, put a stop to Michigan's pillage with an unbelievable 16-14 upset. The Pittsburgh Panthers, led by Tony Dorsett, moved into the top slot.

The Wolverines came back with a 38-7 triumph over Illinois and eyed the Buckeyes with a 9-1-0 record and as the Nation's No. 1 scoring team (40.4); the Nation's No. 1 defensive team against scoring (8.1), and the Nation's No. 4 ranked team.

As "The Big One" approached, Ohio State was rated eighth in the country with an 8-1-1 record that included a 22-21 loss to unpredictable Missouri and a 10-10 tie with UCLA. It's an oddity of sorts that two of college football's most famous "giant-killers"—Purdue and Missouri—were the teams that did the most damage to Michigan and Ohio State in 1976. It's also an oddity that for the first time in seven years, OSU was to face a Wolverine team that had a loss on its record.

As for the bowl stakes, the same scenario that had been in play last year was dusted off for a repeat performance. The winner would smell roses in Pasadena on New Year's, and the loser orange blossoms in Miami.

Michigan went to California; Ohio State to Florida. The Wolverines brought a halt to their spell of frustration against Woody Hayes and the Buckeyes with a convincing 22-0 shutout at Columbus on a bright, crisp afternoon with 88,250 in the stadium and the game's annual television audience of millions.

Maize and Blue supporters all over the country shouted a long and loud, "Halleluiah!"

With the exception of Ohio's only threat of the day, the first half was rather uneventful. The Buckeyes got to the Michigan 10-yard line a minute and a half before intermission but quarterback Jim Pacenla threw one of those "up for grabs" passes into the endzone and the grabber was Michigan's Jim Pickens. There were 11 punts (six by OSU) in the first two quarters and kickers Tom Skaladana and John Anderson booted the ball just over 500 yards.

Halftime score: 0-0.

The story of the second half was an all Michigan story. After the kickoff, the Wolverines went 80 yards in 11 plays, all on the ground, to take a 7-0 lead. Rob Lytle had runs of 15, 11 and nine yards and quarterback Rick Leach rambled for 20 on a third down, busted play to keep the drive in gear. From the three-yard line, Russell Davis scored. Bobby Woods converted.

Ah, Everything Comes Up Roses...
U-M Storms Past Buckeyes, 22-0

Michigan fullback Russell Davis bursts past OSU's Paul Ross (16) in the third quarter for the first of three TDs by the Wolverines in their 22-0 victory

Joe Falls

Bo's Finest Moment: He Did It His Way

COLUMBUS

These Bucks Were Not Awesome

3 Second-Half TDs Break It

BY CURT SYLVESTER
Free Press Sports Writer

COLUMBUS, Ohio — Goodby, Ohio State champ, hello, Rose Bowl.

How U-M Scored

UM-OSU

THIRD QUARTER

7-0 Russell Davis, 3-yard run 9:49 (80 yards in 11 plays, big plays — 20-yard run by Rick Leach) Bobby Wood converted

15-0 Davis, 3-yard run 1:47 (52 yards in 8 plays, big plays — 16-yard runs by Jim Smith and Rob Lytle) Jerry Zuver ran two-point conversion

FOURTH QUARTER

22-0 Lytle, 3-yard run 6:13 (16 yards in 3 plays after Zuver interception big play — 33-yard run by Lytle) Wood converted

Please turn to Page 20, Column 4

The Bowl Picture

ROSE BOWL: Pasadena, Calif., Jan. 1: Michigan (10-1-0) vs. UM (8-1-0).

ORANGE BOWL: Miami, Jan. 1: Big 8 Champ vs. Ohio State (6-3-1).

SUGAR BOWL: New Orleans, Jan. 1: Georgia (9-1-0) vs. Pittsburgh (10-0-0).

COTTON BOWL: Dallas, Jan. 1: Southwest Conference champion vs. Maryland (11-0-0).

FIESTA BOWL: Tempe, Ariz., Dec. 25: Wyoming (8-3-0) vs. Oklahoma (7-3-1).

PEACH BOWL: Atlanta, Dec. 31: Kentucky (7-4-0) vs. North Carolina (8-3-0).

ASTRO-BLUEBONNET BOWL: Houston, Dec. 31: A team to be named later vs. probably a Big 8 team.

SUN BOWL: El Paso, Tex., Jan. 2: Texas A&M (9-3-0) vs. Florida (8-3-0).

GATOR BOWL: Jacksonville, Fla., Dec. 27: Notre Dame (8-3-0) vs. Penn State (7-4-0).

LIBERTY BOWL: Memphis, Tenn., Dec. 20: Alabama (7-3-0) vs. UCLA (9-1-1).

TANGERINE BOWL: Orlando, Fla., Dec. 18: A Big 8 team vs. a team to be named later.

Happy Seniors Whoop It Up
As Famine Ends for U-M

BY CURT SYLVESTER
Free Press Sports Writer

How Top 20 Fared

How the Associated Press Top 20 college football teams fared this weekend:

1—Pittsburgh (10-0-0) did not play.
2—UCLA (9-1-1) lost to Southern Cal, 24-14.
3—Southern Cal (9-1-0) stopped UCLA, 24-14.
4—Michigan (10-1-0) rose above Ohio St., 22-0.
5—Texas Tech (9-1-0) lost to Houston, 27-19.
6—Georgia (9-1-0) did not play.
7—Maryland (11-0-0) shut out Virginia, 28-0.
8—Ohio St. (8-2-1) fell to Michigan, 22-0.
9—Houston (7-3-0) tripped Texas Tech, 27-19.
10—Oklahoma (7-3-1) did not play.
11—Texas A&M (9-3-0) crushed Texas Christian, 59-10.
12—Nebraska (7-3-1) did not play.
13—Notre Dame (8-3-0) stunned Miami, Fla., 40-27.
14—Iowa St. (8-3-0) dumped by Oklahoma St., 42-21.
15—Colorado (8-3-0) beat Kansas St., 35-28.
16—Oklahoma St. (8-3-0) whipped Iowa St., 42-21.
17—Penn St. (7-4-0) did not play.
18—Alabama (7-3-0) did not play.
19—(tie) Missouri (6-5-0) lost to Kansas, 41-14.
—Rutgers (10-0-0) did not play.

Michigan happiness is beating Ohio State. When it's the first time in five years, there's more ecstasy than plain happiness. Rich Leach (7) and Curt Stephensen whoop it up. (Photo courtesy of Michigan Athletic Department.)

Ohio took the ensuing kickoff, ran three plays and punted to the Michigan 48, where another scoring march was launched. This one took eight snaps. A 16-yard run by Lytle, plus another 16-yarder on a reverse by Jim Smith set up Davis' second touchdown of the game, again from the three. Schembechler pulled a real stunner on the conversion attempt when he had Jerry Zuver, holding for the kick, run with the ball instead. It worked for a two-point conversion and a 15-0 lead with 1:47 remaining in the third quarter.

"We felt 14 points weren't enough in this game. We couldn't go to the Rose Bowl with a tie, so we went for two. We put that play in just this week. . .The only question was whether we'd do it after the first or second touchdown," Schembechler told the press after the game.

In the final period, Tom Roche intercepted a Leach pass at the OSU 13 but the Buckeyes gave it right back as Zuver intercepted Pasenla at the 28 and returned it to the 16. A touchdown came in three plays as Lytle, who gained 165 yards in 29 carries during the game, bolted for 11 to the three-yard line, then over for the score. Wood's kick put the final point on the scoreboard with 6:47 left to be played. But OSU was "done."

With the shutout victory, the Wolves got an extra measure of revenge by breaking the Buckeyes' consecutive games scoring streak at 122—one short of tying the all-time collegiate record set by Oklahoma over the 1946-57 period. OSU's last shutout? Michigan did it, 10-0, in 1964.

Twenty-two to nothing. There was rejoicing throughout the State of Michigan that November night in 1976. The dragon had been beheaded.

A subdued Hayes told newsmen after the game, "I'll pick them as No. 1. Any team that can beat us that badly should be No. 1." (Hayes was one of the 43 members of the UPI coaches panel.) He continued, "We got beat by a better coach and a better team. That was a courageous thing Bo has done, to come back (from heart surgery) and coach like that."

Michigan entered the big game as the Nation's top rushing team with a 362-yard per game average and improved on that as Wolverine runners shredded the Ohio defense for 366 yards. Michigan's passing yardage was zero. The winners got more first downs, 23-10 and were penalized 10 yards, one more than the Bucks. Ohio managed only 173 yards (104 rushing and 69 passing).

Michigan went to Pasadena and lost 14-6 to Southern Cal for a final 10-2-0 record and a No. 3 finish behind Pittsburgh and USC; Ohio State went to Miami and defeated Colorado 27-10 for a final 9-2-1 record and a No. 6 finish. It was Ohio State's first football visit to the South since a scoreless game against Auburn in 1917, played in Montgomery, Alabama.

As for the Buckeye-Wolverine series, Michigan led 40-28-5.

1977

GAME 74

TWO IN A ROW FOR BO

In the Michigan-Ohio State football series, there appears a seemingly endless succession of memorable, unique events, or "firsts", as well as many that are not so memorable but at least are interesting to note. For example, a "first" in the 1977 encounter was the first time the Wolverines had taken two straight from the Buckeyes since Woody Hayes arrived in Columbus 26 years earlier.

Both teams went into the '77 clash with 9-1-0 records. OSU's lone loss was a 29-28 heartbreaker to Oklahoma in Columbus, as the Sooners kicked a field goal in the last seconds of the game in the first-ever collision between the two grid giants. Michigan's only setback was to Big Ten foe Minnesota, 16-0 at Minneapolis. The Wolverines at the time had a 113-game scoring streak working.

As the 74th renewal of the series came into focus, once again the participating teams were rated among the Nation's top ten. Ohio was fourth, Michigan was sixth. The winner of the game would go to Pasadena, and for the first time, the loser would get to see what New Orleans had to offer, including Bourbon Street, the fabulous Superdome and the Sugar Bowl.

On paper, the two teams were close. Ohio State went to Ann Arbor with the Nation's No. 1 defense against scoring; Michigan ranked fourth. The Bucks had averaged a 35-7 score per game in 10 outings, and the Wolves, 32-9. An independent national publication showed OSU's opponents' average *power rating* was 95.5, U-M's 95.2. The home field advantage? A check of the records suggests that at least in this series, there's no such thing. At kick-off time, in 73 previous games, the host teams had won 34 and lost 34, and five games ended in ties.

Another record crowd—106,024—showed up and a national television audience of untold millions tuned in to watch as host Michigan called upon the defensive troops to repel repeated Buck-eye threats and to save a hard-fought, drama-filled 14-6 victory.

Once the game started, Ohio moved impressively against the vaunted Michigan defense—until the Buckeyes worked themselves inside the 20-yard line, or until the Wolverines goal line was threatened. On five different occasions, the Bucks operated 19 plays in that territory and came up with a net figure of minus 13 yards, but with two field goals. Otherwise, Ohio rambled around at will as indicated by its 23 first downs and 352 offensive yards. The Wolverines managed only 10 first downs and 196 yards, but as OSU had been doing in recent years, lost the stat battle but won the scoring war.

"I've been there when we got all the statistics, but this one we've got the points. We got two touchdowns and they got two field goals, and that's the only thing that matters," Bo Schembechler told newsmen after the grueling game.

OSU took the opening kickoff and pushed Michigan around on a drive to the 12-yard line. Michigan stiffened and Vlade Janakievski came on for a field goal and a quick 3-0 Buckeye advantage. On Ohio's next possession they stormed back to the seven-yard line and once again had to go for a field goal. This time it was no good and what could have been a 14-0 score early in the game was only 3-0.

That's the way it stayed until midway through the second quarter. This time Michigan was driving 46 yards for the go-ahead touchdown after receiving a punt. The big play in the march came on a third-and-11 situation at the Ohio 30. Junior quarterback Rick Leach hit Ralph Clayton with a 22-yard pass for a gain to the Bucks' eight. Two plays later, Roosevelt Smith scored from the one. Gregg Willner converted and the home team led 7-3 and the home team's fans just loved it.

Moving to early in the third period, U-M's Ron Simkins re-covered a fumble in mid-air at the Ohio 20 to set up a series of downs that ended with Leach's two-yard dive into the endzone. Willner's PAT was on target to make it 14-3.

As in the first quarter, Michigan's defense was tested again. The Bucks took the ensuing kickoff and moved to a first down at the enemy 11. Mike Jolly belted Jeff Logan for a yard loss. A pass was incomplete. On third down, Simkins sacked quarterback Ron Gerald for a big 13-yard loss. It was back to Janakievski, and he pounded a 44-yard field goal to make the score 14-6.

Ohio kicked off and immediately got the ball back by recovering a Smith fumble at the Michigan 31. Two plays gained nine yards to bring up third-and-one at the 22. The ball was given to Campbell, a 212-pound fullback made in the mold of many other of Coach Hayes' big fullbacks, to get the one yard. Michigan's Simkins, a 221-pound linebacker, met Campbell head-on and won the battle. Campbell lost two yards. Janakievski missed a field goal try and the Wolverines maintained their eight-point lead.

The rugged Bucks were soon back knocking on the door, this time at Michigan's 10, where it was fourth-and-one. The 106,000-plus were on their feet roaring encouragement—the great majority for the defensive team. Campbell was called upon again to get the one big yard. This time, linebackers Mel Owens and John Anderson, and tackle Curtis Greer, log-jammed the alley for zero yardage.

The big bowl erupted with even louder cheers.

Michigan then knocked out a couple of first downs in a drive to midfield, but more importantly, it gave the defensive unit a little time to catch its breath. They would need it. The Wolverines punted to the 10-yard line where the Bucks took over and took off. They worked it to the 20. . .the 30. . .the 40. . .and kept on until the line of scrimmage was the Michigan eight and it was first down. At this point in time, the Wolverine fans began to think about a two-point conversion and a 14-14 "loss" more than anything else. It would, after all, be asking too much of their team to stop Ohio State *again*. And a tie would give the Bucks an outright Conference title and the Rose Bowl bid.

Amid the thunderous roar of the record-setting throng, quarterback Gerald brought his Bucks to the line, barked out the signals, took the snap from center, turned and held the ball in Campbell's belly for a second or two, pulled it away and was about to pitch the ball to trailing Ron Springs. While the ball handling was going on, Anderson was coming through from his linebacking position. Anderson whacked Gerald and the ball flew all the way back to the 18-yard line where Derek Howard recovered. Howard wore a blue jersey.

The stadium was rockin' and rollin'! The thousands of rolls of toilet tissue the Michigan fans either brought with them or

341

It's a Michigan touchdown. Roosevelt Smith (barely visible at bottom of stack in middle) plows over from the one, giving his team a 7-3 second quarter lead in the 1977 game at Ann Arbor. Other players include Mike Kenn (78), Russell Davis (33), Luther Henson (54), Mark Donahue (60), Kelton Dansler (32), and Doug Marsh (80). (Photo courtesy of Michigan Athletic Department)

It wasn't a good day for Woody....

purchased at the game were streaming through the stadium. Each of the sheets was imprinted with a picture of Coach Hayes and a caption that read: "PUT WOODY WHERE HE BELONGS."

Mike Freedman, an ABC-TV cameraman, was near Coach Hayes when the devastating fumble occurred and Freedman moved in for a closer shot of Hayes' face. Woody didn't feel photogenic. He let Freedman "hold one."

"He swung at me. Woody Hayes swung at my stomach, but I blocked it," Freedman told the *Chicago Tribune Press Service.* "He (Hayes) showed deep emotion. It's part of my job to capture and report those emotions," explained Freedman.

The Michigan crowd was going absolutely crazy. The Hayes' incident was frosting on the cake of the heroic defensive show their warriors had put on all afternoon. The place was wild! And all the while, the toilet tissue was flying everywhere.

But Hayes' action didn't alter the game's outcome, and for the fifth time in six years, Ohio State and Michigan were co-champions of the Big Ten—Michigan's 28th Conference football title won or shared, and Ohio State's 21st.

It would be the Wolverines going to Pasadena but on this New Year's, even throughout Big Ten country, the Sugar Bowl plucked a good portion of the Rose Bowl's roses. The New Orleans bowl people fell into a matchup of Woody Hayes vs. Bear Bryant. Or was it Ohio State vs. Alabama? If the news releases that began flooding the Nation's sports desks were any indication, the two teams would stand on the sidelines and watch Woody and Bear play a football game. Anyway, it would be Ohio State's first game against a Southeastern Conference team since the Bucks beat Kentucky 19-6 back in 1935.

The Sugar Bowl was a game matching the No. 3 all-time winningest coach (Bryant) against the No. 4 all-time winningest coach (Hayes); and the two winningest active coaches. These elements, plus the colorful personalities involved, made it most difficult for the news media to focus on the teams and the players.

There was another Big Ten bowl participation besides the Rose and Sugar as the Conference, for the first time, sent three teams to post-season games. In Birmingham, Alabama, Minnesota (7-4-0) would play Maryland (7-4-0) in the first annual Hall of Fame Bowl.

But it was not a good bowl season for the Big Ten.

Maryland topped the Golden Gophers 17-7 to start it off. Then on January 2, the Crimson Tide belted the Buckeyes 35-6. When

In This Section

The Inside of Sports   Page 8
Outdoors with Opre   Page 10
Classifica   Pages 11-24

Detroit Free Press
Sports
SUNDAY, NOVEMBER 20, 1977

Ah! Everything Comes Up Roses For Bo's Gutty Wolverines, 14-6

The Sunday News

COLLEGE FOOTBALL	Michigan .. 14 Ohio State . 6	Mich. St. ... 22 Iowa 16	Cent. Mich. 28 West. Mich. 23	Morris ..... 13 Albion 10	Notre Dame 49 Air Force .. 0	Kentucky 21 Tennessee . 17
	Story on page 1D.	Story on page 1D.	Story on page 4D.	Story on page 4D.	Story on page 6D.	Story on page 7D.

'Best game we ever played and lost'.— Woody

No fluke: Michigan does it again!

By JACK BERRY
News Staff Writer

ANN ARBOR — Michigan is going back to the Rose Bowl with new resolve, and an elastic but incredibly tenacious defense, and hopefully not against the kind of all-pro team it faced last season with the University of Southern California.

Fittingly the defense, Michigan's strong point all season, produced the 14-6 victory over Ohio State Saturday before a record crowd of 106,024 and a national television audience that missed some of the Buckeyes' best moments because the network was covering Egyptian President Anwar Sadat's peace mission to Israel.

He should have come to Ann Arbor. Several times war broke out, first when overzealous Michigan lettermen from other sports jostled Coach Woody Hayes and the Buckeyes when they took the field before the game, running under the M Club banner and then in the fourth quarter when Hayes charged ABC-TV cameraman Mike Freedman. Hayes went after the cameraman after Freedman moved in for a closeup when John Anderson crunched Ohio State quarterback Rod Gerald and forced him to fumble as the Michigan side with 2:38 left to play.

It was a typical Michigan-Ohio State game, very, very tough. Hayes said it "was by far the best game we ever played and lost. One big factor was they were able to move us and keep us beating us.

"Damn them! It's always Michigan held it Ohio team playing against a good defense after the

State ran 39 plays inside the Wolverines' 20 and lost six yards to the awesome Michigan defense.

Michigan has held Ohio State without a touchdown in three of the last four meetings and now has stopped the Buckeyes from crossing the goal line for eight straight quarters.

This time it meant the Big Ten co-championship, the seventh time in Bo Schembechler's nine years at Michigan that the Wolverines have shared the title or won it outright.

"This team has overcome more adversity than any team I've had," Schembechler said, referring to the string of injuries that started with All-America

Bowl lineup

ROSE BOWL — **MICHIGAN** vs. Pacific-8 champion.
COTTON BOWL — Southwest Conference champion vs. Notre Dame.
SUGAR BOWL — Alabama vs. Ohio State.
ORANGE BOWL — Arkansas vs. Big Eight champion.
BLUEBONNET BOWL — Loser of Texas-Texas A&M game vs. undetermined opponent.
FIESTA BOWL — Western Athletic Conference champion vs. Penn State.
GATOR BOWL — Pittsburgh vs. Clemson.
HALL OF FAME BOWL — Minnesota vs. Maryland.
LIBERTY BOWL — North Carolina vs. team of Oklahoma-Nebraska game.
PEACH BOWL — North Carolina State vs. undetermined opponent.
SUN BOWL — Stanford vs. Louisiana St.
TANGERINE BOWL — Probably Florida State vs. Texas Tech.

tackle candidate Bill Dufek's broken leg the first day of practice.

"I told them after the game that this team has had more tenacity than any I've had in 25 years of coaching."

And Schembechler clearly regards Michigan as the Big Ten champion even though it shares the title with OSU at 7-1.

"People think of the team that goes to the Rose Bowl as the champion and we're going I've been in games (with Ohio State) where we get all the statistics and they won the game.

"They may have gotten the statistics (they did), but we scored two touchdowns and they scored two field goals.

"I don't care who we play in the Rose Bowl (the picture still is muddled in the Pacific-8), and I'm tired about the Rose Bowl psych about preparation. We're just gonna go out there and play."

It's doubtful Michigan can play any better defensively than it did against Ohio State, the nation's No. 1 rushing team with a 282.6-yard average going into the game.

Michigan's offense wasn't awesome, but it did wind up with 141 yards rushing, 55 passing and quarterback Rick Leach broke Old Blue hero Tom Harmon's touchdown record when he accounted for his 51st score with a two-yard run in the third quarter for Michigan's second TD. And Harmon was in the audience.

The key for Michigan was stopping Ohio State quarterback Gerald.

Gerald bolted Michigan in the first quarter with 55 yards rushing and he virtually

Continued on Page 11D

that one ended, the Nation switched channels and watched as Washington (7-4-0) streaked to a 24-0 lead over Michigan by the middle of the third period. Led by the determined and gritty play of Leach, the Wolverines roared back and had a chance for victory before two interceptions near the Huskies' goal shattered the comeback bid. Washington escaped with a 27-20 win.

Even though OSU lost three games in the 1977 season, it took three outstanding teams to do the job—10-1-0 Oklahoma, 10-1-0 Michigan and 10-1-0 Alabama. For the first time in five years, the Buckeyes failed to make the final top ten. Michigan made the No. 9 spot with a 10-2-0 record.

While a ninth place finish was not up to recent Michigan standards, the Wolverine faithful had much to sustain their spirits in the months ahead. Beating Ohio State for the second year in a row was a plus plus. And in Michigan, just recalling the sight of Woody Hayes losing his cool and punching a television cameraman on the sidelines was good for a basketful of pluses.

In Columbus, the thoughts centered on next year.

1978

GAME 75

A SAD BYE-BYE TO
A GREAT BUCKEYE

Other than Michigan and Ohio State, no team had won or shared the Big Ten football crown since 1967. The Spartans of Michigan State were to break that streak in '78 by tying the Wolverines for the title. It was also the first season in the 1970s that when the time rolled around for the annual Michigan-Ohio State encounter, both teams were not in the top ten. The Wolves did their part to keep the string going with a No. 6 ranking, but the Buckeyes slipped to 16th.

During the period 1968-78 (11 seasons), the "Big Two" of Big Ten football posted a devastating 139-9-0 (.939) record against the other eight Conference members. Michigan was 70-4-0; Ohio State 69-5-0.

The 1978 season also saw the end of Woody Hayes' career as head coach at Ohio State. The tough old ex-Navy officer had roamed the Buckeye sidelines since 1951, exhorting his troops to greater effort, and offering constructive criticism to officials.

Hayes' final edition lost the season opener 19-0 to Penn State, the first shutout loss to a non-Conference team since the Nittany Lions pulled the stunt 14 years earlier. After topping Minnesota and Baylor, the Bucks tangled with the Mustangs of SMU in a thriller at Columbus that ended in a 35-35 draw. Next was a loss to Purdue followed by five consecutive victories, including Hayes' final triumph on November 18 at Bloomington as OSU defeated Indiana, 21-18. Michigan was next on Ohio State's list and the

346

Buckeyes were 7-2-1, even after surrendering 205 points—the most yielded in one season by any Ohio State football team, ever.

The Wolverines had lost only to Michigan State and blasted the nine other opponents by an average score of 38-7. One of the wins was over Notre Dame, 28-14, in the first meeting of the teams in 35 years. Another victory was against Wisconsin, 42-0, in the sixth weekend of the season and it marked the Wolverines' 600th all-time gridiron triumph.

Coach Bo Schembechler's charges, the country's top defense against scoring, were established as solid favorites to take care of OSU for the third straight year. And they did. The score was 14-3, played before 88,358 at Columbus, and the customary nationwide television audience.

Actually, only the ticket holders got to see the first seven minutes of the game. ABC's TV cameras were in Israel for live satellite coverage of the arrival of Egypt's President Anwar Sadat. The network's switchboards were inundated with telephone calls protesting the preempting of football—Michigan-Ohio State football—for mere politics.

The 75th series game featured Michigan's senior quarterback Rick Leach against Ohio's freshman signal caller Art Schlichter. Schlichter and the Buckeyes acted as if they meant business with drives to U-M's 21 and 12-yard lines on the first two possessions. Only three points resulted, in a 29-yard field goal by Bob Atha when the second march stalled.

Michigan took the ensuing kickoff and scored in 59 seconds. Leach hit on three consecutive passes, the last one 30 yards to Rodney Feaster for the touchdown. Gregg Willner converted for a 7-3 lead.

That was it for the first half, and with four minutes left in the third period, the Wolverines put the Buckeyes away for another year with a 13-play, 69-yard drive. Leach tossed an 11-yard pass to Roosevelt Smith for the score. Willner again kicked good. The TD pass by Leach was his 81st touchdown at Michigan—accounted for by both passing and rushing. It is an NCAA record.

The 14-3 lead was enough. The stingy Wolverine defense allowed OSU only one first down in the second half, and that with 3:25 showing on the game clock. Coach Hayes brought quarterback Rod Gerald out of the bullpen late in the contest, but to no avail. As the game ended, the Bucks had not scored a series touchdown since 1975.

Michigan led in first downs 21-11 and total yards 364-216. Leach completed 11 of 21 passes for 161 yards. Ohio was penalized more yards, 35-16.

RICK LEACH

Started in 48 consecutive games (NCAA record) for Michigan at quarterback, 1975-78, and was 3-1-0 versus Ohio State. (Photo courtesy of Michigan Athletic Department.)

For the second straight year, the Big Ten sent three teams to enjoy post-season festivities in warmer climes. Purdue (8-2-1) met Georgia Tech in the Peach Bowl and immediately after the game began it was obvious the Boilermakers could name their score. Coach Jim Young, however, called off his first stringers and won by a final score of "only" 42-21.

Michigan's 200th football defeat came in the Rose Bowl, a controversial 17-10 setback to Southern Cal. Only 200 losses in 836 games over a 99-year period is truly a remarkable record. The defeat was also the 11th straight year in which the Wolverines lost their season's final game. The bowl game ended the four-year career of Rick Leach, who had set another all-time NCAA record by starting 48 consecutive games. During his "M" football days, the Wolverines were 38-8-2 and 3-1-0 against OSU. It was the fifth consecutive "Rosey" win for the West Coast and ninth in 10 years. The Big Ten's lead in the series, which once had been 12-1-0, melted to 18-15-0.

Ohio State was the Big Ten's other bowl contestant—matched against Clemson in the Gator Bowl at Jacksonville. Late in the game the Buckeyes were trailing 17-15 and got the ball for a final crack at go-ahead points. Clemson's Charlie Bauman intercepted a pass just beyond the line of scrimmage and ran to his left, toward the sideline and the Ohio State bench. As he was forced out of bounds, he encountered Hayes.

Television viewers across the Nation knew that something serious happened, but got no immediate visual or narrative clarification. On local station newscasts a few minutes later, Hayes was seen taking a swing at Bauman. Coach Hayes was fired the next morning.

It was a sad ending to a great career.

Hayes' 28-year, 276-game record at Ohio State was 205-61-10 for a winning percentage of .779. His Bucks outscored the opposition 6651-3212 (24-12 average) and his Big Ten record was 152-37-7, .793. Under Hayes, OSU won (or shared) 13 Big Ten crowns, captured three national championships (1954, 1957, 1968) and finished in the top ten a total of 15 times.

Woody Hayes' ground-oriented Buckeye teams gained just over 92,000 yards (334 per game) of which 73 percent was by running. He held a 16-11-1 margin over Michigan and nationally his 238 overall victories then ranked him as the fourth all-time winningest college football coach — behind Amos Alonzo Stagg, Glenn "Pop" Warner, and Paul "Bear Bryant.

WEATHER
Rain and snow mixed tonight.
Low in low 30s. Rain with
high in mid-40s Sunday.
(Map, Data on Page A-2)

The Columbus Dispatch

HOME
FINAL
Associated Press, United Press
International and
Copley News Services

32 Pages OHIO'S GREATEST HOME NEWSPAPER 3 Sections

VOL. 108, NO. 183 COLUMBUS, OHIO 43216, SATURDAY, DECEMBER 30, 1978 15 Cents

WOODY HAYES RESIGNS

©1978, Dispatch Printing Co.

Woody Hayes, Ohio State's legendary head football coach for the last 28 years, announced his retirement Saturday morning following his team's loss in the Gator Bowl on Friday night.

The 65-year-old Hayes, who recorded 238 career wins, told Dispatch sportswriter Paul Hornung by telephone from Jacksonville, Fla., Saturday morning, that "I am resigning as of now."

HAYES DECLINED to make further comment, but apparently his decision was triggered by the events in the Gator Bowl on Friday night. Ohio State was beaten by Clemson, 17-15, and Hayes was involved in a sideline incident involving a Clemson player near the end of the game.

In Jacksonville, one news wire service reported that Hayes has been fired.

OSU Athletic Director Hugh Hindman was quoted as saying that "Coach Hayes has been relieved of his duties as head football coach at Ohio State University. This decision has the full support of the president of the university."

Hindman said he was leaving Jacksonville to return to Columbus and would have no further comment on the

Related stories on Pages A-3, B-1
Woody Hayes picture page on Page B-11

ships during his career at Ohio State, is fourth on the all time win list among college coaches behind Amos Alonzo Stagg, Glenn "Pop" Warner and Paul "Bear" Bryant of Alabama. Hayes' career record is 238-72-10. His record at Ohio State is 205-61-10.

HE BEGAN HIS coaching career at Denison University in 1946, where he stayed three years. He moved on to Miami University in 1949 before taking over the Buckeye helm in 1951.

During his career at Ohio State, Hayes led the Buckeyes to three national championships. His teams also won or shared six straight Big 10 championships from 1972 through 1977, a conference record. Hayes was voted the top collegiate coach following the 1957 and 1975 seasons.

Hayes, born in Clifton, Ohio, on Feb. 14, 1913, was graduated from Denison in 1935 where he majored in English and history. His first high school coaching job was at an assistant at Mingo Junction while his first job as

head coach came in 1938 at New Philadelphia.

HAYES FOLLOWED that with a five year stay in the Navy.

Then came his first college head coaching job at Denison. He won 19 games and lost six from 1946 to 1948, winning two conference titles. While at Miami he won 14 games and lost 5.

He took over at Ohio State in 1951 at a time when the school was fast earning a nickname as the "graveyard of coaches." From 1941 to Hayes' arrival, the Buckeyes had seen four head coaches.

Hayes seemed ready to make the nickname stick when his first three teams combined for a 16-8-2 record. But in 1954, he coached the Buckeyes to a 10-0 record, including a 20-7 win over Southern Cal in the Rose Bowl. In return, Ohio State was named the national champion.

HAYES' TEAMS won two other national championships, but the 1968 team was his only other unbeaten team. It went 10-0.

He coached three Heisman Trophy winners, including two-time winner Archie Griffin. The other two were Vic Janowicz and Howard "Hopalong" Cassady

COACH WOODY HAYES
From small Ohio high schools to small Ohio colleges to The Ohio State
University and the Big Ten. Woody Hayes' life had been Ohio football —
tough, winning football. Only three other college coaches had won more
games at that time. (Photo courtesy of OSU Photo Archives)

1979

SCHEMBECHLER THE SOOTHSAYER

Two days before the 1979 edition of "The Big One" at Ann Arbor, U-M Coach Bo Schembechler told Bill Halls of the *Detroit News*, "The advantage going in, as far as the kicking game, is with Ohio. That's the *only* thing we concede. If our kicking game holds up, we'll be right in there. . . ."

Schembechler's emphasis on kicking was justified: the Wolverines had belted eight of their opponents by an average score of 31-10. However, poor kicking, both punting and field goals, had led directly to a 3-point loss (24-21) to Purdue just a week earlier, and a 2-point defeat (12-10) to Notre Dame early in the season. Furthermore, U-M kickers had hit only three field goals in 18 attempts for the year, and three punts had been blocked.

Ohio State and its army of scarlet-clad fans rolled into town with visions of a national championship. The rambunctious 10-0-0 Buckeyes, featuring sophomore quarterback whiz Art Schlichter, had already registered 356 points and were ranked No. 2 in the land behind Alabama. If that wasn't enough to concern the Michigan coaching staff, OSU's defensive platoon had surrendered a mere four touchdowns in the last six games.

OSU was officially made a 4-point favorite.

As always, there was the madness, hoopla and excitement wrapped around this annual football war. In 1979, however, something was missing. That something was Woody Hayes. How could there be a Michigan–Ohio State game without Woody Hayes? After all, the 1950 Snow Bowl had been the last one without him.

Plus, the whole State of Michigan, both Spartans and Wolverines alike, had grown to *love* to *hate* Woody Hayes. It had become as much a part of "The Big One" as the football itself. Earle Bruce, head coach at Iowa State for the past six years, had taken over the grid reins at Columbus.

With or without Woody, the biggest regular season crowd in NCAA history—106,255—jammed the giant blue bowl on a gorgeous, sun-splashed November 17, the earliest date the game had been played in 46 years. And the throng roared through a suspense-filled, see-saw struggle that saw the lead change hands five times.

For starters, and perhaps indicative of how the day would go, Schembechler shocked everybody by starting a freshman quarterback who had failed to complete either of the two passes he had thrown as a member of the Michigan varsity. His name was Rich Hewlett.

Michigan kicked off, and the exciting afternoon of football was under way. After an exchange of punts, the first big break went to U-M when Mike Hardin intercepted a Schlichter pass and returned 15 yards to Ohio's 31. Hewlett's first completion, a 14-yarder to Ralph Clayton, highlighted a quick march to OSU's 11 and a first down. Lawrence Reid rammed three yards, and Butch Woolfolk got six more to the two. Hewlett was stopped, bringing up fourth-and-inches for a first down, fourth-and-a yard for a touchdown. Schembechler, probably sensitive to his team's "3-for-18" field goal ratio, opted for a touchdown. The call was a Hewlett option to the left, but Buckeye linebacker Alvin Washington spoiled things by slashing through to wrestle Hewlett to the carpet back at the four.

OSU had dodged an early bullet. OSU dodged another bullet three plays later when Schlichter cheated Michigan out of an endzone sack by scrambling free and firing a 25-yard strike to Calvin Murray.

Late in the first quarter and early in the second period, the Michigan offense turned the ball over at its own 38 and 36, but the Wolverine defense blunted both OSU efforts, forcing a punt and a long and futile field goal attempt.

Midway through the second quarter, Ohio State took a punt at its own 25. In the next seven-plus minutes, 13 points would go on the scoreboard.

Three running plays gained 16 yards to the 41 before tailback Jim Gayle, on a delay, burst through left guard for a big 22-yard pickup to U-M's 37. One play later from the 33, the same number

Celebrating 100 Years of Michigan Football

MICHIGAN

OHIO STATE

Michigan Stadium   November 17, 1979   Official Program $1

was called and Gayle ripped off another 22-yarder to the 11. Schlichter got it to the seven, threw incomplete into the endzone, and was then set back five yards by a delay penalty. A pass gained six to the six and Vlade Janakievski came on to hit a short field goal for a 3-0 Buckeye cushion with 3:48 remaining on the first-half clock.

Taking the ensuing kickoff, Michigan worked the ball out 21 yards for a first down at its own 41. Junior quarterback John Wangler, now guiding the offense after Hewlett was injured on the previous series, let go a long one, hitting the speedy Anthony Carter at the Ohio 20. Carter jetted into the endzone to complete the 59-yard touchdown pass—the longest TD pass for Michigan in series history at the time. It was better by 14 yards than the previous record set by Bennie Oosterbaan to Louis Gilbert in the official Dedication Game of Michigan Stadium back in 1927.

Bryan Virgil converted after the record bomb, and the underdog Wolverines had grabbed a 7-3 lead with 1:30 left in the first half.

Schlichter cranked up. From his own 20, he hit on three straight passes—to Gayle for seven, to Doug Donley for 25, to Donley again for 19—and a first down at U-M's 29. After two misses, Schlichter found Gary Williams open for a 21-yard advance to the eight. The clock read "00:22." Following two more incompletions, Janakievski booted his second field goal of the day 11 seconds before intermission to pull his team to within one point.

Even though the score was only 7-6 at half time, the two teams had combined for 406 total yards—244 by the Bucks, 162 by the Wolverines.

Ohio State moved back in front on its first possession of the second half. Taking over at their own 49 after a short 29-yard U-M punt, the Buckeyes executed a grinding 11-play drive that resulted in a first down at the four. Schlichter went to the one, but a holding penalty pushed his team back to the 18. After an incomplete pass, Schlichter aimed one towards Chuck Hunter in the endzone, but Michigan's Mike Jolly broke it up—or so everybody thought. Jolly tipped the ball away, but Hunter, with amazing concentration, stretched out his left hand and seemed to balance the ball on his finger tips. He somehow continued to hold on as he fell to the ground. It was a superb catch.

It was also an Ohio State touchdown! The drought had *finally* been broken, marking the Bucks' first touchdown against hated Michigan in four years. Furthermore, with the exception of Pete

*Fans began arriving early for the 1979 game at
Ann Arbor — on a perfect day for football.*

Johnson in 1975, Hunter became the first Buckeye to score a series six-pointer since Archie Griffin in the 1972 game.

In any event, Ohio led 12-7, and it stayed that way when Jolly intercepted Schlichter's pass on an attempted 2-point conversion.

Michigan once again stormed back. On second-and-15 from the 15, Wangler spotted Carter up field and rifled one his way. Carter took it at the OSU 40 and raced to the 19 for a 66-yard gain before being pulled down by Vince Skillings. Wangler kept for 14 to the five; Roosevelt Smith went to the four; Ohio was penalized to the two, Woolfolk went to the one; Ohio was penalized to the 18-inch line; and Smith plunged over for the score. Now ahead 13-12, Schembechler wanted two more points and got them on Smith's run. With 3:53 left in the third period, the Wolverines were whooping it up with a 15-12 lead.

Roosevelt Smith's touchdown run entitled him membership in a club with only three others—those players who had scored touchdowns in three different Michigan–Ohio State games. Smith joined Bill Heston (1901-02-04), Tom Harmon (1938-39-40) and Paul Warfield (1961-62-63).

Now it was OSU's turn. Sparked by a 43-yard pass from Schlichter to Donley, the Bucks quickly reached Michigan's 14. Disaster! Gayle hit for five but fumbled, and U-M's Jolly came up with the ball at the nine. With 12 seconds left in the third quarter, wearers of the Maize and Blue began thinking about the 1969 game, the year their team pulled off the biggest upset in series history.

Knocking out two first downs, the U-M drive bogged at its own 38. Another disaster! Standing in punt formation at the 25, kicker Virgil never had a chance. Linebacker Jim Laughlin, a senior from Lyndhurst, Ohio, roared through a gap untouched and slammed the kick with both arms. A wild scramble followed. First, Skillings tried to pick up the ball but kicked it instead. As the ball bounded goalward, it suddenly leaped upward at the 18-yard line—right into the hands of Todd Bell, also a linebacker. As Bell waltzed across the Michigan goal at OSU's "end of the stadium," he was engulfed by delirious teammates and frenzied fans who poured from the lower seats onto the field to greet his arrival. It was the tenth time in the series that a blocked punt had directly resulted in a score.

Before things could settle back down, Janakievski missed the all-important conversion. Still, the Buckeyes had clawed back into a 3-point lead, 18-15.

"If our kicking game holds up, we'll be right in there. . . ."

Jim Laughlin blocked a fourth quarter punt that resulted in OSU's winning touchdown in 1979.

Schembechler's pre-game fear—the kicking game—had indeed become a haunting reality.

The stunned Wolverines got the ball back three more times but began 70, 80, and 83 yards away from the Buckeye goal. Final score: Ohio State 18, Michigan 15. The Buckeyes had their 22nd conference football championship.

Why did Schembechler start a freshman quarterback who had never completed a collegiate pass? "We wanted to run the option with him. Our running attack is devised that way, and we planned to have Hewlett run the option and Wangler run the power plays and pass."

What were Schembechler's post-game comments (for the thousandth time this season) about the kicking game? "Our punting has been so bad. Pathetic. Our whole kicking game has been bad. All year."

Season figures of 15 missed field goals, four punts blocked, and only a 35-yard punting average clearly illustrate the coach's point.

The Buckeyes led in first downs, 20-13, yards rushing, 236-151, yards passing, 196-147, and total yards, 432-298. Gayle was the leading rusher with 72 yards in nine carries.

The OSU victory capped an 11-0-0 season and sent the happy Bucks to the Rose Bowl for the first time in four years. Immediately after the loss to Ohio, Michigan accepted an invitation to play North Carolina in the Gator Bowl. Two other Big Ten teams also went bowling—Purdue to the Astro-Bluebonnet and Indiana to the Holiday.

With all four games settled by less than a touchdown, the Big Ten came out with a 2-2 split. At San Diego, the Hoosiers withstood Brigham Young's savage passing attack to escape a 38-37 winner, as BYU missed a field goal from inside the 10-yard line on

Dispatch *Sports*

- Sports At A Glance .... Page D-2
- Purdue Beats Indiana .... Page D-4
- Wisconsin Wins; Big Ten .... Page D-6
- Duke Cagers Nip Kentucky .... Page D-7
- Glen To Lose GP Race? .... Page D-8
- Alabama Rolls; Top 20 .... Page D-10

Section D

Buckeyes Grab The Roses

Punt Block Nets TD To Beat Wolves

By Bob Hunter
Of The Dispatch Staff

ANN ARBOR, Mich. — Ohio State...

the game's final play. At Houston, the Boilermakers built a big lead early, then withstood a furious Tennessee rally for a 27-22 victory.

At Jacksonville, the Tar Heels (7-3-1) pulled off a big 17-15 surprise over Michigan. 17-15? That's the identical score Woody Hayes and Ohio State remembered from the same bowl just a year earlier against Clemson. Now, for the 13th straight year, the Wolverines became losers in their season finale.

In a thriller at Pasadena, Southern Cal rallied for a 17-16 triumph over the Buckeyes. OSU, 11-1-0, finished fourth in the ranking behind Alabama, the Trojans, and Oklahoma. Michigan, 8-4-0, was 18th or 19th, depending upon the poll.

Few feelings sting quite as sharply as in the moments that immediately follow losing the annual "big game." Such was the case that sunny November Saturday in Ann Arbor. While the 18-15 Buckeye-Wolverine score still had a stabbing freshness, a quiet and despondent Michigan rooter moved slowly through the maze of humanity and between the snarled traffic just outside the emptying stadium. Giving it his best shot at self-consolation, he finally said, "Well, there's only one good thing about the whole (expletive deleted) thing. At least we didn't have to lose to Woody Hayes."

359

1980

FINALLY, A HAPPY ENDING
FOR BO AND THE BIG BLUE

Very few, if any, of the undergraduate students attending Ohio State University and the University of Michigan in 1981 could remember when one of the schools did not win or share the Big Ten football championship. They were children either in kindergarten or early grade school the last time it had failed to happen. During this time, the nation had been served by five different Presidents.

For the 13th consecutive year one of the "Big Two" of Big Ten football was the wearer of the 1980 gridiron crown.

Both Ohio State and Michigan finished the regular season with 9-2-0 records. However, those 9-2-0 records had far different meanings to the partisans of the two schools.

For the Buckeyes, it was a miserable 9-2-0—one they wanted to forget, quickly. For the Wolverines, it was a glorious 9-2-0 that brought happy jubilation.

In late summer, when the AP and UPI pre-season polls came out, along with all the other "Top 20" predictions from all kinds of magazines and tabloids, Ohio State hogged just about all of the "No. 1 ink." Of 12 different polls, nine placed the Bucks on top, while the remaining three claimed the Pitt Panthers would be the nation's best. Rounding out the top five were Alabama, Arkansas, and Oklahoma.

Michigan? One poll—just one—thought enough of the Wolverines to have them among the top ten teams. Generally, they were rated about 15th.

Throughout Buckeyeland, it was an upcoming campaign that couldn't begin any too soon. In Michigan, there was plenty of doubt, but a willingness to get on with it, anyway. "Just tee it up," they thought, "play'em one at a time, and see what happens. . . ."

Once the season kicked off, OSU's grip on No. 1 wasn't nearly as secure as it had seemed. Even though the nation's three "top dogs" were equally unimpressive in their season openers, the voters of both polls apparently had sudden changes of thought. Alabama jumped to the top and the Buckeyes fell to second, while Pittsburgh tumbled all the way to fifth—all this after just one game. The Tide topped Georgia Tech, 26-3; OSU overcame Syracuse, 31-21, after trailing by 18; and the Panthers got past Boston College, 14-6.

Three games into the season, the Buckeyes were still No. 2, while at the same time, Michigan was staggering around and given up for dead. After the Syracuse game, Ohio State swamped Minnesota, 47-0, and defeated Arizona State, 38-21. Michigan, looking ahead a week to Notre Dame, sputtered past hapless Northwestern, 17-10, then lost an incredible 29-27 decision to the Irish at South Bend. Next came another loss, 17-14 to South Carolina.

Then, on October 4, Michigan "won a doubleheader" of sorts. At Ann Arbor, U-M was hammering California, 38-13, and, at the same time, Big Blue fans were celebrating the great news coming up from Columbus—UCLA's shocking 17-0 shutout of the Buckeyes.

As so many times in the recent past, Ohio State was put under the pressure of a pre-season No. 1 tag and, once more, it was too much. The run for No. 1 had run out of gas.

Each team then reeled off six straight successes. U-M continued to hold its act together and thumped Michigan State, 27-23, Minnesota, 37-14, and Illinois, 45-14. Then came three shutouts, 35-0 over Indiana, 24-0 over Wisconsin, and 26-0 over Purdue.

Meanwhile, OSU was belting Northwestern, 63-0, Indiana, 21-17, Wisconsin, 21-0, and Michigan State, 44-16. In one of those "Believe It Or Not" games, Illinois gained 695 yards against the Bucks—but lost—49-42. OSU went on to defeat Iowa, 41-7, and awaited Michigan's invasion of the territory the following week.

Both teams were 7-0-0 in conference play, bringing up "showdown time" once again. OSU was 9-1-0 overall and ranked fifth; U-M was 8-2-0 and had worked all the way to 10th. The Buckeyes had outscored their opposition, 37-14, per game and the

Wolverines by 29-12. The Bucks were slight favorites, and a record-setting Ohio Stadium crowd of 88,827 filled the historic old horseshoe. As usual, ABC's television cameras were there to show off the Big Ten's premiere event.

The first half was a standoff. An Art Schlichter-to-Cal Murray pass for 38 yards led a march to Michigan's 16 early in the second quarter. The Wolverines' rugged defense set the Bucks back to the 23, and senior Vlade Janakievski's field goal put his team on top by three. Less than six minutes later, however, U-M's Ali Haji-Sheikh matched it with a 43-yarder.

It was still anybody's ball game at intermission, even though Michigan led in first downs, 13-3. The score stood: Janakievski 3, Haji-Sheikh 3.

The Wolverines moved ahead in the third quarter following an OSU turnover. Schlichter completed a pass to Gary Williams who was stripped of the ball by Marion Body, and Tony Jackson came up with the ball for Michigan at its own 44. U-M then cranked up a 14-play, 56-yard drive. Led by the running of Butch Woolfolk, the game's leading rusher with 141 yards in 31 carries, the Blue reached the Bucks' 12. On third-and-11 from the 13, quarterback John Wangler hit his favorite target, Anthony Carter, just beyond the goal line for a touchdown.

"The touchdown was an audible," Wangler told newsmen after the game. "I called it at the line of scrimmage. I saw them playing man-to-man coverage, and Anthony did a good job of getting open."

That made the score 9-3, and it remained that way when Haji-Sheikh's conversion attempt struck the crossbar.

This game, however, was far from over.

On the first play of OSU's next possession, Michigan intercepted a long Schlichter pass at its 44 and looked ready to put the game away, marching to Ohio's 25-yard line. From there, though, the Buckeyes intercepted a halfback pass by Woolfolk in the endzone. Michigan had let OSU off the hook.

Midway through the final period, an OSU punt had U-M backed to its own five-yard line to set the scene for the final, frantic, seven-plus minutes of the game. On third-and-seven, Wangler rolled out and completed a 17-yard pass to Norm Betts for a big first down. Now, Ohio State had let U-M off the hook.

The souped-up Wolverines then crunched down to the Buckeyes' 27, but were forced to punt, which went into the endzone. With 2:38 remaining in the game, Schlichter & Co. took over at their 20 and in possession of all three of their timeouts. On first down, Schlichter scrambled for 13, but then threw four straight incompletions.

Taking over at the OSU 33, Michigan was surely now ready to seal things. But not quite. After three plays had netted only one yard, the team lined up in punt formation. The snap went instead to running back Stanley Edwards, but the fake didn't work.

Incredibly, Ohio State still had life. But all of its timeouts had been used up on Michigan's last series of downs.

With just under a minute to play, the Bucks started at their 26 and Schlichter threw deep to Doug Donley for a big 42-yard gainer to U-M's 32.

The whole stadium could now see "10-9" figures.

On first down, Schlichter was forced from the pocket and picked up two yards. He then threw out of bounds to stop the clock.

Third down. Twenty-one seconds left. With all 88,000-plus on their feet, it was no place for the faint-hearted. Every eye was on Schlichter as he retreated to pass. He started to scramble but was caught by Michigan's Phil Girgash, an Ohioan from Lakewood. In Girgash's grasp, Schlichter threw anyway. After a 15-yard penalty and loss of down, Schlichter once again retreated to pass. He was sacked by Robert Thompson, U-M's first of the day.

Ball game.

The contest was the 30th anniversary of the infamous Snow Bowl of 1950, won by Michigan, 9-3. The score of the 1980 game? Also 9-3, Michigan. It was the third year in a row that the home team had lost this game, and the fifth in six years.

Offensively, Michigan also dominated, operating 84 plays (rushing and passing) to only 58 for Ohio. U-M led in first downs, 23-14, and total yardage, 317-244. The winners threw 23 passes and connected on 11 for 120 yards, while OSU could manage only 8-for-26 for 130 yards.

Winning Coach Bo Schembechler said he was enjoying this championship more than any previously. "This team has come far beyond all our expectations," said Bo. "They gave us up for dead earlier in the season, but we vowed to come back and win the Big Ten title. Our defense was simply unbelievable."

Buckeye Coach Earle Bruce, losing the first Big Ten game in his two years at OSU, declared, "This is the game that makes our season, isn't it? Our offense sputtered all day. On defense we had to do a great job in containing them like we did."

In this 77-game series dating back to 1897, there was no home field advantage. The host team had won 36 and lost 36 (with

sports
DETROIT FREE PRESS

the scoreboard
Complete sports rundown, Page 4

Today's television highlights:
🏈 1:00 p.m. Lions football: Detroit at Tampa Bay
🏈 1:00 p.m. NFL football: Pittsburgh at Buffalo
🏈 1:30 p.m. CFL football: Grey Cup: Edmonton vs. Hamilton
🏈 4:00 p.m. NFL football: Washington at Dallas

Sunday, Nov. 23, 1980	
LOVE LETTERS	2
INSIDE OF SPORTS	6
MOVIE GUIDE	8
OUTDOORS	9

H

Defense takes U-M to Pasadena

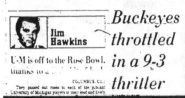

Jim Hawkins

Buckeyes throttled in a 9-3 thriller

U-M is off to the Rose Bowl, thanks to a ...

COLUMBUS, Ohio —

They passed out roses in each of the jubilant University of Michigan players at their loud and lively ...

five ties).

The season wasn't over for either team. Both would be heading to the warm West for bowl dates—the Buckeyes to Arizona and the Fiesta Bowl, the Wolverines to California and the Rose Bowl. Conference member Purdue would also go bowling.

On the day after Christmas, Ohio State lost to Penn State, 31-19, and the next afternoon Purdue sneaked past Missouri, 28-25, in the Liberty Bowl. On New Year's Day, Michigan allowed Washington only two field goals en route to a 23-6 triumph.

The league's 2-1-0 bowl season brought its all-time postseason record to 25-23-0.

Michigan's "Rosey" victory snapped an unbelievable streak. For the first time in 14 long years, the Wolverines managed to win their final game of the season. OSU was now embarked on a four-year streak of losing its last game each season and could count only two final victories in 12 years.

An '80 grid season that had begun on such an exciting note for Ohio State ended a disappointing 9-3-0 (including a loss to Michigan) and a final rating of 15th. Michigan, once 1-2-0, closed with nine straight victories, its 30th conference championship, and a No. 5 national standing behind Georgia, Pittsburgh, Oklahoma, and Florida State. It was some rally for Coach Bo Schembechler and his charges!

Michigan's defense surrendered 120 points in the first seven games (17.1 average), then slammed the touchdown door completely shut for the remainder of the season. The opposition could muster only three field goals over the last five games.

1981

GAME 78

SCHLICHTER RUNS
IN AND RIDES OUT

The biggest Big Ten news during the season was that the conference had finally shaken its "Big 2, Little 8" image, an image the conference had been trying to shake for many years. Six weeks into the '81 campaign saw Iowa, Wisconsin, and Ohio State as the league's three leading teams, while a five-way tie existed for fourth place. Only Michigan State and Northwestern were out of the race.

Furthermore, Wisconsin had already beaten both Michigan and Ohio State, while Iowa had bumped off the Wolverines and was not scheduled to play the Buckeyes.

"Parity," as they love to say in the NFL, had *finally* returned to the Big Ten.

Five weeks later, however, and for the 14th straight year, "The Big One" carried both conference championship and Rose Bowl ramifications. A Michigan victory over Ohio State would give the Wolverines an outright title and, along with it, an automatic Rose Bowl bid.

Just as Ohio State had been the year before, Michigan was the overwhelming pre-season choice as the nation's No. 1 team. The albatross tag did its job in the first game, as Wisconsin shocked the Big Blue and the rest of the collegiate football world with a 21-14 win, while OSU was handling Duke, 34-13. The Bucks later lost, 36-27, to Florida State, and, 24-21, to Wisconsin. However, OSU went to Ann Arbor with five victories in a row, including a 70-6 mashing of Northwestern. U-M was awaiting the

Buckeyes' arrival with four wins in a row, including a 70-21 smashing of Illinois.

It was now time for the 78th meeting between the Wolverines and Buckeyes. U-M was 8-2-0, OSU 7-3-0, and it had been 14 years since the two old rivals met with five total losses. Michigan was made an 8-point favorite, even though the Buckeyes were averaging 442 yards per game, third best in the country behind Arizona State and Brigham Young. Michigan was seventh among the major colleges with 419 yards-per-game offensive figures. The AP poll had the Wolverines rated No. 7, but did not include the Buckeyes.

Gray skies and temperatures hovering in the low thirties greeted the 41st consecutive 100,000-plus throng to Michigan Stadium to see firsthand if the Blue could win and keep the "Big 2" dominance intact. Millions more gathered around television sets to watch.

Michigan blew it.

With two running backs the calibre of Butch Woolfolk and Stanley Edwards, and with an offensive line averaging 6-5 and 257 pounds in size, it seemed astonishing that on four different occasions during the afternoon Michigan could not bang out a few crucial yards, especially while facing a defense that had surrendered tons of yardage and 216 points during the season—the most in Buckeye gridiron history.

As so often happens in this rivalry, the offenses go into a shell and the coaching staffs of both teams seem to place top priority on first "not losing" the game rather than "winning" it.

Over the course of the game, Michigan had: first-and-goal at OSU's four, third-and-two at OSU's six, third-and-three at OSU's seven, and first-and-goal at the OSU eight.

Out of this, Michigan got no touchdowns. What Michigan did get were field goals the first three times and a pass interception in the endzone on the fourth effort.

Anthony Carter electrified the big crowd by returning the opening kickoff 52 yards. It was a promising beginning, but it was wasted when quarterback Steve Smith threw an interception. OSU couldn't move and punted. Carter returned to the Buckeye 29. Michigan held onto the ball this time but settled for a field goal after coming up with fourth-and-goal at the two. Ali Haji-Sheikh, a hometown boy from Ann Arbor, put it through the pipes and Michigan grabbed a 3-0 lead.

On the Wolverines' next possession, they ripped off a 30-yard drive in six plays, reaching the Buckeyes' 36. On second-and-eight, Smith threw a pass that was tipped by OSU's Calvin Bell and picked off by Maurice Marey at the 18-yard line.

Art Schlichter, OSU's senior quarterback, hit on three passes (one to Cedric Anderson and two to John Frank) totaling 31 yards, and along with the power running of Tim Spencer, drove the Buckeyes to a first down at the U-M 12. Fullback Vaughn Broadnax—all 252 pounds of him—blasted for five yards, and Spencer rammed four more. Then Broadnax rumbled for another first down at the one. After Spencer was stopped just inches short of the goal, Schlichter sneaked it over. Bob Atha kicked the conversion, and with 9:57 left in the first half, the underdog Buckeyes had the lead.

Michigan had something going just before intermission, but quarterback Smith was belted for no gain on a fourth-and-one at the Ohio 39-yard line.

Halftime: OSU 7, U-M 3.

Holding the Buckeyes on their first possession of the second half, Michigan started from its own 26. Woolfolk ripped off a 19-yarder and, three plays later, Edwards shot for 15 more to OSU's 25. Edwards took it to the 21, Woolfolk to the 16, then to the 14 and another first down. Woolfolk gained four and Edwards four more, bringing up a third-and-two situation at the Buckeye six. Then, Smith went to his left on a quarterback option and was dragged down for a big three-yard loss by John Gayle.

On came Haji-Sheikh for another chip-shot field goal to bring his team to within one point, 6-7, with just over five minutes remaining in the third stanza.

A few minutes later, Michigan appeared to be in a position to wrap it up for the day. After the kickoff, on second down from the 20, Schlichter threw a wobbler that was tipped by Keith Bostwick and intercepted by Tony Jackson at the OSU 48.

Smith missed a pass on first down and then burst for a 13-yard gain. Woolfolk hit for six, and 15 more yards were tacked on because of a face mask penalty, giving U-M a first down at the 14. Two Woolfolk runs gained seven yards, bringing up a third-and-three at the seven-yard line for Coach Bo Schembechler and his staff to mull over. The Buckeye defense gave Edwards only one yard, and Schembechler was more than ready to settle for another Haji-Sheikh field goal and a 9-7 Michigan lead with 4:44 remaining in the third period.

On the first play of the final quarter, Schlichter was way off target on a long pass, and Brian Carpenter intercepted at the ten and returned it to the 19. On first down, though, a Woolfolk fum-

367

sports

DETROIT FREE PRESS ••

the scoreboard
The complete sports rundown. Page 4H.

Today's television highlights:
- 1:00 p.m. Football: Detroit at Chicago
- 1:00 p.m. Football: Denver at Pittsburgh
- 1:30 p.m. Grey Cup: Edmonton vs. Ottawa
- 4:00 p.m. Football: Miami at NY Jets

Sunday, Nov. 22, 1981
HORSE RACING 5,8
INSIDE OF SPORTS 12
OUTDOORS 13
Call with sports news 222-6600

Mike Downey

Color U-M Rose plans blue

OSU's 'Straight Arrow' Art gets his point across to U-M

ANN ARBOR

"Your Honor," said Jim Nein, now an attorney but once an Ohio State halfback, "this young man is not

Bluebonnet's left after 14-9 Buckeye win

ART SCHLICHTER
Scored both touchdowns in Buckeyes' 14-9 win over Michigan in 1981. He started all 48 games at quarterback in his four years at OSU and rushed/passed for 8,850 yards. He was 2-2 against the Wolverines. (Photo courtesy of OSU Photo Archives)

ble gave it right back at the 27. The Bucks were unable to get anything positive going. A 40-yard field goal try by Atha that would have put OSU back ahead wasn't even close.

Michigan took over and put on another impressive drive. With Smith completing passes to Carter for 16 and 12 yards, and with Woolfolk, Edwards, and Larry Ricks taking care of the ground work, U-M went 44 yards in eight plays. On third-and-eight from the 30, Smith and Vince Bean connected on a beautiful 22-yard pass play to the enemy eight-yard line. Again, Michigan was in great shape to put it away.

Going for the touchdown this time, Smith threw incomplete into the endzone. He came right back with another throw that would have been a touchdown, but the pass was thrown behind a wide-open Craig Dunaway. Buckeyes everywhere breathed a big sigh of relief.

Then came disaster. Retreating once more to pass, Smith lobbed it into the right corner of the endzone where the ball was tipped by OSU's John Gayle into the hands of OSU's Kelvin Bell. It was the third tipped interception of the game.

The ball was brought out to the 20-yard line, with just over eight minutes left. Not only did the visitors trail on the scoreboard at this point, but also in first downs (9-20) and total yards (167-352). It seemed highly unlikely that OSU could get its act together long enough to cover the 80 yards, or even 50 yards to get in field goal position.

After a Spencer gain of five yards, Schlichter passed for six to Frank and a first down at the 31. Moments later, however, Schlichter was faced with a big third-and-eight dilemma at his 33. He dropped back, was forced to scramble to his left, and threw off-balance—complete. Frank grabbed the aerial for a big gain of 11 yards and "a must" first down at the OSU 44. Schlichter, now finally cranked up, threw to Gary Williams for 17 more yards to Michigan's 39. Spencer went to the 35, before a Schlichter-to-Frank connection reached the 29, just inches short of a first down. A Schlichter sneak got it, but he fumbled. However, Lucas fell on the ball for the Buckeyes. Spencer then exploded around the right side for a 20-yard pickup down to Michigan's nine. First down.

Spencer also got the next two calls but got only three yards. On the second-down play he appeared to run just to get position for a forthcoming field goal. The whole stadium, it seemed, was thinking field goal and the lead going back to OSU at 10-9. But not Schlichter.

On third down, Schlichter rolled right, looked into the endzone, couldn't find an open receiver, and decided to run. All the while, Broadnax kept fighting and warding off a Wolverine defender who was between Schlichter and the goal line. Schlichter used the Broadnax interference to perfection and somehow slipped into the endzone just inside the orange rubber pylon. Touchdown! Schlichter's second of the day.

Michigan was stunned. Atha added the conversion and all but "2:50" had blinked off the scoreboard clock.

Ohio State 14, Michigan 9.

The Buckeye defense then stifled U-M's passing game, spotty at best. OSU took over at the enemy 44 and ground out a vital first down as the Wolverines spent all three of their timeouts. From there Schlichter fell on the ball twice, and the clock took care of the rest.

Ohio State had knocked Michigan out of the Rose Bowl.

Art Schlichter, who started every game at quarterback in his four-year career at Columbus, was carried off the field on the shoulders of his equally happy teammates. He left in true hero style. Schlichter lost to Michigan as a freshman and junior, but he won as a sophomore and senior. Overall, his record stood 35-11-1 with one bowl game remaining.

Ohio State's win at Ann Arbor marked the fourth straight year that the visiting team won. Also, in the long history of the series, the home team had now lost one more game than it had won.

The losing Wolverines led in first downs, 20-15, rushing yards, 231-126, passing yards, 136-131, and total yards 367-257. Plus, the losers had to punt only once. Schlichter was 12-for-24 in passing; Smith, 9-for-26.

The Michigan–Ohio State Rose Bowl dominance did indeed end in 1981. For the first time in 14 long years, the Pasadena bowl wouldn't be greeting either the Buckeyes or Wolverines. This time Iowa would represent the Big Ten.

Sending four teams bowling, the Big Ten won two and lost two. Michigan scrubbed UCLA, 33-14, in the Bluebonnet, and Ohio State edged Navy, 31-28, in the Liberty. Losing were Wisconsin (28-21 to Tennessee in the Garden State) and Iowa (28-0 in the Rose to Washington).

Both the Wolverines and Buckeyes posted 9-3-0 records. U-M was ranked No. 12 in the final AP poll, OSU No. 15.

1982

TOO MUCH MARK MAREK,
TOO MANY TURNOVERS

For the first time in 12 years, the names of both Michigan and Ohio State were absent from the Associated Press's pre-season Top Ten list. Since 1970, U-M had been in the August spotlight every year except 1980, while OSU had been ranked among the nation's elite every year except three—1971, 1979, and 1981.

It was different in 1982, with the Wolverines pegged at No. 12 and the Buckeyes two notches lower. Perhaps it was a blessing of sorts. During those 12 years, coaches Bo Schembechler, Woody Hayes, and Earle Bruce, collectively, could push their teams to finish above their lofty pre-season ratings only five times. It also meant there were no pre-season "WE'RE NO. 1!" expectations created among fans and media (*and* the players) as the teams prepared for the '82 campaign. Two years earlier the Buckeyes had to wear that burdensome tag, and in 1981 the Wolverines carried it. Neither team remained No. 1 after its season debut. So with these uncharacteristically humble rankings of 12th and 14th, both Michigan and Ohio State were able to approach the season with the attitude that they had nowhere to go but up.

The Wolverines began with a 20-9 win over Wisconsin but then dropped back-to-back games to Notre Dame and UCLA. Returning to the cozy confines of the conference family, U-M reeled off seven straight victories, including blowouts of Northwestern, 49-14, Minnesota, 52-14, and Purdue, 52-21.

OSU opened up with wins over Baylor and Michigan State. So far so good. Then came three straight setbacks that had Buckeyes everywhere aghast! Why? All three losses were at Ohio Sta-

371

dium, and their beloved Buckeyes had not lost three in a row there since 1922, the year the stadium opened. Pulling off the stunning gridiron hat-trick in 1982 were Stanford, Florida State, and Winconsin.

The Bucks bounced back, however, and as the big day approached, they had only one conference loss—to the Badgers. Michigan had none. Under normal circumstances, the winner of this game would represent the Big Ten in the Rose Bowl. But not this time. In an odd scheduling twist, Michigan had booked, and won, an extra conference game. The Wolverines were 8-0-0 in league play, the Buckeyes 6-1-0. Thus, an Ohio triumph still wouldn't be enough. The Rose Bowl issue was already settled.

Coming into Columbus, the Wolverines' average game score was 31-16, the Buckeyes' 28-18. The visitors from Ann Arbor were made a two-point favorite.

A hard rain drenched Columbus on the morning of the game; more of the same was forecast for the afternoon. As usual, the weather mattered little. Under cool, heavy skies the big horseshoe was jammed with its biggest crowd ever—90,252.

Michigan won the toss, took the football, and in an impressive display of power marched 72 yards in 11 plays to the OSU eight. But as in the previous year's game, once inside the Bucks' ten, momentum fizzled. Quarterback Steve Smith fumbled, and Curt Curtis recovered for Ohio State.

Oh! Those turnovers!

Michigan's next series began at its own 48 after a short OSU punt. Sparked by two Smith keepers for 20 yards, and seven rushes for 29 yards by tailback Lawrence Ricks, the Wolverines were third-and-goal at the one. Smith then pitched out to Ricks for the touchdown. Ali Haji-Sheikh converted and U-M led, 7-0. At this early stage of the game, Michigan had racked up eight first downs to OSU's one and led in total yards, 124-11. Despite the early fumble, it seemed as if it would still be a Michigan kind of day.

Early in the second quarter, Smith rolled right from his 17 and threw into the hands of Buckeye linebacker Rowland Tatum who was celebrating his 20th birthday.

Taking advantage of Tatum's big "birthday present," OSU went to work. Starting at U-M's 29, the Buckeyes were successful, but problems soon beset them. From a first down at the 15, Tim Spencer scored, but the offense was caught holding and OSU was penalized back to the 25. Quarterback Mike Tomczak then lost eight more yards. Suddenly, it was second-and-28 at the 33.

Ohio St. stuns Michigan

Tomczak threw to Spencer for 12, then came right back with a 16-yard strike to Gary Williams to the five. The chain gang came out for a measurement, and the Buckeyes were inches short. Fourth down. Fullback Vaughn Broadnax—up to 260 pounds this year—pounded all the way into the endzone for a touchdown. It was Ohio State's first touchdown against Michigan in Columbus in ten long years! (Archie Griffin's touchdown in a 14-11 win in 1972 had been the last.) Rich Spangler added the conversion for a 7-all score with 6:48 remaining in the first half.

On a carpet now glistening from heavy rain, Michigan took the ensuing kickoff and, keyed by a 28-yard pass from Smith to Craig Dunaway plus two 13-yard completions to Anthony Carter, had a first down at OSU's 12. On an end-around Carter went to the eight, but a holding infraction pushed U-M back to the 22. On third down, and still from the 22, Smith fumbled the snap from center, and Jerome Foster fell on it for the Buckeyes at the 25.

Oh! Those turnovers!

The clock showed just 2:17 left in the half, but it turned out to be adequate time for OSU to score again. Spencer immediately shot ahead for 25 yards to midfield. On third-and-10, Tomczak hit Cedric Anderson for a big gain of 19 yards to the 31. Spencer hammered to the 18 and Broadnax to the 15. Moments later, the Bucks were once again in a fourth-and-inches situation deep in Michigan territory—this time at the eight. Broadnax crashed for the yard and the first down. One play later Spencer powered over for the score from the five. Spangler converted, and OSU took a 14-7 lead. The combined total of 21 points scored in the first half amounted to the greatest first-half point production in the series in 13 years.

Ohio State took the second-half kickoff and drove 64 yards to the 16, but Tomczak was stripped of the ball by Robert Thompson. Michigan's Mike Hammerstein recovered it at the 37, a loss of 21 yards and possession.

It was a costly error, for Michigan capitalized on the opportunity and tied the score in 15 plays. Facing a crucial fourth-and-one at OSU's four, Smith kept the ball himself on an option and scored. Haji-Sheikh's kick made it 14-14 with 2:28 left in the third period.

Ho-hum. Just another Michigan–Ohio State football affair.

The battle continued, and neither side could sustain an advance. It was back and forth in a misty rain on the soggy rug. At 7:52 in the fourth quarter the break, or disaster, came, depending on one's point of view.

After receiving a punt, Michigan began from its own 14. On an option play Smith pitched back to a trailing Carter who was blasted head-on by All-America linebacker Marcus Marek. Fumble! Marek also recovered the loose ball at the 15.

Sheer bedlam at Ohio Stadium!

Spencer bulled to the eight, and Broadnax rumbled to the one. Spencer then went airborne and over for the score. Spangler's kick made it 21-14 with 6:27 left in the game.

Oh! Those turnovers!

In only 22 seconds the raging Buckeyes had the ball again. Who got it? That man Marek. He intercepted a Smith pass and returned the ball 17 yards to the Michigan 20, with Buckeye fans roaring to the heavens. Three plays gained only three yards, however, and Spangler booted a 33-yard field goal.

Oh! Those turnovers!

With a big ten-point lead and only 3:27 showing on the clock, Coach Earle Bruce and his Buckeyes were beginning to savor their second straight victory over Bo Schembechler's hated Wolverines.

After an exchange of punts and with a mere five seconds left to play, happy Ohio State fans jumped the gun and swarmed onto the field. It took about 10 minutes to clear the gridiron, which was minus one set of goal posts. Michigan's last gasp pass was incomplete, and the fans poured back onto the sodden field to celebrate, wet and overjoyed with their hard-earned triumph.

Final score: 24-14. Not since 1968 had so many points been

374

scored in "The Big One."

"We just gave them the game," Schembechler told newsmen after the game. "We handed it to them. We didn't just lose. We gave it away."

Michigan led in first downs, 20-18, and rushing yards, 176-170, while Ohio State was out front in passing yards, 159-127, and total yards by a slight margin of 329-303. The Buckeyes were 10-for-18 in passing, Michigan only 12-for-28. Two strong running backs, OSU's Tim Spencer and U-M's Lawrence Ricks, had impressive afternoons. Spencer gained 119 yards in 23 attempts and Ricks carried 27 times for 111 yards. But the most telling statistic was Michigan's six turnovers. All the Buckeyes' points directly followed Michigan bobbles.

A month later, Ohio State went to San Diego and trounced BYU, 47-17, in the Holiday Bowl. The 9-3-0 season gave the Buckeyes a final national ranking of No. 12, two places better than had been predicted in August.

Meanwhile, Michigan's trip to the Rose Bowl resulted in another 24-14 defeat, UCLA's second success over the Wolverines in three months. U-M, with an 8-4-0 record, failed to crack the final Top 20 for the first time in 15 years.

Two other Big Ten clubs received post-season bids—Wisconsin and Iowa. The Badgers went to Shreveport and beat Kansas State, 14-3, in the Independence Bowl. In Atlanta's Peach Bowl, the Hawkeyes topped Tennessee, 28-22, giving the Big Ten an impressive 3-1-0 bowl season.

Meanwhile, back in Ohio, the Buckeyes were relishing two straight wins over Michigan. On the other hand, the Wolverines could still brag about their overall 43-31-5 lead in the long rivalry.

1983

OSU TRICK
IS U-M TREAT

In 1983 the Big Ten produced two teams that mounted a serious challenge to Michigan and Ohio State for top conference honors and national recognition. Who were these two new bullies on the block? Illinois and Iowa.

Early in the 1983 season, four Big Ten teams were ranked and, suddenly, other league games than the usual season-ending bout from Columbus or Ann Arbor took on national singnificance. When the polls came out after the second weekend in October, there was Ohio State (ranked 6th), Michigan (13th), Iowa (14th), and Illinois (19th).

In the final Associated Press poll of 1982, however, the Buckeyes wound up as the sole Big Ten member to make the Top 20. That had happened only two other times since the inception of the polls—in 1947 and 1972—when Michigan alone represented the conference.

The Buckeyes began their season with a bang, beating Oregon, 31-6, as a warmup before going to Norman, Oklahoma, to meet the No. 2-rated Sooners. Final: OSU 24, OU 14. And the Buckeyes leaped up three notches to No. 3.

At the same time, Michigan, picked by *Sports Illustrated* to capture the national championship, was struggling. There was an unimpressive 20-17 win over Washington State and a 25-24 setback at the hands of Washington.

Ohio State, unable to "get up" for big back-to-back road games, went to Iowa City and lost to the Hawkeyes, 20-14. Back home for the next two weeks, the Buckeyes battered Minnesota, 68-18, and beat Purdue, 33-22. Another road trip, this one to Champaign–Urbana, resulted in a 17-13 loss to Illinois. The next four weeks, however, were just an autumn walk through the woods as OSU pounded Michigan State, Wisconsin, Indiana, and Northwestern by an average score of 44-15.

Back in Michigan, the 1-1-0 Wolverines' next four games were with those same Spartans, Badgers, Hoosiers, and Wildcats, and it was a U-M picnic in the park by a 40-10 average score. Michigan faced Iowa and Illinois next and managed a split, edging the Hawkeyes, 16-13, before losing to the Illini, 16-6. The Wolverines then smothered Purdue, 42-10, and Minnesota, 58-10.

Meanwhile, Illinois had socked Iowa by a shocking 33-0 score and had doubled up on its other five conference foes by a total score of 181-90.

That brought the season to November 19, the last Saturday in the Big Ten season. Illinois enjoyed an 8-0-0 league record, Michigan 7-1-0. But it didn't matter that each team had a game left. Illinois already had the Rose Bowl in hand by virtue of its earlier win over the Wolverines.

Although for only the second time in 12 years there was no Rose Bowl at stake, "The Big One" still carried major bowl implications. The winner would go to the Sugar Bowl, the loser to the Fiesta Bowl—not a shabby deal for either camp.

Joe Falls of the *Detroit News* thought it was a welcome change. "Even though Bo (Schembechler) was raving at the officials, you felt little of the intensity," wrote Falls. "That's because both sides came out knowing they had cushy holiday trips ahead of them. In the old days it was win or devastation. Now they were loose, and what it produced was an entertaining game—not the old pit war of the past when they'd put the nation to sleep on TV."

Joe Falls had a valid point.

Never before had the Michigan-Ohio State game produced as many as 60 passes or 32 completions or 863 total offensive yards. And never before had *both* teams scored more than 20 points. By all standards of the bitter old rivalry, this was a *wild* game.

Sixty passes in a Michigan-Ohio State game? Coach Woody Hayes was in attendance and, most likely, he growled something like, "This isn't football. This is. . . ."

There was little difference on paper as the two teams prepared for the series' 80th collision. Both had 8-2-0 records. OSU's yearly scoreboard averaged 36-16, U-M's 32-13. The Wolverines were ranked No. 8 in the land, the Buckeyes No. 10.

As in Columbus the previous year, on game day Ann Arbor had also been drenched by hard rains. But the usual 106,000-plus fans packed Michigan Stadium, and they were more than ready to "quit all the talk and get it on."

On Michigan's first play from scrimmage, tailback Rick Rogers broke free for 47 yards to Ohio's 28. After the drive stalled at the nine, Bob Bergeron kicked a field goal for an early 3-0 lead.

With just over five minutes left in the quarter, U-M took possession at its 21. Two plays later from the 33, quarterback Steve Smith threw to speedy sophomore Triando Markray. Touchdown! The 67-yard bomb was the longest touchdown pass in the series in 22 years. After Bergeron's conversion, the huge crowd was whooping it up with a 10-0 lead achieved with relative ease.

Ohio State drove deep into Michigan territory in the second period, but Keith Byars lost the ball on a fumble at the five. A 17-yard punt soon put the Buckeyes in business at U-M's 26. Five plays later, Byars scored from the one. Rich Spangler's kick was good, and Michigan's lead had shrunk to three points, 10-7.

The Wolverines flubbed a grand opportunity to grab another ten-point advantage just before intermission. On third down from the Ohio one-yard line, Rogers attempted to leap the pile but was slammed for no gain. Fourth down, 1:22 on the clock. In came the play from the bench. As Smith barked his signals, a delay of game penalty was called.

Schembechler exploded! He screamed that the field judge had started the clock too soon. Into the game went Bergeron to salvage three points from the embarrassing situation.

Bergeron missed.

As the teams departed for the locker rooms, a still-raging Schembechler followed the officials all the way to the tunnel.

Halftime: Michigan 10, Ohio State 7.

The Buckeyes moved ahead on their first possession of the second half, going 80 yards in seven plays, capped by Byars's pile-driving run of 18 yards. Spangler's conversion was perfect, and OSU had rallied to take a 14-10 lead—a lead that the Michigan fans could hardly believe.

It would be a crazy fourth quarter.

U-M's Brad Cochran intercepted a Mike Tomczak pass and returned it 23 yards to OSU's 28. As in the previous year's game, an interception would turn the tide the winners' way.

On third-and-eight from the 26, Smith found Sim Nelson open for an 11-yard advance to the 15. Three plays later, Smith rolled right from the one and scored. Bergeron converted. Michigan 17, Buckeyes 14.

Pandemonium at Ann Arbor!

Ohio State answered with a drive to U-M's 38 with just over 12 minutes left in the game. Here, OSU resorted to a rare tactic for a Michigan–Buckeye game: trickery. Center Joe Dooley snapped the ball to Tomczak who laid the ball on the ground for guard Jim Lachey to pick up—and take off. Instead, Mike Hammerstein, clad in Maize & Blue, grabbed the football.

"We ran the play all week in practice, and it looked like a million dollars, but nobody picked up the ball. It was just a bad call," said Coach Earle Bruce after the game.

Michigan's roarin' and hootin' fans loved the decision by Bruce—especially after their team turned the trick into a touchdown treat.

Nine plays had the Wolverines on the Ohio State eight. Smith calmly pitched a touchdown strike to Eric Cattus, and once again a "million" rolls of toilet paper came streaming down from the student section. Following Bergeron's conversion, the score was 24-14 with 10:08 left in the game.

With Michigan in its "prevent defense," Tomczak systematically passed the Buckeyes downfield, completing six passes to six different receivers. The final 32 yards came on a Tomczak aerial to Cedric Anderson, who made a spectacular catch in the endzone with less than two minutes left. Spangler converted again, but that was it for the game.

Final score: Wolverines 24, Ohio State 21. It would be the Sugar Bowl for Michigan and the Fiesta for the Buckeyes.

The losing Bucks were out front in first downs, 22-20, and in total yards, 448-415. Byars led all rushers with 115 yards in 26 carries, while U-M's Rogers gained 91 yards in 16 tries. Tomczak passed for a personal series-high of 298 yards, completing 21 of 40 attempts. (U-M's Bob Cappius and Bill Culligan combined for 309 passing yards in the 1946 game.) The 863 yards by both teams also broke a series mark of 798 yards set in 1957.

As in the 1982 game, when Michigan lost due to six turnovers, the Buckeyes lost in 1983 because of their four give-aways. They got none in return.

Schembechler's first game as coach at Michigan in 1969 resulted in a 42-14 victory over Vanderbilt. Now, 15 seasons and 173 games later, he would be opposing only his second Southeastern Conference foe—Auburn—in the Sugar Bowl. The outcome? Auburn 9, Michigan 7, on a chip shot field goal in the last seconds

379

■ Bob Welch discusses the dangers of drinking . . . 4C
■ College Tipoff: N.C. State surprises Houston . . . 10C
■ Wisconsin routs MSU, 32-0, in season finale . . . 12C

SUPER SUNDAY
SPORTS

The Detroit News

C

Sunday, November 20, 1983

U-M's victory sweet as Sugar

Wolves win a trip to Bourbon Street

By Lynn Henning
News Staff Writer

ANN ARBOR — Maybe the only thing that can beat Michigan now is top notch steak or too many octopi through Bourbon Street's urban doors.

U-M's Steve Smith (18) threw for two touchdowns and ran for another overshadowing OSU's Keith Byars (41) who ran for two TDs in Michigan's victory.

Wolverines show class, but not Bo and staff

ANN ARBOR — Ah breakfast at breakfast—

Joe Falls

See Falls, 10C ▶

See Michigan, 10C ▶

Brother Rice prevails 28-14

'The best team won,' says Henry Ford Coach Hoskins

By Jim Spadafore
News Staff Writer

Ford's Bryant Warren is grabbed by Paul Konsol

PLAYOFF RESULTS

CLASS A
E. Lansing 14, Traverse City 0
Brother Rice 28, Henry Ford 14
CLASS B
B. Cr Lakeview 21, Durand 10
E. Gr. Rapids 36, Robichaud 6
CLASS C
De Porres 34, Leslie 12
St. Francis 22, Comstock Pk. 14
CLASS D
Hudson 15, Waterford Lakes 0
St. Ignace 26, Beal City 6

See Close A, 8C ▶

NFL pressured by new league

Players, agents use USFL to bolster their paychecks

Associated Press

Abdul-Jabbar primes for life after basketball

News Staff Writer

ANN ARBOR — Maybe the only thing
LOS ANGELES — Kareem Abdul-Jabbar's storied playing career which has extended from the rookie 1980s to the more enlightened 1980s is near its twilight.

Nov 17871 11 ▶

of the game.

Ohio State, however, enjoyed its Fiesta Bowl holiday with a 28-23 win over Pittsburgh.

Two other Big Ten teams also went bowling and both lost. Illinois was beaten, 45-9, by UCLA in the Rose, while Iowa dropped a 14-6 decision to Florida in the Gator.

The final AP poll ranked Michigan No. 8, Ohio State No. 9, Illinois No. 10, and Iowa No. 14. Had "parity" arrived in the Big Ten?

1984

PENNANT FEVER
GRIPS BIG TEN

As the 1984 season wound down, the following quotes appeared in newspapers across the United States:

"Every coach in the Big Ten has predicted this for years. But the thing that is unbelievable is that we've tied and lost our last two games, and we're still in the running for the Rose Bowl." That's what Haden Fry of Iowa had to say.

"The thing is too hard for me to figure out. There are too many circumstances involved for us to go, so I really haven't been thinking about it. Anyway, I'm only thinking about Ohio State." That was the appraisal of Michigan's Bo Schembechler.

"It's been a great year for the Big Ten, but we've destroyed ourselves with the number of losses we've inflicted on each other." Earle Bruce of Ohio State delivered this incisive comment.

These gentlemen and millions of football fans throughout the country were fascinated with what was happening in the Big Ten. Entering the final Saturday of the season, three conference teams had a shot at the Rose Bowl, and five clubs had a chance to win or share the league championship.

It was remarkable. It was unprecedented. It was fun.

Here is a brief summary of the conference's contenders going into the season finales:

Ohio State, 6-2-0, to face Michigan.

Iowa, 5-2-1, to face Minnesota.

Illinois, 6-3-0, season completed.

Michigan, 5-3-0, to face Ohio State.

Michigan State, 5-3-0, to face Wisconsin.

Purdue, 5-3-0, to face Indiana.

Depending on how various games ended, here are some of the outcomes that were being discussed:

If Iowa (a 19-point favorite) beats Minnesota and Michigan (a 10-point underdog) beats Ohio State, the Hawkeyes are outright champions, leaving a possible five-way tie for the runner-up position.

If Michigan, Michigan State, Minnesota, and Purdue all win, there would be a five-way tie among those four teams (plus Illinois) for the title, each with 6-3-0 league records.

Back in August, the pre-season pollsters of the Associated Press had Ohio State pegged No. 9 and Michigan No. 10.

The Wolverines opened with a 22-14 upset of defending national champion Miami. It proved to be a real attention-grabber, as U-M moved all the way to No. 2 (UPI) and No. 3 (AP). But the excitement lasted only a week, until a 20-11 loss to Washington. Then came two wins, a loss, a win, a loss, a win, a loss, and a win. It all added up to 6-4-0 credentials to take to Columbus.

The Buckeyes were waiting with a 9-2-0 record, losing only to Purdue (28-23) and Wisconsin (16-14), good enough for an 11th place national ranking. It was also good enough for the oddsmakers to stake OSU as big ten-point favorites.

The customary Ohio Stadium crowd of 90,000-plus gathered in crisp and mostly sunny weather for the 81st feud between the two old foes.

After an exchange of punts to open the game, the Buckeyes began their second possession 61 yards away. Highlighted by Mike Tomczak passes to Keith Byars for 11 yards and Mike Lanese for 16, plus a 10-yard run by John Woolridge, OSU was first-and-goal at the five. Byars carried the ball on three straight plays and scored to cap the impressive 13-play series. Rich Spangler converted and, 10:13 into the game, Ohio State was off and running with a 7-0 lead.

Michigan came right back. A 13-play, 72-yard march had the Big Blue in fine shape with a first down at the five. After a loss of three, quarterback Chris Zurbrugg was flushed from the pocket, chased right, and, on the run, threw into the endzone. Interception! Sonny Gordon got it for the Buckeyes.

The next five series of downs all resulted in punts. Then, just 17 seconds before intermission, the Wolverines' Monte Robbins lifted a high kick that Lanese decided to field at his 11-yard line. Lanese dropped the football, and Bradley Cochran recovered for

Michigan at the nine.

Nobody—especially Coach Bruce—could believe it!

But once again Michigan couldn't punch out a touchdown. Following an incomplete pass and a sack of Zurbrugg at the 20, the Wolverines had to settle for a field goal by Bob Bergeron with just 00:04 on the clock.

In a defensive-oriented first half, OSU (with only 134 yards total yards) led U-M (with just 95 yards) by a score of 7-3.

To illustrate Michigan's frustration, since 1970, on 11 occasions they had gotten inside the Buckeyes' ten-yard line, only to come away with just three field goals.

Struggling Michigan received the second half kickoff and, in 12 plays, reached a second-and-four situation at OSU's 19. Two plays later, however, the Wolverines were fourth down at the 29. Bergeron was successful with his field goal attempt, making it 7-6.

U-M's next possession began at its two-yard line after a Buckeye punt. Eleven plays later they faced a big third-and-two at OSU's 17. On a keeper inside right tackle, Zurbrugg was zapped by Gordon. No gain. Coach Schembechler once again called upon Bob Bergeron for three crucial points that would give U-M a 9-7 advantage. He missed.

The Buckeyes still led by a thin point.

Five minutes into the fourth period, OSU faced a third-and-12 at its 43. Then came "the play of the game." Tomczak threw a pass intended for Lanese, who made a miraculous, diving catch at the U-M 40 to keep the football in the Buckeyes' hands. Lanese had more than atoned for his first half boner.

Byars cracked to the 38, Tomczak found Chris Carter at the 23, Byars hammered to the 14, Tomczak kept to the 11, and then to the nine. A Tomczak pass to Byars got the ball to the two, and, on the next play, Byars plowed into the endzone. Spangler converted. The scene was sheer bedlam as the scoreboard lights said "14-6" while the clock flashed "06:48" left to play.

The Ohio stomping grounds became even wilder when, ten seconds later, their Buckeye team recovered a fumble. Zurbrugg had passed 17 yards to Sim Nelson, and OSU's William White fell on his fumble at Michigan's 37.

Byars burst to the 20. Two plays later from the 19, Woolridge broke loose to the two. Byars scored—his third touchdown of the game—and Spangler again converted. With 4:43 remaining in the game, it was now 21-6, and that's the way it ended.

OSU led U-M in first downs, 17-15, and in total yards,

Roses bloom for Buckeyes

293-264. Michigan's passing game was 17-for-27, the Bucks' 11-for-15. Keith Byars was held to less than 100 yards for only the second time this season (93 yards in 28 carries), and his 1,647 yards left him just 48 shy of the Big Ten single-season rushing mark set by OSU's Archie Griffin ten years earlier.

In the sizzlin' Big Ten race, only the Buckeyes and Boilermakers (a 31-24 winner over Indiana) survived the pressure. Michigan lost at Columbus; Iowa lost to Minnesota, 23-17; and Michigan State lost to Wisconsin, 20-10.

The Buckeyes were outright champions, and it was on to the Rose Bowl for the first time in five years.

The Big Ten's "bowl-of-plenty" ran over following the 1984 season. Six teams were invited to post-season action, a league record.

Michigan agreed to play No. 1-ranked Brigham Young in the Holiday Bowl and dropped a 24-17 thriller. It's ironic that the Wolverines opened the season with the '83 national champions and closed it with the '84 national champions.

The final record: a dismal (for U-M) 6-6-0—the worst since 1967.

In the conference's other five bowl games, Iowa smashed Texas, 55-17 in the Freedom; Wisconsin lost, 20-19, to Kentucky in the Independence; Michigan State lost, 10-6, to Army in the Cherry; Purdue lost, 27-24, to Virginia in the Peach; and in the "Granddaddy" at Pasadena, Ohio State lost, 20-17, to Southern Cal.

The five losses (by a total of just 18 points) dropped the Big Ten's bowl record below .500 for the first time (32-34-0).

The Buckeyes finished 9-3-0 and received a final ranking of No. 13. With OSU beating Michigan three of the last four years, the Wolverines' series lead was cut to 44-32-5.

1985

AIR MICHIGAN?

Michigan? Michigan who? That's about what the various pre-season football fortune tellers thought of the 1985 Wolverines. Of eight prominent polls examined, only two even mentioned Michigan. *Inside Sports* rated U-M 20th, while *Sport,* picking a Top 40, had the Maize & Blue No. 36.

A team with six losses the previous year—even a Michigan—hardly ever creates much attention the following season.

Ohio State, on the other hand, made everybody's poll. The Buckeyes were slotted somewhere between No. 3 (UPI and *Inside Sports*) to 21st *(Sport).* But getting the most Big Ten attention in August were Iowa and Illinois.

The Wolverines obviously had nowhere to go but up. And up they went. The climb began with an opening 20-12 win over 13th-ranked Notre Dame, after which the AP "discovered" Michigan and admitted it to the No. 19 position. Then came a 34-3 shelling of 15th-ranked South Carolina and U-M went to No. 12. A 20-0 shutout of 17th-ranked Maryland followed, and it was up to No. 7. The next week it was a climb to No. 3 after beating previously unbeaten Wisconsin, 33-6. U-M then blanked Michigan State, 20-0, and the Wolverines advanced to No. 2.

In only five weeks, Michigan had jumped from being ignored to second place. Who was No. 1? Iowa. Who was Michigan's next opponent? Iowa.

It would be only the 19th time in NCAA history that a No. 1 and a No. 2 came face-to-face on the gridiron. The game was at

386

Rich Spangler (left) kicked the longest field goal in series history (48 yards) and also became the first player to score in four U-M—OSU games. Keith Byars (right) became the first player in 83 years to score six touchdowns in the series, and only the second overall.

Iowa City, and even though the host team hammered out 26 first downs to Michigan's nine and led in total yards by the wide margin of 422-182, the Hawkeyes didn't score a touchdown. They did get four field goals, however, the last one on the game's final play, in dealing U-M a bitter 12-10 defeat.

Michigan bounced back with a 42-15 win over Indiana but was tied, 3-3, by Illinois a week later. Rank: No. 9. Then came 47-0 and 48-7 routs of Purdue and Minnesota, and the Wolverines were ready for Ohio State.

Meanwhile, the Buckeyes had topped Pittsburgh, Colorado, and Washington State, before a wild 31-28 loss to Illinois momentarily cooled them. OSU regrouped and captured five in a row, including a big 22-13 victory over the high-flying, still No. 1-ranked Iowa Hawkeyes.

Ohio State was ranked No. 3 by the AP, behind Penn State and Nebraska. Vague dreams of a national championship began to creep in. . . .

Next on OSU's schedule was a home game with Wisconsin, a team which had won only one of its last six games. Next on OSU's mind, however, was Michigan. In a classic example of "looking ahead," it was the Badgers 12, the Buckeyes 7, in an absolutely crushing defeat.

The Ohio press, along with Buckeye boosters everywhere, once again began howling for Coach Earle Bruce's hide.

Approaching the final weekend, the Big Ten title was still in question. Iowa was 6-1-0, Michigan 5-1-1, Ohio State 5-2-0, and Illinois 4-2-1. Thus, "The Big One" would have Rose Bowl im-

It's the greatest rivalry in the game

'This will be war,' Bo says

plications. A Michigan win and an Iowa loss would send the Big Blue to Pasadena.

Michigan was 8-1-1 overall and ranked No. 6. Also, Michigan was ranked No. 1 in scoring defense, having given up a paltry 58 points all season. The Wolverines were made a 7-point favorite over the 8-2-0 and 12th-rated Buckeyes.

In cool, overcast weather more than 106,000 fans filled the huge bowl at Ann Arbor for the 82nd renewal of this great rivalry.

A turnover led to the game's first score. OSU was second-and-10 at its own 19 when quarterback Jim Karsatos threw long—to U-M's Ivan Hicks, who intercepted and returned the ball

10 yards to the Bucks' 38. Seven plays later, Pat Moons kicked a field goal from the 17, and it was 3-0 with 1:59 remaining in the first period.

The second quarter, however, would produce 17 points.

Ohio State took the ensuing kickoff and reached Michigan's 31 after ten plays. On fourth down, kicker Rich Spangler entered the game and slammed the longest field goal the rivalry had ever witnessed. At the same moment, he also became the first player to score in four U-M–OSU games. Spangler's field goal of 48 yards broke the record previously held by Ohio's Tom Klaban since 1974 by one yard.

Spangler's historic kick had also tied the score at 3-all.

It was soon 10-3. On the first down after the kickoff, U-M quarterback Jim Harbaugh tossed a screen pass to Jamie Morris, who fumbled. OSU's Eric Kumeron recovered at the Wolverines' 19. Six plays advanced the ball to the two, and Keith Byars scored. It was Byars's sixth touchdown against Michigan in three years, an achievement that matched a series record which had stood for 83 years. U-M's A. E. Herrnstein scored six touchdowns against Ohio State, all in the 1902 game.

The Wolverines answered. A 12-yard run by Gerald White and a 40-yard pass from Harbaugh to Eric Kattus keyed a nine-play march to OSU's six, where it was fourth-and-one. Harbaugh sneaked for the yard. Soon, however, the offense faced another crucial situation, third-and-goal at the four.

Would the jinx again grab Michigan inside Ohio's ten-yard line?

Harbaugh took the snap and popped a quick pass over the middle to White. Touchdown! Moons's conversion tied the score.

Halftime: 10-10.

After receiving the second-half kickoff, Michigan moved 55 yards before stalling at the 20, where Moons booted another field goal for a 13-10 score.

But U-M cheers quickly became U-M jeers. It was announced that Iowa had defeated Minnesota, 31-9, thus clinching the Rose Bowl.

The Wolverines made it 20-10 on their next possession with a 63-yard scoring drive in 12 plays. Harbaugh completed two 13-yard strikes to White en route, and U-M found itself second-and-goal at the five. Harbaugh rolled right and spotted Kattus open in the rear of the endzone. Moons's kick was good.

After an exchange of punts, OSU began at its 20, and Karsatos cranked up his pitching arm. He completed a 19-yarder to

Believe it—Iowa rules Big 10

Chris Carter, a 13-yarder to Byars, and a 17-yarder to Ed Taggart, sparking a quick advance to U-M's 31 and a first down. Three plays later, however, the Bucks faced fourth-and-15. Karsatos threw long to Carter. Touchdown! After another Spangler conversion, it was a 20-17 game with 10:10 to play.

Would the drama in these games ever end?

The ensuing kickoff went into the endzone, and Michigan began from its 20. White rammed for three. Then came a real, honest-to-goodness Bo Schembechler coaching shocker. Harbaugh faded back and drilled a long spiral straight down the middle. Flanker John Koselar caught the ball in perfect stride at Ohio's 45 and raced the rest of the way—a 77-yard touchdown bomb, Michigan's longest touchdown pass play in the 88-year-old series. It was also the series second longest scoring pass, topped only by Joe Sparma's 80-yarder to Bob Klein for Ohio State in the 1961 game.

Following Moons's conversion, Michigan led by ten. Time left: 9:19.

The Buckeyes got two more shots, but one was fumbled away and the other resulted in a sack of Karsatos on fourth down. The game ended with Michigan on the enemy's four-yard line.

Final score: Michigan, 27-17, the most points the Wolverines had scored on Ohio State since the 58-6 runaway in 1946.

This was the first game of the series to end under artificial lighting. CBS–TV had installed four light towers because of a later than usual (1:50 P.M.) starting time.

Air Michigan? According to the numbers, maybe so, at least in this rivalry. In Schembechler's first 13 games versus Ohio State, his teams averaged 207 yards rushing and 102 passing. In the last three series games, however, Bo's Wolverines had rushed for only 167 yards per game and passed for 272.

In the '85 game, U-M led in first downs, 19-14, yards passing, 230-179, and in total yards, 424-269. Harbaugh completed 16 of 19 passes, while Karsatos was 17-for-31.

As has become customary, the outcome of the Michigan–Ohio

The Detroit News

Sunday, November 24, 1985

Sports scores/983-8424
Circulation/222-2900
Classified/977-7800

Sports

Jerry Green

Michigan stops OSU 27-17

Bo's winners head for a loser's bowl

ANN ARBOR — They played on in the soft half light of the early evening. Artificial lights blazed with the brilliance of lasers at the four corners of Michigan Stadium. The lights had to be imported for the occasion. Tradition disappears everywhere in college sports. But its departure is slow and painstaking at Michigan where tradition may have been invented.

The tradition never is richer than when Michigan plays Ohio State. And now in this strange glow from lights rigged on flatbed trucks, thousands of spectators left the grandstands. They ringed the football field, planning to pounce.

BUT THE PLAY continued. In one marvelous moment, an entire football season was rapturized and shattered. Jim Karsatos, the Ohio State quarterback, stepped back to pass. He raised his arm with true grit. And then suddenly he vanished. He seemed to be gobbled up by the great rush of the Michigan front line. Jim Scarcelli, from the outside, smacked him first. Then the rest got in on the kill. Mark Messner, Bill Harris, Mike Hammerstein.

The last you could see of Karsatos was an arm in a white sleeve waving, and struggling, and then disappearing between the jaws of the defense. Eleven guys stood around in a pack.

Years ago, Bo Schembechler, in a moment of dizzy happiness, said: "I love defense." His eyes burned as he said it. He loves defense. He loves this 1985 Michigan football because it played defense with the spirit of the devil.

This year, this football season, is the proudest, the finest of Bo Schembechler's life.

THIS WAS the team that was supposed to lose, not win. This was the team that could not squeeze anywhere into the Top Twenty when the brains and computers figured out this year's champions — before any of the games were played.

This was the team that was designated to burial somewhere in the middle of a conference that had become insignificant...

Michigan's Eric Kattus (81) heads downfield as Ohio State's Terry White tries to catch up.

Buckeyes show class in defeat

Long pass plays help Wolverines clinch Fiesta spot

By Jack Berry
News Staff Writer

ANN ARBOR — The bomb, of all things, Michigan beat Ohio State yesterday with the bomb, a 77-yard fourth quarter shocker from Jim Harbaugh to John Kolesar just after Ohio State closed the deficit to 3 points.

"That took the starch out of their sails," Coach Bo Schembechler said.

"It's dangerous to blitz us like that. We're in deep the last three weeks."

NOT AGAINST an Ohio State, though, and this one wrapped up a 27-17 victory that sends the sixth ranked and climbing Big Ten runner up Wolverines to the Fiesta Bowl in Tempe, Ariz. on New Year's Day against Big Eight runner up Nebraska.

It gave Michigan a 9-1-1 record. Its best since 1974, the most points Michigan has scored against Ohio State since 1946's 58-6 walloping and the biggest victory margin since 1976's 14-3 victory.

Ohio State finished 8-3 and will play Brigham Young in the 24 Citrus Bowl in Orlando, Fla.

Michigan was ripe to open up. It shredded Purdue and Minnesota the last two weeks with big plays, but probably even one in the crowd of 106,102, fourth largest in Michigan Stadium history, doubted Schembechler would continue to go deep. For years he's lived with the conservative image, especially in the big games.

SO WHAT did he do. Passed on Michigan's first play of the game.

"We're a wide open team we like to open it up, ring it down there." Schembechler joked afterward.

Please see U-M/13C

College report

☐ Iowa clinches a berth in the Rose Bowl by beating Minnesota 31-9. 14C

☐ Yale beats Harvard in 102nd renewal of Ivy League rivalry. 15C

State clash allowed various bowls to fill in blanks on their dance cards. Michigan had agreed earlier to play in the Fiesta, provided the Rose Bowl did not beckon. It didn't, so Michigan packed for Tempe, Arizona.

A Buckeye victory over Michigan would have meant a Cotton Bowl bid. A loss would have sent them to the Orlando and the Citrus. Orlando it was.

For the second straight year, the Big Ten sent six teams to bowl games, and the league came away with a split. Michigan defeated Nebraska, 27-23, and Ohio State topped Brigham Young, 10-7. In the Independence Bowl, Minnesota dropped Clemson, 20-13. Losing were Iowa to UCLA, 45-28, in the Rose, Illinois to Army, 31-29, in the Peach, and Michigan State to Georgia Tech, 17-14, in the Hall of Fame.

Michigan finished 10-1-1 and No. 2 nationally behind Oklahoma. The Buckeyes, interestingly enough, posted their sixth straight 9-3-0 season and a No. 14 or 17 ranking, depending on the poll.

1986

GAME 83

BIG TEN GRIDMASTER RESTORES ORDER, ORDERS ANOTHER CLASSIC

It's the biggest and bitterest and best football bash of them all, this annual Michigan–Ohio State thing. The 1986 game produced still another in the series abundant history of classic and climactic moments.

Sixty-six seconds left to play. The Buckeyes trailed by two points and faced a fourth-and-two at U-M's 28-yard line. Timeout. Ohio Stadium was erupting with frenzied behavior as Coach Earle Bruce sent in his field goal kicker to win the game. . . .

After a few years of rude upstaging by Iowa and Illinois, the Big Ten was back to normal. The conference's great gridmaster had restored order. Once more the other eight members assumed their roles of providing Michigan and Ohio State with a seven-week preliminary card leading up to the main event.

The Buckeyes and Alabama kicked off the season early—in the Kickoff Classic in New Jersey—with the Tide winning, 16-10. Then came a layoff of almost three weeks. OSU journeyed to Seattle and felt the sting of its worst defeat in 40 years, 40-7, to Washington, and the Buckeyes were 0-2 for the first time in the twentieth century. (OSU had lost its first two games of the season only twice before, in 1891 and 1894.)

The Buckeyes rebounded to edge Colorado, 13-10, and then smothered Utah, 64-6. Entering Big Ten competition, except for a 24-22 winning struggle with Indiana, OSU swept through their other six games by an average score of 30-8.

Michigan was just about everybody's pre-season pick as one of

Jim Harbaugh, U-M quarterback, boldly "guaranteed" a victory over OSU in 1986. His 19 completions for 261 yards had much to do with his prediction becoming a reality.

the nation's top five teams. The Wolverines lived up to their billing and rolled up nine straight wins. They were ranked No. 2 behind Miami.

But as Ohio State had done a year earlier, Michigan got caught "looking ahead." And what a mistake! Minnesota, with a 5-4-0 record, which included losses by scores of 63-0, 52-23, and 33-0, went to Ann Arbor as 25-point underdogs, but on the game's final play the Golden Gophers kicked a 30-yard field goal for a 20-17 upset.

Michigan vs. Ohio State. The Wolverines were 9-1-0 overall (6-1-0 in the conference) and ranked No. 6 by both AP and UPI. The Buckeyes were 9-2-0 overall (7-0-0 in the conference) and ranked No. 7 by both AP and UPI. The winner would go to the Rose Bowl, the loser to the Cotton Bowl.

U-M was made a 2½-point favorite.

Harbaugh guarantees U-M win

A la Broadway Joe,
Michigan quarterback
goes out on a limb

By JIM KORNACKI
STAFF SPORTS REPORTER

Buckeyes' boss
pulls no punches
with the press

By JOHN BARTON
STAFF SPORTS REPORTER

The buildup to this bout got off to an early and startling start. On Monday Michigan quarterback Jim Harbaugh boldly predicted a victory. Flat out.

"I guarantee we will beat Ohio State and be in Pasadena New Year's Day," Harbaugh boasted to the press. "People might not give us a snowball's chance in hell to beat them in Columbus. But we're going to. We don't care where we play the game. I hate to say it, but we could play on the parking lot. We could play at 12 noon or midnight. We're going to be jacked up, and we're going to win."

His unbelievable remarks dominated sports news across the nation.

THE RIVALRY: MICHIGAN VS. OHIO STATE

For Roses
Momentum figures to play role in deciding conference crown

Bright sunshine and temperatures in the mid-fifties greeted 90,674 fans to Ohio Stadium for the 83rd game of the series. The Buckeyes won the toss and elected to receive.

This emotional roller coaster affair was poised for takeoff.

Jamie Holland took the kick at his eight and bolted 47 yards to the Michigan 45. Quarterback Jim Karsatos completed three passes (two to Chris Carter and one to Vince Workman) for a total of 28 yards, and Workman rammed out 12 ground yards in four carries, advancing OSU to a first-and-goal at the five. Two plays later from the four, Karsatos lobbed a quick pass to Carter in the the corner of the endzone. Touchdown. Matt Frantz converted and, four minutes after kickoff, it was a quick 7-0 Buckeye lead.

Michigan came right back, staging a nine-play march and a first down at Ohio's 14. Soon, however, the Wolverines faced fourth down at the 15 and had to settle for a Mike Gillette field goal.

OSU scored again on its next possession. Starting from the 20-yard line, Workman gained two. Karsatos passed to flanker Everett Ross who spun, twisted, and broke tackles for a gain of 32 yards to U-M's 46. Workman scored from there. With three minutes still left in the first period, Ohio State was going mad with a 14-3 lead.

Was this Michigan vs. Ohio State or a track meet? Since the game of football had been divided into four quarters in 1910, Michigan and Ohio State had never combined for 17 points in the first period. Fourteen, yes, but never 17.

The raging Buckeyes got the ball right back when Harbaugh threw an interception to David Brown, who returned 17 yards to his own 42. On first down, Workman plowed through the middle for 29 yards to Michigan's 29.

Harbaugh's prediction?

Moments later, Karsatos passed complete to Carter at the one-yard line, but holding had been spotted against the offense. The play that very likely would have put the game away had been nullified. Michigan held, and Frantz missed on a 43-yard field goal attempt.

Ohio State had also missed on a grand opportunity.

Following an exchange of punts, Michigan marched 63 yards to Ohio's 17, and Gillette added another field goal to make the score 14-6.

On their next possession, the Wolverines quickly moved 78 yards for a first down at OSU's eight, and Harbaugh promptly threw his second interception of the game. This one was to Mike

Kee at the goal line.

Harbaugh's prediction?

Halftime: 14-6, Buckeyes.

Michigan received the second-half kickoff. Harbaugh completed passes of 21 yards to Jeff Brown, 11 yards to Greg McMurtry, four yards to Brown, and 15 yards to Bob Perryman, highlighting a 14-play, 83-yard touchdown drive. The final four yards came on a run by Jamie Morris. Gillette's conversion brought his team to within one point, 14-13.

Ohio State took the kickoff and quickly went 61 yards, reaching U-M's 14 and a first down. But the Wolverines held, and this time Frantz got the field goal. With 5:20 left in the third period, the Buckeyes had a 17-13 cushion.

The relentless Wolverines went on the attack again. On first down from his 22, Morris broke through the line, cut down the sideline, and raced for the goal with roverback Sonny Gordon. Gordon won, but not until Morris had gained 52 yards to OSU's 24. One play later, Harbaugh dumped a pass off to Perryman for a gain of 15 to the eight. Morris got the ball on the next play and fought his way into the endzone. Michigan had its first lead of the afternoon. Harbaugh's pass for two failed.

Michigan 19, Ohio State 17.

Time: 3:48 left in the third quarter.

The red-hot Maize & Blue quickly forced another punt. Starting at the 15, Harbaugh connected with Ken Higgins for 23 yards and with Perryman for 23 more; in only seven plays they had a first down at the OSU seven. Thomas Wilcher scored from there, and Gillette converted.

From a 14-3 lead in the second quarter (and threatening to make it more), the Buckeyes were behind by a shocking 17-26 count. Their hated rivals had gone on a 23-3 run.

More Buckeye grief. On first down after the ensuing kickoff, Karsatos threw an interception to Andree McIntyre. U-M had the ball at OSU's 36.

Ohio fans couldn't believe this game's disastrous turnaround.

However, four plays later from the 30, defensive tackle Darryl Lee blocked a field goal attempt by Gillette, pumping new life into the Buckeyes at their own 44-yard line.

Ohio State scored in only four plays, the last 17 yards on a pass from Karsatos to Carter. Frantz converted.

Now it was Michigan 26, Buckeyes 24, with 9:06 remaining to play.

On Michigan's first play from scrimmage from its 18, the

crowd noise became so thunderous and lasted so long that the officials penalized the Buckeyes by taking away one of their time-outs. Order was finally restored, and the teams settled down with an exchange of punts.

Then, with the clock down to 3:17 and Michigan with the ball, Wilcher was belted hard by William White. OSU's Gordon pounced upon his fumble at Ohio State's 38.

Once again an emotional high, or low, depending on the colors, gripped the stadium's already-drained customers.

Eight gut-wrenching plays later, the Buckeyes had advanced to Michigan's 28-yard line. Fourth down. Two yards for a first down.

Timeout. Sixty-six seconds left.

Kicker Matt Frantz, a junior from Cincinnati, trotted onto the field. The snap was good. The placement was good. Frantz slammed his foot into the football.

"The ball was kicked, it rose toward the uprights, and they all just stood helpless and watched," wrote Mitch Albon of the *Detroit Free Press*. "Everybody in red and everybody in blue and everybody in between. . . . The ball carried, the crowd roared. . . . The Michigan players watched that ball rise, rise, saw the Buckeyes' players raise their arms up as if the field goal were good, heard a thunder begin in Ohio Stadium—then felt it die like a blink. . . . No good. Wide left."

Frantz had barely missed, but miss he did. His team would not be going to the Rose Bowl.

Final score: U-M 26, OSU 24.

As Bo Schembechler took a short ride on the shoulders of his victorious players, he had just become the winningest coach in Michigan's football history. It was No. 166 at U-M, one better than the record of Fielding H. Yost.

Harbaugh, fortunate that his "guaranteed" victory prediction had held up, completed 19 passes (29 attempts) for 261 yards. Teammate Morris rushed for 216 yards (7.4 average) on 29 carries. OSU's Workman ran for 128 yards in 21 attempts (6.1), while Karsatos was 15-for-27 for 188 passing yards.

Overall, U-M led in first downs, 27-19, yards rushing, 268-170, and total yards, 529-358. The total fell only two yards short of the series record set by the Wolverines in the 1943 game.

The Big Ten hit another bowl bonanza following the '86 season, sending five teams (17 in the last three years) to post-season games. Iowa won a thrilling 39-38 shootout with San Diego State

Give these men a Rose

Wolverines grow up quickly in game of games

Major bowl matchups

A Michigan classic

Spartans win, miss bowl bid

By JACK SAYLOR
Free Press Sports Writer

U-M wins, 26-24, on missed kick

By TOMMY GEORGE
Free Press Sports Writer

Tyson crushes Berbick with 2d-round KO

By GEORGE PUSCAS
Free Press Sports Writer

LAS VEGAS, Nev. —

in the Holiday Bowl, and the Buckeyes walloped Texas A&M, 28-12, at Dallas. But Michigan lost to Arizona State, 22-15, at Pasadena; Minnesota was beaten, 21-14, by Tennessee in the Liberty; and Indiana dropped a 27-13 decision to Florida State in the All-America.

But would the Big Ten ever win in the Rose Bowl? The West Coast teams had won six straight, 12 of 13, and 17 of 19.

Michigan, for the first time in 44 years, did not end its regular season against the Buckeyes. U-M had a December 6 fun date scheduled in Honolulu; the trip was a 27-10 success over the University of Hawaii Rainbow Warriors.

With Ohio State playing in the Kickoff Classic, both the Buckeyes and Wolverines had 13-game schedules (including bowl dates) the same season. U-M had played that many games only once before, in 1905, when it outscored the opposition by a staggering 495-2—but still lost one—2-0 to the University of Chicago in the unlucky 13th game. OSU had never played 13 games in one season.

In 1986 Michigan posted 11-2-0 figures and finished with a No. 8 ranking. Ohio State was 10-3-0 and ended up in the No. 7 spot.

Head-to-head, U-M's series lead over OSU went to 46-32-5.

WOODY HAYES

Feb. 14, 1913 — March 12, 1987

Hayes erased the "Graveyard of Coaches" reputation Ohio State had built with his iron-fisted rule built on conservative football.

PROFILE

By George Strode
Dispatch Sports Editor

Woody Hayes was a human chameleon.

He could charm. He could lose control. He could show compassion just as well as his infamous temper.

"He's like a volcano waiting to explode," said Esco Sarkkinen, who served as an assistant for all but one of Hayes' 28 years as Ohio State University's football coach.

Hayes — tireless worker, unmatched recruiter, master of the most minute detail — became a legend in his own time for those very reasons.

EVEN IN the face of a June 1974 heart attack and a 1984 stroke, Hayes kept his long, tiring daily schedules against the wishes of his physicians.

Only Alabama's Paul "Bear" Bryant, Amos Alonzo Stagg and Glenn "Pop" Warner ranked ahead of him in career victories when Hayes was fired for slugging Clemson nose guard Charlie Bauman in the waning moments of the 1978 Gator Bowl. Since then, Eddie Robinson of Grambling, with 336 victories, has passed all of them.

Hayes' 33 years of college coaching produced 238 victories, 72 defeats and 10 ties.

"I JUST can't control my temper," Hayes sometimes would admit. And it was a fit of rage over Bauman's defeat-producing interception that triggered it a final time.

Hayes frequently had run-ins with writers, broadcasters and photographers, even to the point of physical contact. One of the most famous incidents came before the 1972 Rose Bowl.

The Ohio State coach was charged by the *Los Angeles Times* with battery, contending he shoved staff photographer Art Rogers' camera back into his face and caused injury to the newsman before the game. The case in a Pasadena, Calif., court was later dropped.

The son of an Ohio high school principal, Hayes erased the "Graveyard of Coaches" reputation Ohio State had built with his iron-fisted rule built on conservative football.

FROM 1951 through 1978, Hayes molded two national championships, 13 Big Ten Conference titles or co-titles, 58 All-Americas and 205 Buckeyes victories.

In the twilight of his career, Hayes seemed to slip. His assistant coaches saw it. His players saw it. Because of the immeasurable respect they had for the man, they said nothing publicly.

"He's senile now. He's an egomaniac," said a longtime Hayes lieutenant during Hayes' final campaign in 1978.

Hayes ran his practices in firm, often uncontrollable fashion. When a player erred in workouts, Hayes sometimes would jerk his wristwatch off and stomp it into the turf. Other times, it was Hayes' hat or his eyeglasses. He would rip his hat into shreds. He would slam his glasses to the ground.

Frequently, Hayes beat on his players' helmets or shoulder pads, uttering a stream of invectives.

YET, VERY few of them ever spoke against him. They all admired him, especially once they left the Big Ten school. Fred Pagac, a tight end for Hayes and now an OSU assistant coach, wept openly in the lobby of the team's Jacksonville, Fla., hotel upon learning of Hayes' firing. Pagac was a graduate coaching assistant at the time.

Hayes relished his relationship with his players. He guarded it jealously against the media. He forbade newsmen from entering the Buckeyes' locker room.

"A newspaperman never won a game for us," a scowling Hayes often said.

As much a curmudgeon as Hayes was, he could become a charmer when he visited a prospective recruit's home.

"He's nothing like I thought he was," one mother of an Ohio State prospect once said of Hayes. "I was really impressed with his honesty."

ONE FACET of Hayes' life that received little attention — perhaps by his design — was his frequent hospital visits to see sick friends, or even people he had never met. He halted his hectic schedule, even going to hospitals at odd hours to lift spirits.

Hayes had very few close friends because of his football devotion.

"Football is my whole life anymore," he would say. "If there was anything else I thought I would like to do, I would get out. But there isn't."

Because of his near total attention to his sport, Hayes' wife, Anne, saw little of him in season.

"I count my blessings," she once said. "While he's absorbed in 80 boys and their problems, I don't have to worry about one thin blonde in an apartment somewhere. I'm his full-time housekeeper and part-time mistress."

Hayes, an offensive lineman in his college days at Denison University, had no desire to jump into professional coaching, if for no other reason than money meant very little to the man. He was among the lowest-paid coaches in the Big Ten and lived in a modest house in suburban Upper Arlington the entire time he coached the Buckeyes.

Hayes once was accused of placing $100 in the church till at the father of Ohio State quarterback Rod Gerald, a minister in Dallas.

"THAT'S RIDICULOUS," one of Hayes' assistants said. "Woody usually has to scrape up enough money from all of us just to get out of town."

Once Hayes departed from coaching, he spent his time helping with charity events, visiting hospitals and speaking throughout the nation.

Ironically, his office was in Ohio State's Military Science Building, just a few steps away from mammoth Ohio Stadium, the scene of some of his greatest triumphs.

Hayes during playing days at Denison.

After Paul Bryant of Alabama passed away four years earlier, of all the quotes from all over the country, it was Woody Hayes who best understood it. He said simply, "Bear coached himself to death."

1987

THE BRUCE BOWL

While it is only a football game, the annual matchup between Michigan and Ohio State has attained the status of an institution in its own right.

Regardless of what might be decided by the outcome, the meeting itself is the dominant event of the week in both states. In both anticipation and remembrance, it stands out like a landmark—a transition point—and as a focus of attention around which other events resolve. Since the end of World War II until 1987, on only three occasions had "The Big One" been conclusively upstaged.

In 1950 Mother Nature grabbed the spotlight. "The Snow Bowl" was played in Columbus before only 50,503 shivering fans and 31,197 unused seats. Games took a low priority that day as the eastern half of the nation struggled to survive the onslaughts of snow, ice, sub-zero temperatures, and the resulting power outages, immobile cars and trains, and impassable streets and highways.

In 1963 the nation was in shock over the assassination of President John F. Kennedy. His death on the day before the game was, appropriately, the center of every American's attention and concern. The Michigan–Ohio State game was postponed one week, but even then only 34,500 used their tickets, while 65,500 decided against it.

In 1966 another football game somehow managed to achieve a big advantage over "The Big One." It was a meeting reminiscent

401

Firing of OSU's Bruce rocks Columbus

Ohio State fires Bruce with 5-4-1 record

Buckeyes' AD Bay steps down in protest

BUCKEYE AFTERSHOCKS

Ohio governor: Comments were misconstrued by press

New A.D.: Search for coach shouldn't hamper recruiting

'Keep Earle, fire Jennings'

Large crowd rallies to support fired Ohio State coach

SPORTS

THE ANN ARBOR NEWS • SATURDAY, NOVEMBER 21, 1987

OSU's not-so-grand finale

Bowl-less Spielman, Buckeyes invade Michigan Stadium

Bruce fires last shot, beats Michigan

of the "Game of the Century" between Army and Notre Dame in 1946 at Yankee Stadium. This time it was Michigan State and Notre Dame at East Lansing in a "Game of the Century," 1966 edition. Both games, it will be remembered, promised more than the participants could deliver. Tie games resulted, and partisans on both sides wound up with much remorse and nothing to celebrate.

On Monday of "Game Week" in 1987, however, Edward Jennings, president of Ohio State University, announced that Coach Earle Bruce had been fired, effective immediately after the Michigan game. It was a bona fide bombshell, front page news. It dominated the sports sections and jammed the electronic media.

In retrospect, perhaps Bruce's dismissal should not have been such a surprise. Ohio State was suffering through a rough season with a 5-4-1 record. On the previous Saturday, the Buckeyes had lost their third straight game, 29-27, to Iowa.

But this was an Ohio State team acclaimed almost unanimously by pre-season "experts" as belonging among the top five in the country. *The Sporting News* placed the Bucks No. 2 in August but also observed, "Earle Bruce finally silences the critics and his Buckeyes may win one (a national championship) for Woody. . . . Ohio State fields a potentially overpowering team."

The '87 Buckeyes, however, never reached their potential. There were wins over West Virginia, 24-3, and Oregon, 24-14. Then a trip to Baton Rouge resulted in a 10-10 tie with LSU in OSU's first regular scheduled game against a Southeastern Conference team in 52 years. After edging Illinois, 10-6, Ohio State lost to Indiana, 31-10, for the first time since 1951, the first year of the Woody Hayes era. After beating Purdue and Minnesota, the Buckeyes lost, 13-7, to Michigan State, 26-24, to Wisconsin, and then to Iowa.

The voices that had been loudly calling for Bruce's ouster got louder. Whether in reaction to the clamor or not, President Jennings made his announcement. Adding to the furor was the resignation of Rick Bay as Ohio State's athletic director, in anger over Bruce's firing.

Within 48 hours, however, Bruce emerged the hero and Jennings the villain. A Columbus television station gave viewers the means to express an opinion on the matter. Of the more than 12,000 "votes" called in, over 90 percent favored Bruce.

The controversy raged all week and—almost forgotten—was the news that on Saturday Ohio State would be in Ann Arbor to play a football game against Michigan.

Ohio State 23, Michigan 20

'Poetic justice'
Bay enjoys last OSU win, hedges toward U-M

The Ann Arbor News

'No sweeter victory in the world'
Bruce departs OSU by beating U-M, 23-20

The Detroit News
Sunday, Nov. 22, 1987
Sports
Section C
Joe Falls
OSU president not welcome on Bruce's day
Fond farewell for Bruce
Buckeyes trip Wolverines 23-20
ANN ARBOR — Earle Bruce went out a stylish winner Saturday as Ohio State defeated Michigan 23-20 and the Wolverines dropped the ball more than OSU President Edward Jennings.
Bruce was as defiant as his players who came out for the opening kickoff wearing headbands emblazoned EARLE.
"I guess anyone has the right to fire me but what I don't like is what they're saying about me and my integrity," Bruce said.
ALL JENNINGS did this week, without divulging a reason, was fire a man who had nine consecutive winning seasons, compiled an 81-26-1 record, the best in the Big Ten during that period, and did something Woody Hayes never did: Get the edge on Michigan Coach Bo Schembechler.
Bruce went out with a 5-4 record against Michigan. Hayes was 4-5-1.
Michigan, which afterward officially accepted an invitation to the Hall of Fame Bowl in Tampa on Jan. 2, certainly helped make it a memorable exodus for Bruce.
The Ohio State coach strode the sidelines in frigid weather wearing a dark blue suit, white shirt, scarlet-and-gray striped tie and a snappy fedora with a red feather. It's the game costume he introduced at the Cotton Bowl last winter in an effort to improve his image after being criticized for a drooping belly.
Please see U-M/6C
Elsewhere . . .
Spartans finish off season, Badgers 30-9

For the first time since 1967, neither of the two teams could be found in the Top Twenty of the AP or UPI polls. Michigan's 7-3-0 record included losses to Notre Dame, Michigan State, and Indiana—U-M's first loss to the Hoosiers in 28 years.

The only bowl implication of the game was the unofficial report that—win or lose—Michigan would go to the Hall of Fame Bowl in Tampa to play the loser of the Alabama–Auburn game. President Jennings had announced that Ohio State would not go bowling under any circumstances.

Seven combined U-M–OSU losses? Neither team ranked? Michigan playing the "loser" in one of the smaller bowls? Ohio State no bowl at all?

"The Big One" in 1987 was not so big. Still, nobody forgot to show up for the game. The customary crowd of more than 106,000 was on hand, plus ABC's television crew and hordes of reporters.

The teams showed up also, with the Buckeyes making a dramatic statement as they tore from the tunnel. The players quickly gathered in the south endzone before heading to their sideline. They ripped off their silver helmets and put on headbands—broad white headbands inscribed in scarlet with the name *EARLE*. It was a surprise gesture even to the coaching staff.

Coach Bruce later said, "I don't believe in headbands. I never have liked them, but when I saw them today, well, in your last game, I guess you've got to let your hair down a little."

After a fussy five and a half days, it was finally time to play ball. The game got under way, and Michigan jumped out to a 13-0 lead by scoring on each of its first three possessions. Jamie Morris's one-yard run for a touchdown, and field goals of 34 and 19 yards by Mike Gillette, capped drives of 73 yards in seven plays, 55 years in 10 plays, and 53 yards in 13 plays. With 5:49 remaining in the first half, U-M led, 9-2, in first downs and, 181-13, in total offensive yards.

It had been that lopsided.

But the Buckeyes, somehow, picked themselves up to dispel any thoughts that the events of the week had left them flat and disspirited. They pieced together a march of 61 yards that took ten plays, the touchdown a four-yard pass from Tom Tupa to Everette Ross. Matt Frantz converted to cut Michigan's lead to 13-7 with 1:36 left in the half.

The Wolverines stormed right back to OSU's 18, but the clock forced Gillette to try a field goal. No good.

At intermission, Michigan had more than tripled the Bucks' offensive output, 281-91, but had only a seven-point lead.

The lead was not to last. On Ohio State's first play in the second half, Tupa hit Carlos Snow with a short swing pass, and Snow took it the distance—70 yards. It was the third longest touchdown pass in the series. Frantz added the conversion, and the Buckeyes were ahead, 14-13.

OSU kept up the pressure. Later in the third period, David Brown intercepted a John Kolesar pass and returned it 32 yards to Michigan's 19. George Cooper carried to the 15, and a Tupa pass to Vince Coleman moved it to the one. Tupa then sneaked for the score to boost the Buckeye lead to 20-13. Frantz missed the conversion attempt, his first miss in 52 tries. A little more than seven minutes remained in the quarter.

On the next two series of downs, U-M lost a fumble at OSU's 36 and OSU lost a fumble at U-M's 46. The Wolverines cashed in on their recovery by scoring in 10 plays. Leroy Hoard covered the last ten yards, and Gillette made his point-after to tie the score at 20-20. It had been an eventful third quarter, and 1:14 remained for even more excitement.

The Michigan kicker, Rick Sutkiewicz, flubbed the kickoff in what had all the appearance of a planned "on-side" kick. Sean LaFountain recovered the ball for Michigan. Fans thought that Bo Schembechler had pulled off an ingenious piece of trickery, but Schembechler later scotched the notion that he would employ such a drastic strategy at this stage of the game.

Planned or not, the development came to naught. Michigan ran three plays and had to punt. Ohio punted it back, and Michigan punted again.

The clock had ticked down to 12:03, and the Buckeyes began to hammer down the field. Fourteen plays, five first downs, 77 yards, and almost seven minutes later, they had reached Michigan's nine, facing a fourth-and-two situation. Time remaining, 5:18.

Matt Frantz entered the game. Earlier in the game, he had missed a conversion to account for the now tied score. More important, a year earlier, he had missed a late field goal that could have beaten Michigan.

Frantz had told Steve Kornacki of the *Ann Arbor News,* "It's been 11 months, 28 days, 11 minutes and five seconds. For 11 months I've been known as Matt, the guy who lost the Michigan game. Of course I'd like another chance at them. I know it sounds selfish, but I'd like it to come down to that last kick again."

Frantz's wish for a second chance had been granted, and he delivered. The kick was perfect, and three big points were added to OSU's total. Frantz was mobbed by happy teammates, and the Buckeyes had a 23-20 lead. Michigan, on the other hand, would have five minutes to overcome the Ohio lead.

Getting the ball, however, is not the same as keeping it. Hoard fumbled 58 seconds later, and Eric Kumerow recovered for OSU at the Wolverines' 46. The Bucks drove all the way to U-M's one with less than 30 seconds left. Rejecting the risks of another field goal attempt (including what might happen on an ensuing kickoff), Coach Bruce was content to settle for low-risk line plunges.

Michigan held. Quarterback Demetrius Brown launched two long passes that failed, and Ohio State had a victory.

A triumphant, smiling, and teary-eyed Earle Bruce was carried off the field in one of the most emotional moments in Ohio State football history.

"I'm not Woody Hayes," he later told newsmen in the locker room. "I could not be Woody when I came here nine years ago, and

In Earle Bruce's nine years as Ohio State head coach, the Buckeyes had the best record in the Big Ten and the seventh best in the nation. At the time of his firing, he was one of only three OSU coaches (out of 18) with a winning record against Michigan.

I won't be Woody when I leave. I'm Earle Bruce. You have to take me as I am, or let me go. The president of Ohio State let me go."

Bruce's record at OSU was 81-26-1, better than that of any other Big Ten team during the same period. His record against Michigan was 5-4-0—the only "active" coach in the conference to hold an edge over Schembechler. On the national scene, just six teams (Nebraska, Brigham Young, Oklahoma, Penn State, Georgia, and Miami) topped Bruce's overall .755 winning ratio.

The '87 U-M–OSU game had been another thriller in a long list of thrillers in this rivalry. It had also been a strange game.

Consider:

First half: U-M led in first downs, 16-6, and total yards, 283-91.

Second half: OSU led in first downs, 11-5, and total yards, 253-91.

Michigan was well ahead in rushing totals, 271-106, while Ohio State had a 238-103 difference in passing. U-M's Morris was the leading rusher with 130 yards in 23 carries, a fine 5.7 average.

Schembechler's record against the Buckeyes became even after the 1987 game, 9-9-1.

Michigan State represented the Big Ten in the Rose Bowl. The Spartans had opened their season with a 27-13 victory over Southern Cal at East Lansing and, four months later, defeated Southern Cal again, 20-17, at Pasadena. It was the Big Ten's best bowl news in the eighties. Elsewhere in Big Ten bowl action, Iowa squeezed by Wyoming, 20-19, in the Holiday, and Michigan beat Alabama, 28-24, in the Hall of Fame, but Indiana lost to Tennessee, 27-22, in the Peach.

1988

OHIO'S KOLESAR
KILLS OHIO STATE

Exit Earle Bruce and enter John Cooper as head football coach at The Ohio State University.

Cooper earned four football letters at Iowa State and held assistant positions at Oregon State, UCLA and Kentucky before becoming head coach at Tulsa in 1977 and Arizona State in 1985. He became the Buckeyes' 21st coach, but only the third in the last 38 years, and would be bringing an 82-40-2 record to Columbus.

At Ann Arbor, meanwhile, Bo Schembechler was entering his 20th season as leader of the Wolverines.

The consensus of five pre-season polls had Michigan ranked 15th, but a sixth, *The Sporting News,* had this to say: "The talent and intangibles are in place for the Wolverines to capture the national crown....The squad will dominate the trenches....The schedule is favorable....The game with Iowa will determine the Big Ten champion and possibly the national champion."

It's difficult to imagine how the schedule could be "favorable" considering UM's first two games were against Notre Dame and Miami of Florida.

The Buckeyes could hardly be found.

It's interesting to note that one publication, *Don Heinrich's College Football '88*, published a Top 20, followed by a group of "teams to watch." Both UM and OSU made the latter list.

Michigan and Ohio State cataloged as "teams to watch?" Fans across the nation, and especially in Big Ten country, were unaccustomed to such late-summer folly.

410

But in the only two polls which really count — *AP* and *UPI* — Michigan was rated 11th and 10th, respectively. OSU was ranked 26th by *AP*.

Cooper's Buckeyes opened with a 26-9 win over Syracuse at Columbus, but were then hammered 42-10 by Pittsburgh. It had been 42 years (1946) since an OSU team surrendered more points on the gridiron in a single afternoon. The Bucks bounced back with a wild 36-33 win over LSU, but lost to Illinois, Indiana and Purdue. They then topped Minnesota, lost to Michigan State, defeated Wisconsin and tied Iowa.

Michigan was stung by two heartbreaking defeats to start the season — 19-17 to Notre Dame at South Bend and 31-30 to Miami at Ann Arbor. An 0-2 start hadn't happened to UM in 29 years, dating back to 1959 when Missouri and Michigan State pulled it off.

But Schembechler, his staff, and his wounded Wolverines gathered the season's shattered pieces and began a slow, week-to-week climb. First was a win over Wake Forest, then Wisconsin, then State. Following a 17-all draw with Iowa came successes against Indiana, Northwestern, Minnesota and Illinois.

It was now time for a trip down to Columbus.

Michigan was 7-2-1 by an average score 31-12 and had labored up to a No. 12 national ranking. Win or lose and UM still had locks on the Rose Bowl bid.

Ohio State was 4-5-1 by a negative average count of 20-25. Never before, in the 84-game series, had Michigan faced a Buckeye team that was so generous in yielding points.

The visiting Wolverines were posted in the daily newspapers as a whoppin' 11-point favorite.

What in goodness sakes would Woody Hayes think of all this November nonsense. The Buckeyes an 11-point *underdog* at Ohio Stadium? And to *"that team up north?"*

No doubt about it, Ol' Woody was lookin' down with a frown.

But what a game! What a thriller this would turn out to be. Just over 91,000 would look on and a customary national television audience would tune in on another electrifying conflict between these old foes.

The first half looked like a stroll through the park as UM led 20-0 and had not allowed its lame opposition past midfield.

In the first period, Michael Gillette's 22-yard field goal and a

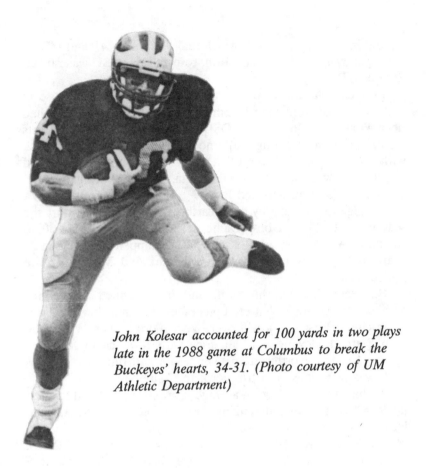

John Kolesar accounted for 100 yards in two plays late in the 1988 game at Columbus to break the Buckeyes' hearts, 34-31. (Photo courtesy of UM Athletic Department)

57-yard pass play from Demetrius Brown to Greg McMurtry made it 10-0. Leroy Hoard scored from 13 yards out in the second quarter, but an illegal procedure nullified the play. No problem. Hoard was given the ball again from the 18 and, breaking three tackles, romped into the endzone. Gillette converted and it was a 17-point advantage.

Gillette later boomed a 57-yard field goal — the longest in series history — topping Rich Spangler's (OSU) 48-yarder in the 1985 game.

The 20-point halftime difference was the largest since 1946 when Michigan led 27-0 on this same field.

SPORTS

Detroit Free Press

Kolesar leaps, grabs a miracle

*In the end,
Kolesar was
Wolverines'
saving grace*

*Wolverines
wrap up
Big Ten
title, 34-31*

BY STEVE KORNACKI
Free Press Sports Writer

COLUMBUS, Ohio — The ball was coming down from the sky, there were two men around him, the angry crowd roaring fire-fresh, he was on the goal line, he bent his legs and he leapt in the air and all he could think of was ... practice.

"A drill," wide receiver John Kolesar would say later, after he made a spectacular jump-ball catch in the end zone to give the Wolverines the final edge, 34-31, in the most exciting Michigan-Ohio State game to never really matter. "We do this drill in practice all the time, throwing the ball up between two men and trying to catch it. I was just thinking of that, really."

And he got it. Oh, how he got it! With just 97 seconds left. Pulled down a miracle in a game that only a miracle would win. His teammates mobbed him. The Wolverines — who had gone from way ahead to seriously behind — were back in the lead. And the Buckeyes' crowd was suddenly silent. Touchdown? Touchdown.

"The biggest," Kolesar, a senior, would claim, "of my career."

Which is saying something, coming from this guy. But then, you had to see this game. Wow. How can you describe it? How had things gotten so crazy that Kolesar had to save the day — twice? This had been a blowout in the first half, Michigan was going through Ohio State the way a ball goes through a fence. U-M led at halftime, 20-0, and it should have been more.

And then, somewhere surely, the gods of ... State swallowed a rusty midget exit timer and mumbled ...

Mitch
Albom

COLUMBUS, Ohio — It was a game of redemption. And in the end, the greatest comeback belonged to John Kolesar, whose 41-yard touchdown reception from Demetrius Brown gave Michigan a 34-31 win over Ohio State.

The Wolverines (8-2-1, 7-0-1) won the Big Ten title outright. The Buckeyes (4-6-1, 2-5-1) lost five games in the conference for the first time.

But the Buckeyes didn't go down easily Saturday before 90,176 fans at Ohio Stadium.

They came back from a 20-0 halftime deficit to take the lead in the fourth quarter. And it looked as if the 11-point underdogs were going to pull it out. Fullback Bill Matlock's 16-yard touchdown run with 2:02 left made it 31-27 for Ohio State.

Kolesar had another ending in mind, though. It was a long-shot for sure, the kind kids dream about when they're too young to know better. But when you have a 4.3 speed over 40 yards and a burning desire, the odds seldom enter your mind.

"I stood back waiting for the kick, and I just told myself to do something," Kolesar said.

Early in the second half, Kolesar botched a kickoff return, deflecting it out-of-bounds at the 13. In the fourth quarter, it got worse. He dropped what could have been a 44-yard touchdown pass.

Assistant coach Cam Cameron no-

Michigan's Leroy Hoard breaks away for an 18-yard touchdown run in the second quarter against Ohio State. Hoard scored again in the fourth. See WOLVERINES, Page 13D

**MSU's win over Wisconsin
feels like Florida sunshine**

BOWLS FILLED
■ ROSE: Jan 2, ...
Michigan (8-2-1) vs. No 2 USC
■ FIESTA: Jan 2, 5 p.m., No. 1 ...

**USC earns Rose Bowl bid,
but Irish are No. 1 priority**

What happened in the Buckeye locker room at intermission? Well, something did — for sure — as they scored on their first four possessions of the second half.

Carlos Snow's run from the four finished a seven-play, 70-yard drive and Pat O'Morrow's PAT made it 20-7.

It was soon 20-14 after the Bucks moved 66 yards in eight plays, capped by Bill Matlock's nine-yard sprint and O'Morrow's conversion.

Getting the ball right back, the Buckeyes set the old concrete horseshoe ablaze with an astounding 90-yard drive in only eight snaps. The highlights were a pass for 27 yards from Greg Frey to

413

Bobby Olive, a 17-yard run by Snow, a blast of 21 yards by freshman fullback Scotty Graham to UM's 17, and Olive's diving catch in the endzone of a Frey pass. O'Morrow converted.

Score: Ohio State 21, Michigan 20. Time: 11:18.

Soon after the ensuing kickoff, OSU nose guard Pat Thomas belted the ball loose from Tony Boles and Ohio linebacker Mike Sullivan recovered at the UM 22.

Buckeye Bedlam!

But the Wolverines saved themselves. OSU worked its way to a first-and-goal at the three. Three plays later, however, it was fourth-and-goal at the four. O'Morrow kicked a field goal.

Score: Ohio State 24, Michigan 20. Time: 8:30.

Michigan bounced right back. Starting from the 24, Brown and McMurtry connected on a 21-yard pass play up to the 45. Hoard went to midfield, then to OSU's 47, where it was third-and-two. Hoard hammered for three. Boles got five to the 39. After no gain, Brown found Boles for 18 yards and another first down at the 21. Hoard carried to the 14, Boles to the eight, and Hoard scored from there. Gillette converted.

Score: Michigan 27, Ohio State 24. Time: 4:27.

It was now the Bucks turn to bounce back — and they did — covering 92 yards in just six plays. The biggies came via a personal foul defensive penalty, Frey passes to Jeff Ellis for 17 yards and to Snow for 22, and Bill Matlock's TD run from the 16. O'Morrow was again on target.

Score: Ohio State 31, Michigan 27. Time: 2:02.

More Buckeye Bedlam!

Ohio State kicked off to John Kolesar, who was from Westlake, Ohio, and who earlier in the game had dropped what would have been a 44-yard touchdown pass. He also dropped a TD pass in last year's 23-20 loss to the Buckeyes.

Kolesar fielded the kick three yards deep, broke free of the first wave, and sped all the way to the Bucks' 41 before being taken down by kicker O'Morrow. Brown threw incomplete. On the next play, though, Brown was forced from the pocket and saw an open Chris Callaway on a shorter route. But Brown instead went deep for Kolesar. And Kolesar made an unbelievable leaping catch, outfighting defensive backs Zack Dumas and David Brown at the goal and tumbling into the endzone. Three plays, 100 yards — and all 100 covered by John Kolesar.

Touchdown, Michigan!

Ohio State refused to believe it....

Gillette, by the way, made the conversion.

The Buckeyes gave it one last shot, reaching UM's 39-yard line with the clock now down to 45 seconds. But on second-and-two, Michigan's Mark Messner and Alex Marshall belted Frey upon his release, the ball fluttered into the air, and Marc Spencer made a diving interception.

Columbus was crushed.

Score: Michigan 34, Ohio State 31. Time: 00:00.

William Kolesar, John's father, was at Ohio Stadium that day in 1988 and he had been involved in "The Big One" three times as a UM letterman during the fifties. In fact, William's last game had occurred 33 years to the day earlier (November 19, 1955) against the Buckeyes at Ann Arbor.

In the '88 thriller, each team banged out 24 first downs. OSU led in rushing yards by a yard (277-276), while UM had more passing yards (223-193), total yards (499-470) and penalty yards (50-42).

The combined total of 969 offensive yards set a series record, topping the 887 figure two years earlier.

Three players rushed for over 100 yards — OSU's Carlos Snow had 170 yards on 25 carries, UM's Leroy Hoard 158 on 23 runs, and Tony Boles 103 on 19 attempts.

How bad was Buckeye ball that fall? They finished 4-6-1, the team's first losing season in 29 years (1959), they surrendered 283 points, the most in OSU history, and they tied with *Northwestern* for seventh place in the conference.

Still, they came within a couple of minutes of upsetting the Wolverines.

Michigan (7-0-1) captured the Big Ten title over Michigan State (6-1-1) and Illinois (5-2-1).

The Rose Bowl featured 8-2-1 UM (ranked 11th) against 10-1-0 Southern Cal (ranked 5th). Michigan handed the Trojans their fourth straight bowl defeat by a 22-14 score.

The Big Ten, now in the full-blown bowl business, sent four other teams packing for post-season play. Indiana smothered South Carolina 34-10 in the Liberty Bowl; Iowa lost to North Carolina State 28-23 in the Peach; Michigan State lost to Georgia 34-27 in the Gator, and Illinois lost to Florida 14-10 in the All-

UM's Mike Gillette slammed the series' longest field goal (56 yards) in the 1988 game and in all booted 26 points against the Buckeyes (1986-87-88).

American.

Michigan's upset victory at Pasadena did indeed cap a magnificent comeback. From an 0-2 start to a 9-2-1 finish and a final No. 4 ranking behind Notre Dame, Miami and FSU. The Wolverines' two slim setbacks? As you can see, they were handed out by the nation's two top-ranked teams.

More good news for Michigan came three months later when it captured the NCAA basketball championship with an 81-80 overtime thriller over Seton Hall at the Kingdome in Seattle.

Hail To The Victors!

On the Buckeyes' side, it had been a long, dreary season and a harsh break-in for Coach John Cooper.

1989

GAME 86

PLATE SAVES SCHEMBECHLER'S SWAN SONG

Back in the 1970s one had to wonder the reasons behind Michigan signing a long-term football contract with Notre Dame.

Except for some additional television revenue, why?

Michigan is going to draw its usual 100,000-plus home crowd no matter who it schedules, and Notre Dame is going to draw its usual 60,000 at South Bend.

Michigan has the Big Ten Conference to worry about. Why have to worry about Notre Dame? Let Notre Dame go elsewhere for its "big games."

For all the obvious reasons, namely Notre Dame's built-in national recruiting base, why schedule the Irish?

The cold, hard fact remains: no collegiate football team in America — not Michigan, not Southern Cal, not Alabama, not Oklahoma, not Penn State, not anybody — is going to beat Notre Dame consistently.

So why schedule them? Over the long haul you're going to get beat. It's guaranteed.

The bottom line reality is that Notre Dame "needs" Michigan more than Michigan "needs" Notre Dame.

The 1989 Wolverines were positioned among the pre-season elite and some polls, including the *Associated Press,* even pegged them as No. 1, followed by the Fighting Irish, Nebraska, Miami, Southern Cal and Florida State.

The Wolverines fell to No. 2 before ever dressing out in their

417

game gear.

On August 31, Notre Dame and Virginia kicked off the season in the Kickoff Classic, the Irish won 36-13, took over the top spot, and sent Michigan to the runnerup role.

Two weeks later the two top teams met at Ann Arbor. Final score: Notre Dame 24, Michigan 19. UM fell to fifth.

Did the Buckeyes cherish UM's "fall?" Sure, but they were also well aware of their own problems, which were numerous.

The Wolverines next went out to Los Angeles and edged UCLA 24-23, but it proved only good enough for a drop a notch to sixth by the *AP* pollsters

But Bo Schembechler's troops then defeated Maryland, Wisconsin, Michigan State, Iowa, Indiana, Purdue, Illinois and Minnesota by a combined score of 254-154.

Ohio State was next.

The Buckeyes split their first four games, beating Oklahoma State and Boston College, with losses to Southern Cal and Illinois.

For the next six weeks, however, Coach John Cooper's boys averaged 37 points a game and along the way topped Indiana, Purdue, Minnesota, Northwestern, Iowa and Wisconsin.

The Wolverines were next at Ann Arbor.

UM (9-1-0) was now No. 3 behind Notre Dame and Colorado, while OSU (8-2-0) had worked its way into the *AP* poll at 20th.

Michigan's season scoreboard figures were 297-149, Ohio State's 307-238. Last year UM was an 11-point favorite, this year it was up to 13½.

As for Pasadena, the prize was already wrapped in Maize and Blue (win or lose) for the second year in a row.

On a mild, gray day, a crowd of 106,137, fourth largest in Michigan Stadium history, was there for the 85th game of the series, along with a national television audience, and they all watched Michigan, who never trailed, pound out a functional 28-18 victory. The Bucks did, however, supply a few anxious moments late in the game.

The Wolverines got the ball at Ohio's 47-yard line midway through the first quarter and nine plays later put up the game's first points on Leroy Hoard's one-yard effort. John Carlson converted and it was 7-0 with 3:13 on the clock.

Michigan went up 14-0 in the second period after staging a 13-

play march which covered 81 yards. Allen Jefferson scored from the two and Carlson's kick was good.

With the clock down to 2:23, Ohio took the ensuing kickoff and, keyed by Scottie Graham's 22-yard run, was in great shape with a first down at the four. Just like last year, however, OSU couldn't punch it over and had to settle for a Pat O'Morrow field goal just seconds before intermission.

Halftime: Michigan 14, Ohio State 3. It could have been worse, though, as UM had lost fumbles at the OSU 16-yard line and later at the 22.

The third period would belong to the Bucks.

After Vinnie Clark intercepted a Mike Taylor pass at his 45, Ohio State once again got down close, this time to the five, but had to call on kicker O'Morrow for points. He got the three but his team still trailed by eight.

The Wolverines couldn't move after the kickoff and a Chris Stapelton punt of only 14 yards enabled OSU to start at the UM 40. Nine plays later, Graham got into the endzone and, even though a two-point conversion try failed, the underdog Bucks were back in business, trailing by only 14-12 late in the third quarter.

However, a fellow by the name of William Todd Plate, UM cornerback, would squelch any Buckeye comeback bid in the final stanza.

On the first play of the quarter, Plate intercepted a Greg Frey pass at the Michigan 47. Highlighted by Hoard's 40-yard burst up the middle, the Wolverines scored in six plays when Taylor pitched a pass to Jarrod Bunch from the five. Carlson converted and the score was now 21-12.

But back came the Bucks with an 80-yard touchdown march. Facing third-and-three at midfield, a Frey-to-Graham pass was good for 14 yards to the 36. Led by Dante Lee's 14-yard run and Frey's seven-yard pass to Jeff Graham, OSU scored on Scottie Graham's four-yard run. Michigan's Tripp Welborne, however, made an enormous play by blocking the conversion try, leaving Ohio State a touchdown — instead of a field goal — shy of winning the game.

With the game clock at 7:04, UM's lead was down to 21-18.

OSU kicked off, got the ball back at its 38-yard line, and suddenly Michigan Stadium was very much alive. Where had that 21-12 lead gotten off to?

BASEBALL
■ Tigers not ready to make
worst-to-first move. Gene
Guidi's column, Page 7E.
Sunday, Nov. 26, 1989

SPORTS

Detroit Free Press

**MICHIGAN 28,
OHIO STATE 18**

It's a Rose Bowl repeat

On first down, Frey drilled a bullet down the middle intended for Greg Beatty at the Michigan 41, but here was that Plate guy again. He swooped in and swiped the ball right from Beatty's grasp. Interception!

Pandemonium in Ann Arbor!

Soon, however, an erie hush fell over the big crowd. Lying face down and motionless was Michigan's Vada Murray, who had collided head-on with teammate Plate an instant after the interception. Murray, with an injured neck, was strapped to a stretcher and carried away on a golf cart to an ambulance.

Good news later arrived from the University of Michigan Hospital. It proved not to be a serious injury.

The Wolverines' offense, meanwhile, went to work and made Plate's big steal pay dividends.

On third-and-five from the UM 46, the Buckeyes were called for pass interference which resulted in a crucial first down — instead of a punt. Later from the OSU 23, Bunch blasted straight ahead for a touchdown, Carlson's kick was good and with only 1:20 left to play, Michigan had a 28-18 triumph in the books. It marked the Wolverines' fourth win in five years over Ohio State and extended their series lead to 48-33-5.

California, Here We Come!

Little did anybody know, but as Bo Schembechler strolled towards the dressing room that November 25 afternoon, it would be his 134th and final game at Michigan Stadium.

UM's victory was also the first time in 23 years that a team had captured outright back-to-back Big Ten football championships. Michigan State last did it in 1965-66.

Leroy Hoard, hard-charging UM fullback, scored four touchdowns in the series (1987-88-89). In the last two years, he ripped OSU defenses for 310 yards on 44 carries (7.0 average). Hoard also became only the seventh player to score TDs in three different series games.

Michigan and Ohio piled up some numbers in their '89 game. OSU led in first downs 25-22, UM in yards rushing 310-200, OSU in passing 220-100, and in total yards by a scant 420-410. OSU's passing game resulted in 14-for-25 figures, UM's 8-for-16. OSU also led in penalty yards 29-10 and possession time 32-28.

UM's Hoard rushed for 152 yards on 21 carries (7.2), OSU's Scotty Graham for 133 yards on 28 attempts (4.8). In the last two years, Leroy Hoard had hammered the Buckeye defense for 310 yards rushing (44 attempts) and a handsome 7.1 average.

BOOM!

Three weeks after the game Bo Schembechler announced his retirement as Michigan coach. It was, to say the least, headline sports news all across the country. He would become Athletic Director, replacing Don Canham, who had held the position for 21 years.

Both Michigan and Ohio State would be playing in New Year's Day bowl games — UM at Pasadena and OSU at Tampa. The Big Ten also sent Illinois (Citrus) and Michigan State (Aloha) bowling.

Oddly enough, last year it was 8-2-1 Michigan against 10-1-0 Southern Cal in the Rose Bowl and UM pulled the upset, 22-14. This year it was 10-1-0 Michigan against 8-2-1 Southern Cal in the Rose and USC pulled the upset, 17-10.

The Buckeyes lost to Auburn 31-14, but the Illini topped Virginia 31-21, and the Spartans beat Hawaii 33-13.

The final *AP* poll had Michigan (10-2-0) No. 7 behind Miami, Notre Dame, Florida State, Colorado, Tennessee and Auburn. Ohio State (8-4-0) placed 24th.

GLENN "BO"
SCHEMBECHLER

He coached 21 years and 247 games at Michigan.
Here are the statistical highlights:

- His record was 194-48-5, .796.
- His teams outscored the opposition 7111-2805 (29-11 average).
- His home record (134 games) was 115-16-3, .869.
- His road record (113 games) was 79-32-2, .708.
- His Big Ten record (170 games) was 143-24-3, .850.
- His non-conference record (77 games) was 51-24-2, .675.
- His 194 wins were by an average score of 33-9.
- His 48 losses were by an average score of just 20-13.
- Thirty-three of his 48 losses were by 7 points or less.
- Nineteen of his 48 losses were by 3 points or less.
- His offenses were shutout only twice (1977 and 1984).
- His defenses pitched 43 shutouts.
- His teams won or shared 13 Big Ten championships.
- Seventeen of his 21 teams finished in the Top 10.
- His bowl record was 5-12-0.
- His record against Woody Hayes was 5-4-1 by a 138-105 score.
- His record against Ohio State was 11-9-1 by a 350-319 score.
- His overall head coaching record (Miami of Ohio/Michigan) was 234-65-8 (.775) and, upon retirement, ranked fifth in all-time NCAA Division I-A coaching victories.
- *His was a job well done.*

1990

GAME 87

"IT'S A GAME OF INCHES, FOLKS"

Woody's gone, now Bo's gone. Would the Michigan-Ohio State annual football feuds ever be the same? No. No way.

The 1990 edition of "The Big One" would be the first time in 34 years that neither Woody Hayes nor Bo Schembechler would be stalking the sidelines.

Woody and Bo — stewing and stomping....cursing and crying.... jerking and jawing....bitching, bullying and bellyaching.

But what fun it all was. And now it's gone. There'll *never* be another pair quite like 'em on one football field.

What a shame.

Schembechler had named Gary Moeller as his successor as Michigan's new head coach last December. Moeller, a native of Lima, Ohio, was a three-year letterman at Ohio State (center and linebacker, 1960-61-62) and played under coach Hayes and then-assistant coach Schembechler. He joined Schembechler's staff at Miami of Ohio in 1967 and made the move to Ann Arbor with him in 1969. Moeller became only the 15th head coach in the 111 years of UM football.

Each college football season now heats up in July when the flood of pre-season publications start hitting the shopping mall racks. And in 1990 it was Notre Dame, Miami, Florida State and Colorado getting all of the topflight ink. Michigan was rated anywhere from fifth (*Heinrich* and *Game Plan*) to 11th (*Street and Smith*). Ohio State was generally found among the worst of the country's best 25 clubs.

However, the *Associated Press* would start the Wolverines in sixth place and the Buckeyes 17th.

Michigan opened the season at South Bend and lost 28-24 to Notre Dame, but bounced back with impressive wins over UCLA (38-15), Maryland (45-17) and Wisconsin (41-3), thrusting the Wolverines into the nation's No. 1 position over Virginia (5-0-0) and Oklahoma (5-0-0).

But the good fortune lasted only a little while as UM then dropped consecutive one-pointers to Michigan State (28-27) and Iowa (24-23).

Six weeks into the season and only three wins? There had not been a worst Wolverine start in 23 years.

Moeller's honeymoon grace period was long gone — even though the team was still ranked (20th).

The next four weeks, however, produced victories over Indiana, Purdue, Illinois and Minnesota.

Ohio State was next.

The Buckeyes began with victories over Texas Tech and Boston College before dropping decisions to Southern Cal and Illinois, and tieing Indiana. OSU then reeled off five wins in a row, which included a big 27-26 upset of sixth-ranked Iowa at Iowa City.

Michigan was next.

As the weeks reeled by during the '90 season, five Big Ten teams were in a dandy chase for the conference championship.

Entering the final Saturday the top looked like this:
Iowa 6-1-0; Ohio State 5-1-1; Michigan 5-2-0; Michigan State 5-2-0, and Illinois 5-2-0.

The schedule:
Iowa vs. Minnesota (4-3-0) at Minneapolis.
Ohio State vs. Michigan at Columbus.
Michigan State vs. Wisconsin (0-7-0) at East Lansing.
Illinois vs. Northwestern (1-6-0) at Champaign-Urbana.
The league's only "meaningless" game that final day was
Indiana (2-4-1) vs Purdue (1-6-0) at West Lafayette.

The Rose Bowl? Only the Hawkeyes and Buckeyes were in a position to go.

Let 'er rip, boys!

In years past, the only conference game this late in the season that mattered was played either at Columbus or Ann Arbor. But not this year. There was wild interest all throughout Big Ten Country.

It was now time to get on with the 87th renewal of this volatile old rivalry. UM had scored 338 season points, OSU 325; UM had yielded 182 points, OSU 181. On paper, they were that even. Also on paper, UM was favored by 2½ points.

The Rose Bowl condition was this: An Ohio State win or tie, coupled with an Iowa loss, and the Bucks go. An Iowa win and it goes — regardless.

Iowa's game would start an hour after Ohio's game.

The last five Michigan-Ohio State games had produced an average of 821 offensive yards and 50 points. The '90 game, then, was a throwback to the Hayes-Schembechler days, as it could manage just 29 points and 532 yards of offense — the lowest yardage output since the 1971 game.

But it was still another classic — in a strange sort of way.

Just over 90,000 showed up and watched as the Buckeyes took a 3-0 lead in the first quarter.

Mark Pelini, OSU free safety, put a hit on UM fullback Jarrod Bunch, the ball flew free and was recovered by Buckeye strong safety Byron Cook at the Wolverines' 21-yard line. On fourth down from the 16, Tim Williams kicked a field goal.

Michigan tied it with 10:12 remaining in the second period, moving 70 yards in 10 plays down to the Bucks' 10, but had to rely on John Carlson's short field goal for points.

UM then went ahead when cornerback Lance Dottin picked off a Greg Frey pass at the OSU 20. On fourth down from the 13, Carlson booted another chipshot field goal, making it 6-3 with 6:05 showing on the first-half clock.

Ohio State answered with a touchdown, moving 78 yards in 13 plays, capped by Frey's 12-yard strike to flanker Jeff Graham. With the time down to 0:44. Williams converted.

Halftime: OSU 10, UM 6.

The Buckeyes made it 13-6 on their first possession of the second half when Williams hit a long 43-yard field goal.

The Wolverines quickly tied it. Derrick Alexander fielded the ensuing kickoff at his 15 and raced all the to OSU's 37, a return of 48 yards. It took 11 plays to cover the distance, the final 12 yards on a pass from Elvis Grbac to Desmond Howard. Carlson's kick made it 13-13 with 7:13 remaining in the game.

OSU punted. UM punted.

With just over three minutes left, the Bucks began from their 20. It was soon third-and-one. Frey, on a deep slant pattern, drilled one to Bobby Olive for a gain of 15 yards and a big first down up at the 44.

But wait!

At the end of the play, OSU's Jeff Graham was flagged by an official for an infraction on UM's Otis Williams.

Clipping!

That brought it back to the 29, still third-and-one. Raymount Harris hit the line, but was met head-on by linebacker John Milligan. Harris was short by a matter of inches.

Fourth down and 1:38 left to play.

Get a first down, run some clock, punt if you have to, settle for a tie if you have to, hope Minnesota beats Iowa, and a Rose Bowl trip belongs to the Buckeyes.

Time-out.

The coaching staff huddled over the big decision. It would be some kind of quarterback option play with Greg Frey.

It didn't work. In fact, it never came close.

Bryan Burwell of *The Detroit News* described the fatal play this way: "It began in the middle of the line, when T.J. Osman somehow burrowed his way past the line, and clogged up the hole that was intended for OSU fullback Raymont Harris. If you understand the precision involved in running an option play like the Buckeyes planned, you can well imagine how disruptive it must have been for Frey when he saw Osman scrounging around there on the ground. But it got much worse when he glared to his right and saw defensive tackle Chris Hutchinson blocking his only other path. Now Frey had nowhere to go. He froze like some frightened deer with headlamps in his eyes....now it was target practice time. Frey clutched the ball, ducked his head and awaited the collision."

Orman grabbed Frey's ankle, Corwin Brown and Mike Evans quickly arrived, then what seemed like the entire defensive unit came swarming in from all directions.

Michigan's ball. From the 20 and with the final seconds ticking away, John Carlson kicked a field goal.

The Columbus Dispatch
Sunday
NOVEMBER 25, 1990

Sports

SECTION **E**

Frey's 4th-down run was doomed all along

DICK FENLON

On the biggest play of Ohio State's season, Greg Frey took the snap and headed east.

Oops, wrong direction.

The first down the Buckeyes gambled for — the necessary first step in the victory over Michigan they longed for — lay a mini-yard to the north yesterday.

The quarterback, a senior, playing his last game in Ohio Stadium, never had a chance to turn it *that* way.

At crunch time, somebody identified as Michigan tackle Chris Hutchinson was in the Ohio State backfield to gum up offensive coordinator Jim Colletto's wild and curious spin of the play-calling wheel, dooming the Buckeyes to yet another painful defeat by Michigan and sending them whirling off to Memphis, Tenn., for a blue Christmas.

"I've got about five or six choices, and it's like playing the lottery," Colletto said. "If I pick the right one I'm a hero, and if I don't pick the right one I'm a horse-manure coach."

Ohio State didn't win the lottery on Michigan Day, that's apparent. And it's apparent, too, that football has changed immensely since the days of the old curmudgeon, Woody Hayes, the coach who never forgot that the next yard was a block and a blast straight ahead.

But the certitude that the shortest distance between two points is a straight line hasn't changed.

FREY IS NO OPTION QUARTERBACK

When the game was on the line — when Ohio State could have been headed off to Pasadena to play Washington in the Rose Bowl instead of to Memphis to play Air Force in the Liberty Bowl — the Buckeyes gave an option look to a quarterback running diagonally whose strength has been anything but running the option.

"Don't second-guess that call," the head coach and overseer, John Cooper, would argue. "If we block out, we make a first down."

If Ohio State gets the first down — this with 1:38 left — maybe it has the time and the machinery to go north for a winning field goal. Helped by a Minnesota upset of Iowa, it then goes to the Rose Bowl.

Cooper, burned by playing for a tie at Indiana six games earlier, is correct to go for it. For, as it turns out, Iowa did lose yesterday, and if the other part happens, he's in Roses.

The call is what boggles.

The call is what will always boggle.

"I'll stay up all night tonight and debate whether I called the right play," Colletto confessed, when all the stonewalling was done.

The Ohio State center, Dan Beatty, goes 6 feet 4 and 285. A sneaking quarterback tucked in behind a rolling boulder of a center can often find a foot or two, even when the other side is in its goal-line defense. The Ohio State fullback, Scottie Graham, is a 220-pound chunk who averaged 4.2 yards in five blasts.

There are a couple of the options beyond Four Base, wherein Frey, Colletto said, is to fake to the fullback, head right, find the tackle angling outside, cut and dive for what's needed.

PLAY HAD WORKED BEFORE

"We've done this many times in the last three years and made the first down," Colletto said. "But we didn't make it."

Bottom line, that.

But there were others yesterday very near the bottom that could have changed it, too.

The one that hurt Frey the most was the clip that Jeff Graham put on Michigan safety Otis Williams two plays before the snuffed option. It erased a 15-yard strike to Bobby Olive. When linebacker John Milling stopped Raymont Harris for no gain at left tackle, it left the Buckeyes at fourth-and-short on their 29.

Five plays later, with the final second ticking off, Michigan had J.D. Carlson's winning 37 yard field goal, a 16-13 triumph and the Gator Bowl bid OSU would have earned even with a tie.

"It hurts," Frey said. "That's all I can say.

"We just made mistakes we don't ordinarily make. We put the ball on the ground. There were interceptions (he threw three) and penalties. It seemed every time we got a big play it turned around and went back the other way."

The completion to Olive would have put Ohio State in business on its 44 with a timeout left. "I thought that play would make a difference," Frey said.

It didn't. So it came down to Four Base, described by Cooper as "really not an option," identified by Frey as a play in which "the basic option is to get the ball outside and make the pitch, or cut it up to get the first down."

And when he cut?

"Nothing was there," Frey said.

Hutchinson was.

"It's been a really successful play for us," Frey said, "but the nose guard or somebody had me by the legs, and I didn't have a chance to do anything with it. They guessed right."

And somebody else, you have to guess, guessed wrong.

Dick Fenlon is sports columnist for The Dispatch.

Rose fails to blossom for OSU

Chris Russell/Dispatch

Michigan kicker J.D. Carlson (38) and holder Ken Sollom celebrate winning field goal

Carlson's field goal at 0:00 lifts Michigan to 16-13 win

By Tim May
Dispatch Sports Reporter

It was close. It was won on the last play of the game. It featured some ferocious, timely defense and some . . . well, some offense.

But Michigan's 16-13 victory over Ohio State yesterday in Ohio Stadium was no classic. At least not from Ohio State's point of view.

It was a tragedy.

When quarterback Greg Frey was stopped for no gain on a fourth-and-18-inches option keeper with 1:38 left at his 29 — that was devastating.

When Michigan kicker J.D. Carlson kicked his third field goal of the day, a 37-yarder as time expired to win it, that was depressing.

But when Minnesota knocked off Big Ten leader Iowa 31-24 an hour later . . .

"I don't even want to know the score," Ohio State senior center Dan Beatty said.

A fan had just presented him a bottle of champagne intended for the celebration that was to follow victories by Ohio State and Minnesota. The parlay would have given the Buckeyes the outright Big Ten championship and a trip to the Rose Bowl.

What happened yesterday simply left Iowa, Michigan, Illinois and Michigan State in a four-way tie for the conference title.

It sent Iowa (8-3, 6-2), which beat the other three, to the Rose Bowl and Michigan (8-3, 6-2) to the Gator Bowl. Illinois (8-3, 6-2) is going to the Hall of Fame Bowl and Michigan State (7-3-1, 6-2) to the John Hancock Bowl.

As for the Buckeyes (7-3-1, 5-2-1), as Carlson's kick floated toward victory, OSU senior cornerback Vinnie Clark — his block attempt in vain — was sprawled on the grass.

"I'm laying there thinking, it's over," Clark said. "We . . . by three points. My last game.

"The Rose Bowl's gone. The Gator Bowl's gone. The Liberty Bowl."

That's where the Buckeyes are headed, Dec. 27 against Air Force.

While ecstatic about his team's victory and trip to the Gator, first-year Michigan coach Gary Moeller said, "I know how Ohio State feels going to the Liberty Bowl."

Probably not, OSU split end Bobby Olive said.

"I'm not looking forward to it at all," he said.

He thought he was headed anywhere but Memphis when he took a pass on a deep crossing route and gained 15 yards with just over two minutes left. It came on third-and-1 from the OSU 29, and the pass, from Frey, seemed to send the Buckeyes well on their way to at least a winning field goal attempt.

But at the end of the play, senior flanker Jeff Graham was called for a clip on Michigan strong safety Otis Williams. A replay showed he clearly caught Williams from behind.

Instead of a first down at their 44, the Buckeyes faced

Please see OSU page 2E

Turnovers kill DeSales in state title game

St. Marys wins 14-3 on big defensive plays

By Ray Stein
Dispatch Sports Reporter

MASSILLON, Ohio — When the DeSales passing game worked last night, it was very friendly to the Stallions. But when it didn't, it was very costly.

St. Marys Memorial took advantage of five turnovers, including four interceptions, to beat DeSales 14-3 in the Division II state high school football championship in Paul Brown Tiger Stadium.

Shane Dysert had two interceptions for the Roughriders (14-0), but it was a 90-yard interception return by Mike Elston for a third-quarter touchdown that hurt the most.

"(St. Marys) played an excellent defensive game against us," DeSales coach Bob Jacoby said. "They caused those turnovers we made. We got beat by a very good team."

On paper, it was DeSales (11-3) that looked like the better team. The Stallions had 16 first downs and 218 yards of offense. The DeSales defense limited St. Marys to nine first downs and 131 yards, including 27 in the second half.

But the Stallions self-destructed inside the St. Marys 40-yard line, losing one fumble and throwing two interceptions.

"We just made too many mistakes," DeSales center Adam Asbeck said. "We were getting the job done on offense until we hurt ourselves."

St. Marys hurt DeSales early, driving 45 yards in eight plays on its first possession to take a 7-0 lead on Fred Fry's 1-yard run with 6:48 remaining in the first quarter.

DeSales struck back, driving to the St. Marys 30 in seven plays. But sophomore quarterback Brian Emmerling was intercepted by Dysert inside the 15.

"We didn't think they'd be able to run inside on us," St. Marys coach Skip Baughman said. "We thought they'd have to throw the ball, and that's what we wanted."

Emmerling almost made Baughman eat his words in the first half by completing 6 of 9 passes for 52 yards. But the Stallions were able to score only when John Mahle kicked a 24-yard field goal with 2:21 left in the half.

"We definitely felt like we could win the game at halftime," Jacoby said. "We were moving the ball pretty well against them."

After DeSales forced a punt on the Roughriders' first series of the third quarter, its offense continued the trend.

With the help of two fourth-and-1 conversions, the Stallions drove from their 33 to the St. Marys 16 in 11 plays.

On the 12th, Emmerling dropped back and looked for tight end Luke Fickell on a hitch pattern.

But Emmerling's pass was underthrown — Jacoby said his arm may have been hit as he released — and Elston stepped in to take the ball at the 10. He wasn't touched until teammates mobbed him in the end zone 90 yards away.

"He's a very gifted young man," Baughman said of Elston, a 6-foot-4, 200-pound sophomore. "He's the kind of kid who makes those kind of plays."

Jacoby took the blame for the play, which made it 14-3 with 2:56 left in the third quarter.

"I put our kids in tough situations with a few calls," Jacoby said. "That was one case. I think that pass was a matter of going to the well once too often. We probably should have run the ball."

After that, the Stallions didn't run or throw with much success. Halfback Steve Smith was intercepted by Dysert late in the third quarter and Emmerling was picked off by Andy Liming midway through the fourth quarter to end any comeback chances.

"Our offense stayed in the game (mentally) the whole second half," DeSales running back Chad Young said. "We performed pretty well. We just shut down when we got close to the end zone."

■ St. Henry captures Division V title / 16E

Games that count begin for Buckeyes

By Mike Sullivan
Dispatch Sports Reporter

Randy Ayers . . . *eager to start*

■ **Tipoff** — 8:07 p.m.
■ **TV-radio** — WSYX-Channel 6; WBNS-AM (1460), WBNS-FM (97.1).

If the Ohio State basketball team is going to feature a viable inside power game, as advertised, the time has come to exploit it. . . .

"We'll see if we can deliver the ball inside and take advantage of our size," said OSU coach Randy Ayers, looking ahead to the season opener at 8:07 tonight against Bethune-Cookman in St. John Arena.

The Wildcats, who opened Friday night with a 96-83 loss to Florida A&M, have just one player taller than 6 feet 6 — sophomore center Thel Sergeant, who stands 6-8.

By contrast, OSU will start Perry Carter and Treg Lee, both 6-8, at center and power forward, respectively, and rotate 7-foot Bill Robinson off the bench.

"I think our players are extremely anxious to get going," Ayers said. "It's finally time for the games that count.

"To me, it's exciting that we're facing coach (Cy) McClairen. I've heard about him when coaches sit around and tell basketball stories: He's been one of the real innovators in this game. I guarantee you they'll throw things at us we won't be ready for."

McClairen graduated from Bethune-Cookman in 1952 and has coached at the Daytona Beach, Fla., school for 28 seasons, compiling a 373-331 record.

McClairen's disciplinary touch has not softened with the years, a point driven home Friday when starting point guard Chris Carter and reserve guard Terry Taylor watched the opener in street clothes.

Both players were serving the first of a three-game suspension for curfew violations, forcing McClairen to move 6-4 senior Clifford Reed from shooting guard to point guard and start Jeff Robinson, a 6-5 freshman, at small forward.

"I think we'll be a better team when we get all our troops back, although I don't think that made the difference against A&M," McClairen said. "But it will make things easier for Clifford."

If things were hard for Reed, his numbers didn't show it. He led Bethune-Cookman with 29 points, making 10 of 18 shots from the field, and had five steals and six assists.

Joe Parham, a 6-6 senior, added 18 points and Reggie Cunningham had 13. Sergeant had seven rebounds and two points, Robinson eight points and two rebounds.

Buckeyes assistant Dave Cecutti, who scouted the game, said the Wildcats will show Ohio State a variety of looks.

"They change defenses often, and we'll have to adjust during the course of the game," Cecutti said. "We'll have to communicate on the court and be aware of matchups."

Ayers said Mark Baker, who missed two exhibition starts because of classroom attendance, will start at point guard next to Jamaal Brown. Sophomore Jim Jackson will join Lee and Carter on the front line.

INSIDE SPORTS

Sports editor: George Strode/461-8522
Latest scores: 469-9909

WHAT NOW, BENGALS?

Inconsistency has been a hallmark of the Bengals' season, so don't assume they'll handle the Colts today. With tough games against Pittsburgh, San Francisco and the Raiders coming up, Sam Wyche's team might get caught looking ahead/15E

ONE TOUGH DEFENSE

In just one season, the Miami defense has risen from the ashes to become one of the best in the NFL: It will give Cleveland a stern test today/14E

DEER SEASON LOOMS

If the weather cooperates, Ohio hunters could take a record number of deer during gun season, which opens Monday/19E

Sports capsules/8E

The clock showed 00:00 as UM kicker John Carlson (38) and holder Ken Sollom revel after Carlson's successful field goal and the Wolverines' 16-13 thriller over OSU in 1990 at Columbus.

Final score from Columbus: Michigan 16, Ohio State 13.

Final score from Minneapolis: *Minnesota 31, Iowa 24.*

The Buckeyes were crushed. Crushed!

What easily could have been a trip to sunny Pasadena instead turned into a trip to frigid Memphis.

Both hard-core and casual Buckeye boosters would remember for a long time their 1990 loss to Michigan.

The other three conference scores that memorable Saturday were: Illinois 28, Northwestern 23, Michigan State 14, Wisconsin 9, and Indiana 28, Purdue 14.

It all flushed out as a four-way tie for the championship, as the Hawkeyes, Wolverines, Spartans and Illini each finished 6-2-0.

Back at Columbus, OSU led in first downs 16-13, passing yards 157-104, total yards 284-248, and penalty yards 66-15. UM led in rushing yards 144-127 — and in scoring 16-13.

UM's Richard Powers rushed for 128 yards in 27 carries (4.7).

The Big Ten shipped six teams off to bowls, but only two returned as winners. In the Gator, Michigan manhandled Ole Miss 35-3, and Michigan State edged Southern Cal 17-16 in the Sun.

The Buckeyes, still fretting over their disaster against Michigan, lost to Air Force 23-11 in the Liberty, Indiana lost in the final seconds to Auburn 27-23 in the Peach, and Illinois was blanked 30-0 by Clemson in the Hall of Fame.

Pollwise, the Wolverines experienced an extremely strange season. They began No. 6, worked up to No. 1, tumbled all the way to 20th, then climbed back to seventh, behind Colorado, Georgia Tech, Miami, Florida State, Washington and Notre Dame.

Ohio State posted a disappointing 7-4-1 record.

In their 87 all-time football feuds, UM now leads OSU 49-33-5 in wins and 1,388-993 on the scoreboard.

1991

NOT AT ALL LIKE UM-OSU

QUESTION 1: Is Michigan and Ohio State football "always overrated?"

QUESTION 2: Do UM and OSU fans, year after year, grow weary over their teams' big pre-season build-up, only to feel "let down" at season's end?

ANSWER TO QUESTION 1: No.

ANSWER TO QUESTION 2: Most likely, yes.

For sure, collegiate football fans all across the nation would cherish the "problem" that these two Midwest powers have had over the past two decades.

That problem? High expectations. Too high, for the most part.

Created by whom? The pre-season prognosticators.

How? By "overrating" almost all of the nation's elite programs. It's the price they pay for success.

In the period 1970-1991 (22 seasons), the *Associated Press'* top 10 ranked teams (listed alphabetically) were Alabama, Michigan, Nebraska, Notre Dame, Ohio State, Oklahoma, Penn State, Southern Cal, Texas and UCLA.

A formula was established. For example, if a team was a pre-season eighth pick and finished third, it received a plus-five points for that particular year. If a team was a pre-season second pick and finished ninth, it was given a minus-seven points, etc.

The formula also takes into consideration pre-season unranked teams that finish in the Top 20, and vice-versa.

After tabulating each of the 10 teams' year-by-year figures, only one (UCLA) "lived up" to its pre-season billings over that time frame.

430

UCLA finished a +1, Alabama was next at -5, followed by Penn State -28, Texas -45, Michigan -47, Nebraska -48, Oklahoma -55, Ohio State -69, Notre Dame -83 and Southern Cal -85.

The conclusion is that the *AP* pollsters, for the period 1970-1991, hit the closest with UCLA and Alabama, and missed the most on Notre Dame and Southern Cal.

In all, these 10 teams combined for 199 pre-season rankings (of a possible 220). Nebraska, Oklahoma and Penn State were listed each of the 22 years; Michigan, Notre Dame and Alabama 21 times; Southern Cal 20; Ohio State and UCLA 17, and Texas 16.

To begin the '91 season, the *AP* boys pegged Florida State, Michigan and Miami as 1-2-3. The Buckeyes were 22nd.

Even though the Wolverines opened with wins over Boston College and 7th-rated Notre Dame, they fell a notch to third in favor of Miami, who had beaten Arkansas and 10th-ranked Houston.

On September 21, it was No. 1 Florida State against No. 3 Michigan at Ann Arbor. FSU 51, UM 31. Even though it wasn't that close, it did amount to the most points ever scored by a visiting team at Michigan Stadium.

The Wolverines went on to thrash seven conference opponents by a lopsided 285-88 score and were all set for Ohio State.

The Buckeyes were 4-0-0 after beating Arizona, Louisville, Washington State and Wisconsin, and had worked up to a No. 11 ranking.

But a 10-6 setback at Illinois and later a 16-9 loss to Iowa at Columbus, nixed all Rose Bowl chat.

Up next was a trip to Ann Arbor.

UM was rated fourth on the strength of a 9-1-0 record, OSU was 8-2-0 and ranked 18th. UM's average score was a flashy 38-17, OSU's 26-13. Guess who was made a big 14-point favorite?

Also guess what head coach in town was awarded a three-year contract extension on the morning of the game? If you said Gary Moeller, go to the back of the line. It was Ohio State's John Cooper. In a surprise move, OSU athletic director Jim Jones offered — and Cooper gladly accepted.

Win or lose, the Wolverines already had their Rose Bowl jetliner all confirmed.

Before a crowd of just over 106,000 on a drizzly, overcast afternoon, it was UM all the way, 31-3, in a game highlighted by

431

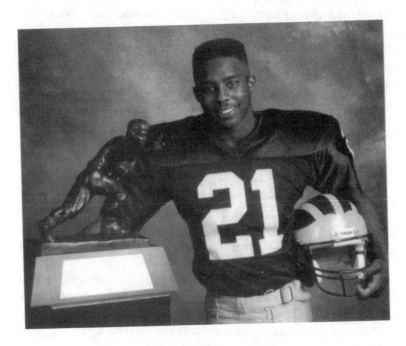

**MICHIGAN'S DESMOND HOWARD
THE 1991 HEISMAN TROPHY WINNER**

He won the award by the second largest margin in the trophy's history. In three seasons, Howard scored 23 touchdowns and 138 points. He became the seventh Heisman winner to play in the series, joining UM's Tom Harmon (1940), and OSU's Les Horvath (1944), Vic Janowicz (1950), Howard Cassady (1955) and two-time winner Archie Griffin (1974-75). Against the Buckeyes in '91, Howard returned a punt 93 yards which represents the second longest scoring play in the series.

the second longest touchdown play in series history.

FIRST QUARTER:
■ UM — Went 76 yards in 10 plays, capped by Burnie Legette's 1-yard dive. John Carlson converted, 7-0.

SECOND QUARTER
■ OSU — Tim Williams slammed a 50-yard field goal, 3-7.

■ UM, Lance Dottin intercepted a pass at the Ohio 12. Jesse Johnson later scored from the one. Carlson converted, 14-3.

■ UM — Carlson kicked a 37-yard field goal, 17-3.

■ UM — Desmond Howard returned a punt 93 yards. Carlson converted and it was 24-3. Desmond's long run is topped only by Alfred Barlow's (UM) 113-yard return of a missed field goal in the 1905 game before 8,000 fans at old Regents Field in Ann Arbor.

Howard's play also marked only the fourth punt returned for a touchdown in the series (1935-1940-1971).

THIRD QUARTER
UM — Howard's 50-yard pass reception from Elvis Grbac set up Tyrone Wheatley's six-yard run. Carlson converted, 31-3.

FOURTH QUARTER
Moeller called off the Wolves.

A 28-point difference in a UM-OSU bash? It was the most lopsided score in 30 years going back to a 50-20 Buckeye victory in 1961.

The losers led in first downs (19-16), possession time (34-26) and turnovers (3-1). The winners led in rushing yards (198-109), passing yards (125-124), total yards (323-233) and penalty yards (75-30). UM's passing game was 9-for-15, OSU's 13-for-25. Wheatley led all rushers with 79 yards in 12 carries (6.6).

It was Michigan's fourth straight win over Ohio State and also its fourth consecutive Big Ten football title (three outright).

The Big Ten's bowl season was a disappointment. Indiana blanked Baylor 24-0 in the Copper, Iowa and Brigham Young tied 13-13 in the Holiday, but the other three entries lost — Illinois 6-3 to UCLA in the John Hancock, the Buckeyes 24-17 to Syracuse in the Hall of Fame, and the Wolverines 34-14 to Washington in the Rose.

By the way, the Hawkeyes' tie was the Big Ten's first in post-season play, and the Buckeyes' game was the league's 100th bowl

The Detroit News

Sunday
NOVEMBER 24,
1991

Section E

FORUM 6E
WEATHER 12E

■ **Road test:** Lions must get passing grade against Vikings in Minnesota. **4E**

■ **Champs:** Ann Arbor Pioneer, Zeeland take swimming titles. **9E**

Michigan 31, Ohio St. 3
Michigan St. 27, Illinois 24
Indiana 24, Purdue 22
Iowa 23, Minnesota 8
Wisconsin 32, N western 14
E.Tex St. 38, Grand Valley 15
Allegheny 24, Albion 21

Miami 19, Boston College 14
Washington 56, Wash. St. 21
Stanford 38, California 21
Tennessee 18, Kentucky 7
Texas A&M 65, SMU 6
E. Carolina 30, Cincinnati 19
College report, 2-4F

Sports

HIGH SCHOOLS
STATE SEMIFINALS

Tecumseh's Scott Meredith absorbs defeat.

CLARENCE TABB JR. / The Detroit News

Scoreboard

CLASS AA
■ S. Arthur Hill 29, Ann Arbor 6
■ Detroit Catholic Central 10, Detroit King 7 (OT)

CLASS A
■ E. Lansing 10, South Lyon 7
■ Birmingham Brother Rice 21, Ypsilanti 14 (3OT)

CLASS BB
■ Cheboygan 35, Three Rivers

CLASS B
■ Farmington Harrison 32, Tecumseh 7

CLASS B
■ Cooperville 24, Kingsford 7
■ Monroe St. Mary Catholic Central 21, Ridgewood 0

CLASS CC

MICHIGAN STATE 27, ILLINOIS 24

Victory Perles' last stand? He says no

■ **'No matter what':** George defiantly stakes his claim to retaining his coaching job at MSU.

EAST LANSING — The miniscene and motor drives raise crowding amid George Perles as he made his way slowly out of Spartan Stadium late Saturday afternoon, everyone eager to record one emotional outburst that would foreverer symbolize his farewell as Michigan State's football coach.

BRYAN BURWELL

But there would be no teary farewells on this day. In fact, there would be no farewells of any kind. Perles was in no mood to say goodbye. As he marched off the field, he fought back the tears, then defiantly proclaimed that this 27-24 upset victory over Illinois was by no means his final appearance as Michigan State's head football coach.

He did not mince words. He did not speak in vague terms. Others could think what they wanted about what the future held for Perles as he sinks deeper and deeper into this sorrow.

Please see Burwell, 4F

George Perles: "This won't be my last game. Underline that."

KIRTHMON F. DOZIER / The Detroit News

■ **MSU opportunist:** Spartans turn three third-period turnovers into 17 points, beat Illini.

By Terry Cabell
THE DETROIT NEWS

EAST LANSING — As the final seconds ticked off the scoreboard clock Saturday to signal Michigan State's 27-24 victory over Illinois, several MSU players lifted George Perles upon their shoulders and carried the him to midfield. As they did, the crowd of 61,721 in Spartan Stadium — at least those who stuck around and braved the cold, rainy day — stood and applauded Perles and his team's effort.

It was a moving moment, especially since many thought Saturday's game would be Perles' last as MSU coach. But during his postgame interview Saturday, Perles, who has always remaining on his contract made it perfectly clear that he intends to return as the Spartans coach in 1992.

"I'm positive we can work things out," Perles said. "Of course, we have to get around the table together and haven't had that opportunity in long, long time."

It has been a long time since

Please see MSU, 4

MICHIGAN 31, OHIO STATE 3

It's Wolverines all the way

■ **Hail to Howard:** Move over A.C., Heisman hopeful is U-M's greatest.

■ **Big Ten champs:** Buckeyes prove no match; Huskies in Rose Bowl are next.

THE DETROIT NEWS

---

date. The Wolverine-Huskie encounter later that New Year's Day made it 101.

The record stood at 47-53-1.

Miami *(AP)* and Washington *(USA Today*-CNN-Coaches) split the national championship. The Wolverines finished No. 6 in both polls behind the two champs, Penn State, Florida State and Alabama. The Buckeyes were 8-4-0.

Michigan, with six wins over Ohio State in seven years, now held a commanding 50-33-5 series advantage.

1992

THE BIG TEN CRY:
"BREAK-UP MICHIGAN!"

Michigan began the season as the country's fifth best team, according to the *Associated Press* and its pollsters. Ohio State was rated 17th.

But the Wolverines stumbled out of the gate, blowing a 17-7 fourth quarter lead against third-ranked Notre Dame at South Bend and were forced to settle for a 17-all tie.

Boom! The next six weeks saw Gary Moeller expose the opposition to some rather harsh Saturday afternoon therapy, grinding Oklahoma State 35-3, Houston 61-7, Iowa 52-28, the Spartans 35-10 and Indiana 31-3. That brought the season to October 24 and Homecoming against Minnesota.

It would be Michigan's 1,000th all-time football game.

Final score: Wolverines 63, Golden Gophers 13, and the Little Brown Jug would remain where it had rested for six years.

The record after all that time: 728-238-34, .745.

Michigan edged Purdue 24-17, followed up by a surprise! surprise! Illinois, with a 5-4-0 record, went to Ann Arbor and forced the Wolverines to kick a field goal in the final seconds to salvage a 22-22 tie. But it was still good enough for a fifth straight Big Ten title and Rose Bowl journey.

Ohio State was next.

John Cooper's '92 Buckeye edition impressed nobody in the early stages — not even Cooper and certainly not the Ohio Stadium Boo-Bucks — after grappling past Louisville 20-19, then Bowling Green 17-6, dropping the team to 22nd.

However, some instant attention came the following week when OSU went to the Carrier Dome and smothered ninth-ranked

Seniors tired of losing to Michigan

▪ *This group says they'd like to hear talk of a win over the Wolverines for a change.*

By Tim May

hour about it 12 months out of the year." What's at stake for Herbstreit, middle linebacker Steve Tovar and 15 other OSU seniors is hearing about it for the rest of their lives. The kickoff at 12:10 p.m. today in Ohio Stadium against the Wolverines (8-0-2, 6-0-1) will mark those Buckeyes' last chance at grabbing a pair of gold pants, symbolic of a victory over Michigan.

▪ **Rivalry still fires up Michigan;** Moeller recalls OSU days; Seniors get some inspiration / 3B

because they're 8-0-2 and we're 8-2. It's a pretty close match as far as records go, and things of that nature.

No. 2 in the league in rushing offense. Except Michigan — powered by Tyrone Wheatley's league-leading 113.6-yard average — is averaging 270.9 yards per game rushing while OSU is averaging 196.2. The Wolverines, a seven-point favorite, also have a 121-yard advantage in total offense (484.9) over No. 2 Iowa.

Syracuse 35-12, and a poll hurdle to 12th.

Lurking straight ahead was Coach Barry Alvarez and his woeful Wisconsin squad, winners of only five conference games in the last five years.

Upset! Badgers 20, Buckeyes 16.

Another loss followed, 18-16 to Illinois, and OSU disappeared from the poll boards.

OSU somehow got its act together and in the next five weeks posted victories over Northwestern, Michigan State, Iowa, Minnesota and Indiana.

Mean ol' Michigan was next.

The Wolverines were 8-0-2 by an average score of 38-13 and ranked No. 5. The Bucks were 8-2-0 by an average of 24-12, ranked 18th and were 7-point underdogs.

It was sullen Saturday. Murky clouds hung low, the Columbus traffic was snarled to a standstill and rain gear was everywhere.

Ahh, just right. It was a typical Michigan-Ohio State kind of football day. Everything was outstanding for the big game.

The second biggest crowd ever, 95,330, inched their way into the old horseshoe bastion and Buckeye boosters went in ready for action. Bring on those *hated* Wolverines!

OSU received the opening kickoff, drove 53 yards down to the 20, stalled, and attempted a field goal. But Jean-Agnus Charles stormed through and blocked Tim Williams' kick.

After an exchange of punts, UM quarterback Elvis Grbac was intercepted by Chico Nelson at his 36. Aided by an interference call, the Bucks reached Michigan's 22, stalled again, but this time Williams' kick reached its target, and it was 3-0 with 3:58 left in the first quarter. It marked Ohio State's 999th point against the Wolverines.

Columbus was a wet place for the 1992 game.

UM answered, going 67 yards in 11 plays, all on the ground. Keyed by Ricky Powers' five straight carries for 28 yards, the Wolverines faced a third-and-one at the OSU's 30. Burnie Legette got six, and Tyrone Wheatley blasted 17 yards down to the seven. Grbac, on a QB draw, later scored from the three. But Peter Elezovic's kick sailed wide, Michigan's lead remained at 6-3, and worst news than the missed PAT was the fact that Grbac was hurt.

He had been whacked in the ribs and kidney, began coughing blood and, of all things, lost his voice — or enough voice that he couldn't shout-out the signals over the loud hometown crowd.

Grbac would warm up on the sideline repeatedly throughout the remainder of the game, but he would never return. He was replaced by sophomore Todd Collins.

Neither team seriously threatened and the half ended 6-3, the lowest score at intermission in 12 years.

Collins cranked up the offense midway the third period, moving his club 80 yards in a dozen plays. On third-and-nine at his 21, Collins threw complete to Amani Toomer for 13 yards and a big

Buckeyes celebrate game-tying TD in the '92 game at Columbus.

first down. Two Wheatley runs for 21 yards, two by Jesse Johnson for 17 yards, plus two completions from Collins to Tony McGee for 23 more yards, had UM at the five. Johnson, in two tries, got it to the one. Collins then faked a handoff to Johnson, kept the ball himself, and ambled untouched into the endzone with 1:33 left in the third period. Elezovic converted this time and the Wolverines' small portion of the stadium was whoopin' it up over their big 13-3 lead.

OSU took the ensuing kickoff, reached the UM 13, and Williams came on to kick a field goal, putting the Buckeyes over the 1,000 mark in all-time points against the Wolverines.

Score: Michigan 13, Ohio State 6.

Time remaining: 12:16.

Even though the weather conditions never turned the field into one of those mud baths, everything was soppin' wet by now.

The Bucks kicked off, held UM to three-and-out, and received the punt at their own 43.

Ohio Stadium was an absolute madhouse.

Fifth-year quarterback Kirk Herbstreit, on first down, scrambled from the pocket and picked up 14 yards.

On third-and-eight from the UM 40, Herbstreit threw to Jeff Cothran for 14 yards to the 26.

On third-and-eight from the UM 24, Herbstreit threw to Greg Beatty for 12 yards to the 12.

OSU was soon first-and-goal at the three.

OSU was soon fourth-and-goal at the five.

Herbstreit got the snap, took two quick steps back, looked left, then rifled one to the right, right into the hands of a sliding Beatty who, by the way, had slipped down at the line, scrambled to his feet and got himself open — all in a matter of seconds.

Touchdown, Ohio State!

Williams put the pressure-packed point-after through the pipes and it was 13-13 with 4:24 left.

The Buckeyes quickly forced a punt and got the ball in great shape at their 45 with plenty of time — 3:19 — left.

But the Wolverine "D" held and on fourth-and-four, Joel Kessel lifted a towering punt that hit UM's return man Derrick Alexander in the face mask.

Suddenly, the football was bouncing around deep in Michigan territory.

OSU's Steve Tovar had a good shot at it, but UM's Shawn Collins barely beat him, pouncing on the ball at the nine-yard line with 63 seconds left in the game. Had the Bucks recovered the stadium would have fallen down.

On the game's final play, Collins heaved a long desperation pass which was intercepted by Walter Taylor and returned 51 yards to the Michigan 34.

Final: 13-13, the series' sixth tie, but the first since '73.

Joe Falls of *The Detroit News* reported, "The fans made so much noise near the end of the game, screaming and beating their feet on the floor, that the press box began swaying. This did not bother anyone, except those writers who were part of the San Francisco earthquake during the 1989 World Series."

Coach Moeller bemoaned the field conditions and crowd noise.

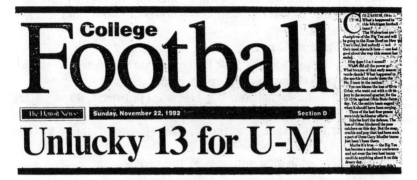

The Detroit News | Sunday, November 22, 1992 | Section D

Unlucky 13 for U-M

The Detroit News

"That field was the biggest joke in the world," he told the press afterwards. "It was like trying to play football on an ice rink. It's a joke."

As for the noise, he said, "Our players couldn't hear a thing, and we got no help from the officials there....Just go ahead and write it. I'll get it worse next time I come down here, because that's the way it works. I don't care who you write for...."

But Michigan quarterback Elvis Grbac had other ideas about the crowd's rowdiness. "I'd love to play here every Saturday because of the noise....but on the other side, the credit goes to the fans. They were great support, and they made it hard for us to get things done."

Over on the other side, you betcha, the question was thrown at Coach John Cooper about not going for two points and a possible 14-13 win — or a possible 13-12 defeat.

"You want to gamble, guys, but you want to gamble with my chips. We went for it down here a couple of years ago and lost the game, and all I see is that we lost the game."

When asked about his job security, he said, "I'm not getting into that, You have to ask who makes those decisions. Either the Board of Trustees, or Dr. Gee (OSU president), or Jim Jones (OSU athletic director), or maybe the local press makes those decisions. I'm outa here."

And he was gone.

As for the game stats, OSU had sizable advantages in first downs (24-16), total yards (362-271) and possession time (33-27),

440

while UM led in the negative departments of turnovers (2-0) and yards penalized (59-34).

Michigan's Wheatley was the game's big ground gainer with 100 yards in 19 carries (5.3).

Herbstreit's 28 completions and 47 attempts are second-highest (both catagories) in OSU history to Art Schlichter's 31-for-52 in 1981 against Florida State.

Herbstreit's 271 passing yards is also second most in the series, topped only by Mike Tomczak's 298 yards (21-for-40) in the 1983 game.

Speaking of Kirk Herbstreit, his father, James, also played in the series and even caught a TD pass in the Buckeyes' 20-14 win at Columbus in 1958. He also caught a 2-point conversion in a 23-14 loss to Michigan in 1959.

Some odd series numbers pop out over the last five years. Even though the Buckeyes are winless (0-4-1), they lead in first downs (108-88) and total yards (1769-1751).

Amazingly, only three Big Ten teams finished with winning records — UM, OSU and Illinois. All three went bowling.

The Illini lost to Hawaii 27-17 in the Holiday, and the Buckeyes lost to Georgia 21-14 in the Citrus, but the Wolverines captured a 38-31 thriller from Washington in the Rose.

The *AP* had the Wolverines and Buckeyes pegged just about right that year.

UM began the season ranked fifth behind Miami, Washington, Florida State and Notre Dame. And, with an odd 9-0-3 record, finished fifth behind Alabama, Miami, Florida State and Notre Dame.

OSU started out 17th and, with an 8-3-1 record, finished 18th.

1993

OHHH, NO, OHIO!

Nationally, Michigan finished fifth last January and began in September as the third-ranked team. Ohio State ended 18th and started out 18th.

So, nothing had changed among the two camps. It was the same song that had been sung for the past several seasons.

Three months later....

The Bucks ranked fifth in the land and were just 60 minutes away from a Big Ten title and Rose Bowl bid.

The Blue was 60 minutes away from being kicked 60 feet under and forgotten as blatant underachievers.

For the first time in 40 years there was a change in Big Ten football, as Penn State was officially included as the 11th member. But the league's lords decided to keep the proud old "Big Ten" name. And well they should. A designer took care of the unusual situation by cleverly incorporating an optical illusion "11" inside the association's logo.

The presidents of the 10 conference schools and the president of Penn State (along with Joe Paterno) hurriedly put together the merger. However, the great majority of the Big Ten athletic directors and head coaches were incensed over the move — particularly since they were never consulted.

Paterno was determined, one way or the other, to play in a Rose Bowl.

To the absolute delight of the Big Ten's "old guard," both Michigan and Ohio State welcomed the Nittany Lions aboard with solid victories.

OSU opened with wins over Rice, Washington and Pittsburgh and, just like that, jumped all the way to No. 7. Then came victories over Northwestern, Illinois and Michigan State, and a No.

442

3 ranking behind the nation's '93 glamour teams, Florida State and Notre Dame.

It was the Bucks' highest poll order in nine years, retreating back to the Earle Bruce days of October 1, 1984, and a No. 2 ranking behind Texas.

After popping Penn State, the Buckeyes hopped off to Madison, suffered a 14-all tie with Wisconsin, and dropped a couple of notches to fifth. They remained there after beating Indiana.

"We want the Wolverines! We want the Wolverines! We...."

Things weren't going the Wolverines' way.

They wasted Washington State 41-14 in a preliminary to the main event — No. 3 Michigan versus No. 7 Notre Dame at Ann Arbor — and the Irish plundered still another Michigan grid season. The score was 27-23, that close only because of a UM touchdown in the final seconds.

Since these grid giants resumed their series in 1978, Michigan is 5-8-1. Three games (1979-80-88) were settled on the *final* play. Notre Dame won all three. In 1989, UM held ND to only 226 yards, but the Irish returned two kickoffs for touchdowns and won 24-19. In 1990 and 1992, the Wolverines carried 10-point leads into the fourth quarter — and won neither (0-1-1).

Of the 25 games scattered over a 106-year period, Michigan leads the series 14-10-1.

Coach Gary Moeller and his staff undertook the struggle of mending the damage and later defeated Houston, Iowa, Penn State (at Happy Valley, no less), Purdue and Minnesota, but thrown in were losses to the Spartans, Illinois and Wisconsin.

Wisconsin? It was UM's first loss to the Badgers in 12 years and only the second in 31 years (24 games).

The Big Ten's final week had the Buckeyes at 6-0-1, surprising Wisconsin 5-1-1, then Illinois and Penn State at 5-2-0. UM and the Spartans were tied for fifth with 4-3-0 records.

It was now time for "The Big One" — for the 90th time.

Fifth-ranked Ohio State was 9-0-1 by an average score of 32-14. Unranked Michigan was 6-4-0 by an average of 27-15.

Michigan was officially a 1½-point favorite. What?

On Wednesday, Bob Baptist of *The Columbus Dispatch* got a few reactions from around the country.

Malcolm Moran of *The New York Times* told Baptist, "If I

Sports

OSU can fulfill its Rose Bowl dream

The Atlanta Journal / The Atlanta Constitution

Ohio St. stumbles on Rose run

Buckeyes' day and maybe their dream season spoiled in 28-0 whitewashing by Michigan

---

The Columbus Dispatch
Sunday
NOVEMBER 21, 1993

Sports

SECTION **E**

Michigan won all categories, Cooper says

By George Strode
News + Sports Editor

ANN ARBOR, Mich. — Coach John Cooper said Ohio State was out-coached, out and flat in its 28-0 loss to Michigan yesterday.

"How can you be overconfident when you're playing Michigan?" he said.

"If they had played all season the way they did today, maybe they would have won the championship again."

Instead, Ohio State has at least a share of the Big Ten title and most of a trip to the Rose Bowl if Michigan State beats Iowa or Wisconsin or loses to Penn State.

"We're the Buckeyes for 'Big Daddy.' The Wolverines said no, Cooper wouldn't come out.

"I don't think we were flat. You guys have a tendency when a team gets beat to say that team was flat, that team won't ready to play. I don't believe in that," Cooper said.

He was asked what a fifth loss to Michigan in six as Ohio State years did to the season. The Buckeyes tied the Wolverines 13-13 last year.

"It leaves a lot of danger of our season," Cooper said. "We've had a great year. We actually haven't had a fantastic season.

"We were in a posture to have a Cinderella-type season. We let it slip away. I don't think you have a great season at Ohio State when you get beat 28-0 at Michigan."

He said he was shocked by the margin.

"If you had told me we were going to get beat 28-0, I'd probably have stayed home," he said. "I'm still proud of the team. You're not going to get me to bad-mouth the players. They've had a great year."

Asked whether he is a snake-bitten against Michigan, Cooper said, "I don't know if snake-bit is the right word," he said. "It's

Michigan gives OSU a goose egg

Buckeyes' frustration against Wolverines continues in 28-0 loss

By Tim May
Dispatch Sports Reporter

ANN ARBOR, Mich. — Some days, it just isn't meant to be.

Ohio State had one of those days yesterday, the only one, really, of this football season. Talk about bad timing.

Michigan 28, Ohio State 0.

The streak continues. That's six straight times the Buckeyes have left the 90-game rivalry without a win. However, they did leave yesterday with a souvenir and a great big kind upside their head.

"We were outplayed in every way," an obviously dejected OSU coach John Cooper said.

Six times he's gone against the Wolverines as head coach at OSU, and only last year's 13-13 tie is an upward blip on the chart. Yesterday, he'd have taken a tie, no doubt, over what happened. Even a tie would have put the Buckeyes (9-1-1) in the Rose Bowl for the first time in nine years.

■ OSU flat, Wolverines says / 6E
■ Michigan kind of cocky / 7E
■ OSU-UM photos on page / 8E
■ Buckeyes have bowl options / 9E

Instead, they were shut out for the first time since Wisconsin turned the trick 6-0 in the fifth game of the 1982 season. They were shut out by Michigan for the first time since a 22-0 loss in 1976. The 28-point deficit was the same as in the 31-3 defeat in Ann Arbor two years ago.

Now it's going to take a win or a tie by Michigan State against Wisconsin (8-1-1, 3-1) on Dec. 4 in Tokyo to send the Buckeyes to the Rose Bowl. Illinois could have done it yesterday, but the Buckeyes prevailed 30-10.

Wherever the Buckeyes end up for the holidays, more from the canvas after that knockout yesterday might be the toughest chore. Michigan (7-4, 5-3), entering the repeat game-season finale with as many as four losses for the first time since 1984, the record

Mike Burch (7) of Michigan leaps to knock down a pass intended for Joey Galloway of Ohio State.

Fred Squillante / Dispatch

Old nemesis leaves Cooper red-faced

were setting the line according to how I felt about the relative strengths of the two teams, I would make Ohio State a fairly serious favorite. But I wouldn't go overboard, because of where the game is being played. I think there is a sentiment out there that despite all the things that have happened to Michigan, they have one blast left."

Moran picked the Buckeyes, 21-17.

Ed Sherman of the *Chicago Tribune* said, "My bottom line is that Ohio State will be the more uptight team with the Rose Bowl and (John) Cooper's winless streak on the line. It just seems that Michigan has a little voo-doo on Ohio State. You've probably got to say Michigan has the edge until Ohio State beats them."

Sherman picked the Wolverines, 20-17.

Baptist also got predictions from:

Ivan Maisel, *Dallas Morning News* — OSU, 19-14.

Gene Wojciechowski, *Los Angeles Times* — OSU, 20-17.

Austin Murphy, *Sports Illustrated* — OSU, 24-21.

Mike Lopresti, *Gannett News Service* — OSU, 21-17.

Time for talk had run out.

It was November 20 and what an explosive Saturday afternoon of college football it would turn out to be.

An NCAA-record crowd of 106,867 jammed the big bowl and countless more looked on in disbelief via ABC-TV as Michigan bushwhacked the befuddled Bucks by a 28-0 count.

The first score came about nine minutes into the game with an 81-yard drive in only five plays, keyed by Tyrone Wheatley's 43-yard blast and capped by an "impossible" reception by Mercury Hayes.

From the Ohio 25, QB Todd Collins lofted one towards a streaking Hayes, who made a diving, twisting, over-the-shoulder grab before landing hard in the endzone. Peter Elezovic converted and it was 7-0, and counting.

Michigan added two more touchdowns in the second period.

After UM's Ty Law intercepted a Bret Powers pass to stop a serious Buckeye surge at the five, the Wolverines staged another five-play series, this one covering 95 yards. From midfield, Collins faked an end-around, then drilled a long one down the middle that a diving Derrick Alexander snagged at the one. Jon Ritchie scored a play later. With 5:30 left, Elezovic's kick was good.

Two drives, 10 plays, 176 yards.

TYRONE WHEATLEY

ED BECK

In three games (1991-92-93) against Ohio State, Wheatley rushed 47 times for 285 yards (6.1 average). Beck scored Michigan's 200th touchdown against the Buckeyes in the '93 game at Ann Arbor. UM's 100th series TD was scored by Vincent Mroz on a 10-yard pass from Jack Wink 50 years earlier to the day — November 20, 1943 — also at Ann Arbor.

More bad Buck luck. Chuck Winters picked off another Powers' pass and returned 19 yards to the OSU 31. On third-and-nine, Collins found his "Mercury Man" for 10 yards to the 20. Ed Davis, on a draw, drove down to the seven, a penalty moved it to the three, and Collins pitched one to Che' Foster for the TD. Elezovic converted.

Halftime: 21-0. The big ol' blue stadium was buzzing. But for the band of Buckeyes who journeyed up, their much-anticipated Rose Bowl preview had turned into a house of horrors.

Early in the third period, OSU punter Tim Williams dropped to one knee to field a low snap. He kicked it anyway, but of course it didn't count, and Michigan took possession at the Ohio 32.

It was that kind of day for the visitors....

On first down, Alexander, on a reverse, circled for 16 yards to the 16, fumbled the football, but it bounced right back his way, and he gained another five yards down to the 11. On third down from the five, Ed Davis notched Michigan's 200th series touchdown. Elezovic's conversion concluded the Wolverines' afternoon of frolic.

Final score, 28-0, as OSU absorbed its first shutout in 11 years (6-0 to Wisconsin in 1982), and their first to UM in 17 years (22-0 in 1976).

Actually, Ohio State still had a chance at the Rose Bowl, even after it was announced that Wisconsin had beaten Illinois 35-10. The conference's two top teams were now the Bucks (6-1-1) and Badgers (5-1-1). But everybody would have to wait another two weeks for the Pasadena Sweepstakes outcome.

Officials at Wisconsin and Michigan State had agreed to switch their original October 2 date to December 4 (or was it the 5th?) and the site from Madison, USA, to Tokyo, Japan — all in the name of ESPN-TV.

The Badgers were most impressive in a 40-21 win. That meant a tie for the conference title, but they got the bonus on the basis that OSU had been to Pasadena since UW.

A Rose Bowl berth decided some 6,000 miles from the Rose Bowl? Wisconsin a Big Ten co-champion? Both were rare.

The Badgers had not seen the Rose Bowl in 31 years and, furthermore, the eight seasons leading up to this one had produced a miserable 12-52-0 (.188) league record and 25-64-0 overall (.281).

Barry Alvarez had pulled off a coaching miracle. Hats off to the big fellow.

Back to that drama-filled November 20.

■ Top-ranked Notre Dame was astounded beyond words when Dave Gordon of Boston College (17th) kicked a 41-yard field goal on the game's final play to edge the Irish 41-39, costing them a national championship.

■ Probation-shackled Auburn (6th) defeated Alabama (11th) 22-14 to conclude an unbelievable 11-0-0 season.

■ West Virginia (9th) surprised Miami (4th) 17-14.

■ UCLA (16th) dramatically got past USC (22nd) to cinch a Rose Bowl spot of its own. The Trojans were first-and-goal at the three-yard line, but the Bruins held on and escaped with a 27-21 victory. A USC win would have sent Arizona to Pasadena.

■ Then, of course, there was Ohio State losing to Michigan by the unlikely 28-0 score.

In that game, UM led 22-14 in first downs, 281-58 in rushing yards, 421-212 in total yards, 45-19 in penalty yards, and 36-24 in possession minutes. OSU led 154-140 in passing yards and 4-0 in turnovers (all interceptions).

The leading rushers were UM's Tyrone Wheatley (106 yards in 16 carries) and Ed Davis (96 yards in 22 attempts).

Three times (1974-82-83) the Southeastern Conference sent seven teams bowling and the Big Ten matched that NCAA record in 1993. Which teams *failed?* Illinois, Minnesota, Purdue and Northwestern.

Even though the Buckeyes got a bowl trip to southern California, it definitely wasn't what they had in mind in late November. San Diego's Jack Murphy Stadium just isn't the same as Pasadena's Rose Bowl.

The Big Ten bowl season unfolded....

Liberty — Louisville 18, Michigan State 7.

Holiday — Ohio State 28, Brigham Young 21.

Independence — Virginia Tech 45, Indiana 20.

Alamo — California 37, Iowa 3.

Hall of Fame — Michigan 42, N.C. State 7.

Citrus — Penn State 31, Tennessee 13.

Rose — Wisconsin 21, UCLA 16.

It came out a successful 4-3-0. But the best news (by far) emerging from post-season play was the Big Ten's second straight

In Gary Moeller's first four years as UM coach, the Wolverines posted a 36-9-3 (.781) record, including a 3-0-1 against Ohio State.

triumph over the Pac-10 in the Rose Bowl. Since their pact following the 1946 season, it's all even at 24 wins apiece, while the Big Ten leads in scoring 960-900.

Even though Ohio State's 10-1-1 finish was its best in 14 years, the way it turned out had to be a bitter disappointment to the Buckeye team and its boosters. Just ask 'em.

Michigan was 8-4-0.

Florida State won the national title, followed by Notre Dame, Nebraska, Auburn, Florida and Wisconsin. Ohio State was 11th, Michigan 21st.

Michigan versus Ohio State continues as one of the nation's premier intercollegiate football rivalries.

Michigan dominated the early games, but over the last 75 years the series has been close. Since 1918, UM has won 38, OSU 33, and four have ended all even.

Overall, Michigan leads 51-33-6 in games and 1,460-1,009 in scoring.

Some years its the Wolverines. Other years its the Buckeyes. But every year it's *something* to see.

Michigan versus Ohio State.....Ohio State versus Michigan. Either way, it's "The Big One." The *real* Big One.

APPENDIX
Records Section

THE MICHIGAN-OHIO STATE FOOTBALL SERIES, 1897-1993

G	YEAR	DATE	AT	*M-REC	*OSU-REC	WINNER	SCORE	SERIES
1	1897	Oct 16	AA	1-0-1	1-1-0	M.......34--0		1-0-0
	1898-1899 - No games							
2	1900	Nov 24	AA	7-1-0	7-1-0	tie......0--0		1-0-1
3	1901	Nov 9	COL	5-0-0	4-0-1	M.......21--0		2-0-1
4	1902	Oct 25	AA	5-0-0	4-0-0	M.......86--0		3-0-1
5	1903	Nov 7	AA	7-0-1	6-1-0	M.......36--0		4-0-1
6	1904	Oct 15	COL	4-0-0	4-0-0	M.......31--6		5-0-1
7	1905	Nov 11	AA	9-0-0	6-0-2	M.......40--0		6-0-1
8	1906	Oct 20	COL	1-0-0	3-0-0	M........6--0		7-0-1
9	1907	Oct 26	AA	3-0-0	3-0-1	M.......22--0		8-0-1
10	1908	Oct 24	COL	2-0-1	2-2-0	M.......10--6		9-0-1
11	1909	Oct 16	AA	1-0-0	3-0-0	M.......33--6		10-0-1
12	1910	Oct 22	COL	1-0-1	4-0-0	tie......3--3		10-0-2
13	1911	Oct 21	AA	2-0-0	2-0-1	M.......19--0		11-0-2
14	1912	Oct 19	COL	2-0-0	2-0-0	M.......14--0		12-0-2
	1913-1917 - No games							
15	1918	Nov 30	COL	4-0-0	2-0-0	M.......14--0		13-0-2
16	1919	Oct 25	AA	2-0-0	3-0-0	OSU......3-13		13-1-2
17	1920	Nov 6	COL	3-0-1	5-0-0	OSU......7-14		13-2-2
18	1921	Oct 22	AA	3-0-0	2-1-0	OSU......0-14		13-3-2
19	x1922	Oct 21	COL	1-0-1	2-0-0	M.......19--0		14-3-2
20	1923	Oct 20	AA	2-0-0	1-0-1	M.......23--0		15-3-2
21	1924	Nov 15	COL	5-1-0	2-1-3	M.......16--6		16-3-2
22	1925	Nov 14	AA	5-0-1	4-1-1	M.......10--0		17-3-2
23	1926	Nov 13	COL	5-1-0	6-0-0	M.......17-16		18-3-2
24	y1927	Oct 22	AA	3-0-0	2-1-0	M.......21--0		19-3-2
25	1928	Oct 20	COL	0-2-0	3-0-0	OSU......7-19		19-4-2
26	1929	Oct 19	AA	3-1-0	2-0-0	OSU......0--7		19-5-2
27	1930	Oct 18	COL	3-0-1	2-1-0	M.......13--0		20-5-2
28	1931	Oct 17	AA	3-0-0	1-1-0	OSU......7-20		20-6-2
29	1932	Oct 15	COL	2-0-0	1-0-1	M.......14--0		21-6-2
30	1933	Oct 21	AA	2-0-0	2-0-0	M.......13--0		22-6-2
31	1934	Nov 17	COL	1-5-0	4-1-0	OSU......0-34		22-7-2
32	z1935	Nov 23	AA	4-3-0	6-1-0	OSU......0-38		22-8-2
33	1936	Nov 21	COL	1-6-0	3-3-0	OSU......0-21		22-9-2
34	1937	Nov 20	AA	4-3-0	5-2-0	OSU......0-21		22-10-2
35	1938	Nov 19	COL	5-1-1	4-2-1	M.......18--0		23-10-2
36	1939	Nov 25	AA	5-2-0	6-1-0	M.......21-14		24-10-2
37	1940	Nov 23	COL	6-1-0	4-3-0	M.......40--0		25-10-2
38	1941	Nov 22	AA	6-1-0	6-1-0	tie.....20-20		25-10-3
39	1942	Nov 21	COL	6-2-0	7-1-0	OSU......7-21		25-11-3
40	1943	Nov 20	AA	7-1-0	3-5-0	M.......45--7		26-11-3
41	1944	Nov 25	COL	8-1-0	8-0-0	OSU.....14-18		26-12-3
42	1945	Nov 24	AA	6-3-0	7-1-0	M........7--3		27-12-3
43	1946	Nov 23	COL	5-2-1	4-2-2	M.......58--6		28-12-3
44	1947	Nov 22	AA	8-0-0	2-5-1	M.......21--0		29-12-3
45	1948	Nov 20	COL	8-0-0	6-2-0	M.......13--3		30-12-3
46	1949	Nov 19	AA	6-2-0	6-1-1	tie......7--7		30-12-4
47	1950	Nov 25	COL	4-3-1	6-2-0	M........9--3		31-12-4

G	YEAR	DATE	AT	*M-REC	*OSU-TRC	WINNER	SCORE	SERIES
48	1951	Nov 24	AA	3-5-0	4-2-2	M. 7--0		32-12-4
49	1952	Nov 22	COL	5-3-0	5-3-0	OSU. 7-27		32-13-4
50	1953	Nov 21	AA	5-3-0	6-2-0	M. 20--0		33-13-4
51	1954	Nov 20	COL	6-2-0	8-0-0	OSU. 7-21		33-14-4
52	1955	Nov 19	AA	7-1-0	6-2-0	OSU. 0-17		33-15-4
53	1956	Nov 24	COL	6-2-0	6-2-0	M. 19--0		34-15-4
54	1957	Nov 23	AA	5-2-1	7-1-0	OSU. 14-31		34-16-4
55	1958	Nov 22	COL	2-5-1	5-1-2	OSU. 14-20		34-17-4
56	1959	Nov 21	AA	3-5-0	3-4-1	M. 23-14		35-17-4
57	1960	Nov 19	COL	5-3-0	6-2-0	OSU. 0--7		35-18-4
58	1961	Nov 25	AA	6-2-0	7-0-1	OSU. 20-50		35-19-4
59	1962	Nov 24	COL	2-6-0	5-3-0	OSU. 0-28		35-20-4
60	1963	Nov 30	AA	3-3-2	4-3-1	OSU. 10-14		35-21-4
61	1964	Nov 21	COL	7-1-0	7-1-0	M. 10--0		36-21-4
62	1965	Nov 20	AA	4-5-0	6-2-0	OSU. 7--9		36-22-4
63	1966	Nov 19	COL	5-4-0	4-4-0	M. 17--3		37-22-4
64	1967	Nov 25	AA	4-5-0	5-3-0	OSU. 14-24		37-23-4
65	1968	Nov 23	COL	8-1-0	8-0-0	OSU. 14-50		37-24-4
66	1969	Nov 22	AA	7-2-0	8-0-0	M. . . . . . .:.24-12		38-24-4
67	1970	Nov 21	COL	9-0-0	8-0-0	OSU. 9-20		38-25-4
68	1971	Nov 20	AA	10-0-0	6-3-0	M. 10--7		39-25-4
69	1972	Nov 25	COL	10-0-0	8-1-0	OSU. 11-14		39-26-4
70	1973	Nov 24	AA	10-0-0	9-0-0	tie. 10-10		39-26-5
71	1974	Nov 23	COL	10-0-0	9-1-0	OSU. 10-12		39-27-5
72	1975	Nov 22	AA	8-0-2	10-0-0	OSU. 14-21		39-28-5
73	1976	Nov 20	COL	9-1-0	8-1-1	M. 22--0		40-28-5
74	1977	Nov 19	AA	9-1-0	9-1-0	M. 14--6		41-28-5
75	1978	Nov 25	COL	9-1-0	7-2-1	M. 14--3		42-28-5
76	1979	Nov 17	AA	8-2-0	10-0-0	OSU. 15-18		42-29-5
77	1980	Nov 22	COL	8-2-0	9-1-0	M. 9--3		43-29-5
78	1981	Nov 21	AA	8-2-0	7-3-0	OSU. 9-14		43-30-5
79	1982	Nov 20	COL	8-2-0	7-3-0	OSU. 14-24		43-31-5
80	1983	Nov 19	AA	8-2-0	8-2-0	M. 24-21		44-31-5
81	1984	Nov 17	COL	6-4-0	8-2-0	OSU. 6-21		44-32-5
82	1985	Nov 23	AA	8-1-1	8-2-0	M. 27-17		45-32-5
83	1986	Nov 22	COL	9-1-0	9-2-0	M. 26-24		46-32-5
84	1987	Nov 21	AA	7-3-0	5-4-1	OSU. 20-23		46-33-5
85	1988	Nov 19	COL	7-2-1	4-5-1	M. 34-31		47-33-5
86	1989	Nov 25	AA	9-1-0	8-2-0	M. 28-18		48-33-5
87	1990	Nov 24	COL	7-3-0	7-2-1	M. 16-13		49-33-5
88	1991	Nov 23	AA	9-1-0	8-2-0	M. 31--3		50-33-5
89	1992	Nov 21	COL	8-0-2	8-2-0	tie. 13-13		50-33-6
90	1993	Nov 20	AA	6-4-0	9-0-1	M. 28--0		51-33-6

*Records at game time.
xFirst series game at Ohio Stadium.
yFirst series game at Michigan Stadium.
zSeries began what is now the season-ending tradition.

OSU's all-time record at series time is 477-120-29, .785.
 UM's all-time record at series time is 479-135-21, .771.

MICHIGAN VS. OHIO STATE AT:

ANN ARBOR	G	W	L	T	UM–OSU	AVG
Regents Field.........5		4	0	1	196---0	37--0
Ferry Field...........7		5	2	0	110--33	16--5
Michigan Stadium.....34		17	14	3	531-466	16-14
TOTALS..............46		26	16	4	837-499	18-11

COLUMBUS	G	W	L	T	UM–OSU	AVG
Ohio Field............8		6	1	1	106-29	13--4
Ohio Stadium........36		19	16	1	517-481	14-13
TOTALS..............44		25	17	2	623-510	14-12

SERIES TOTALS........90		51	33	6	1460–1009	16–11

SCORING BREAKDOWN, 1897-1993

	MICHIGAN			OHIO STATE		
4-point touchdowns..............6	for	24	pts	0	for	0 pts
5-point touchdowns.............47	for	235	pts	3	for	15 pts
6-point touchdowns............147	for	882	pts	130	for	780 pts
2-point kick conversions........5	for	10	pts	0	for	0 pts
1-point kick conversions......149	for	149	pts	93	for	93 pts
2-point run/pass conversions....5	for	10	pts	3	for	6 pts
4-point field goals.............5	for	20	pts	0	for	0 pts
3-point field goals............42	for	126	pts	37	for	111 pts
Safeties.......................2	for	4	pts	2	for	4 pts
TOTALS.................................1,460 PTS						1009 PTS

Michigan has scored 200 touchdowns, Ohio State 133.

SCORE BY QUARTERS

Games 1-11 (game divided into two halves)
```
MICHIGAN.....................185    134 - 319
OHIO STATE...................  6     12 -  18
```

Games 12-90 (game divided into four quarters)
```
MICHIGAN.......217   366   260   298 - 1141
OHIO STATE......199   247   211   334 -  991
```

UM has scored 768 points in the first half and 692 in the second half. OSU is 452-557. Of the series' 2,469 points, 1,220 have been scored in the first half (49%) and 1,249 in the second half (51%).

The last 79 games of the series (since 1910) have been played on the quarter system (316 quarters). UM has scored in 142 quarters (45%) and held scoreless 174 times. OSU is 131-185 (41%).

"THE 20-POINT CLUB"

Players who have scored at least 20 points in the series.

PLAYER-TEAM	TD	PAT	FG	TOTAL	YEAR(S)
Tom Harmon, UM	5	7	0	37	1938-39-40
Keith Byars, OSU	6	0	0	36	1983-84-85
A.E. Herrnstein, UM	6	0	0	30*	1902
Bob Ferguson, OSU	5	0	0	30	1960-61
Jim Otis, OSU	5	0	0	30	1968-69
David Allerdice, UM	2	6	4	29*	1907-08-09
Tom Hammond, UM	0	14	3	26*	1903-04-05
Mike Gillette, UM	0	8	6	26	1986-87-88
Bill Heston, UM	5	0	0	25*	1901-02-04
Herbert Graver, UM	5	0	0	25*	1903
Les Horvath, OSU	4	0	0	24	1943-44
Pete Johnson, OSU	4	0	0	24	1973-75
Leroy Hoard, UM	4	0	0	24	1987-88-89
Harry Kipke, UM	3	0	1	21	1922-23
Louis Gilbert, UM	3	3	0	21	1927
John Carlson, UM	0	9	4	21	1989-90-91
Roosevelt Smith, UM	3	1**	0	20	1977-78-79

*By today's point standards, Herrnstein would have scored 36 points, Allerdice 30, Heston 30, Graver 30 and Hammond 23.
**2-point conversion.

LONG SCORING PLAYS (50 yards or more)

RANK	YARDS	PLAYER-TEAM	YEAR	TYPE OF PLAY
1	113*	Alfred Barlow, UM	1905	Returned missed field goal
2	93	Desmond Howard, UM	1991	Punt return
3	90	David Ramsey, UM	1961	Kickoff return
4	85	Millard Gibson, UM	1908	Run off fake punt
4	85	Tom Campana, OSU	1971	Punt return
6	81	Paul Kromer, UM	1940	Punt return
7	80	Bob Klein, OSU	1961	Pass from Joe Sparma
8	77	John Kolesar, UM	1985	Pass from Jim Harbaugh
9	70	Bill Heston, UM	1902	Run from scrimmage
9	70	Carlos Snow, OSU	1987	Pass from Tom Tupa
11	69	Paul Warfield, OSU	1961	Run from scrimmage
12	67	Triando Markray, UM	1983	Pass from Steve Smith
13	65	Tippy Dye, OSU	1935	Punt return
14	62	Harold Cunningham, OSU	1924	Pass from Bill Hunt
15	60	Merle Wendt, OSU	1934	Pass from Frank Fisch
15	60	Bob Shaw, OSU	1942	Pass from Paul Sarringhaus
15	60	Rodney Swinehart, OSU	1946	Pass from Fran Doolittle
18	59	Anthony Carter, UM	1979	Pass from John Wangler
19	57	Greg McMurty, UM	1988	Pass from Demetrius Brown
20	52	Richard Fisher, OSU	1941	Pass from Jack Graf

*Playing field was 110 yards long.

Each team has 10 long scoring plays.

Amazingly, only two of the long scoring plays are runs from scrimmage (1902 and 1961).

SERIES TOUCHDOWN PASSES

NO.	YEAR	PASSER-RECEIVER	TEAM	YARDS
1	1907	Bill Wasmund - Paul Magoffin............Michigan		25
2	1918	Frank Steketee - Robert Dunne..........Michigan		10
3	1923	Irwin Uteritz - Herbert Steger.........Michigan		25
4	"	Irwin Uteritz - Harry Kipke............Michigan		32
5	1924	Bill Hunt - Harold Cunningham..........Ohio State		62
6	1926	Benny Friedman - Bennie Oosterbaan.....Michigan		7
7	"	Bennie Oosterbaan - Leo Hoffman........Michigan		8
8	1927	Bennie Oosterbaan - Lewis Gilbert......Michigan		45
9	"	Bennie Oosterbaan - Lewis Gilbert......Michigan		40
10	"	Bennie Oosterbaan - Lewis Gilbert......Michigan		13
11	1928	Alan Holman - Wes Fesler...............Ohio State		16
12	"	Alan Holman - Charles Coffee...........Ohio State		27
13	1929	Alan Holman - Wes Fesler...............Ohio State		22
14	1932	Harry Newman - John Regeczi............Michigan		10
15	"	Harry Newman - Ivan Williamson.........Michigan		40
16	1934	Frank Fisch - Merl Wendt...............Ohio State		60
17	"	Tippy Dye - Frank Cumiskey.............Ohio State		20
18	1935	Matt Patenelli - John Bettridge........Ohio State		8
19	1936	Tippy Dye - Frank Cumiskey.............Ohio State		14
20	"	Tippy Dye - John Rabb..................Ohio State		31
21	1937	Nick Wasylik - James Miller............Ohio State		4
22	"	Nick Wasylik - Richard Nardi...........Ohio State		4
23	1938	Tom Harmom - Ben Frutig................Michigan		15
24	1939	Don Scott - Vic Marino.................Ohio State		5
25	"	Don Scott - Frank Clair................Ohio State		18
26	"	Tom Harmon - Frank Evashevski...... ...Michigan		4
27	1940	Tom Harmon - Frank Evashevski..........Michigan		17
28	"	Tom Harmon - Ben Frutig................Michigan		16
29	1941	Tom Kuzma - Harlin Fraumann............Michigan		19
30	"	Jack Graf - Richard Fisher.............Ohio State		52
31	1942	Paul Sarringhaus - Les Horvath.........Ohio State		15
32	"	Paul Sarringhaus - Bob Shaw............Ohio State		60
33	"	Paul Sarringhaus - Les Horvath.........Ohio State		33
34	1943	Jack Wink - Vincent Mroz...............Michigan		10
35	1946	Bob Chappuis - Bob Mann................Michigan		16
36	"	Bob Chappuis - John White..............Michigan		32
37	"	Bill Culligan - Richard Rifenburg......Michigan		40
38	"	Fran Doolittle - Rodney Swinehart......Ohio State		60
39	1948	Charles Ortmann - Harry Allis..........Michigan		44
40	1949	Walter Teninga - Leo Koceski...........Michigan		15
41	1952	John Borton - Bob Joslin...............Ohio State		8
42	"	John Borton - Bob Joslin...............Ohio State		28
43	"	John Borton - Bob Grimes...............Ohio State		19
44	1954	Bill Legitt - Fred Kriss...............Ohio State		15
45	"	Bill Legitt - Carl Brubaker............Ohio State		9
46	1956	James VanPelt - Terry Barr.............Michigan		21
47	1957	James VanPelt - Bradley Myers..........Michigan		28
48	1958	Robert Ptacek - Gary Prahst............Michigan		7
49	"	Robert Ptacek - Gary Phahst............Michigan		32

TOUCHDOWN PASSES (continued)

NO.	YEAR	PASSER-RECEIVER	TEAM	YARDS
50	"	Jerry Fields - James Herbstreit.........Ohio State		15
51	1959	Stan Noskin - Darrell Harper...........Michigan		9
52	"	Roger Detrick - James Houston..........Ohio State		2*
53	1961	Joe Sparma - Bob Klein.................Ohio State		80**
54	"	Joe Sparma - Sam Tidmore...............Ohio State		10
55	1963	Don Unverfeth - Paul Warfield..........Ohio State		35
56	1964	Bob Timberlake - James Detwiler........Michigan		17
57	1965	Don Unverfeth - Billy Anders..........Ohio State		5
58	1966	Dick Vidmer - Clayton Wihite...........Michigan		23
59	1967	Dennis Brown - James Berline...........Michigan		13
60	"	Dennis Brown - John Gabler.............Michigan		13
61	1969	Rex Kern - Stan White..................Ohio State		22
62	1970	Rex Kern - Bruce Jankowski.............Ohio State		26
63	"	Don Moorhead - Paul Staroba............Michigan		13
64	1974	Dennis Franklin - Gil Chapman..........Michigan		42
65	1975	Cornlius Greene - Pete Johnson.........Ohio State		7
66	"	Gordon Bell - Roosevelt Smith..........Michigan		11
67	1978	Rick Leach - Rodney Feaster............Michigan		30
68	"	Rick Leach - Jim Smith.................Michigan		11
69	1979	John Wangler - Anthony Carter..........Michigan		59
70	"	Art Schlichter - Charles Hunter........Ohio State		18
71	1980	John Wangler - Anthony Carter..........Michigan		13
72	1983	Steve Smith - Triando Markray..........Michigan		67
73	"	Steve Smith - Eric Kattus..............Michigan		8
74	"	Mike Tomczak - Cedric Anderson.........Ohio State		32
75	1985	Jim Harbaugh - Gerald White............Michigan		4
76	"	Jim Harbaugh - Eric Kattus.............Michigan		5
77	"	Jim Karsatos - Chris Carter............Ohio State		36
78	"	Jim Harbaugh - John Kolesar............Michigan		77
79	1986	Jim Karsatos - Chris Carter............Ohio State		4
80	"	Jim Karsatos - Chris Carter............Ohio State		17
81	1987	Tom Tupa - Everrette Ross..............Ohio State		4
82	"	Tom Tupa - Carlos Snow.................Ohio State		70
83	1988	Demetrius Brown - Greg McMurtry........Michigan		57
84	"	Greg Frey - Bobby Olive................Ohio State		14
85	"	Demetrius Brown - John Kolesar.........Michigan		41
86	1989	Mike Taylor - Jarrod Bunch.............Michigan		5
87	1990	Greg Frey - Jeff Graham................Ohio State		12
88	"	Elvis Grbac - Desmond Howard...........Michigan		12
89	1992	Kirk Herbstreit - Greg Beatty..........Ohio State		5
90	1993	Todd Collins - Mercury Hayes...........Michigan		25
91	"	Todd Collins - Che' Foster.............Michigan		3

*Shortest. **Longest.
UM has 49 TD passses (average 23 yards), OSU 42 (average 24 yards). The five longest are: 80 yards (1961), 77 yards (1985), 70 yards (1987), 67 yards (1983), and 62 yards (1924).
Bennie Oosterbaan (1926-27) and Tom Harmon (1938-39-40) have thrown the most TD passes (4).

SERIES FIELD GOALS

NO.	YEAR	PLAYER	TEAM	YARDS
1	1904	Tom Hammond	Michigan	32
2	"	Tom Hammond	Michigan	25
3	1905	Tom Hammond	Michigan	20
4	1906	John Garrels	Michigan	36
5	1908	David Allerdice	Michigan	38
6	1909	David Allerdice	Michigan	25
7	"	David Allerdice	Michigan	*
8	"	David Allerdice	Michigan	*
9	1910	Fred Conklin	Michigan	23
10	"	Leslie Wells	Ohio State	23
11	1911	Thomas Bogie	Michigan	26
12	1919	Cliff Sparks	Michigan	37
13	1922	Paul Goebel	Michigan	30
14	"	Harry Kipke	Michigan	37
15	1923	Jack Blott	Michigan	17
16	1924	R.A. Rockwell	Michigan	40
17	1925	Ben Friedman	Michigan	38
18	1926	Myers Clark	Ohio State	6
19	"	Ben Friedman	Michigan	42
20	1936	William Booth	Ohio State	19
21	1945	Max Schnittker	Ohio State	30
22	1946	James Brieske	Michigan	*
23	1948	Leslie Hague	Ohio State	30
24	1950	Vic Janowicz	Ohio State	37
25	1955	Fred Kriss	Ohio State	24
26	1957	Don Sutherin	Ohio State	33
27	1959	Darrell Harper	Michigan	29
28	1963	Bob Timberlake	Michigan	28
29	1964	Bob Timberlake	Michigan	26
30	1965	Bob Funk	Ohio State	28
31	1966	Richard Sygar	Michigan	24
32	"	Gary Cairns	Ohio State	26
33	1967	Gary Cairns	Ohio State	37
34	1968	Nick Roman	Ohio State	32
35	1969	Tim Killion	Michigan	25
36	1970	Fred Schram	Ohio State	28
37	"	Dana Coin	Michigan	31
38	"	Fred Schram	Ohio State	27
39	"	Dana Coin	Michigan	28
40	1972	Mike Lantry	Michigan	35
41	1973	Blair Conway	Ohio State	35
42	"	Mike Lantry	Michigan	30
43	"	Mike Lantry	Michigan	37
44	1974	Tom Klaban	Ohio State	47
45	"	Tom Klaban	Ohio State	25
46	"	Tom Klaban	Ohio State	43
47	"	Tom Klaban	Ohio State	45
48	1977	Vlade Janakievski	Ohio State	29
49	"	Vlade Janakievski	Ohio State	44

FIELD GOALS (continued)

NO.	YEAR	PLAYER	TEAM	YARDS
50	1978	Bob Atha..................Ohio State		29
51	1979	Vlade Janakievski........Ohio State		23
52	"	Vlade Janakievski........Ohio State		25
53	1980	Vlade Janakievski........Ohio State		40
54	"	Ali Haji-Sheikh..........Michigan		43
55	1981	Ali Haji-Sheikh..........Michigan		19**
56	"	Ali Haji-Sheikh..........Michigan		26
57	"	Ali Haji-Sheikh..........Michigan		23
58	1982	Rich Spangler............Ohio State		33
59	1983	Bob Bergeron.............Michigan		26
60	1984	Bob Bergeron.............Michigan		37
61	"	Bob Bergeron.............Michigan		45
62	1985	Pat Moons................Michigan		34
63	"	Rich Spangler............Ohio State		48
64	"	Pat Moons................Michigan		38
65	1986	Mike Gillette............Michigan		32
66	"	Mike Gillette............Michigan		34
67	"	Matt Franz...............Ohio State		27
68	1987	Mike Gillette............Michigan		34
69	"	Mike Gillette............Michigan		19**
70	"	Matt Franz...............Ohio State		26
71	1988	Mike Gillette............Michigan		22
72	"	Mike Gillette............Michigan		56***
73	"	Pat O'Morrow.............Ohio State		21
74	1989	Pat O'Morrow.............Ohio State		20
75	"	Pat O'Morrow.............Ohio State		22
76	1990	Tim Williams.............Ohio State		38
77	"	John Carlson.............Michigan		27
78	"	John Carlson.............Michigan		30
79	"	Tim Williams.............Ohio State		43
80	"	John Carlson.............Michigan		37
81	1991	Tim Williams.............Ohio State		50
82	"	John Carlson.............Michigan		37
83	1992	Tim Williams.............Ohio State		39
84	"	Tim Williams.............Ohio State		30

*Unknown. **Shortest. ***Longest.

Michigan has kicked 47 field goals, Ohio State 37.

Since 1960, there have been 57 field goals — 29 by OSU, 28 by UM. The average line of scrimmage has been the 15-yard line.

UM's Mike Gillette has the most field goals with 6. OSU's Vlade Janakievski and Tim Williams each have 5.

The series' first 56 games (1897-1959).....27 field goals.
The series' last 34 games (1960-1993).....57 field goals.

PLAYER	TD	PAT	FG	TOTAL	YEAR(S)
Frank Hogg	1	5	0	14	1897
Fred Hannan	1	0	0	4	1897
Pingree	1	0	0	4	1897
Stuart	3	0	0	12	1897
Bill Heston	5	0	0	25	1901-02-04
Neil Snow	2	0	0	10	1901
Bruce Shorts	0	1	0	1	1901
Hugh White	1	0	0	5	1901
A. E. Hernstein	6	0	0	30	1902
Paul Jones	1	0	0	5	1902
James Lawrence	2	8	0	18	1902
Joe Maddock	1	0	0	5	1902
Dan McGugin	2	0	0	10	1902
Everette Sweeney	0	3	0	3	1902
Palmer	2	0	0	10	1902
John Curtis	2	1	0	11	1903-05
Herbert Graver	5	0	0	25	1903
Tom Hammond	0	14	3	26	1903-04-05
Harry Hammond	1	0	0	5	1904
Alfred Barlow	1	0	0	5	1905
William Embs	1	0	0	5	1905
John Garrells	2	0	1	14	1905-06
Harry Patrick	1	0	0	5	1905
David Allerdice	2	6	4	29	1907-08-09
Walter Graham	0	1	0	1	1907
John Lowell	1	0	0	5	1907
Paul Magoffin	1	0	0	5	1907
Walter Rheinschild	2	0	0	10	1907
Charles Feeney	1	0	0	5	1909
George Lawton	1	0	0	5	1909
Stanfield Wells	2	0	0	10	1909-11
Fred Conklin	1	1	1	9	1910-11
Thomas Bogle	0	0	1	3	1911
George Thomson	2	0	0	11	1911-12
James Craig	1	0	0	6	1912
George Patterson	0	2	0	2	1912
Robert Dunne	1	0	0	6	1918
Angus Goetz	1	0	0	6	1918
Frank Steketee	0	3	0	3	1918-20
Cliff Sparks	0	0	1	3	1919
Jack Dunn	1	0	0	6	1920
Paul Goebel	0	1	1	4	1922
Harry Kipke	3	0	1	21	1922-23
Jack Blott	0	2	1	5	1923
Herbert Steger	2	0	0	12	1923
Phillip Marion	1	0	0	6	1924
F. A. Rockwell	1	1	1	10	1924
Ben Friedman	0	3	2	9	1925-26
John Molenda	1	0	0	6	1925
Leo Hoffman	1	0	0	6	1926
Bennie Oosterbaan	1	0	0	6	1926
Louis Gilbert	3	3	0	21	1927
Leo Draveling	1	0	0	6	1928
Joe Gembis	0	1	0	1	1928
Harry Newman	2	3	0	15	1930-32
DuVal Goldsmith	0	1	0	1	1931
Ivan Williamson	2	0	0	12	1931-32
John Regeczi	1	0	0	6	1932
Chris Everhardus	1	0	0	6	1933
Bill Renner	1	0	0	6	1933
Mike Savage	0	1	0	1	1933
Ben Frutig	2	0	0	12	1938-40
Tom Harmon	5	7	0	37	1938-39-40
Fred Trosko	2	0	0	12	1938-39
Forest Evashevski	2	0	0	12	1939-40
Paul Kromer	1	0	0	6	1940
Harlin Fraumaan	1	0	0	6	1941
Tom Kuzma	1	0	0	6	1941
William Melzow	0	2	0	2	1941
Robert Westfall	1	0	0	6	1941
James Brieske	0	11	1	14	1942-46-47
Robert Wiese	3	0	0	18	1942-43
Walter Dreyer	1	0	0	6	1943
Elroy Hirsch	0	1	0	1	1943
Don Lund	1	0	0	6	1943
Earl Maves	1	0	0	6	1943
Vincent Mroz	1	0	0	6	1943
Rex Wells	0	2	0	2	1943
Bob Nussbaumer	1	0	0	6	1943
Bill Culligan	3	0	0	18	1944-46
Joe Ponsetto	0	2	0	2	1944
George Chiames	0	1	0	1	1945
Henry Fonde	3	0	0	18	1945-46
Bob Chappuis	2	0	0	12	1945-46
Bob Mann	2	0	0	12	1946
Richard Rifenburg	1	0	0	6	1946
John White	1	0	0	6	1946
Chalmers Elliott	1	0	0	6	1946
John Wisenburger	1	0	0	6	1947
Harris Allis	1	3	0	9	1948-49-50
Tom Peterson	1	0	0	6	1948
Leo Koceski	1	0	0	6	1949
Tony Momsen	1	0	0	6	1950
Stan Noskin	1	0	0	6	1951
Don Peterson	1	0	0	6	1951
Russell Rescarla	0	2	0	2	1951-52
Frank Howell	1	0	0	6	1952
Louis Baldacci	0	2	0	2	1953
Richard Balzhiser	1	0	0	6	1953
Tony Branoff	1	0	0	6	1953
Dan Cline	2	0	0	12	1953-54
Ron Kramer	0	2	0	2	1954-56
Terry Barr	2	0	0	12	1956
James Maddock	1	0	0	6	1956
Bradley Myers	1	0	0	6	1957
James Pace	1	0	0	6	1957
James Van Pelt	0	2	0	2	1957
Gary Prahst	2	1*	0	14	1958
Darrell Harper	1	2	1	11	1959
Tony Rio	1	0	0	6	1959
Bruce McLenna	1	0	0	6	1961
David Rainey	1	0	0	6	1961
James Ward	1	1*	0	8	1961
Richard Rindfuss	1	0	0	6	1963
Bob Timberlake	0	2	2	8	1963-64
James Detwiler	2	0	0	12	1964-66
David Fisher	1	0	0	6	1965
Richard Sygar	0	3	1	6	1965-66
Clayton Wilhite	1	0	0	6	1966
James Berline	1	0	0	6	1967
John Gabler	1	0	0	5	1967
Fran Titas	0	5	0	5	1967-69
Ron Johnson	2	0	0	12	1968
Tim Killian	0	2	1	5	1968-69
Garvie Craw	2	0	0	12	1969
Don Moorhead	1	0	0	6	1969
Dana Coin	0	1	2	7	1970-71
Paul Staroba	1	0	0	6	1970
Mike Taylor	1	0	0	6	1971
Clinton Haslerig	0	1*	0	2	1972

MICHIGAN SCORING (continued)

PLAYER	TD	PAT	FG	TOTAL	YEAR(S)
Mike Lantry	0	2	3	11	1972-73-74
Ed Shuttlesworth	2	0	0	12	1972-73
Gil Chapman	1	0	0	6	1974
Rick Leach	2	0	0	12	1975-77
Jim Smith	1	0	0	6	1975
Bob Wood	0	4	0	4	1975-76
Russell Davis	2	0	0	12	1976
Ron Lytle	1	0	0	6	1976
Jerry Zuver	0	1*	0	2	1976
Roosevelt Smith	3	1*	0	20	1977-78-79
Gregg Wilner	0	4	0	4	1977-78
Rodney Feaster	1	0	0	6	1978
Anthony Carter	2	0	0	12	1979-80
Bryan Virgil	0	1	0	1	1979
Ali Haji-Sheikh	0	2	4	14	1980-81-82
Lawrence Ricks	1	0	0	6	1982
Steve Smith	2	0	0	12	1982-83
Bob Bergeron	0	3	3	12	1983-84
Triando Markray	1	0	0	6	1983
Eric Kattus	2	0	0	12	1983-85
Pat Moons	0	3	2	9	1985
Gerald White	1	0	0	6	1985
John Kolesar	2	0	0	12	1985-88
Mike Gillette	0	8	6	26	1986-87-88
Jamie Morris	3	0	0	18	1986-87
Tom Wilcher	1	0	0	6	1986
Leroy Hoard	4	0	0	24	1987-88-89
Greg McMurtry	1	0	0	6	1988
Allen Jefferson	1	0	0	6	1989
Jarrod Bunch	2	0	0	12	1989
John Carlson	0	9	4	21	1989-90-91
Desmond Howard	2	0	0	12	1990-91
Burnie Leggett	1	0	0	6	1991
Jesse Johnson	1	0	0	6	1991
Tyrone Wheatley	1	0	0	6	1991
Elvis Grbac	1	0	0	6	1992
Todd Collins	1	0	0	6	1992
Peter Elezovic	0	5	0	5	1992-93
Mercury Hayes	1	0	0	6	1993
Jon Ritchie	1	0	0	6	1993
Che' Foster	1	0	0	6	1993
Ed Davis	1	0	0	6	1993
Safeties (2)	-	-	-	4	1906-1950

*2-point conversion

172 UM players have scored against OSU.
131 have scored touchdowns.
4 have scored a TD, PAT and FG. They are:
David Allerdice (1907-08-09), Fred Conklin
(1910-11), F.A. Rockwell (1924) and Darrell
Harper (1959).

OHIO STATE'S INDIVIDUAL SCORING, 1897-1993

PLAYER	TD	PAT	FG	TOTAL	YEAR(S)
Bill Marquardt	1	0	0	5	1904
Ralph Hoyer	0	1	0	1	1904
Millard Gibson	1	0	0	5	1908
Walter Barrington	0	1	0	1	1908
Chelsea Boone	1	0	0	5	1909
Leslie Wells	0	1	1	4	1909-10
James Flowers	1	0	0	6	1919
Charles Harley	1	1	0	7	1919
Herbert Henderson	1	0	0	6	1920
Iolas Huffman	1	0	0	6	1920
Gaylord Stinchcomb	0	1	0	1	1920
Harry Workman	0	1	0	1	1920
John Stuart	1	0	0	6	1921
Charles Taylor	1	0	0	6	1921
Lloyd Pixley	0	2	0	2	1921
Harold Cunningham	1	0	0	6	1924
Myers Clark	0	1	1	4	1926
Byron Eby	2	0	0	12	1926
Martin Karow	1	0	0	6	1926
Charles Coffee	1	0	0	6	1928
Fred Barratt	0	2	0	2	1928-29
Wes Fesler	2	0	0	12	1928-29
William Carroll	2	0	0	12	1931
Carl Cramer	1	0	0	6	1931
Bob Haubrich	0	1	0	1	1931
Louis Peppe	0	1	0	1	1931
Frank Antenucci	1	0	0	6	1934
Sam Busich	0	3	0	3	1934-35
Frank Cumisky	2	0	0	12	1934-36
Richard Heekin	3	0	0	18	1934-35
John Monohan	0	3	0	3	1934
Merle Wendt	1	0	0	6	1934
Damon Wetzel	1	0	0	6	1934
Arthur Boucher	1	0	0	6	1935
Wm. "Tippy" Dye	1	0	0	6	1935
Nick Wasylik	2	0	0	12	1935-36
John Bettridge	1	0	0	6	1935
William Booth	0	0	1	3	1936
John Rabb	1	0	0	6	1936
James McDonald	0	1	0	1	1937
James Miller	2	0	0	12	1937
Richard Nardi	1	0	0	6	1937
Frank Clair	1	0	0	6	1939
Victor Marino	1	0	0	6	1939
Don Scott	0	2	0	2	1939
Richard Fisher	1	0	0	6	1941
Jack Graf	1	0	0	6	1941
John Hallabrin	0	2	0	2	1941
Tom Kinkdale	1	0	0	6	1941
Eugene Fekete	0	3	0	3	1942
Leslie Hovath	4	0	0	24	1942-44
Bob Shaw	1	0	0	6	1942
Ernest Parks	1	0	0	6	1943
John Stungis	0	0	1	1	1943
Oliver Cline	1	0	0	6	1944
Max Schnittker	0	0	1	3	1945
Rodney Swinehart	1	0	0	6	1946
Leslie Hague	0	1	1	4	1948-49
Fred Morrison	1	0	0	6	1949
Vic Janowicz	0	0	1	3	1950
John Borton	1	0	0	6	1952
Bob Grimes	1	0	0	6	1952
Bob Joslin	2	0	0	12	1952
Thurlow Weed	0	6	0	6	1952-54
Carl Brubaker	1	0	0	6	1954

OHIO STATE SCORING (continued)

PLAYER	TD	PAT	FG	TOTAL	YEAR(S)
Howard Cassidy......2	0	0	12	1954-55
Fred Kriss..........1	0	1	9	1954-55
Don Vicic...........1	0	0	6	1955
Joe Cannavino.......1	0	0	6	1957
Fred Kremblas.......1	0	0	6	1957
Charles LaBeau......3	0	0	18	1957-58
Don Sutherin.......0	4	1	7	1957
Jerry Fields........0	1*	0	2	1958
James Herbstreit....1	1*	0	8	1958-59
Loran White.........1	0	0	6	1958
Roger Detrick.......1	0	0	6	1959
James Houston......1	0	0	6	1959
Bob Ferguson.......5	0	0	30	1960-61
Ben Jones...........0	1	0	1	1960
Robert Butts........1	0	0	6	1961
David Francis.......1	0	0	6	1961
David Katterhenrich.1	0	0	6	1961
Robert Klein........1	0	0	6	1961
Sam Tidmore........1	1*	0	8	1961
Dick Van Raaphorst..0	8	0	8	1961-62
Paul Warfield.......3	0	0	18	1961-62-63
Charles Mamula......0	4	0	4	1962
Don Uverferth.......1	0	0	6	1963
Billy Anders........1	0	0	6	1965
Bob Funk............0	0	1	3	1965
Gary Cairns.........0	3	2	9	1966-67
Rudy Hubbard........2	0	0	12	1967
Bill Long...........1	0	0	6	1967
Rex Kern............2	0	0	12	1968
Jim Otis............5	0	0	30	1968-69
Nick Roman..........0	5	1	8	1968
Larry Zelina........1	0	0	6	1968
Stan White..........0	0	0	6	1969
Leophus Hayden......1	0	0	6	1970
Bruce Jankowski.....1	0	0	6	1970

PLAYER	TD	PAT	FG	TOTAL	YEAR(S)
Fred Schram.........0	3	2	9	1970-71
Tom Campana.........1	0	0	6	1971
Blair Conway........0	3	1	6	1972-73
Archie Griffin......1	0	0	6	1972
Harold Henson.......1	0	0	6	1972
Pete Johnson........4	0	0	24	1973-75
Tom Klaban..........0	3	4	15	1974-75
Vlade Janakievski...0	0	5	15	1977-79-80
Bob Atha............0	2	1	5	1978-81
Charles Hunter......1	0	0	6	1979
Todd Bell...........1	0	0	6	1979
Art Schlichter......2	0	0	12	1981
Vaughn Broadnax.....1	0	0	6	1982
Tim Spencer.........2	0	0	12	1982
Rich Spangler.......0	11	2	17	1982-83-84-85
Keith Byars.........6	0	0	36	1983-84-85
Cedric Anderson.....1	0	0	6	1983
Chris Carter........3	0	0	18	1985-86
Vince Workman......1	0	0	6	1986
Matt Franz..........0	5	2	11	1986-87
Everette Ross.......1	0	0	6	1987
Carlos Snow.........2	0	0	12	1987-88
Tom Tupa............1	0	0	6	1987
Bill Matlock........2	0	0	12	1988
Bobby Olive.........1	0	0	6	1988
Pat O'Morrow........0	4	3	13	1988-89
Scottie Graham......2	0	0	12	1989
Jeff Graham.........1	0	0	6	1990
Greg Beatty.........1	0	0	6	1992
Tim Williams........0	2	5	17	1990-91-92
Safeties (2)........-	-	-	4	1937-1955

*2-point conversion.
130 OSU players have scored against UM.
92 have scored touchdowns.

STATISTICAL HIGHLIGHTS OF THE SERIES, 1930-1993 (64 GAMES)

	UM	OSU	AVG/GAME
Record..............32-28-4		28-32-4	---
Points scored...........968		899	15-14
First Downs............970		938	15-14
Yards Rushing........11,520		10,824	180-169
Yards Passing.........7,058		6,362	110--99
TOTAL YARDS..........18,578		17,186	290-268
Passes Attempted......1,123		1,067	18-17
Passes Completed.......532		476	8-7
Yards Penalized.......1,071		1,145	17-18

MICHIGAN COACHES VS. OHIO STATE

NO.	COACH	PERIOD	G	W	L	T
1	Gustave Ferbert................1897		1	1	0	0
2	Langdon "Biff" Lea.............1900		1	0	0	1
3	Fielding Yost.........1901-23, 25-26		20	16	3	1
4	George Little...................1924		1	1	0	0
5	Elton "Tad" Wieman...........1927-28		2	1	1	0
6	Harry Kipke..................1929-37		9	3	6	0
7	Fritz Crisler...............1938-47		10	7	2	1
8	Bennie Oosterbaan...........1948-58		11	6	4	1
9	Chalmers "Bump" Elliott......1959-68		10	2	8	0
10	Glenn "Bo" Schembechler......1969-89		21	11	9	1
11	Gary Moeller.................1990-93		4	3	0	1
	TOTALS...................................*90*		*90*	*51*	*33*	*6*

OHIO STATE COACHES VS. MICHIGAN

NO.	COACH	PERIOD	G	W	L	T
1	David Edwards...................1897		1	0	1	0
2	John Eckstrom................1900-01		2	0	1	1
3	Perry Hale...................1902-03		2	0	2	0
4	E. R. Sweetland..............1904-05		2	0	2	0
5	A. E. Herrnstein.............1906-09		4	0	4	0
6	Howard Jones....................1910		1	0	0	1
7	Harry Vaughn....................1911		1	0	1	0
8	John Richards...................1912		1	0	1	0
9	John Wilce...................1918-28		11	4	7	0
10	Sam Willaman.................1929-33		5	2	3	0
11	Francis Schmidt..............1934-40		7	4	3	0
12	Paul Brown...................1941-43		3	1	1	1
13	Carroll Widdoes..............1944-45		2	1	1	0
14	Paul Bixler.....................1946		1	0	1	0
15	Wes Fesler...................1947-50		4	0	3	1
16	Woody Hayes..................1951-78		28	16	11	1
17	Earle Bruce..................1979-87		9	5	4	0
18	John Cooper..................1988-93		6	0	5	1
	TOTALS...................................*90*		*90*	*33*	*51*	*6*

Only three OSU coaches — Schmidt, Hayes, Bruce — have winning records against UM. In 44 series games they are 25-18-1. The other 15 coaches (in 46 games) are 8-33-5. Hayes has 16 wins, all others have 17.

Oddly enough, neither school's "OWN" has had much success as head coaches in the series.

"Michigan Men" (Ferbert, Wieman, Kipke, Oosterbaan, Elliott) are only 13-19-1 (.409) against the Buckeyes. All others are 38-14-5 (.711).

Just three Ohio State University football lettermen (Willaman, Widdoes, Fesler) have been head coaches at the school. Against UM they are .318 (3-7-1). All others are .411 (30-44-5).

Combined, both school's "own" are 16-26-2 (.386) in the series.

SERIES HIGHS AND LOWS SINCE 1930

MOST FIRST DOWNS
28	OSU	1968
27	UM	1986
25	OSU	1989
24	OSU	1934
24	UM	1947
24	UM	1958
24	UM	1988
24	OSU	1988
24	OSU	1992

FEWEST FIRST DOWNS
0	UM	1950
2	OSU	1943
3	OSU	1933
3	UM	1934
3	OSU	1950

MOST YARDS RUSHING
426	UM	1943
421	OSU	1968
372	OSU	1957
366	UM	1976
333	OSU	1965

FEWEST YARDS RUSHING
6	UM	1934
8	UM	1937
12	UM	1935
16	OSU	1950
24	UM	1933

MOST YARDS PASSING
300	UM	1946
298	OSU	1983
271	OSU	1992
261	UM	1986
258	UM	1958

FEWEST YARDS PASSING
0	OSU	1944
0	UM	1950
0	OSU	1973
0	UM	1976
4	OSU	1955

MOST TOTAL YARDS
531	UM	1943
529	UM	1986
512	OSU	1961
509	UM	1946
499	UM	1988

FEWEST TOTAL YARDS
27	UM	1950
40	UM	1934
41	OSU	1950
45	UM	1937
70	OSU	1933

MOST PASSES ATTEMPTED
47	OSU	1992
40	OSU	1983
35	UM	1958
32	UM	1947
32	UM	1949

FEWEST PASSES ATTEMPTED
3	OSU	1931
3	OSU	1955
3	OSU	1972
4	OSU	1944
4	OSU	1973

MOST PASSES COMPLETED
29	UM	1958
28	OSU	1992
21	OSU	1983
19	UM	1986
19	OSU	1987

FEWEST PASSES COMPLETED
0 by OSU in 1944-73-76,
by UM in 1950.

MOST YARDS PENALIZED
89	UM	1966
75	UM	1991
74	UM	1953
70	UM	1955
66	OSU	1990

FEWEST YARDS PENALIZED
0 by OSU in 1939-43-62-73.

SOME INDIVIDUAL SERIES HIGHS

CATAGORY	NO.	PLAYER	TEAM	YEAR
MOST YARDS RUSHING	210	Jamie Moris	UM	1986
MOST YARDS PASSING	298	Mike Tomczak	OSU	1983
	261	Jim Harbaugh	UM	1986
MOST TOTAL YARDS	310	Mike Tomczak	OSU	1983
	232	Jamie Morris	UM	1986
MOST PASSES ATTEMPTED	46	Kirk Herbstreit	OSU	1982
	40	Mike Tomczak	OSU	1983
	35	Bob Ptacek	UM	1958
MOST PASSES COMPLETED	28	Kirk Herbstreit	OSU	1992
	24	Bob Ptacek	UM	1958
MOST PASSES CAUGHT	12	Brad Myers	UM	1958
	12	Bryan Stablein	OSU	1992
MOST PUNT RETURN YARDS	166	Tom Campana	OSU	1971

ALL-TIME BIG TEN FOOTBALL
STANDINGS, 1896-1993
(conference games only)

TEAM	G	W	L	T	PCT
MICHIGAN (1896).............533	533	375	140	18	.720
OHIO STATE (1913)...........515	515	354	137	24	.711
Michigan State (1953)........302	302	170	124	8	.576
Chicago (1896-1939).........233	233	120	99	14	.545
Minnesota (1896)............573	573	281	264	28	.515
Illionis (1896).............604	604	287	287	30	.500
Purdue (1896)...............560	560	247	285	28	.466
Wisconsin (1896)............591	591	247	305	39	.451
Iowa (1900).................528	528	218	286	24	.436
Northwestern (1896).........592	592	187	384	21	.334
Indiana (1900)..............531	531	164	343	24	.331
Penn State (1993)............8	8	6	2	0	.750
TOTALS....................5570	*5570*	*2656*	*2656*	*258*	---

Note: Michigan left the conference for nine years, 1908-1917.

Listed in order of games played:
Minnesota 604, Northwestern 592, Wisconsin 591, Minnesota 573, Purdue 560, MICHIGAN 533, Indiana 531, Iowa 528, OHIO STATE 515, Michigan State 302, Chicago 233 and Penn State 8.

Through the 1993 season, 2,785 conference games have been played.

SERIES ODDS 'N ENDS

- As strange as it may seem, there has been no home field advantage in the series at Michigan Stadium or Ohio Stadium. The home team is 33-33-4. Overall (since 1897) the home team is 43-41-6.

- In the series' first 46 games (1897-1949) the team that scored first had a 36-6-3 record (there was one scoreless tie). Since then it has changed dramatically, as the team scoring first has only a 23-19-2 record. UM has scored first 51 times (37-12-2), OSU has scored first 38 times (22-13-3). Overall, the team that scores first has a 69% chance of winning the game (59-25-5).

- There have been 601 kickoffs in the series and only one returned for a touchdown — by Michigan's David Raimey in the 1961 game.

- Of the 90 series games, they have met nine times with identical records and six games have ended in ties. In the other 75 games, the team with the best record has posted a 51-24 record, giving the "favorite" a 68% chance of winning the game.

- Ohio State kicker Rich Spangler is the only player to score in four series games (1982-83-84-85).

- Michigan's 100th and 200th series touchdowns came on the same date 50 years apart. On November 20, 1943, Jack Wink threw a 10-yard pass to Vincent Mroz for No. 100. Then on November 20, 1993, Ed Davis scored from the five for No. 200. Both games were played in Ann Arbor.

- Ohio State's 100th touchdown was scored by two-time Heisman Trophy winner Archie Griffin on a 30-yard run on November 25, 1972 at Columbus, as his team won 14-11.

- There has been only one game settled by one point, 17-16, won by Michigan in 1926 at Columbus.

- Thirty-two of the series' 90 games have been settled by 7 points or less (36%).

- Fifteen times the game has been tied at halftime and UM went on to post a 7-5-3 record. In the other 75 games, the team leading at intermission has a 60-13-2 record (81%). UM is 39-8-1 after leading at the half, OSU 21-5-1.

■ Strange, but true: The most touchdown passes thrown in the series by any one player is four — still held by UM's Bennie Oosterbaan (1926-27) and Tom Harmon (1938-40). The record for the most TD receptions is three, first set by UM's Lewis Gilbert in the 1927 game (all three from Oosterbaan) and not matched until 59 years later by OSU's Chris Carter (1985-86).

■ Of the series' 2,469 points, 1,220 have been scored in the first half and 1,249 in the second half.

■ The series has produced 998 points at Ohio Stadium (36 games) and 997 points at Michigan Stadium (34 games). UM's record at the two plants is 36-30-4.

■ Average attendance of the series each decade beginning in 1930:

```
1930s........62,421
1940s........77,800
1950s........85,245
1960s........77,925
1970s........96,613
1980s........98,070
1990s........99,602
```

Total attendance for the 64 games has been 5,379,135, an average of 84,049. The 32 games in Ann Arbor have averaged 88,980, the 32 in Columbus 79,118.

■ How they've scored:

Michigan has scored 200 touchdowns in the series — 137 by rushing (69%), 49 by passing (24%) and 14 by other means (7%).

Ohio State has scored 133 touchdowns — 83 by rushing (62%), 42 by passing (32%) and eight by other means (6%).

How they've scored (both teams): Of the series' 333 touchdowns, 220 have been scored by rushing (66%), 91 by passing (27%) and 22 by other means (7%).

MICHIGAN'S RECORD VS. OHIO STATE ON:

DATE	YEAR(S)	W-L-T
Oct 15 --	1905-32	2-0-0
Oct 16 --	1897-1909	2-0-0
Oct 17 --	1931	0-1-0
Oct 18 --	1930	1-0-0
Oct 19 --	1912-29	1-1-0
Oct 20 --	1908-23-28	2-1-0
Oct 21 --	1911-22-33	3-0-0
Oct 22 --	1910-21-27	1-1-1
Oct 23 --		
Oct 24 --	1908	1-0-0
Oct 25 --	1902-19	1-1-0
Oct 26 --	1907	1-0-0
Oct 27 --		
Oct 28 --		
Oct 29 --		
Oct 29 --		
Oct 30 --		
Oct 31 --		
Nov 1 --		
Nov 2 --		
Nov 3 --		
Nov 4 --		
Nov 5 --		
Nov 6 --	1920	0-1-0
Nov 7 --	1903	1-0-0
Nov 8 --		
Nov 9 --	1901	1-0-0
Nov 10 --		
Nov 11 --	1905	1-0-0
Nov 12 --		
Nov 13 --	1926	1-0-0
Nov 14 --	1925	1-0-0
Nov 15 --	1924	1-0-0
Nov 16 --		
Nov 17 --	1934-79-84	0-3-0
Nov 18 --		
Nov 19 --	1938-49-55-60-66-77-83-88	5-2-1
Nov 20 --	1937-43-48-54-65-71-76-82-93	5-4-0
Nov 21 --	1936-42-53-59-64-70-81-87-92	3-5-1
Nov 22 --	1941-47-52-58-69-75-80-86	4-3-1
Nov 23 --	1935-40-46-57-68-74-85-91	4-4-0
Nov 24 --	1900-45-51-55-62-73-90	4-1-2
Nov 25 --	1939-44-50-61-67-72-78-89	4-4-0
Nov 26 --		
Nov 27 --		
Nov 28 --		
Nov 29 --		
Nov 30 --	1918-63	1-1-0
TOTALS		51-33-6